Perspecta 51, The Yale Architectural Journal

Medium

Medium

Shayari de Silva, Dante Furioso & Samantha Jaff

Editors' Statement May 2018

We wish we could say that the title and content of *Perspecta* 51 are the products of clairvoyance, as the editorial process began well before the election of Donald Trump, discussions of fake news, and the heightened sense that media are inextricable from contemporary life and politics. Yet, to contemplate the spatial nature of media, to ask what a medium is and how it can be understood in architectural terms, seems impossibly broad. As students of architecture, we began with the hunch that form and content are inextricable from their mediums, that the means of conveyance is part and parcel to all architectural and spatial phenomena. The way we draw and communicate architectural ideas is bound up in something larger, more complex—perhaps more invisible—than we have the means to readily express. Nevertheless, to ask the basic question—what is a medium?—is to reveal the contested nature of the term. We also have a sense of déjà vu: the more we read about the preceding decades at our school, the more we believe that any exploration of architecture's relationship to medium should also be a reflexive investigation into the medium of this journal itself.

In 1967, the editors of *Perspecta* 11 were also concerned with the intangibles that shape architecture's relationship to society, as they included an article by Marshall McLuhan titled "The Invisible Environment." McLuhan reflected on "the new and potent electronic environment," proclaiming that "in the case of environments that are created by new technologies, while they are quite invisible in themselves, they do tend to make visible the old environments." Prophesying the internet and today's hyper-networked world, he understood that "the really total and saturating environments are invisible." As we searched for a way to explore architecture's intangibles—the "invisible environment" of today—we drew from the work of our professors, architect Keller Easterling and media theorist Francesco Casetti. If Easterling has reframed architectural discourse around a re-reading of McLuhan's elemental notion of medium—pure information in a web of cybernetic feedback loops—then Casetti is making inroads into spatial-architectural territory through the development of a theory of media-ecology that began with the study of the media themselves.

In fact, we have once more come full circle. Many of the same aspirations and challenges present in the previous eras remain unresolved today. How can architecture engage with a broader society that is patently unjust and mired in conflict? How can we understand the relationship between architecture and the diffuse slurry of culture, art, money, power, politics, and technology? Society is increasingly fixated on media, yet it's increasingly difficult to identify what a medium is.

Today, notions of medium are complicated and elemental. On the one hand, much of the world has edged closer to a cyborg culture. Billions stare into the glowing glass of their smartphones, comforted by the seductive stream of information accessed by these portable computers. Indeed, we are addicted to the media that flow from our nomadic devices. This phenomenon affects our politics, our relationships, our humanity, our architecture, and our environment. Though today architecture and space are bound up in the invisible environment created by media technology, the effects of global warming and a changing climate are palpable. This renews the elemental notion of weather as medium connecting our globe in a complex system of feedbacks. Humans are a crucial part of this system, and architects are uniquely positioned to analyze, visualize, and make tangible these complex sets of relationships.

Thus, *Perspecta* 51 does not focus exclusively on the new media of today. Instead, it presents a conversation among varied theories on medium set against a series of architectural case studies. These include articles about the forensics of the digital image as medium, heating systems and thermostats as progenitors of architecture becoming a medium, and the digital commons as an exemplary medium for the creation of public space. There are stories about sea-level rise and flood-monitoring apps, search lights and public space, media walls and megastructures, social media capitals and suburban sprawl, and surveillance and library architecture grounded in theories of medium design, mediascapes, and media politics. The range of these articles illustrates the degree to which the study of medium is an ever-expanding endeavor, exemplary of the breadth of our current media environment. Everything yet nothing is possible. Nevertheless, *Perspecta* 51 provides new histories and fresh responses to the notion of medium that might illuminate possibilities for its productive use (and misuse) by architects.

6 *Thumbs That Type and Swipe*, 2018

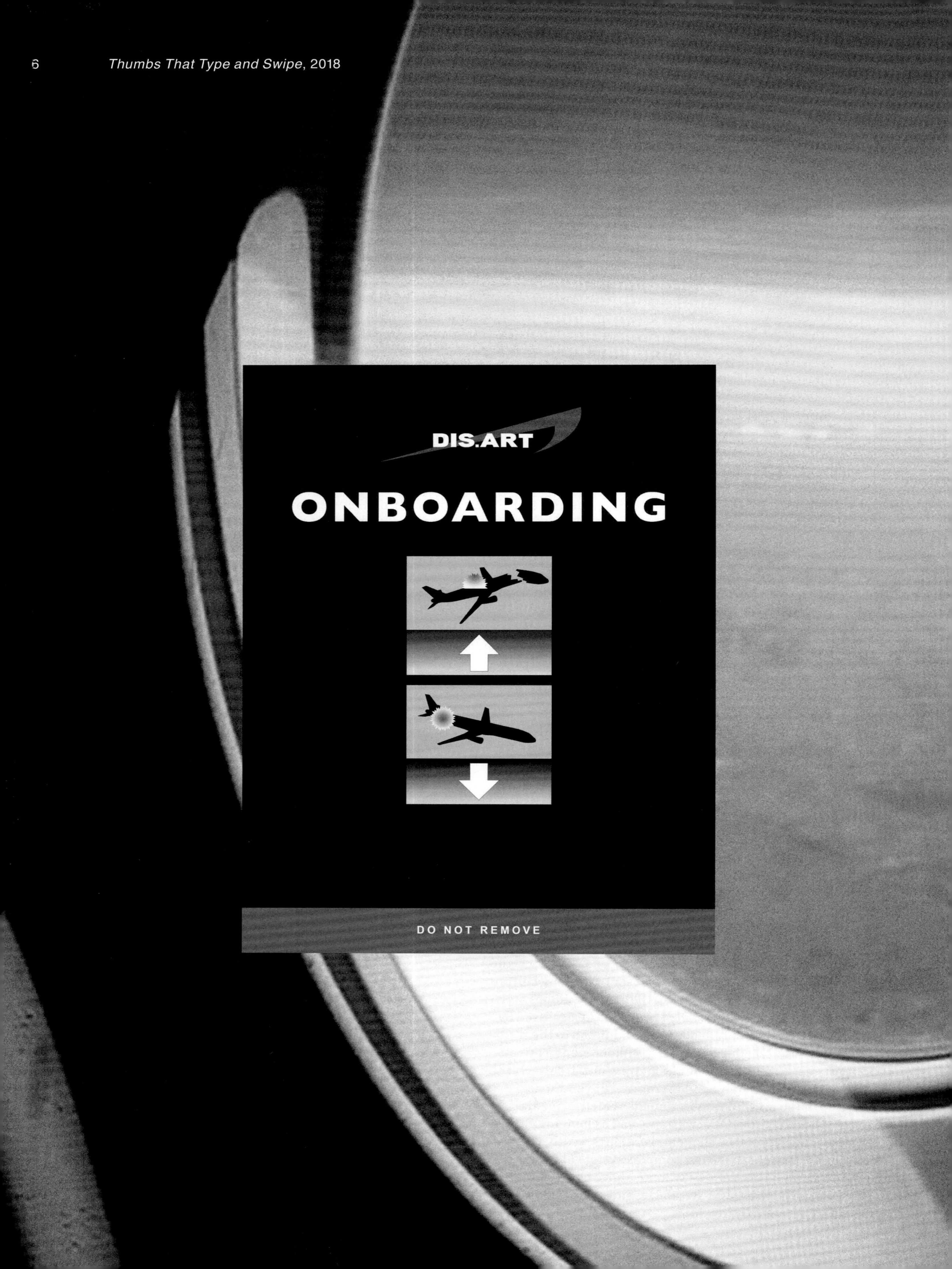

Luminotectonics (An Archaeology of the Searchlight)

PRELUDE

What I am calling *luminotectonics* is the art and science of mounting large-scale, public light shows, displays, or environments: one of the defining spectacle forms of the early-to-mid-twentieth century. What I am calling *luminotechnics* is, instead, the art and science of casting light upon features of the built environment to enhance the usability or the nocturnal appeal of the urban décor.

Luminotectonics is not to be confused with *luminotechnics*, even if the two are intertwined and the dissemination of both depends upon the success of the electrification campaigns that were undertaken in the course of the 1930s.

Luminotectonics belongs to a realm of spectacle whose historical roots are to be found in forms of display such as fireworks shows. Like fireworks shows, its genesis is shaped by the development of military technologies of battlefield projection, reconnaissance, and surveillance. Its setting of choice is the exceptional occasion: the battlefield, inauguration, premiere, or revolutionary festival. Its protagonist is the arc-lamp searchlight and, more recently, the laser. Dependent upon battery and mobile power-generation technologies, as well as the power of telephonic networks to ensure precise sequencing and synchronization, the essence of luminotectonics is mobility.[1]

Luminotechnics, on the other hand, belongs to the realm of effects achievable by casting direct and indirect light on everything from buildings to streets to public spaces. Its genesis is shaped by the development of civil engineering research on everything from urban power grids to reflectors to lighting systems. Dependent upon ubiquitous electrification but not upon precise sequencing and synchronization, its setting of choice is the everyday life of the industrial city. Its protagonist is the incandescent floodlight, deployed in banks, locked into fixed positions.

Because luminotechnic effects often are not merely practical, but spectacular, and because of the frequent intermixing of luminotechnic effects with luminotectonic shows, labels like "light architecture" (*Lichtarchitektur*) conflate the two. However, I would like to differentiate them, even as I acknowledge a shared ontology. Visibility is power, and the sorts of intensified forms of visibility achieved by means of light shows or the augmentation and animation of physical structures by means of electric lighting hint at the presence of a logic of transcendence embedded within the act of projection. But transcendence toward what? The triumph of liberty, progress, or science? The rise of an economy of 24/7 productivity? Or the return of magic, myth, the holy, the absolute? Or some combination of all three in the language of humanity, democracy, empire, or national sovereignty? This essay will suggest that the answer is "all of the above" and that there are features to this story specific to the 1930s, as well as ones that span two centuries of media history.

SPECIAL EFFECTS

Whether from the standpoint of luminotectonics or luminotechnics, the 1930s represent a golden era, directly presaging the augmented cityscapes of our times.

Techniques of outline lighting once reserved for Luna Parks and world exhibitions, now augmented by banks of floodlights, colored fluorescent tubes, mercury-vapor lamps, and other such devices, all contribute to the transformation of buildings into animated fairy palaces and of urban landscapes into vast theaters dominated by nocturnal special effects. Neon, first employed for commercial purposes in 1923, invades the facades of American cities. Within a decade it has crossed the Atlantic, "Americanizing" facades in London, Paris, and Berlin.

In the luminotectonic domain, aerial assault becomes so central to military strategy and searchlights so integral to defense planning, that large-scale production initiates, with the ancillary result that a commercial market begins to develop by the 1920s. First in the United States, next in France, later in the rest of Europe, the searchlight enters the culture of mass advertising and communications. Accompanying store openings, the celebration of historical recurrences, and film premieres, its presence clearly extends and adapts a prior half century of showmanship associated with performances of military might addressed to civilian populations. Searchlights also invade the realm of spectacle: from stadium performances to mass pageants and rallies to new, distinctively industrial-era forms of religious practice.

There are only a few comprehensive studies of this history, among them Dietrich Neumann's *Architecture of the Night: The Illuminated Building*, a work whose primary emphasis, as the title suggests, falls on luminotechnics as applied to architecture.[2] But at the center of Neumann's richly informed account is a luminotectonic event that, on the contrary, is so overrepresented in the historical record that it has become an enduring icon in 1930s historiography and a key leitmotif in post–World War II discussions regarding the cultural politics of spectacle. That event (or rather cluster of events) is Albert Speer's "light cathedral" or *Lichtdom*, featured at the 1934, 1936, and 1937 Nuremberg Rallies of the Nazi party, as well as the 1936 Berlin Olympics. It has most often been approached as both a culminating event and a singularity, situated within a rigorously Germanic chain of cultural transmission, colored by the conviction that the very medium of such light constructions may be implicated in totalitarian models of culture.

My aim in these reflections will be to sketch out an expanded framework: to enfold this key event in the media history of the Third Reich within an overall archaeology of the searchlight whose protagonists are engineers like Walter D'Arcy Ryan, entrepreneurs like Otto K. Olesen, companies like General Electric and Sperry, and the director-designers of military shows. This is a history that antedates, flanks, and extends beyond the transformation of Nuremberg from a place of Party Day assemblies to one remembered for the war crimes tribunal where Speer was tried alongside members of the Nazi Party hierarchy. Even if its heyday has passed, it is a history that continues to this day: both in the form of critical art interventions such as Rafael Lozano-Hemmer's *Vectorial Elevation* (2000) and the Tokyo Skytree, and in revisitations of mid-century models of sublimity, if in an elegiac key, like the annual Twin Towers *Tribute in Light* in New York. The fact that post-Speer projections inevitably summon up the specter of Speer's luminotectonic work suggests at once an overvaluation and a misunderstanding.

Within the expanded frames of reference proposed here, Speer doesn't loom as a culminating figure. He appears neither in the role in which he cast himself nor in that in which post–World War II memory has just as resolutely cast him. Rather, Speer appears as one figure among several who, working with techniques and practices codified by the leading armies of the industrial world and transformed into a worldwide vernacular by the pioneers of luminotectonics, stripped away complexities in the name of simplified geometries and adapted them to a German cultural-political script that zigzags through Romantic understandings of the Gothic cathedral, Richard Wagner's Bayreuth, Bauhaus visions of socialist cathedrals, the Crystal Chain circle's crystallographies of light, and National Socialist dreams of total order.

1. The topic has been valuably explored by scholars in the field of media archaeology; see Erkki Huhtamo, "The Sky Is (Not) the Limit: Envisioning the Ultimate Public Media Display," *Journal of Visual Culture* 8, no. 3 (2009): 329–48 (esp. 330–37), and, more broadly, Huhtamo, *Illusions in Motion: Media Archaeology of the Moving Panorama and Related Spectacles* (Cambridge, MA: MIT Press, 2013).

2. Dietrich Neumann, ed., *Architecture of the Night: The Illuminated Building* (London: Prestel, 2002); but see also his *Luminous Buildings: Night Architecture / Leuchtende Bauten: Architektur der Nacht* (Ostfildern, Germany: Hatje Cantz, 2006). For some of the prehistory see also one of the first comprehensive works in this field, Matthew Luckiesh, *Artificial Light: Its Influence upon Civilization* (New York: The Century Co, 1920), http://www.gutenberg.org/ebooks/17625/.

CHIMERIC STIRRINGS

In a late entry in his *Spandau* diaries, Speer reflects on his legacy in ways that echo his official memoir, *Inside the Third Reich*. Speer writes:

> Today I finished August Köhler's book on lighting technology; he cites me as one of the fathers of light architecture. If my own view is correct, I took the first step in that direction on the occasion of the Paris World's Fair by bathing the German pavilion in dazzling brightness at night by means of skillfully arranged spotlights. The result was to make the architecture of the building emerge sharply outlined against the night, and at the same time to make it unreal. Nevertheless, it was still a combination of architecture and light. Somewhat later, I did without the constructed architecture altogether. At the Party Rally I experimented with antiaircraft searchlights; I had 150 of them pointed vertically into the night sky, forming a rectangle of light. Inside the rectangle the ritual of the Party Rally took place—a fabulous setting, like one of the imaginary crystal palaces of the Middle Ages. ... I feel strangely stirred by the idea that the most successful architectural creation of my life is a chimera, an immaterial phenomenon.[3]

Strange or not, the architect's stirrings are wound in a dense skein of factual errors and half-truths that requires some unwinding. Let's start with "August Köhler." August Köhler is *not* the author of the 1956 book, *Lighting in Architecture*, referred to by Speer.[4] The author was the lighting engineer Walter Köhler, whose sympathies lay not with Speer but with the Bauhaus and its postwar successors. The actual August Köhler was an author Speer might well have preferred to Walter Köhler: the optician and Jena professor responsible for inventing Köhler illumination, a groundbreaking technique for achieving even illumination still widely employed in digital imaging techniques.

Second, not only is Speer not cited as one of the founding fathers of "light architecture" in the book in question, but there is no reference to him at all. Rather, in his discussion of display architecture, Köhler sandwiches an allusion to the 1937 Paris Exposition between praise for French *son et lumière* shows and postwar glass pavilions at the Fiera di Milano. The luminous amplification of built structures was one of the Paris Exposition's defining themes and, along with the United States, France had established itself as one of the world's leading laboratories for luminotectonic experimentation in the late decades of the nineteenth century. (From the time of its construction, the Eiffel Tower was repeatedly framed in searchlights, staged as a luminous billboard, and transformed into a kind of lighthouse casting beams out across the cityscape of the City of Light.)[5] Elsewhere in his diaries, Speer betrays an abiding anxiety about French precedence in this domain and hints that the true object of his design for the German pavilion was to outshine Gustave Eiffel's tower, not the rival Soviet pavilion.

Third, Speer has skewed the sequence of events so that it seems as if he began by outlining buildings against the night with spotlights and later expanded his research to luminotectonics. In point of the fact, the 1934 torch-and-searchlight spectacles at Nuremberg coincide with initial development of the floodlighting system at the Zeppelin Field. The work would continue over subsequent years, with the 1936 Olympic Games closing ceremonies serving as a major stepping stone (followed closely by the *Lichtdom* of 1936) and drawing inspiration from the preceding Olympics in Los Angeles. In all of these cases, luminotectonic work was intertwined with the luminotechnic. Hence, in the 1936 closing ceremonies, the *Lichtdom* is woven into a sequence of in-stadium lighting effects. Moreover, these shows were never the creation of Speer alone. The noted lighting engineer Eberhard von der Trappen, Speer's collaborator on the street lighting plan for Berlin, also played a determining role. So even the diaristic "I" that speaks as if engaged in a solitary act of creation is itself a projection.

Finally, the "imaginary crystal palaces" that Speer associates with his chimerical *Lichtdom* are medieval only to the degree that nineteenth-century medievalism perceived in Gothic cathedrals the promise of a light architecture to be fulfilled in visionary imaginings like Bruno Taut's architectural crystallography and the glass architectures of the subsequent decades. The more concrete lineage to which they belong is that of the crystal palaces and augmented constructions of world's fairgrounds, from the 1851 Crystal Palace in London to the 1933 Chicago Century of Progress exhibition, which predated Speer and von der Trappen's experiments.

3. Albert Speer, Entry for July 9, 1965, in *Spandau: The Secret Diaries*, trans. Richard and Clara Winston (New York: Macmillan, 1976), 428.

4. Walter Köhler, *Lichtarchitektur: Licht und Farbe als raumgestaltende Elemente* (Berlin: Bauwelt, 1956); the book was translated into English as *Lighting in Architecture: Light and Color as Stereoplastic Elements*, trans. Bertrand Languages (New York: Reinhold, 1959).

5. The competition between French and American efforts to pioneer new techniques of outdoor lighting had begun decades before and remained intense. The topic is examined in Shelly Wood Cordulack, "A Franco-American Battle of Beams: Electricity and the Selling of Modernity," *Journal of Design History* 18, no. 2 (Summer 2005): 147–66. For discussion of both earlier and later French developments, see the writings of Éric Monin, among them "The Speculative Challenges of Festival Architecture in Eighteenth-Century France," in Sarah Bonnemaison and Christine Macy, eds., *Festival Architecture* (London: Routledge, 2008), 155–80; and "La naissance des premiers spectacles son et lumière: Les très riches heures de Chambord," in Robert Carvais, André Guillerme, Valérie Nègre, and Joël Sakarovitch, eds., *Édifice et Artifice: Histoires constructives* (Paris: Picard, 2010), 196–201.

Fig. 2
Cover of Albert Robida, *Le vingtième siècle: La vie électrique*, showing Paris's Eiffel Tower as a searchlight platform.

THE SCINTILLATOR

So if Albert Speer isn't one of the "fathers of light architecture," who might they be?

If there is a single figure to whom this title can be assigned, it is probably the Canadian-born lighting engineer Walter D'Arcy Ryan. In 1899, Ryan founded the world's first laboratory dedicated exclusively to illumination engineering for the General Electric Company. Based in Schenectady, New York, he directed the lab until the time of his death in 1934.[6]

In an era when lighting was still routinely considered an afterthought—something to be added into already built environments, with manufacturers of light bulbs, fixtures, architects, city planners, and engineers all operating separately—Ryan formulated an integrated approach that clearly differentiated *illumination* from *lighting*. Illumination belonged to the realm of function and consisted of the casting of light on a given target. Lighting, by contrast, belonged to the realm of spectacle. It was the art and science of producing effects by means of the context-sensitive design and distribution of lighting sources. It presupposed the integration of light and fixture design, architecture, and planning, and complex choreographies of darkness and light.

Luminotechnics were the point of departure for Ryan, the world's most celebrated illumination engineer during the first three decades of the twentieth century. Ryan's initial studies concerned the design of fixtures capable of transforming city streets into pleasurable, glare-free round-the-clock sets for modern life. To this end, light sources and their diffusion patterns had to be not only standardized, but also calibrated to the scale, dimensions, and chromatics of the street. Among the most famous early outcomes of this work were the White Way built through downtown New Haven, Connecticut, in 1911 and the Path of Gold built along San Francisco's Market Street in 1916.[7] During this period, Ryan also worked out systems for floodlighting the facades and interiors of building, developing the 1906 facade illumination for the Singer Building in New York City and the fully integrated interior/exterior illumination system for the General Electric Tower in Buffalo, New York, thereby establishing a model that would be adopted worldwide in 1920s and '30s commercial architecture.[8]

Ryan's true passion, however, lay in the luminotectonic realm. Already in 1907, he was able to persuade the Niagara Falls Board of Trade and several interested railroads to experiment with the first-ever nighttime illumination of a natural landscape. To this end, he assembled multiple platforms linked by a telephone network for light shows carried out nightly during the month of September. These experimented both with shifting architectonics of vision and with a polychrome effect that would become the object of several decades of research: the electric or artificial aurora borealis, achieved by the use of misting machines or, as in this case, by "noiselessly exploding loose giant powder in front of the main battery" to produce sunset effects in the sky that were mirrored in the water.[9]

The technique, dubbed "the Scintillator," became the centerpiece of Ryan's work at the 1915 Panama-Pacific International Exposition in San Francisco, where he served as Chief of Illumination.[10] For the first time in history, an entire city within a city—buildings, streets, and all—was designed as a function with a unified lighting program. Fairs from the 1889 Paris Exposition onward had employed outline lighting and attention-grabbing searchlights mounted atop structures like the Eiffel Tower. But Ryan achieved effects on a par with Bruno Taut's wildest dreams via, for example, the draping of the fair's centerpiece, the 150-meter-tall Tower of Jewels with colored crystals that, swaying with the wind, cast a kaleidoscopic mesh of color and light about the edifice. The entire site was built around a light show that included searchlight framings of the Tower of Jewels, simulated military battles carried along on the water's edge, projected "phantom flags," and "fireless fireworks" generated by an express locomotive whose effects bore titles like Fairy Feathers, Sun-Burst, Chromatic Wheels, Plumes of Paradise, and Devil's Fan. A polychrome backdrop, visible from many miles away, was provided by a battery of forty-eight 36-inch searchlights with alternating color filters that produced artificial aurora borealis shows titled "Birth of Color," "Ghost Dance," "Fighting Serpents," and "Spook's Paradise." Approximately three hundred scintillator effects were developed for the occasion.[11]

Over the next few decades, Ryan expanded on the formula at such events as the Rio de Janeiro World's Fair in 1922, the Edison Golden Jubilee in 1929, the Los Angeles Olympics in 1932, and Chicago's Century of Progress fair.[12] All were widely celebrated in period newsreels that conveyed Ryan's gospel of electric showmanship to audiences worldwide. By now the effects included neon cascades, buildings topped by crowns of vertical columns, and scintillator shows drawing on a total of 1.44 billion candlepower.

Fig. 3
Scintillator at work at a fireworks exhibition, Panama-Pacific International Exhibition, San Francisco, 1915.

6. For Ryan's bibliography and biography, see the entry in the *American National Biography* by Daves Rossell. Ryan's biography is also traced in the obituary that marked his death, "W. D'A. Ryan Dead; Famous Engineer," *New York Times*, March 15, 1934, 24.

7. The New Haven model was widely imitated throughout the United States during this period; see David E. Nye, *Electrifying America: Social Meanings of a New Technology, 1880–1940* (Cambridge, MA: MIT Press, 1990), 54–57. The racial coding of early electric street lighting projects has been explored by Conor Harrison, "Extending the White Way: Municipal Streetlighting and Race, 1900–1930," *Social & Cultural Geography* 16, no. 8 (2015): 950–73.

8. On Ryan and his context, see John A. Jakle, *City Lights: Illuminating the American Night (Landscapes of the Night)* (Baltimore, MD: Johns Hopkins University Press, 2001); and David E. Nye, *American Technological Sublime* (Cambridge, MA: MIT Press, 1994), 143–224.

9. The work was described by Ryan himself in "Illumination of Niagara Falls," *General Electric Review* 10, no. 3 (February 1908): 115–19. The experiments are discussed by Nye in *Electrifying America*, 58–62.

10. On this subject, see J. M. Anderson, "Lighting the Pan-Pacific Exposition: Origin of Illuminating Engineering," *IEEE Power Engineering Review* 18, no. 2 (February 1998): 24–25.

11. For Ryan's description, see his "Illumination of the Panama-Pacific International Exposition," *General Electric Review* 18, no. 6 (June 1915): 579–82. For an overall period description of the fair, see Rose V. S. Berry, *The Dream City: Its Art in Story and Symbolism* (San Francisco: Walter Brunt, 1915). Fritz Lang's designs in *Metropolis* show the impact of these shows on the urban imagination.

12. Ryan described his work at the A Century of Progress Exhibition in "Lighting the Exposition," *Architectural Forum* (July 1933): 47–50.

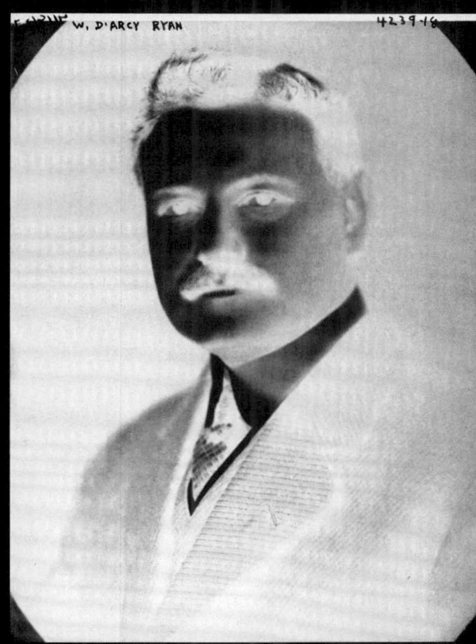

THE WORLD'S MOST SPECTACULAR BUSINESS

Though in 1927 Ryan did develop a "light gun" designed to "fire" logos, signs, and drawings for distances up to five miles, he was far more committed to research than to the commercialization of luminotectonics. Such roles he left in the hands of others like the Danish-American businessman Otto K. Olesen, who carried on Ryan's work. Olesen bought his first klieg light from an abandoned San Diego Navy shipyard in 1920, mounted it on a pivoting stand, and promptly proclaimed himself Hollywood's "King of Illumination." Armed with the slogan "We Light the World," over the next decade Olesen's company would develop fleets of power generation and lighting trucks, the former yielding up to 200 amperes in electric power and the latter mounted with 325 million candlepower searchlights flanked by arc floodlights, gas-filled incandescents with high-powered reflectors, and stacks of spotlights. This mobile army was deployed to light cityscapes for the nocturnal shooting of diurnal film scenes, to inaugurate buildings by means of the construction of light geometries, to stage artificial Northern Light performances (imitative of Ryan's) and to mark exceptional inaugurations, whether of films (at Grauman's Chinese Theatre) or of such structures as the Boulder Dam in Nevada. His fleet's autonomy and candle power was such that it was called upon to address natural disasters like the Long Beach earthquake of March 1933. It was designated as part of the US Naval Reserve in the case of an aerial attack on Southern California.

Aside from translating Ryan's research into a commercial vernacular that traveled the world thanks to its regular presence in newsreels, Olesen was directly involved in a number of events that provide a bridge to the European scene. Along with Ryan, he appears to have been an active force in the luminotechnic and luminotectonic backstage of the 1932 Los Angeles Olympic games, where much of the pregame attention was riveted on the inauguration of a new $50,000 lighting system for the Coliseum that made nighttime competitions possible for the first time ever. No less significant is Olesen's central role in the history of the Hollywood Bowl—the large open-air amphitheater opened in 1922 and equipped with various acoustical band shells during the 1920s—where he directed the annual Easter sunrise mass for 20,000 (accompanied a battery of special effects including a "living cross"). In the fall of 1934, he worked as the lighting and sound engineer on Max Reinhardt's mass production of Shakespeare's *A Midsummer Night's Dream*, attended by 200,000 people over ten performances. In a later press article, Olesen observed:

> Due to the huge area of the Bowl, the power of the lamps must be ten to twenty times the ordinary theater and it is not unusual, particularly when a color scheme is sought, for 1,000,000 watts to be needed. ... When productions require the entire area of the Bowl's sixty-five acres it is necessary to use projectors capable of throwing beams in colors over a distance of some 2000 feet.[13]

Similar stunts followed for the Bowl performance of Wagner's *Die Walküre* (including the shooting of burning butane gas under high pressure 14 meters into the air). Olesen continued into the wartime period with similar displays, alternately working as a light showman and as a defense contractor. During the postwar period he became the postmaster of Los Angeles. The business of luminotectonics now spread from coast to coast.

13. Otto K. Olesen, "Outdoor Lighting Requires Many Revolutionary Devices," *Los Angeles Times*, July 13, 1937. See also Dean Owen, "Olesen Turns Night into Day," *The Billboard Outdoor Equipment Review* (April 9, 1949):12–13.

Fig. 5
Advertisement for Otto K. Olesen Illuminating Company from *Los Angeles Times* (1923–25).

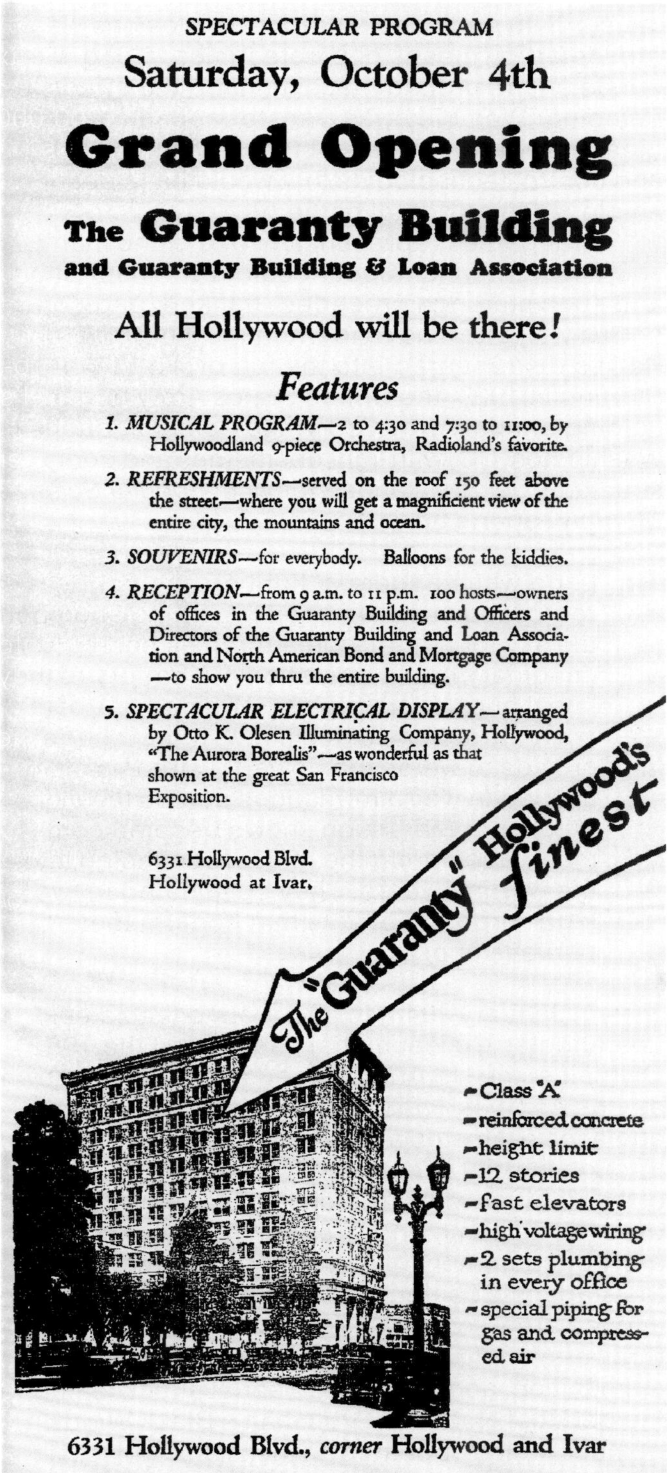

Fig. 6
Advertisement for grand opening of the Guaranty Building in Hollywood, featuring "The Aurora Borealis" by the Otto K. Olesen Illuminating Company; *Los Angeles Times*, October 3, 1924.

THEATERS OF WAR AND REVOLUTION

What Ryan brought to world's fairgrounds and Olesen brought to open-air theaters and stadia during the 1930s already had a venerable history in the realm of military simulations on both sides of the Atlantic. Starting in the 1880s, port calls began to be routinely accompanied by searchlight displays on the part of naval forces. Sometimes these assumed the form of freestanding luminotectonic shows; but they were also held in concert with national holidays or featured events at World's Fairs (Paris in 1889 and Chicago in 1893).

As searchlights migrated from fixed positions on the decks and masts of naval ships to aircraft and then to mobile ground units, these performances shifted in their orientation. Initially, searchlights were used bidirectionally, in criss-cross patterns, with beams cast upward from deck-level interwoven with beams cast downward from elevated positions. The predominant orientation was downward during the World War I era, as early searchlight-equipped military aircraft were designed to throw so-called "artificial moonlight" on potential bombing and reconnaissance targets.

In the course of the 1920s that directionality was reversed. The exclusive direction of luminotectonic displays, as in films like Fritz Lang's *Metropolis* and at Nuremberg, was upward. Ground-based mobile searchlight batteries became the bulwarks of anti-aircraft defense systems, as a result of which they also soon became standard fare in military rituals and parades. By the 1930s they were regularly integrated into performances of synchronized marching, aircraft overflights, simulated bombing runs, and stagings of physical, projected, or human banners and flags.

Sometimes these shows were training exercises. At other times they were explicitly theatrical in nature, as in the case of the Royal Air Force's annual Hendon Pageants (held every summer between 1920 and 1937) and London Defended, "a stirring torchlight and searchlight spectacle," performed between May 9 and June 1, 1925, during the British Empire Exhibition within the very grounds where soon would rise Wembley Stadium.[14] Like similar displays at the 1915 Panama-Pacific International Exhibition (and not unlike several earlier RAF performances), the squadron overflew the Wembley grounds in Sopwith aircrafts painted red and equipped with lights on the wings, tail, and fuselage. Blank ammunition rounds were fired into the stadium audience; shrapnel explosions were replicated by means of pyrotechnics, along with bursts on the ground that simulated the effects of bombing. Wembley was transformed into a literal theater of war by means of the very command and control technologies that would have been employed in an actual battle.[15]

War games represent just one of the many sources from which Speer could draw inspiration, and such stagings preceded, flanked, and continued well after the time when the Nuremberg Rallies disappeared into the fog of World War II. Starting in 1929, the United States Army began holding annual Army Ordnance demonstrations in Washington, DC, with light geometries and dome structures being a standard device. *Popular Science Monthly* reports how:

> Long white fingers of light crossed and recrossed in the darkness ... as they combed the sky for night-flying aircraft as part of imaginary battle operations. A battery of the latest huge searchlights ... formed one of the main attractions of the show. It drew huge crowds to watch the powerful streams of light moving in weird formations across the sky.[16]
> Wildly popular, such shows became commonplace during the 1930s, continuing into the wartime years. They culminated in two long-forgotten events that confirm their pervasiveness.

In January 1944, in and around the same Los Angeles Coliseum that had hosted the 1932 Olympics, the US Army staged a spectacle known as *Los Angeles Attacks* on two nights before an audience estimated at 205,000. A uniformed parade through the city streets was followed by an invasion of the stadium, with one thousand American soldiers dressed as commandos attacking a Japanese army encampment on the Bikini Atoll, recreated at the stadium's center. A chorus of one thousand intoned army songs to the accompaniment of flame throwers, the firing of thousands of rounds of ammunition, and a simulated aerial attack featuring the debut of Northrop Grumman's Black Widow bomber, which appeared, in messianic guise, at the center of a light dome formed by an enormous battery of military searchlights. Audience members were asked to participate by lighting matches. Gary Cooper, Jack Benny, and Bob Hope provided a comic interlude. One participant sustained actual injuries.

Such simulations were so integral to the culture of the American armed forces that within a year of the army's triumphal arrival in Paris in late August 1944, the US Strategic Air Forces in Europe decide to stage a military equipment exhibition for the civilian population at the base of the very tower that had served as the home of French luminotectonic experimentation. Aircraft were arrayed around the Eiffel Tower's base. Four 60-inch searchlights outlined the tower's structure toward a single pinnacle. The fifth searchlight was split to forge a victory sign that would transform the upside down V of the tower's form into a sign of victory that could be seen from the air, throughout the city, and the surrounding countryside.

14. On the Hendon pageants, see David Oliver, *Hendon Aerodrome: A History* (Shrewsbury: Airlife, 1994); and Brett Holman, "Ending Hendon—1: 1920–1922," Airminded: Airpower and British Society, 1908–1941, November 9, 2011, http://airminded.org/2011/11/09/ending-hendon-i-1920-1922/.

15. I note in passing the crossovers between these forms of showmanship and the sorts of theater experiments featured both in Soviet revolutionary festivals like Nikolai Evreinov's three-year anniversary staging of *The Storming of the Winter Palace* (1920) and Alessandro Blasetti's 1934 fiasco *18 BL*; in both cases searchlights provided the central means for guiding the attention of large audiences that were assembled in outdoor urban locations. On this subject see Jeffrey Thompson Schnapp, *Staging Fascism: 18 BL and The Theater of Masses for Masses* (Stanford, CA: Stanford University Press, 1996).

16. "Searchlight Battery a War Game Spectacle," *Popular Science Monthly* (January 1929), 72.

Fig. 7
Program for "London Defended," an air display performed by the Royal Air Force's Squadron #32 between May 9 and June 1, 1925, at Empire Stadium in Wembley Park.

Fig. 8
Battle scene from the Army-Navy War Show at the Los Angeles Memorial Coliseum, held on January 8 and 9, 1944.

THE ELECTRIC LIGHT MASSAGE

The fabric of such events is dense. But proliferation is very much the point inasmuch as it underscores the heterogeneity of the cultural and political freight borne by searchlight shows. Like so many other chapters of media history intertwined with that of architecture, the story of luminotectonics is less one of single inventors than of experimental processes distributed in time and collectively or collaboratively authored.

Within the overall heterogeneity, there are some core commonalities that are worth summing up, by way of a conclusion:

- the leading role performed by the military in the development of projection technologies as well as civic-use scenarios for luminotectonics;
- the importance of supporting media (such as newspapers, magazines, and newsreels) in shaping the worldwide dissemination of luminotectonic shows;
- the enduring presence of religious fantasies with regard to ghostly luminous structures "built" at the boundary line between the material and the immaterial;
- the overall rescaling and reshaping of public spaces during the 1930s as networked and electrified projection spaces where nighttime assembly was increasingly the norm, rather than the exception;
- the persistence of nineteenth-century notions of technology as a kind of artificial nature into (but not beyond) World War II, marked by the resilience of phrases such as "artificial aurora" or "artificial moonlight" with reference to searchlights;
- the defining role played by anxieties regarding Americanization, often merged with fears of Soviet materialism, in the path toward modernization pursued throughout the world.

Doubtless, other conclusions offer themselves up as well. Yet the one with which I will close is media-historical: namely, that Marshall McLuhan may well have gotten the story *exactly* right when, in the opening of *Understanding Media*, the first mature articulation of his theory of communication, it is electrical light that sets the stage for the passage from the era of industry to the electric information age.

McLuhan writes:

> The electric light is pure information. It is a medium without a message. ... The electric light escapes attention as a communication medium just because it has no "content." And this makes it an invaluable instance of how people fail to study media at all.
>
> For it is not till the electric light is used to spell out some brand name that it is noticed as a medium. Then it is not the light but the "content" (or what is really another medium) that is noticed. The message of the electric light is like the message of electric power in industry, totally radical, pervasive, and decentralized.[17]

I have often read this passage and puzzled over the choice of electric light (rather than, say, the cinema) as the entry point to McLuhan's book. The arguments become familiar in the course of subsequent chapters. Like other media, electric light reshapes the space and time of human interactions. It gives rise to new scales and forms of individual and collective action, as well as to new cognitive affordances (individualized looking equals involvement in depth). It succeeds by becoming so pervasive that it can be perceived only with respect to the activities that it enables: everything from brain surgery and nocturnal sporting events to office work and advertising.

Electric light also provides the exit point to *Understanding Media*. Having concluded his fast-paced dash through the media of the electronic age, from telegraphy, typewriting, and telephony to radio, television, and automation, McLuhan returns, by way of a valediction, to electric light:

> Since electric energy is independent of the place or kind of work-operation, it creates patterns of decentralism and diversity in the work to be done. This is a logic that appears plainly enough in the difference between firelight and electric light, for example. Persons grouped around a fire or candle for warmth or light are less able to pursue independent thoughts, or even tasks, than people supplied with electric light. In the same way, the social and educational patterns latent in automation are those of self-employed or artistic autonomy. Panic about automation as a threat of uniformity on a world scale is the projection into the future of mechanical

> standardization and specialism, which are now past.[18]

A paradox is at work (behind which lies a momentous historical transition). As a feature of everyday life in the mechanical age, electric light gradually loosens bonds, decentralizes fundamental forms of social aggregation (huddling around the campfire for heat and light), breeds new individual freedoms (artistic autonomy), and individualizes the workplace (self-employment). On the other hand, when raised to the power of a campfire for an entire city or nation thanks to luminotectonic wizardry on a special occasion, it summons that disaggregating society together in the name of mass entertainments or technoprimitive scenes of communion. But only so long as the mechanical era succeeds in promulgating its gospel of "standardization and specialism." In the course of the electric information age, the situation changes, the fireworks go cold. Their theater shifts from the sky to cathode-ray tubes flickering away in every living room.

17. Marshall McLuhan, *Understanding Media: The Extensions of Man* (New York: Signet, 1964), 23–24.

18. McLuhan, *Understanding Media*, 311.

Fig. 9
Cover of the original hardcover edition of Marshall McLuhan, *Understanding Media* (New York: McGraw-Hill, 1965).

Thumbs That Type and Swipe, 2018

The current evolution of media is surprising. Media are conceived to be available everywhere, and yet their way of working and ultimately their identities depend on where they are located. This is true for traditional media: their survival is tied to migration. Cinema exits the movie theater and reaches domestic and individual contexts; newspaper travels from sheets to electronic pages; videogames quit arcades and consoles and turn up in the palms of our hands. This is even truer for more recent media: their performances regard space. Surveillance cameras provide protection from the outside; hand held devices can create an existential bubble in which users can find an intimacy and refuge even in public spaces; Global Positioning Systems (GPS) parse territories; pixelated media-facades envelop and enmesh entire buildings. Both established and emerging media increasingly work through, within, and on the territory. As a consequence, space is no longer a neutral container in which media can simply take place or come to pass; it responds to the presence of media, aligning their actions with its assets and in turn readjusting its internal configuration to the media's affordances. Space grounds media, and media reshape space. We can even expand the picture. When the convergence of media and space reaches a certain degree, it elicits a mutual transformation. Indeed, if understood as components of physical and social landscapes, media display a distinctive and decisive set of qualities: more than tools for recording, storing, and transmitting information, they appear as resources for negotiating with reality and with others within a particular situation. Media ultimately become tools for a situated mediation. Conversely, space appears not just as the place where information circulates and becomes available, but as the environment where a situation comes into being and consequently where a negotiation becomes necessary. This allows a space to acquire in itself a certain quality of mediation: space mediates—it becomes a medium. Rooted in space, media reveal their decisive nature. Pervaded by media, space becomes the bedrock of mediation. The idea of a *mediascape* provides a conceptual grid able to explain these processes and their contextual and conjunctural implications.

Mediascapes: A Decalogue

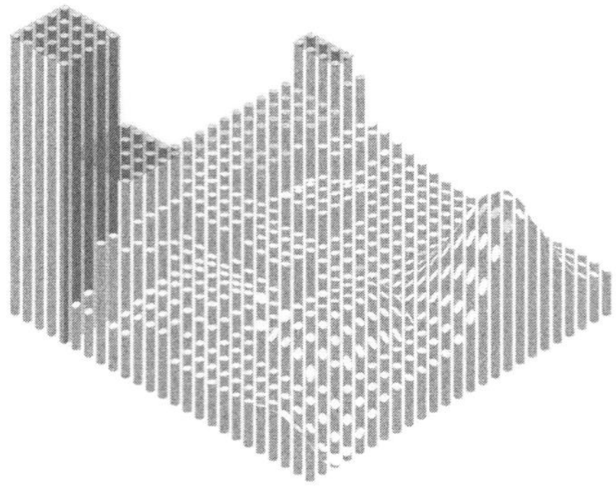

I. Space as Construct

Let's start from the beginning. We perceive the space around us as something that is given and natural. Even strikingly artificial environments—for example, the urban context in which at this moment I am located—tend to withdraw from consciousness and appear as entities which are just "there."[1] And yet it suffices to be affected by some disturbance—for example, by some phobia, like agoraphobia or claustrophobia[2]—to realize that space is a construct, something that we delineate.

There are at least four processes by which we arrange space: through perceptual schemata, through physical manipulations, through techniques of the body, and through discourses and narratives in the imagination. The cultural techniques[3] developed at each of these levels—techniques of observation, techniques of foundation or maintenance of a locality, urban planning, mapping or rendering, utopian imaginations, strolling—transform place into space,[4] or a surrounding into an environment.[5] A territory defined by the simple coexistence of elements becomes the theater of our action.

According to Michel de Certeau, this transformation recalls the process of enunciation by which a speaker takes possession of the possibilities of

1 On withdrawing from consciousness, see Martin Heidegger, *Being and Time* (New York: Harper, 1962).

2 Anthony Vidler, "Agoraphobia: Psychopathologies of Urban Space," in *Warped Space: Art, Architecture, and Anxiety in Modern Culture* (Cambridge, MA: MIT Press, 2000), 24–49.

a language and creates her own discourse, thereby inscribing herself into the utterance as its ideal source—as "I."[6] The parallel is revealing. Indeed, in the construction of a space, we deal with a twofold movement: on the one hand I manipulate a place, to transform it into "my own" space; on the other hand the space affects me and makes me one of its components. The former is a process of *appropriation* (a place becomes "my" space); the latter is a process of *inclusion* (I become a component of the space). This is what happens in the process of enunciation, where an utterance is at the same time an appropriation of the linguistic possibilities and an inclusion of the subject in her discourse.[7]

At this point three qualifying remarks are in order. First, a place can host several subjects (human and nonhuman), all internally differentiated in a rich typology. Each of them will shape its own space. That means that a surrounding can generate many possible environments. They will coexist, each of them being unique for the subject that shapes it, or will overlap, if a subject switches from one world to another. All spaces are in principle multilayered and multifaceted.[8]

Second, the construction of space does not by necessity require direct (or unmediated) human agency. It can be the effect of an intentional human action, but also the outcome of the arrangement of a set of physical and anthropological presences. The parallel with enunciation is again useful: an utterance can be considered as the product of someone's activity, but also as an output of the internal mechanism of a language. In this sense, the space can be seen as a product in itself. What matters is the process, the cultural techniques that carry out an act of appropriation and inclusion.

3 See Bernhard Siegert, *Cultural Techniques: Grids, Filters, Doors, and Other Articulations of the Real* (New York: Fordham University Press, 2015).

4 Michel de Certeau, *The Practice of Everyday Life* (Berkeley: University of California Press, 1984), in particular Part 3, "Spatial Practices."

5 Jacob von Jakob von Uexküll, *A Foray into the Worlds of Animals and Humans* (Minneapolis: University of Minnesota Press, 2010).

6 De Certeau, *The Practice of Everyday Life*, 97ff.

7 On the process of enunciation, see Emile Benveniste, *Problems in General Linguistics* (Coral Gables, FL: University of Miami Press, 1971).

8 This issue is largely underlined by von Uexküll, *A Foray into the Worlds of Animals and Humans*.

Third, once established, a space or environment appears as something that is taken for granted, or that has a natural existence, unless an unsettling or disclosing practice comes to the fore. There is a sort of permanent loop between naturalization and artificiality.

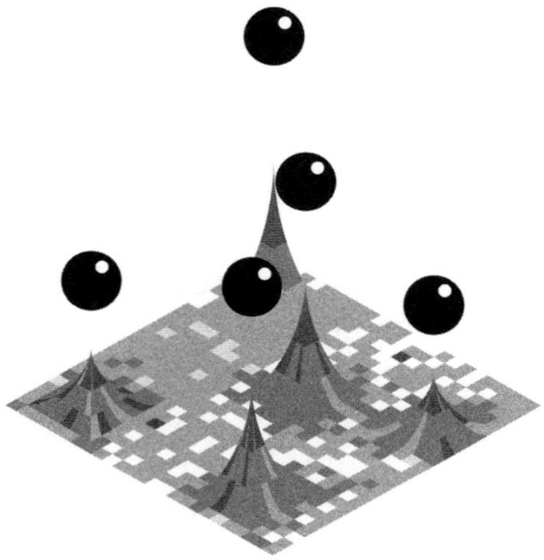

II. The Role of Media

If space is a construct, we can expect media to be a relevant component of this construction. Indeed, there are many ways in which media operate as active agents in the transformation of a place into a space, or of a surrounding into an environment. The most common action is tied with the process of representation. Space always comes through images, either mental or physical, and maps fulfill better than anything else such a function. Maps include not only the cartographic representation of a Zterritory, but any kind of discourse able to delineate a space. As James W. Carey remarked, a territory can be mapped "by producing a poetic or musical description," as well as through a "danced ritual." Every medium can offer a spatial representation. What matters is the fact that a map "is capable of ... transforming undifferentiated space into configured—that is, known, apprehended, understood—space."[9] The map establishes territory's arrangement, and in doing so not only it provides a means of orientation, but moreover it helps the territory to become what it is. In this sense a map *is* the territory.[10]

The role of media is often performed by elements that belong to a territory. A river, a rift, or a peak can mark a space and show up its configuration: they work like lines and points on a map. As for a map, they equally can act as means for orientation: they identify possibilities and interdictions, right routes and no-man's-lands, and consequently they predict possible behaviors. In this sense there is no substantial difference between natural elements—"elemental media," to quote the felicitous term coined by John Durham Peters[11]—and technical devices, i.e. media in a more traditional sense: both parse a territory and provide guidelines for an action; both push a space to become itself.

Media go beyond the fact of providing a representation or an orientation: they can directly interfere with the territory. In connecting people, they break down distances; in distributing information, they create privileged or deprived zones; in keeping records, they add or subtract values; in allocating technological features, they change the landscape. Their physical presence within the space can perform a range of functions. Sometimes media are components that identify an environment: it is the case of a screen that makes a room to appear as a theater, be it a movie theater or a home theater. Sometimes they are additions that enhance an environment: loudspeakers and monitors in a train station reinforce the idea of a point of transit. Sometimes they build a totally new territory, as a virtual reality or mixed reality do.

Whether we consider media as tools aimed at representing a territory and at orienting passage through it, or as active presences able to identify, enhance, and recreate a territory, spatial constitution is always media-driven, or at least media-related. It is no surprise that today, as the media expand their extent and scope, their interrelations with space become more and more evident. Such an intersection elicits integrated

9 James W. Carey, "A Cultural Approach to Communication," in *Communication as Culture: Essays on Media and Society* (New York: Routledge, 1992), 21–22.

10 Bernhard Siegert, "The Map Is the Territory," *Radical Philosophy* 169 (September–October 2011): 13–16.

11 John Durham Peters, *The Marvelous Cloud: Toward a Philosophy of Elemental Media* (Chicago: University of Chicago Press, 2015).

milieus: a television set or a surveillance system are not just supplements to a domestic space, they are fixtures of what we now consider home; a screen in a square or a control camera are not just a surplus, they are essential elements of a contemporary urban landscape; cables or hotspots are not an improper addition to a natural environment, they are what makes an environment more livable.[12]

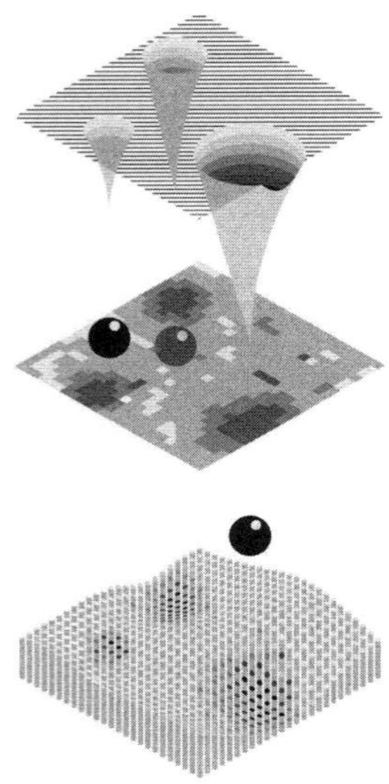

III. Mediascapes

When a medium is intimately integrated into a space, or when it constitutes a prominent presence within it, we may consider this space to be a *mediascape*. I borrow the term from Arjun Appadurai, who intended it as a concentration of tools for communication and expression in a world dominated by flows.[13] More properly, I want to consider a mediascape as an environment that promotes or facilitates mediation between individuals and reality, thanks to technological artifacts placed in it. In this perspective, media are far more than simple presences in a space: they are components that *innervate* the territory.

Walter Benjamin, to whom we owe the idea of "innervation," speaks of it in a threefold sense.[14] To innervate means to provide an individual or collective body with new organs that were previously external to it.[15]

Media are those organs. As Marshall McLuhan has already suggested,[16] media work as the "nervous system" that keeps the different points of a territory connected and makes the circulation of information possible. In this respect, they appear first and foremost as *infrastructure* that implements and underpins an environment.[17]

To innervate also means to create a new sensibility. The improvement of a sensory system implies a refinement or an update in the way things and events are perceived.[18] Media are such a sensory system, and when they sustain a territory, the territory can display new kinds of responsiveness. Some infrastructures make a space more *feverish,* as others allow it to

12 On television sets at home and outside, see Lynn Spigel, *Make Room for TV: Television and the Family Ideal in Postwar America* (Chicago: University of Chicago Press, 1992); and Anna McCarthy, *Ambient Television: Visual Culture and Public Space* (Durham, NC: Duke University Press, 2001). On screens in public spaces, see Scott McQuire and Meredith Martin, eds., *The Urban Screens Reader* (Amsterdam: Institute of Network Cultures, 2009). On the new geography of a networked society, see the pioneering research of Manuel Castells, *The Internet Galaxy: Reflections on the Internet, Business, and Society* (Oxford: Oxford University Press, 2001).

13 See Arjun Appadurai, *Modernity at Large: Cultural Dimensions of Globalization* (Minneapolis: University of Minnesota Press, 1996).

14 On innervation, see Walter Benjamin, *One-Way Street*, in *Selected Writings*, vol. 1 (Cambridge, MA: Belknap Press of Harvard University Press, 1996); "Surrealism: The Last Snapshot of the European Intelligentsia," in *Selected Writings*, vol. 2; and "The Work of Art in the Age of Its Technological Reproducibility," in *Work of Art in the Age of Its Technological Reproducibility, and Other Writings on Media*, ed. Michael W. Jennings, Brigid Doherty, and Thomas Y. Levin (Cambridge, MA: Belknap Press of Harvard University Press, 2008), 19–55.

15 "Revolutions are the innervation of the collective—or, more precisely, efforts at innervation on the part of the new, historically unique collective, which has its organs in the new technology." Benjamin, "The Work of Art in the Age of Its Technological Reproducibility," 45, n. 11.

16 Marshall McLuhan, *Understanding Media: The Extension of Man* (New York: McGraw-Hill, 1964).

17 For media as infrastructure, see Lisa Parks and Nicole Starosielski, eds., *Signal Traffic: Critical Studies of Media Infrastructures* (Champaign: University of Illinois Press, 2015).

18 "In technology a *physis* is being organized through which mankind's contact with the cosmos takes a new and different form from that which it had in nations [*Völkern*] and families." Benjamin, *One-Way Street*, 487.

be more *reflexive* or even more *indifferent*. There are diverse styles of feeling: they regulate the intensity and the tone of mediation.[19]

Finally, innervation requires a mutual adaptation. Something penetrates a body, changing the latter's performance; in turn the body, in incorporating something, gives what is incorporated a ground in which to settle down and develop its action.[20] In the media the physical and anthropic territory finds the backbone that sustains the whole, and in exchange it locates the media, assigning to them their range, their jurisdiction, their sphere of activity, and their proximities. Consequently, the infrastructure that underpins the territory takes the place of the territory, and at the same time displays its affordances.

A *highway* is a good example of contemporary mediascape. It is deeply innervated by a set of infrastructures: the traditional traffic signals are now integrated by a permanent wireless connection that makes it possible to get information about the traffic, listen to the radio, have phone conversations, and so on. Outside the car, surveillance cameras help to keep the traffic under control and allow a central station to make decisions if necessary. Inside the car, the GPS regulates speed and route and, at the same time, provides warnings about possible obstacles on the road. The GPS data are collected and added to other drivers' data to create an overall picture of the situation. The driver's sensibility, so different from the past, implies a reckoning with an expanded array of cues—not only visual, but multisensorial. The transference of bodies overlaps with the conveyance of information; transportation and communication become synonymous again.

19 McLuhan's distinction between "hot" and "cool" media was an attempt in this direction. For a reconsideration of this distinction, see Francesco Casetti and Antonio Somaini, "The Conflict between High Definition and Low Definition in Contemporary Cinema," *Convergence* 19, no. 4 (November 2013): 415–22.

20 Benjamin speaks of interpenetration (*One-Way Street*) and of interplay ("The Work of Art in the Age of Its Technological Reproducibility").

21 On the interplay of a set of elements as a process underpinning a territory, or a zone, see Keller Easterling, *Extrastatecraft: The Power of Infrastructure Space* (New York: Verso, 2014).

IV. Configuration, Assemblage, Disposition

A mediascape is characterized by a deep interplay among communicative technologies, human practices, and physical milieu.[21] Such interplay has a twofold property: it retroacts over the parts, defining or redefining their functions—a technology, a practice, a milieu are what they are because of their mutual interrelation—and its actions condition the whole setup, defining its structure—a technology, a practice, a milieu become part of a comprehensive design. This twofold action allows us to say that a mediascape is never characterized by the simple presence of a single medium or a single use, but by its *configuration*—the overall outline that holds together infrastructures, human traces, cultural technics, and physical fixtures in a unique conglomeration and at the same time circumscribes the property of each component.[22] Two caveats are necessary. First, the mutual relationships between elements are strong, but not constrictive. If it is true that a configuration affects the whole, as well as the parts, it is also true that there is not necessarily a strict determination. What matters is the convergence of parts toward a being-together of some sort, more than a perfect synchrony. We can consider a mediascape as an *assemblage* of technologies, environmental affordances, social practices, and so on, instead of an apparatus—that is, a compact machine.[23] Taking into account such a "loose determinism" helps capture how often mediascapes are not planned realities, but the result of a bottom-up process. For example, the domestic space has progressively become a mediascape, thanks to the progressive and often accidental integrations of devices and functions.

Second, the overall outline is not just an allocation of components; it provides an orientation of the whole. In other words, what matters in a configuration is its *disposition*. The idea of disposition has been recently invoked by Keller Easterling, who sees in it the propensity of an infrastructure to work in a certain way and to develop its potential.[24] Yet the concept has a long history. The word *disposition* has two parallel meanings. As the Latin translation of the Greek *taxis*, the term was a component of ancient rhetoric: precisely, the set of operations aimed at organizing the great parts of a discourse and orienting it toward its ending.[25] As the Latin translation of the Greek *oikonomia*, it referred to the way God arranges things in order to reach His purposes—the redemption of mankind—and consequently the way humans use resources to accomplish their goals.[26] What we have is an oriented set of sentences or an oriented course of action. A mediascape is deeply marked by orientation. The parts, while assembling together, take a direction that expresses and adapts to either the fulfillment of a vocation or a response to a current or future need.[27] At the same time, the reference to discourse and action is equally crucial: a mediascape always finds a way to express its orientation through stories that reckon with its past and future; and it always implies different forms of economy—not only financial investments, but a certain way of negotiating with scopes, desires, and affects—that orient it.

These two aspects—assemblage and disposition—explain how a configuration can have internal points of friction or dissipation, how it can coexist

22 On configuration and reconfiguration provided by media, see Pietro Montani, *L'immaginazione intermediale: Perlustrare, rifigurare, testimoniare il mondo visibile* (Rome: Laterza, 2010); and *Tecnologie della sensibilità: Estetica e immaginazione interattiva* (Milan: R. Cortina, 2014).

23 On *assemblage* as opposed to *apparatus*—and as a more correct translation of the Foucauldian and Deleuzian idea of *dispositif*—see Francesco Casetti, *The Lumière Galaxy: Seven Key Words for the Cinema to Come* (New York: Columbia University Press, 2015), 74–92.

24 Easterling, *Extrastatecraft*, 71–94.

with other manners of arranging the same surrounding, and, finally, how it can be contingent. Yet once established, the configuration of a mediascape permeates its single components and the whole so effectively that it is able to reinvest some components with new functions and even to assign to them the status of medium. If it is the presence of media that firstly identifies an environment as a mediascape, it is a mediascape that ultimately defines what works as media within its perimeter. This is true for elemental media—a star or a fire becomes means of orientation or traces of a passage on the ground because the situation requires signs and points of reference. This is equally true for modern mediascapes; once identified as a mediascape and not simply as a crossroad, Times Square redefines many fixtures as components of a space of vision, such as steps on the roof of a ticket booth that become seats for spectators.

It is against this backdrop that we can detect the emergence of a territory characterized by a concentration of practices aimed at recording data, transferring information, facilitating expression, distributing knowledge, connecting people, making texts workable, and so on. Through these practices, what comes to the fore is a process of mediation with—a special relationship that in some circumstances must be highlighted, intensified, tested, and maintained. A mediascape is precisely a site of mediation—a space where processes that usually underpin our everyday existence find a specialized mode of functioning.

What distinguishes a mediascape from other environments is this concentration at the level of assemblage and this specialization at the level of disposition. The examples that first come to mind are religious spaces (churches, temples, mosques). Here a mediation (maybe *the* mediation) that could occur anywhere is performed in a dedicated site that enhances typical characters of a relationship with divinity, such as an overlapping of closeness and distance, exposure and intimacy, immanence and transcendence, and communality and individuality. With a touch of irony, we can say that a localized meditation (with a "t") lets a mediation (without a "t") express itself in its purest and most radical form.

These observations invite us to consider a mediascape as a medium in itself. More than single devices, it is the environment that provides mediation. Even the bubble that we build around ourselves while watching a movie on a tablet or calling a friend on a smartphone provides a sense of intimacy that neither the tablet nor the smartphone possess as such, but that the situation requires. Media today are either mediascapes or they are mere technical gadgets.

25 For a reconstruction of the ancient rhetoric that underlines the central role of *dispositio*, see Roland Barthes, "L'ancienne rhétorique: Aide-mémoire," *Communications* 16 (1970): 172–222, in particular 213–17.

26 Tracing the birth of the concept of *oikonomia* in Byzantine thought, Marie-José Mondzain writes, "In the same way that God chose a manner of showing himself in order to make himself better understood, his servants, in imitation of him, will make instrumental, specifically focused choices of word and images in demonstrating the foundations and legitimacy of the cause they are defending." Marie-José Mondzain, *Image, Icon, Economy: The Byzantine Origins of the Contemporary Imaginary* (Stanford, CA: Stanford University Press, 2005), 12. On the translation of *oikonomia* into *dispositio*, see Giorgio Agamben, *What Is an Apparatus? And Other Essays* (Stanford, CA: Stanford University Press, 2009), 8–11. Agamben also reminds that the French word *dispositif*—as well as the English *dispositive* and the Italian *dispositivo*—come from *dispositio*.

27 For the opposition between the fulfillment of a vocation and the accumulation of resources in order to respond to a new need, see Martin Heidegger, "The Question Concerning Technology," in *The Question Concerning Technology and Other Essays* (New York: Garland Publishing, 1977), 3–35.

V. Evolution, Adaptation, Collapse

The interplay among communicative technologies, human practices, and physical milieu allows us to grasp not only the configuration of a mediascape, but also its evolution. Indeed, if we consider mutual determinations within an assemblage as a set of *feedback* that continually affects the elements of the whole, we inevitably highlight a mediascape's inner dynamics. Ongoing feedback forces a mediascape to continually adjust itself. The adjustment tends to be conservative, as the outputs fed back into the system are mostly aimed at preserving the overall configuration. There is room for innovation, however. When a feedback signals a possible modification that endangers the system, the system can adapt itself to the new conditions. The choice between preservation and adaptation also emerges when feedback originates not from within the system but from outside—from other environments with which the mediascape comes in contact. This results in either an isolation of the mediascape, or a new step toward harmony with the greater ecosystem.

The picture I have briefly mentioned recalls the process of niche construction, in which an organism creates its own environment through a complex circuit of feedback. Indeed, mediascapes are in many respects specialized niches whose components survive and evolve by reacting to and adjusting the environmental conditions. And yet a mediascape implies something more than a set of responses based on actual outputs. To mediate, an organism also must take into account unexpected solutions, and do so in anticipation of the situation. The presence of hypotheses, projections, and suppositions would enable the organism to face and counter whatever event may occur and to take whatever direction is available.

Such actions demand not only feedbacks, but also *imagination*—intended in a Kantian sense as the faculty that lies between perception and intellect. If feedback highlights the capacity of an entity—both in its single components and as a whole—to react to what happens, imagination underlines its capacity to deal with what may happen. It recalls not only the actual, but also the possible. Mediascapes imagine—I am not saying that the humans in a mediascape imagine, but the mediascape itself does so. Indeed, a configuration logically includes possibilities that have been excluded, but that nevertheless are present, even though in reserve; for a mediascape, to imagine means that these possibilities are recalled. Such an evocation is not necessarily instrumental: possibilities highlight paths that an entity is able to take, not only resources that an entity must exploit. Hence, a dimension that we must take in account: the development of a mediascape through a preemptive exploration of its possibilities, in order not simply to fit its task, but also to make itself available to a different destiny. Mediascapes conceived by architects or urbanists in the form of visionary cities or futuristic buildings, or, especially today, conceived by artists in the form of installations, generally activate this dimension, either as something aimed at the critique of the present or as something aimed at instantiating a utopia.

Yet the evolution of a mediascape implies not only a progressive adaptation or a creative expansion in scope and range, but also the risk of failure. Every environment hosts points of resistance, malfunction, and counterproposals. Mediascapes can slow down their action, reverse their mode of working, and ultimately disconnect their components. If an adjustment becomes either impossible or useless, a *communicative catastrophe* intervenes. The collapse of a mediascape is not necessarily a loss: it is the critical moment that can also initiate forms of reconstitution.

Urban spaces today are a good example of coexistence of these three tendencies. First, an increasingly elaborate system of feedbacks is provided by surveillance cameras, detectors, police monitors, and so on, mostly aimed at the preservation of the whole, or at modest adjustments. Second, they contain creative districts, or small business areas, or visionary complexes, generally supported by an intense presence of personal and social media, able both to connect users with different worlds (including virtual ones) and to reinvent a sense of communality. They represent well spaces of imagination. Third, within urban spaces there arise no-man's-lands, a consequence of the collapse of social routes and the evacuation of well-established functions. These discarded districts, lacking in media, host forgotten citizens, but that can also be the cradle of utopian ideas of a city.

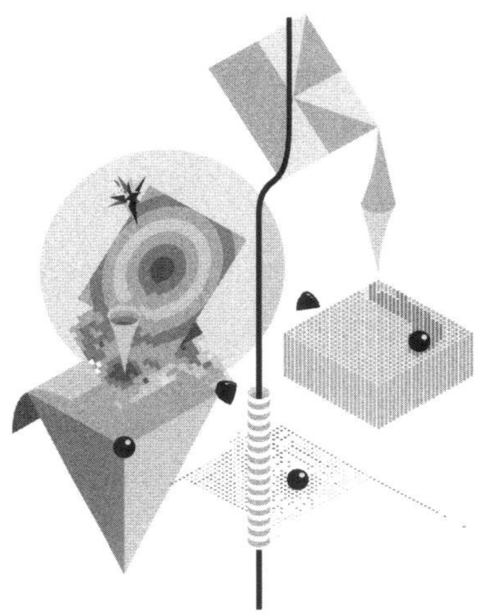

VI. Hybrid Profiles

Traditional mediascapes were relatively stable, largely specialized, and easily identifiable. Changes were possible, but generally they happened over long periods. More frequently, a mediascape gave rise to a set of variants, each one invested in a more circumscribed function. Take the movie theater: whatever size or location, whichever film was screened, the theater was a space with recurring characters. At the same time, there were a certain number of subtypes that fulfilled specific needs—from the film palace to the drive-in, the open-air projection to the home theater. Today, mediascapes are less established in both their prototypes and their variants, and they are less unidimensional, as they are often conjured from semiautonomous components. A movie theater can take multiple and even divergent instantiations—as a public space or as an installation in a gallery, as a permanent site of exhibition or as a temporary venue—and it can be supported by unspecific tools, like computers or LED screens, in different circumstances. Mediascapes increasingly respond to contingency and become conjunctures.

This indetermination of current mediascapes reflects tensions along three axes that, instead of defining clear alternatives, tend to overlap.

i. *The site and the flow*: the components of a mediascape are often in movement. This means that they belong to more than one location. A mediascape has to intercept these elements, keep them for a while, and then lose them—sometimes rotating or substituting them. Hence a provisional or a shifting existence of a mediascape.

ii. *The global and the local*: it is increasingly difficult to define what a locality is; its borders are more and more porous, unstable, and open. Hence the difficulty in identifying a mediascape with a specific territory. From the existential bubble in which I am included to a geographical entity such as a city or a region, its extension can span the dimensions of the globe.

iii. *The actual and the virtual*: we live in a regime of possibilities that are coexisting, rather than mutually exclusive. Traditionally, the possible was what could happen if something else did not happen instead. Today

28 "In an age of media ubiquity . . . a distinction between physical and virtual space does not provide a stable principle of orientation." Nanna Verhoeff, *Mobile Screens: The Visual Regime of Navigation* (Amsterdam: Amsterdam University Press, 2012), 20.

29 On "mixed reality" see Joshua A.T. Fairfield, "Mixed Reality: How the Laws of Virtual Worlds Govern Everyday Life," *Berkeley Technology Law Journal* 27, no. 1 (Spring 2012): 55–116; on the melting of effectual and possible, see the idea of Image crystal in Gilles Deleuze, *Cinema 2: The Time-Image* (Minneapolis: University of Minnesota Press, 1989).

the possible is identified with a set of events that, notwithstanding their incompatibility, happen at the same time and together. Instead of a mutual exclusion of actual and virtual, we have the coexistence of virtual and actual, of what is and what could be.[28] Augmented reality (the recent fascination with *Pokémon GO* being an example), with its set of information overlapping the image of an actual landscape, was the first step in this merging of the two dimensions. Virtual reality, with a user placed in physical space and experiencing a possible environment, was the second step. Mixed reality, with its merging of real and virtual worlds in a unique environment, can be the third step.[29]

VII. Relocations

Current mediascapes are characterized not only by blurred configurations, but also by ambivalent transformations. Traditional media tend to migrate into new environments. The resettlement of film or television in home theaters, public spaces, or individual tablets is a good example of this movement. In doing so, media do not dissolve: they reiterate some of their characters and at the same time they adapt them to a new context. Media rarely die; more often, they *relocate*.[30]

Relocation implies multiple paths. One is the almost meticulous reconstitution, elsewhere, of a previous territory. This is the logic of the traditional colonies—I will call it the "New England effect." It is characterized by a sort of aesthetics of obsolescence, in which the old is kept alive in a new context. Its opposite is a migration that ends with the creation of a new nation—I will call it the "war of independence." In relocating, media create a new type of situation that changes the configuration of a preexisting mediascape. More often, relocation triggers a hybrid situation, in which old and new coexist, or in which the persistence of the old is the ground upon which the new can more easily grow.

These dynamics recall the movement of deterritorialization and reterritoriazation explored by Deleuze and Guattari in what they call a rhizomatic space.[31] What previously was a compact entity is deassembled and then reassembled in an expanded territory. Once again, cinema is exemplary: its previous apparatus (the projector–film strip–theater–screen system) falls apart. Some elements, such as the film strip, are no longer in use; other elements become key components of other dispositives, changing their mode of working, such as the screen becoming luminescent instead of reflective, and in exchange, new devices can be integrated into the assemblage—for example, computers.

Such a movement implies the end of the traditional idea of specificity, based on the technical components of a medium: in relocating, a medium is no longer the machine it used to be. And yet, while the specificity is lost, the medium is not. In relocating it can perform, by other means, the same type of experience that traditionally is associated with it. The persistence of a medium is precisely the persistence of its experience. Cinema no longer relies on its traditional apparatus, but the idea of cinema survives even when we watch a movie at home.

30 I have tried to illustrate the process of relocation of cinema—and to distinguish between remediation and relocation—in *The Lumière Galaxy*.

31 Gilles Deleuze and Félix Guattari, *A Thousand Plateaus: Capitalism and Schizophrenia* (Minneapolis: University of Minnesota Press, 1987).

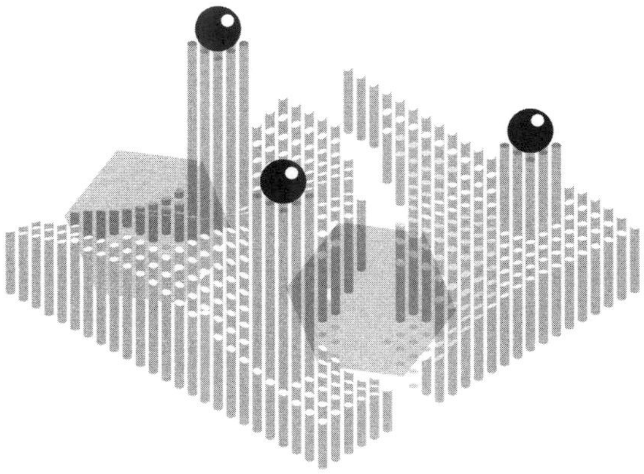

VIII. Screenscapes

Among the mediascapes, the ones based on the presence of screens are of particular interest, as most media today incorporate some form of screen or display, and because screens provide a wide and sometimes conflicting variety of environments. Indeed, it may be in the essential character of the screen to play a privileged role in the environmental conditions of media.

A first group of *screenscapes* implies the presence of a support for representation. Movie theaters, television sets at home, and public displays are instances of this type of screenscape: screen and audience are separated, yet the representation provides a space of immersion. A second group is based on touching more than viewing: the user enjoys a physical proximity with the screen, which in turn works as an ideal worktable. Video games are the typical media that innervate these spaces of privacy and performance. The mobility of the screen is the main character of a third group of screenscapes: if the screen-device is handheld, a personal bubble that the user creates around him or her represents a shelter or refuge, wherever the user may be. Traditional media based on screens, in their relocation, can migrate from one to another of these environments: film typically can migrate to the home theater, keeping most of the characteristics of its previous space, but can also migrate to a tablet, eliciting a more individual and intimate form of experience. Film can also be conceived for a touchscreen, but in this case it bears assimilation within the category of video games.

We can even extend our idea of the screen. Retracing its original meanings, we can think of the screen as a shelter, filter, or tool for camouflage instead of a simple support for representation, whether visible or touchable or mobile. Augmented reality, in which the physical reality passes through the scaffold of a system of information, is exemplary of screenscapes based on filtering. Surfaces intended to hide something—for example, facades of buildings under construction or restoration—are exemplary of screenscapes based on camouflage. Waiting rooms in train and bus stations, with their monitors bringing information and images of surveillance, are in some respect like shelters. And so on.

IX. Mediascaping

Much as a landscape invites a concept of landscaping, today a mediascape demands a concept of *mediascaping*. Mediascapes should not be considered as an enduring reality, but a continuing process of crafting space *by* media and *as* media—they inscribe themselves in a "becoming" more than in a "being." In this framework, what matters are the conditions that make possible the emergence of a locality and an environment.

The notion of mediascaping addresses the inevitable difficulty of sketching a typology of discrete and stable mediascapes. Mediascapes are active things that graft themselves on previous territories and in doing so, reshape both those territories and themselves. Mediascapes are mutants. We find them at work in urban space, domestic space, private space, virtual space, and what we might call infraspace (spaces that interconnect other spaces: for example, the ones we pass through while traveling).

They redefine the previously understood geography. For example, a space of intimacy, as our bedroom is expected to be, loses part of this characteristic when we bring a laptop with us and work as if we were in our office—but it keeps the sense of intimacy when we use the same laptop for a chat with a close friend. The bedroom changes status and cedes a place to a mediascape that in turn oscillates between these two states.

The emphasis on the becoming-mediascape recognizes a change in the way we think of a space: if a territory devoted to mediation helps to localize it, the mediation performed in this territory upends the usual concepts of border, distance, size, trajectory, and so on. Mediascaping geography goes beyond any geography. If it is useful to consider the great geopolitical questions that mediascapes raise—for example, their connections with centers where power, control, and decisions are concentrated, or their uneven location or relocation in different geographical areas—it is even more useful to understand such problems not as inert facts to be solved and defined, but processes to be tracked and followed.

Finally, the concept of mediascaping captures current negotiations that underpin the spaces in which we live. As it is, our ecosystem is a mélange of natural milieus, environments for specialized purposes, and spaces for mediation. We live among landscapes, taskscapes, and mediascapes. These -scapes coexist side by side, often with porous borders, but they also compete to expand their presence. The becoming-mediascape casts a light on this open fight. The increasing impact of human activities on earth's ecosystem—with the advent of the so-called Anthropocene epoch—requires this conflict to be acknowledged against the background of the increasingly technological presence of ecologies.

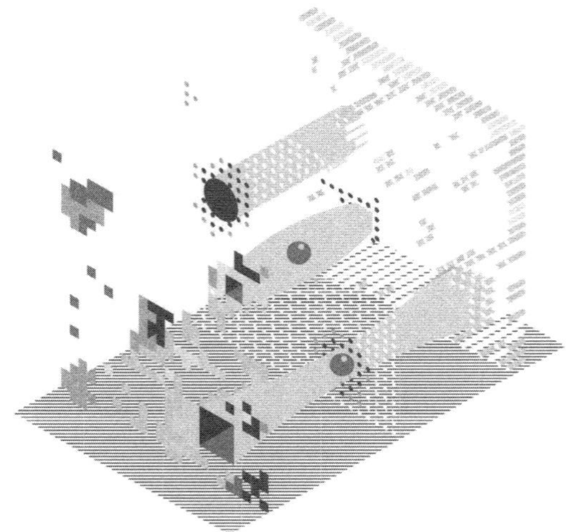

X. From Media Archeology to Media Ecology

The notion of mediascaping brings us to the problem of a media ecology. The concept of a "media ecology" was first proposed by Neil Postman in the early 1970s, in reference to McLuhan and Harold Innis.[32] It underlined the emergence of a new cultural space, characterized by a dense presence of media that elicited strong effects on our collective mentality. Now it is time to reassess—and even to overturn—this approach. We have to take the sense of space as a physical and cultural entity more seriously, and we have to retrace the interplay of a place, the media, and the practices that interconnect them. In other words, we should no longer ask what a territory is, what media are, or how the former is affected by the latter, but rather we must detect how media are intimately a spatial reality and vice versa.

A media ecology complements and rivals the burgeoning media archeologies. Media archeology is interested in retracing the long history of a device: it identifies borrowings and debts, ancestors and lost relatives, a possible lineage and the creation of new families.[33] Media ecology, on the other hand, focuses on media as components of an environment or as environments as such. Media are not defined on the basis of identities that are stable regardless of the space they occupy; on the contrary, media are identified by the positions they occupy in a space, and by the articulation or re-articulation they produce within a space. Here, what is at stake is a different becoming-media, no longer depending on technological exchanges, but on the different forms and assets of an environment. Mediascapes let space regain its relevance in the face of time.

32 Neil Postman, "The Reformed English Curriculum," in A.C. Eurich, ed., *High School 1980: The Shape of the Future in American Secondary Education* (New York: Pitman, 1970), 160–68.

33 Erkki Huhtamo and Jussi Parikka, eds., *Media Archaeology* (Berkeley: University of California Press, 2011); François Albera and Maria Tortajada, *Cinema Beyond Film: Media Epistemology in the Modern Era* (Amsterdam: Amsterdam University Press, 2010); Thomas Elsaesser, *Film History as Media Archaeology* (Amsterdam: Amsterdam University Press, 2016).

Illustration by Dimitri Brand and Gregory Cartelli

Christina Varvia

Fig. 1 Palestinian Resistance Press, video still (August 1, 2014).

On the Retrieval of Depth

Fig. 1 Palestinian Resistance Press, video still (August 1, 2014).

X – Y

On August 1, 2014, a videographer positioned his camera on the ledge of a window overlooking the sprawling buildings of Rafah, the westernmost city of Gaza bordering Egypt. After three seconds of stillness, the frame was completely overwhelmed by a cloud of dust from an explosion. The videographer zoomed out as the cloud grew and revealed the aftermath of two one-ton bombs that had fallen in a residential area. Later, this video was interpreted by both sides of the Israeli–Palestinian conflict. Was this another piece of propaganda? Why was the videographer there? How did they know to expect the bomb? How did they have such a perfect frame? Did someone notify them prior to the attack? What was the target? Did people die? Were they militants or civilians?

Although the bombing was perfectly captured in the watermarked image frame, the answers to these questions reside elsewhere—in other images, hospital records, and the memories of those who witnessed the bombing and survived it. Israel argued it was targeting terrorists and trying to protect its own soldiers, while Hamas used the video to demonstrate the extreme force inflicted upon Rafah on that day. The video is just one instance of the events that unfolded during the deadliest day of that summer in Gaza.

In fact, this is just one of hundreds of videos and images produced that day. The 2014 Gaza war was conditioned by the media field in which it took place. Images were not only produced by professional photographers, but also by civilians fleeing the bombings and using their smartphones to capture what was taking place. Most of them captured smoke and explosions. Together these pieces of footage formed a disparate cloud of data, thousands of viewpoints, and peeks into the history of the day. And while the war unfolded, the history of the events took shape based on those images. To paraphrase Paul Virilio, a war of militaries is also a war of media, a battle of perceptions, where the historical outcome of events is argued upon between citizen journalists, activists, official press, and government representatives.[1] Subsequently, the war in Gaza of 2014 was utterly conditioned by the proliferation of cheap recording devices. But the abundance of images did not candidly clarify the historical narrative; rather, it confused it. Although images were available, they lacked interpretation. As Eyal Weizman often highlights, a photograph or a video rarely captures the perpetrator, the victim, and the act of violence all in one frame. Therefore, the frame is the primary constraint of perception. It is the first parameter distancing the image from the reality it represents. In order to unravel the course of history, one must ask what exists beyond the frame.

This was the task at hand for the "Rafah: Black Friday" project that we undertook as Forensic Architecture in collaboration with Amnesty International. Forensic Architecture is a research agency comprising architects, filmmakers, journalists, scientists, programmers, and others that undertakes spatial and media analysis and presents it as evidence for human rights cases.

In this project, we analyzed and established the perceptual fields of each of hundreds of images and videos that resulted from the offensive in Rafah on the first of August 2014. We then composed these disparate perspectives through a three-dimensional model of the city, reconstructing the spatial relations embedded in the footage. We established the time of each strike by looking at the metadata of the images. When metadata was not available, we looked for shadows that allowed us to conduct sun simulations to reveal the time the footage was captured. When shadows were not available either, we examined the morphology of the smoke clouds. The clouds acted as fingerprints that allowed us to recognize the same bombings in multiple photographs or videos and create a chain of relations that would eventually lend the metadata of one image to a whole sequence of footage. We fought against the image frame by creating an *image complex*, the spatial and temporal relationship between the disparate footage that allowed us to narrate the events of the day. Within this complex, we also cross-referenced the testimonies of witnesses and their trajectories in the city as it was being bombarded. Thus, we were able to see how each perspective fit with the rest—all crystallizations of the same events, depicting the same reality.

However, the frame is not the only limitation of the image as a media object. In the becoming of images, the three-dimensional environment gets compressed into an abstracted two-dimensional medium. This representation is conditioned by multiple parameters.

Within the digital image canvas, information is arranged on the surface in pixels. Weizman writes extensively about the way violent events are often concealed under the veil of low resolution, from the silver halide crystals that make up the chemical composition of the film negative to the single digital pixel that represents a space of fifty square centimeters in satellite photography.[2] Resolution, the second most important factor in the resulting image, acts as a representational sieve that captures only the bits of reality that are larger than the given pixel or silver grain. The image canvas then hangs dry of any excess detail that has not passed the threshold of visibility or detectability. Depending on resolution, trees and cars are often depicted as only a few pixels, and people often escape representation.

Z

On October 28, 2015, the photographer Richard Mosse and his crew set up their equipment on a hilltop on the Greek island Lesbos, looking out toward the Turkish border. Their military-grade super-telescopic lens captured heat values and portrayed them as different shades of gray. They zoomed in about 4.4 kilometers to capture a shipwreck of a migrant's boat and the rescue operation that was unfolding on the stretch of sea between Greece and Turkey. It was a crowded scene. In the image frame, one can see boats by the Greek coast guard, the European border patrol Frontex, jet skis by nongovernmental organizations such as Proactiva Open Arms, fishermen's boats, and a helicopter. The footage is shaky, but the events are portrayed in an almost perfect perspectival

Fig. 2 Forensic Architecture, *The Image-Complex*, from the "Rafah: Black Friday" project (2015). The story of the events in Rafah, Gaza, on the first of August, 2014, lies somewhere between hundreds of images and video clips existing in disparate locations on the smartphones of activists, press clippings, and social media posts. Three-dimensional models provided an optical device and means of composing the relationships between multiple images and videos in space and time. This evidence-assemblage allowed a narrative of events to emerge.

Fig. 3 Richard Mosse, film still from footage captured during the production of *Incoming* (2014–2017), three-screen installation with 7.2 surround sound, 39 mins 25 secs, in collaboration with Trevor Tweeten and Ben Frost, commissioned by the Barbican Art Gallery and National Gallery of Victoria.

Fig. 2 Forensic Architecture, *The Image-Complex*, from the "Rafah: Black Friday" project (2015). The story of the events in Rafah, Gaza, on the first of August, 2014, lies somewhere between hundreds of images and video clips existing in disparate locations on the smartphones of activists, press clippings, and social media posts. Three-dimensional models provided an optical device and means of composing the relationships between multiple images and videos in space and time. This evidence-assemblage allowed a narrative of events to emerge.

Fig. 3 Richard Mosse, film still from footage captured during the production of *Incoming* (2014–2017), three-screen installation with 7.2 surround sound, 39 mins 25 secs, in collaboration with Trevor Tweeten and Ben Frost, commissioned by the Barbican Art Gallery and National Gallery of Victoria.

elevation. From such a distance, the migrants still at sea are visible only as a few pixels of higher heat value. As the waves swell, they temporarily mask the people's heads that are still afloat. In these instances, the migrants are in the shadow of the wave. The z-axis that determines the depth of field arranges objects in an ultimate hierarchy of proximity. Thus, the relative size of the waves in perspective manages to periodically conceal human life as it is portrayed in these few bright pixels.

This is just one of hundreds of videos depicting the so-called migration crisis that culminated during the long summer of 2015. Over 250,000 people crossed the wet border to Europe that year. On the 28th of October alone, approximately sixty people lost their lives on a stretch of sea only 4.2 miles wide, making it the deadliest incident in the Aegean's recent history. Forensic Architecture was asked by one of the survivors to investigate how in such a crowded scene there was still such significant loss of life.

In order to reconstruct space from image, one needs at least two distinct points of view. This is the principle of stereoscopy that allows humans to read depth by constantly calculating the binocular parallax between the two images perceived by our eyes. We collected videos from survivors, activists, and mainstream media as well as photographers like Mosse in order to unpack the space where this event took place and to understand the role of the actors who were involved.

In digital platforms, one might reconstruct space either by juxtaposing the images in three-dimensional models or through a computer process called photogrammetry that analyzes the difference between multiple photographs of the same objects and derives depth. The results of photogrammetry are three-dimensional models called point clouds, which are essentially colored pixels arranged in space. However, the challenge of measuring depth through images of the sea is significant, as the repetitive patterns of the waves deny any recognition of depth. It is difficult to distinguish between waves that are closer to the camera and others that are further away. Floating objects that might be used to measure the relative distance from the photographer are in a state of constant drift, and therefore cannot be reliably referenced across frames. The sea presents a representational challenge when it comes to reading depth. Photogrammetry mostly fails.

Even on ground conditions, when point clouds can be obtained and one is able to read space backwards from images, most often there will be voids—informational lacunas at the places where objects stood in the way and concealed the view. The shadows of such objects perforate the image-space of photogrammetry models. And even when the pixels of a point cloud are merged together to form a mesh, the mesh remains an image-surface that unfolds in space to describe the relief of an object. In other words, no matter how three-dimensional those models may become, they will always be hollow. They are limited to the fact that they are images draped over non-existent digital objects. What exists on the dark side of the image-plane, its "backside,"[3] still remains unknown.

If there are people behind the pixels depicting waves, we cannot know.

This becomes an issue of geopolitical importance when considering the military operations that different states employ at a subterranean level. Ryan Bishop writes about an initiative called "Transparent Earth," launched by the US Department of Defense in 2010 in order to detect and visualize underground military bases by using sound waves and lightening technology.[4] In an effort to create an image of the underground, to see beyond the image mask of the surface, the “Transparent Earth” project employed a telestethoscope that could listen to the density of the earth and reveal structures underground. Sound can transgress the materiality of soil and reflect the consistency of objects underground.

The surface of the sea is a very different threshold condition than the crust of the earth. However, similar detection technologies are used to reveal objects underwater through sonar, as well as objects on the surface of the sea through radar. By using light, sound, or radio waves, these technologies measure echo in order to calculate the depth and relative position of objects within range. As with the lightening technology of Transparent Earth, sonar and radar are highly susceptible to interference—what scientists call noise.

Acoustic, electromagnetic, and other types of interference will often distort the image of a sonar or radar scan, and even create false apparitions on the ocean bed. Reading depth brings forward the challenge of materiality as one is forced to consider the substance between the sensing device and the objects sensed. For instance, when set to detect boats, radar may often detect concentrations of mist that exceed a determined threshold and water particles might appear on screen as solid objects. Seafarers call these apparitions “sea clutter” or “angel echoes,” and in the past they may have been mistaken for ghost ships. These phenomena reveal the materiality of the plasma that fills the space between the object to be represented and the apparatus of perception.

When depicting the surface of the sea, the boundary between sea surface (the object of representation) and air (the medium of representation) dissolves as water particles evaporate. We can consider this zone of mist not only as an obstacle in the imaging practice, but also as another layer of inscription. Water is both a body to be represented and the medium through which information travels. As light is reflected on water particles, they carry forward visual information about the surrounding environment. Mist is often perceived as a blurry filter, blending together images of adjacent objects, a phenomenon famously captured by William Turner in his paintings of the sea. By using similar brushstrokes, Turner treats both sea and atmosphere as continuous particles of matter. In this way, he reveals that there is no void between viewing lens and object of viewing (whether a ship, the sea, or clouds), but rather a different kind of materiality—in his case that of misty air. Turner’s fluid perception suggests a way of viewing in which the world is a formulation of particles of different material qualities. Though mist may form noise in

Fig. 4 J. M. W. Turner, *Margate (?), from the Sea* (1835–40). The sea and sky are depicted with the same material quality in Turner's paintings, as the mist blurs the boundary between the two.

Fig. 4 J. M. W. Turner, *Margate (?), from the Sea* (1835–40). The sea and sky are depicted with the same material quality in Turner's paintings, as the mist blurs the boundary between the two.

an image and conceal certain objects from view, it also reveals the collapsing of depth onto the surface of the image.

Through Mosse's lens, the mist also plays an important role in the representation of the shipwreck. As people struggle to stay alive at the surface of the sea, they occupy exactly this zone of mist. They occasionally emerge as distinguishable figures and then blend again within the material quality of the sea. In fact, it is almost impossible to detect a human at sea from this distance by looking only at a still frame. It is the motion of the bodies that reveals what is human and what is noise. Between multiple sequential frames, the few concentrations of pixels representing people still afloat move at a different speed from the constantly shifting mist, allowing the viewer to faintly distinguish human bodies among the forms of the waves.

T

The x- and y-dimensions can be sufficiently described through a still image. But the challenges of reading depth, the z-axis, often require a plethora of images, specifically sequential ones illustrating motion over time and from multiple perspectives. In his essay "Techniques of the Observer," Jonathan Crary places the question of depth, or, as he terms it, "relief," in absolute conjunction with time, quoting nineteenth-century scientist and inventor Sir David Brewster: "the relief is not obtained from the mere combination or superposition of the two dissimilar pictures. The superposition is effected by turning each eye upon the object, but the relief is given by the play of the optic axes in uniting, in rapid succession, similar points of the two pictures."[5]

In human vision, time facilitates the composition of image-space. Our eyes accumulate images that vary slightly in perspective and feed them to the brain, which processes the micro-differences to create three-dimensional images. This processing stage is the moment when interpretation comes into play, and with it, subjectivity. Though our eyes cannot see beyond our own visual frame, behind the shadows of objects or through the mist of the atmosphere, certain assumptions are made in order to read depth and understand the world in its three-dimensionality.

Therefore, perception is far from an instantaneous mechanical function, but rather a real-time cinematic process that blends images together through time.[6] This process takes place at the mental space where memory and subjectivity reside: the way images are interpreted by the viewer is subject to all the previous images and experiences to which the viewer has been exposed. In the cognitive process of imaging space, there is an amalgamation of past and present. Subjectivity enters the epistemology of optics when time is introduced to the equation, as the mind carries forward the memory of the past while creating or interpreting images.

Thus, the photograph as a form of visual language contains a dialectic feature: it is an interface that mediates between the physicality of the world and the subjectivity of the self. As monadic crystallizations of events, images are a priori conditioned by the intentions of their makers.[7] The choice of subject, framing, exposure, and method of capturing the image is already calibrated to fit the personal and political agenda of the author. Therefore, the image depicts not only a representation of events, but moreover the political background that has conditioned the photographer, videographer, or image maker to see through that specific lens. Additionally, the image reader also brings forth his or her own political imaginary that conditions the act of viewing. The reader of the image projects back onto the surface of the image plane the expectations and presumptions that he or she carries as a result of past experiences. Therefore, the Benjaminian notion of images as "dialectics at a standstill"[8] has the power to bring together a dialogue between past and present, and between the two conditioned points of view of the image maker and image reader.

Likewise, dialectics begin at the image plane, but extend and further intensify at the limits of the image itself. Although some consensus can be obtained as to what an image depicts, that which is beyond the image plane, outside the frame, between the pixels, behind the shadows of objects, or masked by the noise is exposed to limitless speculation. Those thresholds of perception are in fact the locale of political struggle, and they are fought over often with the same rigor as nations fight for their physical borders. For what is argued upon is sovereignty over truth; whoever wins the battle of media determines history, controls the way we perceive the past, and establishes the collective understanding and memory of an event.[9]

To read depth from a flat image, one needs to deconstruct it, to analyze how it was captured and to corroborate it with material that sits outside the frame, both spatial and temporal. As previously noted, there is rarely a single image or video that captures the entirety of an event. Truth is argued between images, in a "machinic assemblage of images in a state of universal variation in which privileged instances of subjective perception are always subsumed in a mobile constellation of relationships with other images."[10] Similar to Turner's paintings, we exist within a liquid mode of perception. We sample reality through images and speculate what happens beyond the mist. Our compromised optics allow images to blend together to create narratives of events. But what joins the disparate pixels is fabulation.

The efforts of investigative practices such as Forensic Architecture are to anchor the drifting images in space, to give them gravity through revealing their connections with other images, facts, and experiences. Either through the image complex that considers planar relationships or through photogrammetry that considers pixels arranged in space, we try to reveal the space that exists between images—we problematize depth—in order to come closer to the reality of an event. Though we cannot determine how images will be read, we can reveal the conditions of their making, we can unfold the space they try to represent and we can bring forward the voices of those who have experienced violent events and who have been concealed by representation.

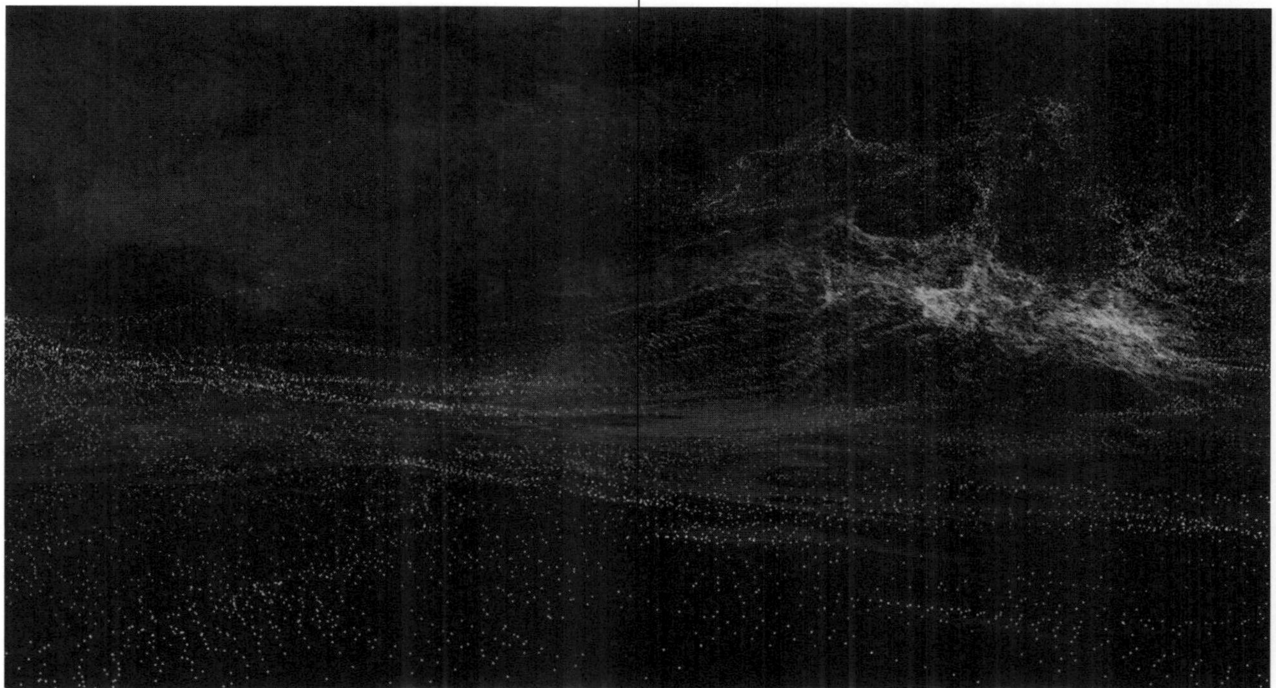

Fig. 5 Christina Varvia, still from *Shipping Tales* (2014), produced as part of the Unknown Fields Division of the Architectural Association. When read through navigational instruments such as radar, the sea becomes data. In this mediatization, there are often glitches and, in some cases, concentrations of mist appear on screen as solid objects. These whimsical apparitions can be the site of a new maritime mythology of ghost ships and mystical islands.

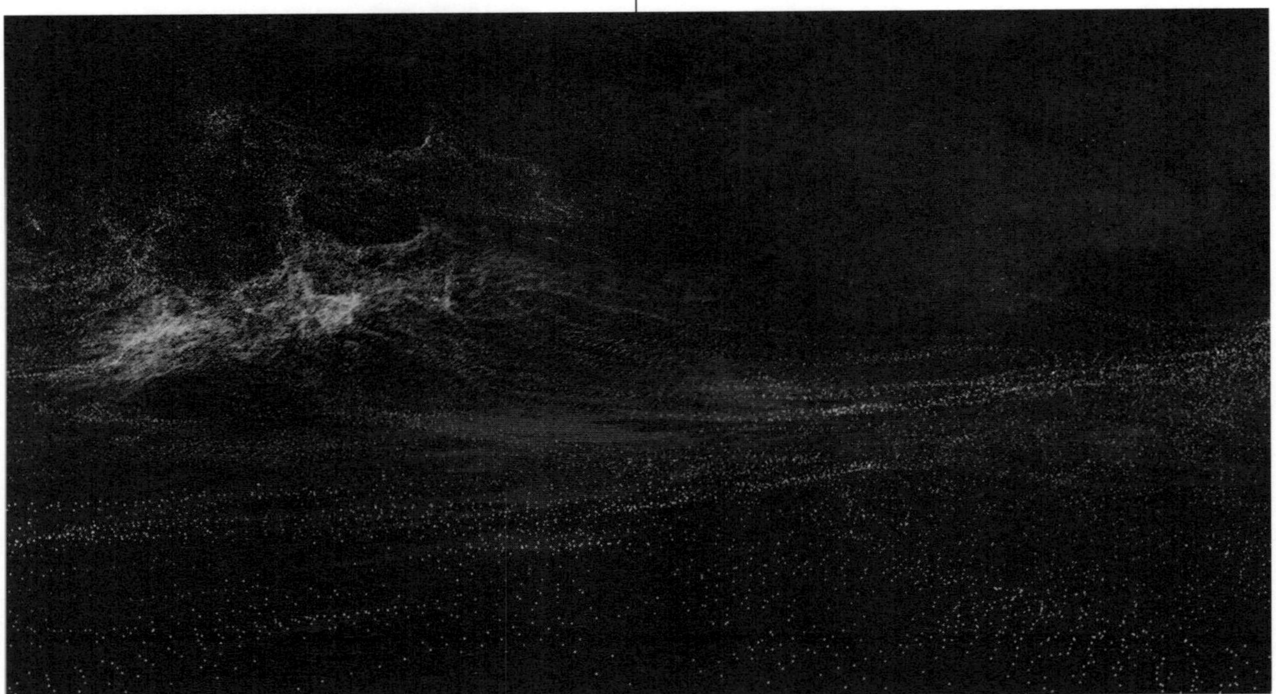

Fig. 5 Christina Varvia, still from *Shipping Tales* (2014), produced as part of the Unknown Fields Division of the Architectural Association. When read through navigational instruments such as radar, the sea becomes data. In this mediatization, there are often glitches and, in some cases, concentrations of mist appear on screen as solid objects. These whimsical apparitions can be the site of a new maritime mythology of ghost ships and mystical islands.

1 "There is no war, then, without representation, no sophisticated weaponry without psychological mystification. Weapons are tools not just of destruction but also of perception." Paul Virilio, *War and Cinema: The Logistics of Perception* (New York: Verso, 1989), 8.

2 Eyal Weizman, *Forensic Architecture: Violence at the Threshold of Detectability* (New York: Zone Books, 2017).

3 Jean-Luc Nancy, *The Ground of the Image* (New York: Fordham University Press, 2005), 2.

4 Ryan Bishop, "Transparent Earth: The Autoscopy of Aerial Targetting and the Visual Geopolitics of the Underground," *Forensis: The Architecture of Public Truth* (Berlin: Sternberg Press and Forensic Architecture, 2014), 580–90

5 Sir David Brewster, *The Stereoscope: Its History, Theory, and Construction* (London: John Murray, 1856), quoted in Jonathan Crary, "Techniques of the Observer," *October* 45 (Summer 1988): 27–28.

6 Gilles Deleuze, *Cinema 1: The Movement-Image*, trans. Hugh Tomlinson and Barbara Habberjam (Minneapolis: University of Minnesota Press, 1986).

7 A monad, in Gottfried Leibniz's theory of Monadology is an object that contains all others. It can act as a prism through which one can view the world. Similarly, images often carry with them a collapsed version of the world they come to depict, as well as the relationship between the creator of the image and the subject that is depicted.

8 "It's not that what is past casts its light on what is present, or what is present its light on the past; rather, image is that wherein what has been comes together in a flash with the now to form a constellation. In other words, image is dialectics at a standstill. For while the relation of the present to the past is a purely temporal, continuous one, the relation of what-has-been to the now is dialectical: is not progression but image, suddenly emergent." Walter Benjamin, "Awakening, n2a, 3," *The Arcades Project* (Cambridge, MA: Belknap Press of Harvard University Press, 1999), 462.

9 Paul Virilio notes that "the history of battle is primarily the history of radically changing fields of perception. In other words, war consists not so much in scoring territorial, economic or other material victories as in appropriating the 'immateriality' of perceptual fields." Virilio, *War and Cinema*, 8. Equally in every struggle for occupation whether that is territorial occupation or economic dominance, there is always a constant representation of space as a means of exercising control.

10 John Johnston, "Machinic Vision," *Critical Inquiry* 26, no. 1 (Autumn 1999): 35.

Thumbs That Type and Swipe, 2018

In 1978, the Paris-based architect Yona Friedman submitted a proposal to the United Nations Educational, Scientific and Cultural Organization (UNESCO), titled "l'UNESCO pour tous," suggesting that the organization popularize or "vulgarize" its educational materials to better address impoverished populations in the Global South.[1] While Friedman was clearly thinking of the didactic cartoon pamphlets he had started producing several years earlier for UNESCO, he also proposed another medium, a "wall-journal," which would consist of enlarged educational cartoons (several square meters in area) to be posted on building exteriors. This medium would not only save costs relative to printing pamphlets but also, given its public visibility, hopefully encourage community discussion as a spur to economic and cultural transformation.[2] Friedman enumerated dozens of topics that could form the content of these wall-journals, including personal hygiene, home economy, and agricultural sustainability, as well

Between Survival and Citizenship: Yona Friedman's "Vulgar" Media

as more abstract questions of urban development.[3] These "vulgar" media would, he explained, address matters "useful to survival, development, and culture."[4]

Leaving aside for a moment the question of "culture," I would point out that "survival" and "development" were quite different objectives, and arguably conflicting ones, even if it were impossible to strictly delimit where survival left off and development began. At what point could health care, education, labor, nourishment, and shelter exceed the functions of survival and become transformative agents of a hopefully better life? The ambiguous distinction between survival and development was further complicated by Friedman's choice of media. Addressing the fact of widespread nonliteracy in the Global South, Friedman explained that educational cartoons and wall-journals were appropriate for nonliterate people.[5] While graphic formats could be seen as a pragmatic stopgap measure within UNESCO's mandate to instate universal literacy, they also lend themselves to another interpretation.[6] The cartoons and murals normalized nonliteracy, indefinitely deferring one the most basic objectives of UNESCO's founding mission.[7] In this sense, vulgar media transpose the textual knowledge of foreign expertise into simplified, semiotic form to be easily digested by barely literate or nonliterate people.[8]

In his many cartoon pamphlets for UNESCO (produced between 1971 and 1992), Friedman revealed his discomfort with the organization's educational mission. In a 1976 pamphlet, where he first mentioned the idea of wall-journals, he disavowed the medium's educational function, drawing a distinction between *forming* people (the function of education) and *communicating* knowledge.[9] This vexed effort to formulate a noninterventionist mode of intervention characterized Friedman's entire career in the Global South, as he struggled to organize the architecture and indeed the entire culture of impoverished communities in such a way that they might resist change. That is, he sought to *develop* a citizenry capable of *resisting development*, regardless of urgent calls from the decolonizing world for technical assistance and development as a means toward economic independence.

In the 1970s, Friedman advocated a return

to a "poor world" of regional economic self-reliance to stave off impending ecological and human disaster.[10] Several years later, he produced a cartoon pamphlet for UNESCO titled *Programme modeste pour survivre dans un monde en pleine crise* (A modest program for surviving in a world of total crisis), envisaging a global shortage of resources. His "modest" proposal was to abolish monetary currency and reinstate barter as the standard mode of economic exchange, thereby impeding surplus accumulation. A poor world was seen as the solution not only to resource depletion, but also to economic dependency and the threat that globalization posed to cultural diversity.

Friedman's attitude reflected contemporaneous debates among Western experts (and indeed within UNESCO) concerning the advantages and disadvantages of modernization in the Global South and the subsequent turn to cultural preservation.[11] In this context, his work highlights how specific media were intended agents of intervening-without-intervention, of modernizing-without-modernization.[12] Concerning his preference for vulgar media, it should be recalled that for postcolonial and Marxist thinkers

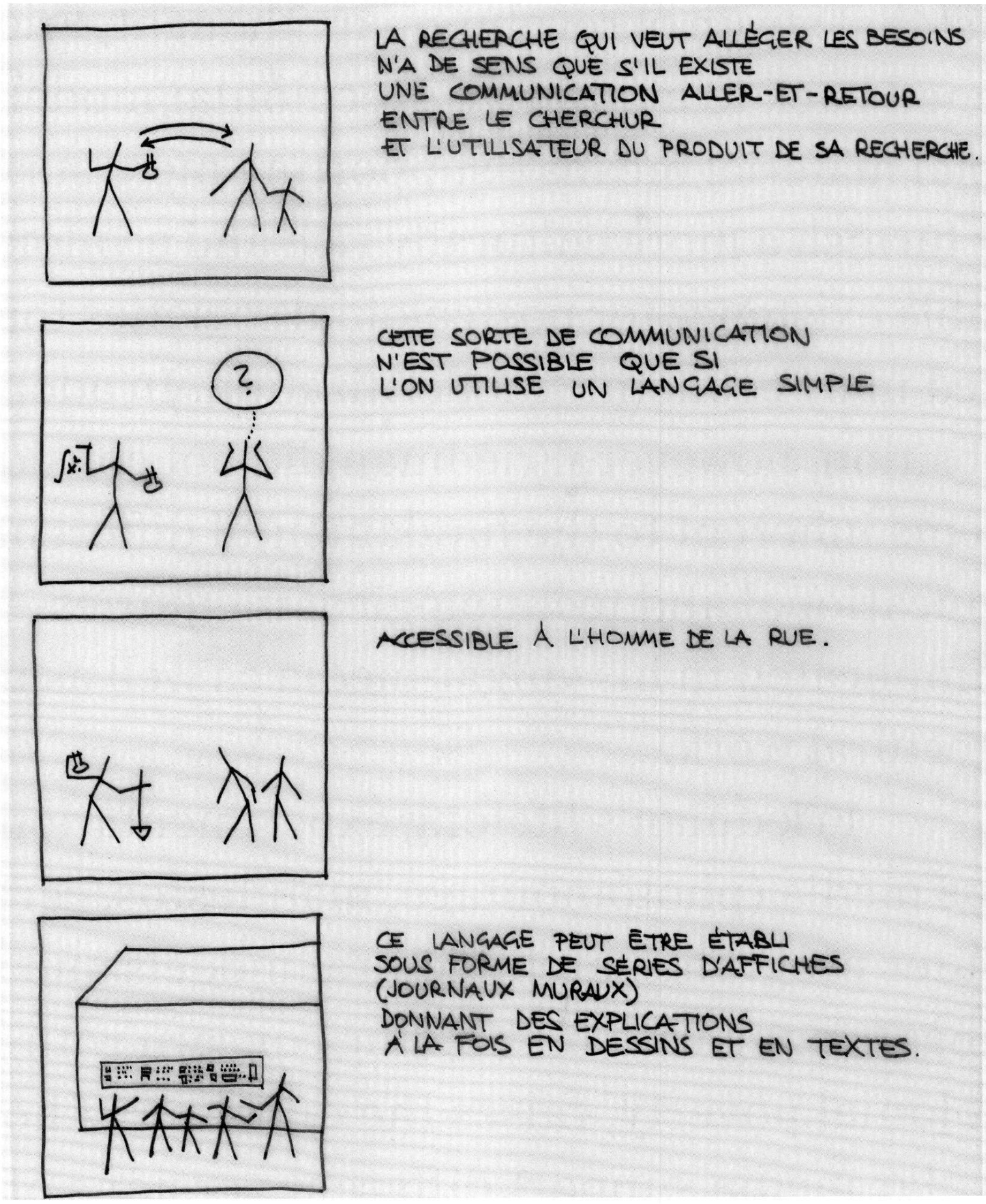

Fig. 1 UNESCO pamphlet: "*Programme modeste pour survivre dans un monde en pleine crise*" (1976), E3.

such as Frantz Fanon, Paulo Freire, and Antonio Gramsci, education and literacy were absolutely requisite to combatting colonialism and hegemony. Against that strain of revolutionary thought, Friedman harkened back to a putative precolonial model. Minimal material means—supporting mere survival—might furnish a more culturally rich and economically equitable existence for postcolonial societies than one ushered in by economic modernization. In adopting this position, however, Friedman did not consider the problems inherent to the fundamental differentials—the educational and technological inequities—that were implicated in his vulgar media as well as in his architectural work.

Friedman's lifelong experimentation with various media (photomontage, manifestos, cartoons, computer programs, architectural models and drawings), along with his abiding concern with postcolonial poverty, raises the question of how particular media support different versions of post-colonial citizenship and different relations of power between media producers and media consumers. Vulgar media take on an ambivalent role in this

COMMUNICATION CENTRE
OF SCIENTIFIC KNOWLEDGE FOR SELF-RELIANCE

UNDER THE AUSPICES OF THE UNITED NATIONS UNIVERSITY
WITH THE PARTICIPATION OF THE INTERNATIONAL COUNCIL OF SCIENTIFIC UNIONS

TALES IN THE AFRICAN MODE

YONA FRIEDMAN

Fig. 2 “Tales in the African Mode” (cover page), circa 1983–1986.

regard. On the one hand, they run the risk of accommodating (rather than helping eradicate) educational difference, while on the other hand, they can be seen as attempting to resist cultural and economic globalization.

Indeed, Friedman wrote of the need to preserve culture, native architectural convention, and oral tradition against the incursions of development and mass media.[13] Yet, he was hardly unique in equating orality and vernacular architectures with cultural authenticity, or in arguing that these aspects of culture must be protected against development.[14] Nevertheless, his architectural strategies for cultural preservation differed from those typically implemented through the self-help housing movement in the mid-twentieth century.[15] Whereas most self-help housing schemes endeavored to camouflage modernist planning through the reproduction of local building types, Friedman conspicuously flouted prevailing modernist architectural conventions in Africa by proposing space-frame megastructures as a platform for housing. In this scheme, the vernacular was within the purview of individual residents who were to design and build their own housing units within the provided infrastructure. The buildings' occupants would insert and preserve native culture within the larger spatial and economic frameworks of urbanization—frameworks that were physically manifest as megastructures.

Many of Friedman's space-frame designs, including *blocs à l'enjambée* and several of his proposals for Africa, defined a discrete role for each of two competing *topoi* of humanitarian discourse: survival-as-cultural-preservation versus modernization-as-development.[16] Culture-survival was carried out within the sphere of individual habitation, while modernization-development constituted the space-frame through which individual cultures would be integrated within the scope of industrial urbanism and at the same time, safeguarded from it. In this respect, the megastructures would operate like media to be filled with the content of diverse cultures. Friedman envisioned these space-frames as grammar-like structures within which individual habitation would operate as semiotic signs. Echoing structuralist anthropology, Friedman described the megastructure as a "support that would allow the realization of any term within a repertoire [of architectural possibilities] or the transformation of one term within the repertoire into another."[17] Similar to that of Claude Lévi-Strauss, Friedman's thinking was guided by a cybernetic logic he deemed perfectly compatible with the goal of preserving cultural authenticity.[18] The technological incursions of modernization would be warded off by Friedman's own technological incursions. That is, engineering and eventually digital computation would behave as neutral structures enabling the free play of cultural signifiers within them.

As a form of vulgar media, the megastructures served as instruments of deferral. Just as Friedman's UNESCO cartoons facilitated the deferral of literacy, his proposed megastructures would operate as mechanisms for deferring basic modern housing standards, effectively reproducing existing slums in the sky. Raised on pilotis, the megastructures appear as bulwarks against the economic and cultural invasions of the surrounding city, while clearly replicating—indeed intensifying—urban density.

In light of Friedman's preoccupation with subsistence and economic independence in the decolonizing world, the sublime scale of the megastructures and the imported expertise required for their design is surprising. Why should a "poor world" of subsistence and autonomy require this kind of massive infrastructural intervention from foreign architects?

Although vulgar media could be understood as a minimal technology, Friedman employed complex systems and programs for their production. This constant movement between minimal and maximal technologies is repeated throughout his career. For example, while designing a Museum of Simple Technology in Madras (now Chennai) and using Indian agricultural journals to instruct rural workers in low-tech methods of survival, Friedman collaborated with the Architecture Machine Group at the Massachusetts Institute of Technology (MIT) to develop Flatwriter, a software program intended to help impoverished people design their own apartment units. In 1971, Friedman copublished a small piece, "La Ville Totale," with R. Buckminster Fuller, Nicholas Negroponte, and Kenzo Tange. In his

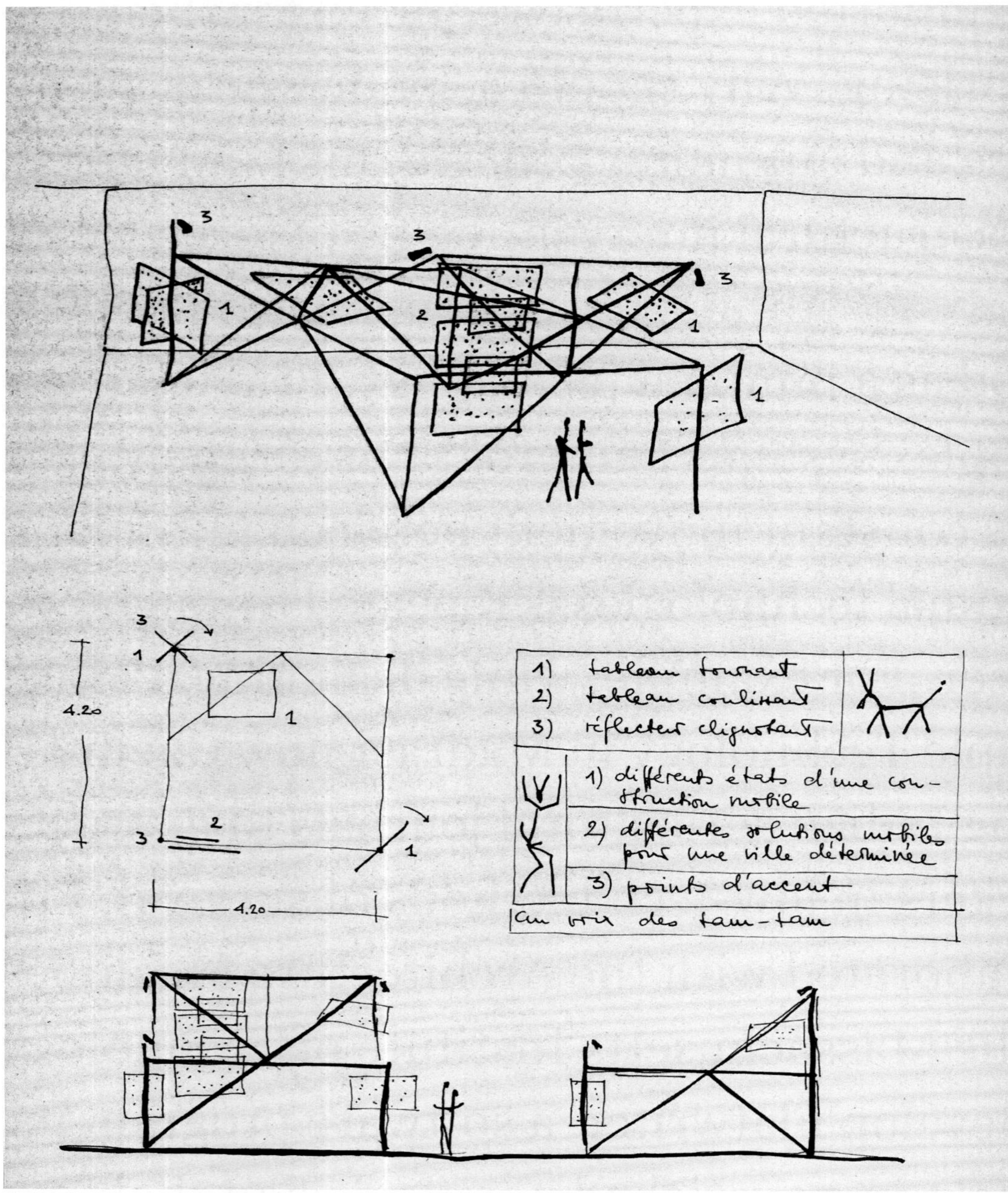

Fig. 3 "Africa: Cote d'Ivoire," n.d.

media promulgate?[21] In light of Friedman's radical push toward a "poor world," his work to some extent reevaluated the values assigned to the minimal and maximal: to dearth versus excess; to survival versus opulence. In fact, his inversion of the hierarchical relationship between survival and development can be read as a prolepsis to Giorgio Agamben's conception of biopolitics, grounded on the distinction between *bios* (the good and politically enfranchised life of the *polis*—this is, of citizenship) and *zôe* (the depoliticized life of mere survival).[22] For Friedman, the good political life consists of electing to relegate one's material existence to the narrow bounds of survival. Meager subsistence was to secure economic, cultural, and political independence against hegemony. Not acknowledging any dichotomy between survival and politics, Friedman saw the pursuit of mere survival as a form of politics. Against Agamben's notion of "bare life," Friedman's cartoons suggest that human life might never be bare or merely biological, impelled as it is by an inexorable drive toward the fantastic. Even amid material penury, an innate cognitive excess coaxes forth the plenitude of art and ritual. It is this human proclivity toward embellishment that Friedman sought to preserve—against something we now call biopower—through his minimal media of cartoons and his maximal media of space-frame megastructures.

Yet, Agamben's grim image of biopolitics cannot be so easily discredited. Even as Friedman's oeuvre sought to deflect bare life, it was haunted by the specter of bareness. The specter of a bleakly regimented and depoliticized life lurks not in the content of Friedman's work, but rather in the media he employed: the very conception of vulgar media implied a stark imbalance in semiotic power between the producers and consumers of that media. The imbalance is visible in the looming, sprawling space-frames that express the power differential between infrastructure and domestic infill. It lurks between the intended users of Flatwriter and the vast financial and military power (leveraged by MIT) that supported the software's development. Although the content of these media conveys an idealistic vision of cultural diversity pursued through simple material and technical means, the media themselves are developed through absolutely maximal means, through international developmental agencies and the research apparatus of military superpowers. In other words, Friedman's choice of media suggests that cultural authenticity and simplicity can only be preserved by dint of enormous assemblages of international expertise, ones arising from the same global imbalances Friedman sought to deflect.

This vexed position stands in contrast to the strategy Fanon advocated in the early 1960s. Although supportive of industrial development, Fanon wrote:

> If the building of a bridge does not enrich the consciousness of those working on it, then don't build the bridge. ... The bridge must ... be the product of the citizens' brains and muscles. And there is no doubt architects and engineers, foreigners for the most part, will probably be needed, but the local party leaders must see to it that techniques seep into the desert of the citizen's brain so that the bridge in its entirety and in every detail can be

> integrated, redesigned, and reappropriated.
>
> The citizen must appropriate the bridge.[23]

Fanon suggests here that a differential in technical knowledge reproduces neocolonial relations. One way to understand the contradictions in Friedman's work is by pointing to what could be called a media differential: an imbalance of power between the intellectual work of encoding and decoding a medium's message. Flatwriter sought to bridge architectural expertise and laymen's nonexpertise to enable residents to actively shape their habitations. Yet the software actually exacerbates the distinction between experts and laymen, transposing class difference into a media differential. The difference between architect and nonarchitect is reborn as a difference between computer user and computer science (with all the power underlying that science), a difference mediated and obfuscated by simple user interfaces designed to communicate across this difference.[24] Secondly, the software instates a process of depoliticization by replacing architecture, an object of oppression but also political contestation, with an impoverished form of participation and, thus, consent.

Regarding whether Friedman's media bolsters resistance to neocolonial power, recall how he imagined his wall-journals inspiring democratic discussion through their placement in prominent public spaces and popular graphic form. The wall-journal presupposed two architectural conditions: first, a central space around which a public tended to convene, and second, the existence of a wall in the immediate vicinity of that public space. However, what disappears in Friedman's proposed megastructures is not only a centralized space for accommodating a public, but even the walls upon which a wall-journal could be posted. Intended to support flexibility, transience, and decentralization, the ephemeral housing infill of Friedman's looming architectures privileged individual freedom and unsettlement over the organization, centralization, and stability of political community.

Friedman writes that his global infrastructural "proposition boils down to the elaboration of an organizational schema for the processes of

Fig. 7 *Community Participation in the Construction of Educational Buildings* (Paris: UNESCO, 1984), 61.

Even children
can make a house beautiful.

Women too, often have
a particular sense of decoration.

Everybody who lives in the house
can decorate some part of it:
front walls,
porch,

or even the ground
in front of the house.

'choice' and the establishment of a code, that is to say, a writing."[25] In other words, the cultural richness of nonliteracy was to be preserved through expert forms of writing capable of effacing writing *per se* by transposing it through code into other media. Democracy was to be encoded by writers for the benefit of societies that couldn't write back. While it is dubious to situate democracy within the media differential between development-*qua*-writing and survival-*qua*-nonwriting, Friedman's trick was to represent cultural survival as equivalent to democratic politics. He did this by making self-help housing the basis for both cultural robustness and free choice, and by making his space-frames serve as the legitimizing mechanism of freely built housing.

Despite the inadequacies of this proposal, there remains something compelling in Friedman's ideas of a return to survival. Yet for survival to be a form of political action (rather than a form of neocolonial oppression), media differentials would need to be ironed out; semiotic apartheid would need to be resisted rather than embraced. The most generous reading of Friedman's visions of survival would be to see them as a model for affluent society, as a utopian repudiation of the material excesses of the wealthy. Although to some extent his depictions work in that direction, for the most part Friedman addressed his work to rural-urban migrants in the Global South, working primarily in Africa, India, and Indonesia. His work was thus not an enjoinder for the wealthy to impoverish themselves as an act of political responsibility so much as it was a resignation to the modes of survival imposed on poor populations through an inequitable global division of labor. Indeed, the only one of Friedman's megastructures that was ever constructed was a prototype, the Sahara Cabins, designed between 1953 and 1958. He urged the French government to deploy the cabins in its North African colonies as workers' housing. This project, seminal to his later work, presented an astounding contrast of scale: between the looming monolithic repetition of its steel space frame and the minuscule and miserable capsules intended for habitation.

In 1989, Friedman wrote some notes proposing that the 1948 Universal Declaration of

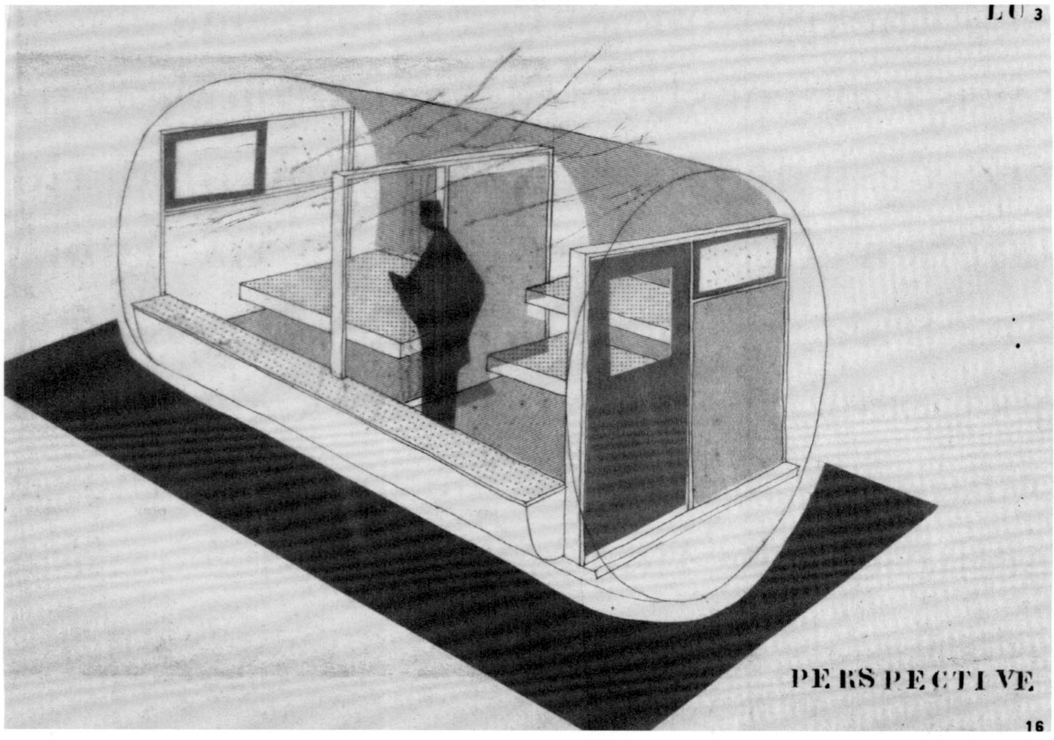

Fig. 8 Cylindrical Shelters, n.d.

Fig. 9 Perspective (Cylindrical Shelters), n.d.

Human Rights be severely abridged into two succinct formulations: "1) Each person has the right to existence, and the duty to promote the existence of others; 2) Each person has the right to have his or her selfhood respected, and the duty to respect others' selfhood."[26] Agamben has echoed Hannah Arendt's arguments, showing that the idea of universal rights is vexed by an internal contradiction, namely that the primary subject intended by human rights—the refugee—is the very person who is *de facto* excluded from these rights as he or she has no nation-state to guarantee them.[27] For Agamben this contradiction reveals the inadequacy of human rights to protect against the expansion of bare life. Friedman's complaint against the declaration is different, claiming that the declaration is of a "juridical" nature and is therefore too difficult to understand. Thus, it "would be necessary, *in order to educate* the public, to *simplify* the content of the Declaration."[28]

In fact, the 1948 declaration was written in a fairly straightforward style. It goes without saying that a nonliterate person would be unable to parse it, but is Friedman claiming that such a person would be any more capable of parsing his abridged version? The problem with Friedman's simplified version is that "the right to existence" could feasibly amount to nothing more than just that, the right to *exist*—in a concentration camp, prison, homeless shelter, or any other such coercive provision. In asserting this as a universal right and thus intoning a standard of justice, Friedman attempts to dislodge bare life from the category of political and economic oppression, situating it instead as a standard to be upheld.

Clearly, Friedman's second formulation concerning respect is more promising, offering a possible supplement to the right to mere existence, but this potential is too easily undermined by Friedman's first formulation: What if respect for selfhood is interpreted only as respect for the right to survival? And after all, wasn't colonial paternalism framed as respect for the cultural authenticity of the colonized (that is, for economic and educational underinvestment)? Notably absent from Friedman's formulation is, *inter alia*, the provision of Article 26 from the Universal Declaration of Human Rights:

Everyone has the right to education.

> Education shall be free, at least in the elementary and fundamental stages. Elementary education shall be compulsory. Technical and professional education shall be made generally available and higher education shall be equally accessible to all on the basis of merit.[29]

Article 26 tacitly recognizes the fact that decolonization and civil rights movements were led by people well-versed in literature, and that among the many rights for which they fought was the right to universal education. Friedman's proposed version of human rights effectively abrogates the right to education on the grounds that people are not educated enough to understand the inscription of that right.

The architectural corollary to this line of reasoning can be seen in technologies such as Flatwriter that threaten to foreclose urban politics by instating—in place of political struggle—the right to exist and the architectural provisions for that existence. In the case of Friedman's architectures, the right to exist indicates the right to hover somewhere just above and beyond the city, suspended in a "zone of indistinction."[30] Friedman proposes this alternative to standardized public housing because the latter—like public education—he deems too rigidly regimenting. However, to claim that maximal architectures, maximal technologies, and maximal infrastructures—in lieu of political negotiation—provide a viable safeguard against the excesses of modernity is to be guilty of an illogic so glaringly vulgar that it could only be obfuscated when presented through vulgar media.

1 I am using "vulgarize" for the French *vulgariser*, although a more idiomatic translation might be to "vernacularize" or "popularize," the latter being used by Friedman in his own translation of the title. In other words, "vulgar" here is in intended in its older sense of sacred texts translated into vulgate. See Yona Friedman, "l'UNESCO pour tous," June 1978, box 8, folder 9, Yona Friedman Papers, Getty Research Institute.

2 Friedman apparently understood the *journaux-muraux* (wall-journals) as a native form of communication: "Dans les quartiers pauvres de très nombreux pays, les gens n'achètent qu'un seul exemplaire d'un journal; ils l'affichent sur un mur et tout le monde vient lire les nouvelles." Yona Friedman, "l'UNESCO pour tous," June 1978, box 8, folder 9, Yona Friedman Papers.

3 For example, Friedman proposed cartoons on topics such as "Where does the city begin" (*Où commence la ville*) and "What is 'development'" (*Qu'appelle-t-on 'développement'?*). See Friedman, "l'UNESCO pour tous," 7.

4 Friedman, "l'UNESCO pour tous," cover.

5 Friedman, "l'UNESCO pour tous," 3–5.

6 In 1946, as part of formulating UNESCO's mission, Julian Huxley wrote a pamphlet advocating the goal of universal literacy as necessary to combatting racial injustice. Huxley, *UNESCO: Its Purpose and Its Philosophy* (London: Preparatory Commission of the United Nations Educational Scientific and Cultural Organisation, 1946). On UNESCO's early endeavors in literacy, see Jens Boel, "UNESCO's Fundamental Education Program, 1946–1958: Visions, Actions, and Impact," in *A History of UNESCO: Global Actions and Impacts*, ed. Poul Duedahl (New York: Palgrave MacMillan, 2016), 153–67.

7 Huxley, *UNESCO*, *passim*.

8 Friedman writes: "Communiquer des connaissances ce *n'est pas* éduquer. Car il ne s'agit pas de 'former des gens.'" Friedman, "Programme modeste pour survivre dans un monde en pleine cirse," 1976, box 21, folder 3, E6, Yona Friedman Papers.

9 Yona Friedman, "Vers un 'monde pauvre' ou comment la pénurie nous évitera de courir à la catastrophe," 1973, box 5, folder 22, Yona Friedman Papers.

10 On UNESCO's turn to world heritage, see Aurélie Elisa Gfeller and Jaci Eisenberg, "UNESCO and the Shaping of Global Heritage," in Duedahl, *A History of UNESCO*, 279–99.

11 There is a growing literature on self-help housing, but most pertinent to the themes dealt with here is Ijlal Muzaffar's work. See Muzaffar, "The Periphery Within: Modern Architecture and the Making of the Third World" (Ph.D. diss., Cambridge: Massachusetts Institute of Technology, 2007).

12 On the presumed relation between orality and authenticity, see Jacques Derrida, Of *Grammatology*, trans. Gayatri Chakravorty Spivak (Baltimore, MD: Johns Hopkins University Press, 1998).

13 I am referring especially to the Western philosophical tradition Jacques Derrida describes in Of *Grammatology*. See Derrida, *Of Grammatology*.

14 Muzaffar, "The Periphery Within."

15 My discussion of the tension between developmental agenda and ideas of cultural preservation is much indebted to Muzaffar's reading of the First World's efforts at intentionally "incomplete" modernization in the Third World. See Muzaffar, "The Periphery Within," *passim*.

16 Yona Friedman, "La Ville Totale," with Kenzo Tange, Nicholas Negroponte, and Richard Buckminster Fuller in *2000* 24 (1971), 7, box 5, folder 33, Yona Friedman Papers.

17 Friedman writes: "Ma proposition se résume donc à l'élaboration d'un schéma d'organisation du processus du 'choix' et à l'élaboration d'un 'code', c'est-à-dire d'une écriture. … En effet, l'infrastructure n'est autre chose que le 'support qui permet la réalisation de n'importe quel terme du répertoire, ou la transformation d'un terme du répertoire en un autre terme du même répertoire, de telle manière que les conséquences à attendre correspondent à celles prédites lors de l'avertissement." Friedman, "La Ville Totale," 7.

18 Ibid.

19 Yona Friedman, "Sept villes-ponts reliant les quatre continents," n.d., box 61, folder 2, Yona Friedman Papers.

20 Elsewhere, I have discussed Jean-Jacques Rousseau's idea of the *moi-en-commun* ("common self") and how this construct of citizenship is produced through media. See Nolan, "Quasi-Urban Citizenship: The Global Village as '*Nomos* of the Modern,'" *Journal of Architecture* 23 (2018, forthcoming). On Rousseau's *moi-en-commun*, see Étienne Balibar, *We, the People of Europe? Reflections on Transnational Citizenship*, trans. James Swenson (Princeton, NJ: Princeton University Press, 2004). See also Balibar, "'Possessive Individualism' Reversed: From Locke to Derrida," *Constellations* 9, no. 3 (September 2002): 299–317. See also Jean-Jacques Rousseau, *The Social Contract and The First and Second Discourses*, ed. Susan Dunn; trans. Susan Dunn and Henry Tozer (New Haven, CT: Yale University Press, 2002), 164.

21 Giorgio Agamben, *Homo Sacer: Sovereign Power and Bare Life*, trans. Daniel Heller-Roazen (Stanford, CA: Stanford University Press, 1998), parts 2 and 3.

22 Frantz Fanon, *The Wretched of the Earth*, trans. Richard Philcox (1961; New York: Grove Press: 2005), 141.

23 I write about this more extensively in Nolan, "Savage Mind to Savage Machine: Techniques and Disciplines of Creativity, c. 1880–1985," (Ph.D. diss., Columbia University, 2015), chap. 4.

24 Friedman writes: "Ma proposition se résume donc à l'élaboration d'un schéma d'organisation du processus du 'choix' et à l'établissement d'un 'code', c'est-à-dire d'une écriture." Friedman, "La Ville Totale."

25 Yona Friedman, "Déclaration universelles des droits de l'homme" (1989), box 37, folder 11, Yona Friedman Papers.

26 Hannah Arendt, *The Origins of Totalitarianism* (1951; repr. San Diego: Harcourt, 1994), chap. 9.

27 Giorgio Agamben, "Beyond Human Rights" in *Cities Without Citizens*, ed. Eduardo Cadava and Aaron Levy (Philadelphia: Slought Books, 2003): 3–8.

28 Friedman, "Déclaration universelles." Emphasis added.

29 United Nations, "Universal Declaration of Human Rights" (1948), accessed October 11, 2017, http://www.un.org/en/universal-declaration-human-rights/.

30 Giorgio Agamben, *State of Exception*, trans. Kevin Attell (Chicago: University of Chicago Press, 2005), chap. 1.

Reinhold Martin
with Shayari de Silva,
Dante Furioso
& Samantha Jaff

What Architects Do Is Boring: A Conversation about Technocracy and Mediapolitics

11.18.2017
Hungarian Pastry Shop,
NYC

Perspecta 51: How do you understand the concept of media in your work?

Reinhold Martin: Lately I've written a lot about what I've called "mediapolitics." *In The Urban Apparatus,*[1] **I try to think about cities both infrastructurally and organizationally, as media systems. Understood in this sense, "media" translates as something like mediating infrastructures, or infrastructures that do the work of producing and maintaining order.**

P51 You've written and spoken about how media organize. They create patterns and relationships. In terms of architecture's relationship to infrastructure, what is the role of legibility?

RM *The Urban Apparatus* **begins with an axiom: the city is hardware. Yet it's a different kind of hardware than the gramophone-film-typewriter sequence studied by Friedrich Kittler and others. It's a flux of relations at many scales. In** *The Organizational Complex,*[2] **I discuss how humans and machines came together to produce patterns and organizational processes out of which a certain kind of corporate organism arose and was reproduced. That leads to rather technical things like how curtain walls are put together.**

My research involves empirical work on technical systems, on architecture's technicity as it interacts with the urban field, but also as it intensifies what another form of media theory would call "inner experiences" like thought and reflection. Don't forget that IBM's command is to "think," and of course, Apple's command is to "think different." So, there's an intensive and extensive aspect to these hardwares and their systems. Architecture is very well positioned to think critically about and to elucidate their tacit, silent functions.

The drawings architecture students do in school and the drawings architects do in offices all belong to these media apparatuses. They're all forms of mediation. Concerning the role of drawing and visualization, pattern making and order making—graphically and visually—in drawings and models, these and other media constitute what we call architecture; they are how we know it and how architects work with it, with colleagues, with clients, and with various regimes that include buildings but do not necessarily begin or end with them.

P51 Could we talk a little about architecture's media versus architecture as media? In an article you wrote for *Perspecta* **back in 2001, "Atrocities. Or, Curtain Wall as Mass Medium," one of the key points is that there is this moment where architecture realizes that it's one among many media.[3] So, there's a tension between the ideas of media that serve architecture and architecture that functions as a form of media.**

RM Well that's the thing. You could say that architecture's medium specificity is given in something like a curtain wall, but not only in a curtain wall. Thinking relationally highlights one of the methodological limits of classical media theory, where the first move is usually to isolate the medium. For example, we might say that, like television, a smartphone is a medium that does certain things. But such a description tends to isolate the phone from the infrastructural complex to which it belongs. As one among many media, the thing that we call "architecture," which is in some ways a figment of our collective imaginations, enables us to think relationally and at many scales simultaneously.

Scale is another question. Today, our media increasingly train us into new scalar relations. We habitually move our fingers in a certain way on a screen and we expect that the image will zoom in. I'm not talking about a *Powers of Ten* kind of scale. In "The Curtain Wall," when I write about J.G. Ballard, it's to invoke a universe of clashing forces and technical systems, where the atrocities of the subtitle refer to the Vietnam War and to other violent, technologically mediated conflicts. For Ballard, such historical violence was condensed into the television screen. But you can also see that violence in other kinds of screens, including curtain walls.

What relationship exists between one screen and another? A more traditionally humanist idea about scale exemplified by the Eameses' film, *Powers of Ten* (1977), repeats the Albertian idea of the city as a large house and the house as a small city. It posits an integrated, harmonious continuum. In *Powers of Ten*, zooming in and zooming out is all about establishing a continuity of patterns from the microscopic to the cosmic. History, however, disrupts that continuity. Life—meaning social life, social being, and social processes including conflict, desire, and many other things—doesn't add up and needs to be organized, integrated into the body of a city, a society, or a building.

P51 *Powers of Ten* is intensely visual and focused on a visual subject. Returning to the question of legibility, when we talk about these patterns, how do you reckon with the things that are inherently invisible or not visual by nature when we talk about this kind of pattern making or the ways the city can be read? This is an age-old question: How do we understand difficult scales like the modern metropolis or global systems in a visual way?

RM One last thing on *Powers of Ten*. Speaking of visuality, the principal organizing mechanism in that film is actually the voice. As you remember, there is a very male voice—

P51 The voice of god.

RM Exactly. It's the voice of a patriarch telling you about the order of the universe and instructing you to concentrate visually on these patterns. This happens transparently; we don't normally think about that voice. In that sense the film is, of course, a multimedia environment, like so many other things that the Eameses produced. We could certainly investigate the role of sound, listening, and voice in work that, like *Powers of Ten*, has so often been received as primarily visual.

On the other hand, one of the things that visual media do is produce invisibility. They construct frames. In this case, the filmmakers ask us to see patterns, where each pattern is by definition an edit. It excludes more than it includes. And, as they organize and integrate, these kinds of patterns also exclude what communications theory calls "noise," the background noise of being, of the universe, of life, including the background noise of vision and of audition.

A film like this is also carefully edited to exclude the cuts, to manage the montage, in order to produce the effect of continuity. The result is really an excess of order. Discontinuities within and between patterns are like the dust and dirt of a city that other kinds of ordering systems—like infrastructure: plumbing, sewers, wiring, etc.—are meant to hold at bay. Indeed, this is not to say that there's an absolute distinction between order and disorder, between light-and-air and dust-and-dirt. In fact, each side possesses both characteristics. There's an order of dust.

In terms of invisibility, one of the great epistemic questions of our era is how to see climate. More specifically, how to make visible and knowable at a variety of scales, the risks associated with climate change, which of course are on a potentially different time scale than the decades or even centuries that historians use to periodize human events. This is another important aspect of what we're talking about: the time axis, as opposed to the x-y-z spatial axes. Thus, future risk, unpredictability, and probability—these are not easily or transparently visualized. Many have attempted to do just that, but the debates and the concerns around climate change turn in part on a structural impossibility: the necessity to make the future knowable based on facts that, unlike most historical events, humans do not experience directly, at least at first. The presence of carbon dioxide in the atmosphere is not immediately tangible in the way that pollution is. We don't experience these phenomena and their effects in quite the same way. They're mediated in different ways as knowable things.

P51 On this question of invisibility, is there a difference, or what's the relationship between invisibility and immersion? When you say media produce invisibility, there's also this classical discourse on immersion and the idea that media seek to immerse a subject. Has subjectivity changed? Do media still operate in that same way?

RM I'll give you an example. In *Utopia's Ghost*, one of the chapters is called "Mass Customization."[4] It's about computers. The central object is the Union Carbide building designed by Kevin Roche. What's quite distinct about that building are its immersive characteristics, in a specifically architectural sense. It's not immersive in the sense of going to the movies and getting trapped in a spectator–spectacle relationship, but in a more everyday, nine-to-five sense. First of all, it's a building that you drive into—a big parking garage, basically. You park next to your office, theoretically, and walk into that office. There's comparatively little spatial hierarchy; the plan is a branching pattern. Every office is a corner office. In each office, you have a thermostat in which you can control your own technical environment. In this way, every Union Carbide mid-level manager is implicitly considered and treated as an individual human being. This technique is a product of human relations discourse, which began much earlier and developed in American corporate culture in a series of stages.

Yet, if you recognize what was happening at this time, another function of the building was to make invisible what Union Carbide was actually doing—which turned out to be killing people, in huge numbers, with the gas leak at a poorly maintained manufacturing plant in Bhopal, India. Thus, the contest over subjectivity and over the humanization of the white middle-class suburban office worker is infrastructurally, experientially, and cognitively tied to the dehumanization of the people producing the products that the office worker is selling.

P51 You've written about the current political situation, including Charlottesville. Can you speak about how these current political events relate to your understanding of architecture's boundaries?

RM With architecture, the further inside you go (like the further inside that Kevin Roche building) the more you see, the better you are able to see the outside world. For example, in order to help understand the current situation, critical architectural discourse can think more deeply about how certain spaces and certain semantic fields are made sacred, including the space of the nation itself.

Here in New York we can go downtown to Ground Zero. We should take that site very seriously. A good deal of what we're talking about today when we refer to American nationalism, including white nationalism, is crystallized at Ground Zero, which has been an important stage on which the current authoritarian spectacle has been built. As stage, prop, backdrop, and theater, architecture helps to assemble a scene in which we are participants, although we may feel like we are merely witnesses. Bracket out Ground Zero as a theater of rebuilding the national soul, and you potentially have a different story, if not a different history.

P51 You mentioned the way the stage is constructed in terms of the current regime, and you've also mentioned the Vietnam War as the first media war. Was there a moment for you when the relationship between media, current events, and atrocities began to crystallize?

RM I don't know. Surely, we all are historical actors and historical subjects, but I try not to write my autobiography into my work. Historically speaking, as a student of modernism and a participant in its endgame, I did and still do consider myself a card-carrying member of what has to be called at this point a neo-avant-garde, or a neo-neo-whatever. Nonetheless, I remain skeptical of terms like "radical" or "avant-garde," especially when applied to the arts or culture. We cannot simply repeat the modernist ideological fantasy of symbolic transformation standing in for the infrastructural transformation of political-economic systems, including those systems to which architects and architecture contribute day in and day out, mostly unnoticed. Cultural work is infrastructural in its own way, but we miss the bigger picture when we dramatize personal narrative (as our field still tends to do), since most of what architects do is, in fact, boring. The same goes for architectural theorists.

P51 Sometimes you need a personality, or someone to identify, right?

RM Actually, you need patience.

That's one reason I've continued to work on histories of administration, of bureaucracy, of paperwork. This is another way to think about media; these are all expressions of power. So if we want to understand power and to raise questions about its effects, I think we would do well to exercise our patience but also our impatience, a kind of permanent impatience with systems of domination and forms of oppression in which the professions participate on a regular basis.

P51 How does this relate to your role as an educator involved in the university?

RM I think academics, but also in our case practicing architects, can do the work of what Michel Foucault called a "specific intellectual." This is a little different from a "public intellectual" or other characterizations of the role of intellectuals in society. It presupposes that one has technical knowledge by virtue of one's expertise. Foucault's example is *highly* technical: J. Robert Oppenheimer, the nuclear physicist who opposed the proliferation of atomic weapons after the war—and specifically the hydrogen bomb. Oppenheimer used his expertise, his knowledge of nuclear physics and of the defense program, to mount his opposition.

The specificity of architectural knowledge is different. It's more immanent to society. It's more layered. It's less specialized, more diffuse. Or to put it differently, architecture's special quality is making the kinds of connections that we've been talking about. But, the point is to use that technical knowledge as leverage.

P51 You see opposition to the border wall or to the design of prisons in a similar vein?

RM Absolutely. A long time ago, while teaching a course at Yale on the "organizational complex," I met Raphael Sperry, who went on to the Bay Area to lead Architects/Designers/Planners for Social Responsibility (ADPSR). Sperry and his colleagues have been doggedly, uncompromisingly mounting a campaign to get architects to divest from the prison industry. Specifically, they tried to get the AIA to divest from or to disavow the design of execution chambers. The shame of our field is that as far as I know, they have been unsuccessful in achieving this small but important defeat of barbarism, at least so far.

P51 Why do you think that is?

RM *[Laughs]* Well, you saw what the AIA did right after the election?

P51 Right, we know. It was shameful. Well, do you think that architecture is inherently conservative?

RM No, no, no, and this is where I really am a card-carrying member of the neo-avant-garde and absolutely identify with radical programs. There are many things we can be proud of, but this is not one of them. And I don't know exactly why—you could ask Raphael, he's doing great work that is largely unsung because it's not dramatic or theatrical. My sense is that in this as in so many others, it is a positive change blocked by a combination of capital and technocracy, because that's what we're talking about: negotiating with the technocrats at the AIA. This is the same technocracy that came out in support of Trump's infrastructure plan.

If we want to look for politics in architecture then this is where we should start. Start with the AIA. That is politics. Precisely because most technocrats imagine their jobs to be apolitical and refer what they think of as political decisions to their constituents. This is the work of what Foucault famously called governmentality, or the biopolitics of management and administration. I want to insist that it is also the work of mediapolitics. Writing specifications—in fact, architecture is generally written much more than

it is drawn, beginning with the specifications, but ending with the scripts that are written in order that you draw a line—that work is commercial work, but it is also intensely political work. Raphael and his colleagues have been attempting to intervene in that domain, in the everyday, boring, deadly, bureaucratic work that is the design of prisons. They attempted to intervene in the technocracy, the world of mediapolitics, and they were rebuffed. This shows you how recalcitrant and strong that domain can be.

1 **Reinhold Martin,** *The Urban Apparatus: Mediapolitics and the City*. **(Minneapolis: University of Minnesota Press, 2017).**

2 **Reinhold Martin,** *The Organizational Complex: Architecture, Media, and Corporate Space*. **(Cambridge, MA: MIT Press, 2003).**

3 **Reinhold Martin, "Atrocities. Or, Curtain Wall as Mass Medium,"** *Perspecta* **32 (2001): 78–93.**

4 **Reinhold Martin,** *Utopia's Ghost*. **(Minneapolis: University of Minnesota Press, 2010).**

5 **On November 9, 2016, the American Institute of Architects sent a letter congratulating the recent president-elect, Donald Trump, who had pledged $500 billion in infrastructure spending, stating "We stand ready to work with him and with the incoming 115th Congress." ("Updated: AIA pledges to work with Donald Trump, membership recoils,"** *The Architects Newspaper*, **November 11, 2016, https://archpaper.com/2016/11/aia-pledges-work-donald-trump-membership-recoils/.)**

Space Hacks

The concept of commons entered the digital realm from physical space in order to interpret the types of communities, relationships, and production (code and infrastructures built using that code) that started to appear with the development of the free as opposed to the proprietary. In fact, the concept itself was enriched when it was implemented in digital fields. Framing urban space through the lens of digital commons enables additional imagination and knowledge to be applied to the urban commons. Yet, the notion of urban commons is often complicated by the memory of historic models of organization and management—frequently viewed as "the pastures we once knew how to share"—conveniently omitting the fact that common pastures belonged to feudal rulers. There is a tendency to idealize a return to past models. However, in digital realms, there is no return to Middle Age pastures. Digital commons started from scratch, defining their own protocols of production and reproduction, of caring and sharing.

Digital commons can be a source of inspiration and example when addressing urban commons, going beyond nostalgia in search of future models. Indeed, as free-software activist Marcell Mars has argued, given what we now know about digital networks, if we could redefine the way we address land regulations, we could create a more appropriate system for today's world. According to Mars, "That property wouldn't be private, maybe not even property, but something else. Only then can we say we have learned something from the digital."[1] Therefore, it is useful to approach the commons through the definition developed by Harvard Law professor and scholar of digital networks and collaboration, Yochai Benkler, who sees commons as "a particular type of institutional arrangement for governing the use and disposition of resources," defined in contradistinction to property, ensuring "that no single person has exclusive control over the use and disposition of any particular resource."[2]

Digital commons originated with the resistance to scarcity, which was artificially imposed onto the world of software code in wake of the systematic enclosure of the 1970s and 1980s. This was part of a process that anthropologist Gabriella Coleman describes as "a tidal wave of commercialization." Coleman's work focuses on hacker and free-software culture and communities, arguing that software was converted from a "technical object" into a market-based commodity protected by intellectual property law. In fact, this "tidal wave" was part of a larger tsunami of privatization that took place more broadly in the 1980s as part of the development of neoliberal capitalism. At the same time, urban space became increasingly privatized, eventually rendering it the ultimate commodity. The primacy of rent extraction, delegitimization of the right to housing and public provisions for housing, leading to various right-to-buy privatization schemes, and the absolute dominance of the free market as sacrosanct put new pressures on public space and housing, not only endangering the reproduction of everyday life in the city, but threatening bare life itself.

Within this context, computer programmer Richard Stallman devised an alternative software licensing system to resist the new restrictions imposed by intellectual property law. He named this new licensing system "GNU's Not Unix! General Public License" (GNU GPL). The first part of the name, GNU, was a recursive acronym referring to Unix, the closed-source operating system that was dominant at the time, of which Stallman was set to program the free version. The second part, GPL, was to show that this license was ported on the idea of public domain. He called all software published using this new system "free software" and developed a slogan, "free as in freedom." The license enabled programmers to share the joy of coding without worrying about breaking the (intellectual property) law.[3]

Stallman understood that in order to subvert the system of intellectual property, he would have to intervene in the protocols that regulate the conditions under which the code is produced, and not the code itself. In other words, digital commons were not created by a perfect line of code. The complex field of digital commons, the creation of the free software community, was the product of an intervention into the logic of the production of code itself. The creation of the GNU GPL was a legal hack aimed at counteracting the imposition of intellectual property law on code. In the early 1980s, when Stallman published the GNU GPL for the first time, the only license available to programmers who wished to keep code free was public domain, which gave no protection against the code being appropriated—that is, used as a basis or part of copyrighted software, and closed as soon as it was made available. Everything built using a free code published under the GNU GPL had to be made available under the same conditions. This structure ensured that programmers could continue sharing without breaking the law, thus enabling free code to become self-perpetuating.

If the creation of the GNU GPL was successful because the design intervened in the very logic that governs the creation of code, architects and planners have for too long taken the opposite approach, believing that good design can subvert the logic of enclosure that dominates the production and reproduction of physical space. They believe that good design can keep space open and public by the sheer strength of its spatial intervention. Stallman understands that no design is strong enough to protect against private ownership. Furthermore, digital and urban commons, despite operating in completely different realms and economies, are under attack from the same market processes that base their monopoly on the extraction of rent. This power stems from a legalized ownership over the means of production (of surplus value). As geographer David Harvey reminds us, all rent "is a return to the monopoly power of private ownership of some crucial asset, such as land or a patent. The monopoly power of private property is therefore both the beginning-point and the end-point of all capitalist activity."[4] Stallman envisioned a bleak future, but found a way to relate the means to the ends to try to prevent said future from fulfilling itself.[5] In other words, he found a way to intervene in the system,

preventing code from being controlled by profit-driven companies. In this way, he allowed workers (programmers) to maintain a level of control over the means of production and distribution of their work. New tools and methodologies for creating code and sharing knowledge had to be developed, and through the negotiations of those involved in the process, protocols guiding the use of code emerged. Moreover, a broader free software community emerged as well. It can be said that while coding the free software project, the community coded itself.

The appearance of commons points to the limits of property as a system for the allocation of resources. The digital, more than any other field, reveals property as a construct ill-suited for contemporary relationships. As Berlin-based computer scientist Stefan Meretz argues, the digital offers this possibility, as it is nonmaterial, non-rival, and nonexclusive.[6] Indeed, it is unlike anything in the physical world. The digital sphere shows how renegotiating regulation can transform scarcity into abundance. In the past decade, telecommunication, radio, and television have shifted from analog to digital transmission. As digital signals require less frequency space than analogue signals, this shift in protocols and technologies has influenced the redistribution of a finite territory of the radio frequency spectrum. The management of the radio frequency spectrum was renegotiated, increasing the available space by an order of magnitude, while the absolute size of the spectrum stayed the same.

Legal hacking in and of itself is not a novel procedure. As the legal scholar and commons activist Saki Bailey points out, "Legal hacking is going on all the time," but it's legal because "they are the parliament, they are Microsoft," and they can afford to hire lawyers to defend their legal hacks.[7] When it comes to physical space, one of the most obvious regulatory reconfigurations is the public–private partnership. This mechanism has become the dominant tool for financing the construction and maintenance of public spaces and infrastructure throughout the world. Unlike legal hacks by corporations that aim to perpetuate the process of accumulation through dispossession, Stallman's hack is anticipatory. It tries to limit the impact of the market and to create a new space of freedom for the creation of code and of shareable knowledge. To do this, the hack challenges one of the central pillars of liberal jurisprudence: (intellectual) property law.

Good legal hacks require expertise and specialized knowledge. Advocates against the privatization of code have used the right to free speech as an argument for why code should not be considered property; advocates for public space could similarly use the free speech argument in their favor, since we need public space to exercise our right to free speech and assembly. However, when it comes to public space and free speech, the balance that needs to be achieved is between protecting the individual and public interest. This was at the center of the case tried at the European Court of Human Rights (ECHR) in *Appleby v. United Kingdom* in 2003. The case was brought by members of an environmental group who claimed their freedom of expression and assembly had been breached when they were refused entry into a privately owned shopping center to set up campaign stands. While ECHR found that no rights were infringed, the partly dissenting opinion of Judge Maruste offers an important insight into what is at stake in future:

> In my view, the property rights of the owners of the shopping mall were unnecessarily given priority over the applicants' freedom of expression and assembly. The case raises the important issue of the State's positive obligations in a modern liberal State where many traditionally state-owned services like post, transport, energy, health and community services and others have been privatized. In this situation should private owners' property rights prevail over other rights or does the State still have some responsibility to secure the right balance between private and public interests?[8]

The most important lesson urban commons can take from their digital counterparts is at the same time the most difficult one: how to make a structural hack that will perpetuate free and open urban commons. Digital commons remind architects and planners that urban commons should be structured as inclusive, self-regulating communities that are open for inclusion of others. This socializes knowledge, produces and reproduces the commons, and creates a space for political emancipation capable of resisting and expanding the realm that is outside of the market. The big task for both digital and urban commons is building the common-core infrastructure, and it is precisely at this point that digital commons can offer a cautionary tale. When scaling up, it is not possible to rely on the strength of a structural hack. In fact, after the romantic 1990s when it was still possible to think that GNU GPL was immune to enclosure, today most of the infrastructure of information-communications technology is based on the collection of individual servers running the flavors of the Linux operating system (still the most important example of GNU GPL free software). In fact, the continued development of this technology is highly influenced by Google and Facebook.[9]

The pressure on cities to go smart—that is, to delegate the management of space and services allocation to proprietary controlled information protocols—bears an urgency to form alliances between free software hackers and public space activists to develop strategies for porting GNU GPL legal hacks to the scale of infrastructure. Barcelona, under the new local bottom-up radical democratic government led by antiforeclosure activist and architect Ada Colau, has been working toward this end by developing Barcelona Digital City, a strategy for digital sovereignty.[10] Developed by a team led by Barcelona's chief technology and digital innovation commissioner, Francesca Bria, the project aims to rethink the smart city by putting citizen needs and a city's political questions at its core, turning municipal data into a public asset. Barcelona Digital City, based on understanding that the smart city is the extension of the ongoing process of privatization and outsourcing by technological means, does not reject technology, but tries to articulate "technological sovereignty"[11]

Space Hacks

by designing protocols to ensure that the digital platforms create commons in digital realm and sustain the production of urban commons, not jeopardize it. Seeing the connection between space and digital platforms as crucial, Bria and Evgeny Morozov have articulated nine principles for the Right to the Digital City as a guideline for achieving the technological and spatial sovereignty. The principles are (1) promote alternative data ownership regimes; (2) move information services to open source, open standards, and adopt agile delivery; (3) transform procurement to make it ethical, sustainable, and innovative; (4) control digital platforms; (5) build and grow alternative digital infrastructures; (6) develop cooperative models of service provision; (7) maximize innovation with public value; (8) rethink welfare schemes and complementary currency systems at the local level; (9) promote digital democracy and digital sovereignty.[12] Although digital infrastructure lacks physical presence, data collection is a profitable enterprise that not only extracts value from citizens, but is also used to shape the (spatial) development of the city and to regulate access to assets. It is inadequate to merely establish a different legal regime for data; what is needed is to complement this with a strategy to reclaim infrastructure as a whole. This offers an opportunity for urban social movements and free software hackers to work in coalition to find ways to replicate Stallman's hack on the scale of the platform, thus creating an ecosystem in which the digital and the spatial mutually enrich each other. While cities like Barcelona can lead the way, it is important to share the solutions implemented in various cities across continents, as well as to form alliances in order to counter the domination of the digital solutions proposed by private, multinational companies.

1 Marcell Mars, interview with the author, 2013.

2 Yochai Benkler, "The Political Economy of Commons," *Upgrade* 4, no. 3 (June 2003): 6.

3 E. Gabriella Coleman, *Coding Freedom: The Ethics and Aesthetics of Hacking* (Princeton, NJ: Princeton University Press, 2012), 88.

4 David Harvey, "The Art of Rent," in *Rebel Cities: From the Right to the City to the Urban Revolution* (New York: Verso, 2012), 94

5 Richard Stallman, "The Right to Read," *Upgrade* 4, no. 3 (June 2003): 26–28.

6 Stefan Meretz, "Commons in a Taxonomy of Goods," keimform.de, January 11, 2010, http://keimform.de/2010/commons-in-a-taxonomy-of-goods/.

7 Saki Bailey, interview with the author, 2013.

8 Judgment, *Appleby and Others v. the United Kingdom* May 6, 2003, 16, www.internationalhumanrightslexicon.org/hrdoc/docs/echrappleby.doc/.

9 According to the last Linux Kernel Development Report, beside 1681 individuals who actively work on it, development of Linux kernel is partly influenced by the corporate interests of 225 companies involved in it. ("2017 State of Linux Kernel Development," Linux Foundation, https://www.linuxfoundation.org/2017-linux-kernel-report-landing-page/.) Similarly, while Google's web browser Chrome/Chromium is de facto open source, it is fully controlled by the company, which, together with Facebook, has a duopoly over internet advertising, still the main source of income for most digital natives. Another example is Google's Android Open Source Project (AOSP) initiated in 2007 as a free software platform for mobile phones, which at the time helped foster the image of Google as a corporation which worked for good of the community. However, since then Google has been slowly enclosing some of the most important pieces of code in its other proprietary projects, such as Google Play services, established in 2012, thus preventing the possibility of an open source phone with full functionality.

10 Official website of the Barcelona Digital City initiative, http://ajuntament.barcelona.cat/digital/en.

11 The concept of technological sovereignty is introduced by Bria and Evgeny Morozov in Francesca Bria and Evgeny Morozov, *Rethinking the Smart City: Democratizing Urban Technology*, City Series 5 (New York: Rosa Luxemburg Stiftung, 2018), 21–24.

12 Ibid, 30–53.

Thumbs That Type and Swipe, 2018

Nashin Mahtani & Etienne Turpin

Neuroecologies of Attention and Intelligence in the Megacity

> *Power relationships, hierarchies, technological mutations linked to the rise of semiotization machines such as computers are an intrinsic part of new assemblages of enunciation.*
>
> —Félix Guattari, "Institutional Intervention"[1]

February 21, 2017

With shifting climate patterns in the tropics, it has become increasingly difficult to anticipate the time and location of flooding. No longer restricted to the channels, spillways, and reservoirs designed to segregate water from urban residents, the flood disobeys the system of pumps and canals meant to guide and govern its behavior. During twelve-hour downpours, torrents of water gush from upstream neighborhoods, water seeping through the crumbling infrastructure that permeates the coastal megacity. Thus, the river declares its *residency*. It saturates the city, blocking traffic; it wreaks havoc, forcing emergency evacuations.

The torrent of water and waste in Jakarta also it makes itself known most potently through its social media and instant messaging semiotization, as human residents relay this news with the torrential signifiers *#banjir* or *#flood*. An alpha-numeric message is keyed in to a mobile device through a series of taps on a touch screen. Transformed into a binary code of 1s and 0s, the message travels in fragmented segments, at the speed of light, through undersea cables. On its journey to a vast and anxious audience of residents, the message is detected through an automated process. CogniCity Open Source Software (CogniCity OSS) processes the message: it originated from within the geographical bounding box of Jakarta and contains the key word "banjir." The match triggers a series of automated responses to the messenger:

> *Is it flooding? Text #flood to @petabencana to submit your flood report.*

A second message travels over 1,200 kilometers to reach CogniCity's Singapore cloud servers. After confirming this second set of terms—flood and @petabencana—CogniCity delivers the next set of instructions:

> *To submit a flood report, click on this link.*

The resident swipes through a "microsurvey" designed to structure the data being shared. She takes note of her surroundings as she completes the report: water height, description, photograph, submit. Within a second, CogniCity has received and responded to the report, and sends another message:

> *Thank you for submitting your flood report. Click here to see it on the map.*

The resident is directed to a map, where her report appears as a water droplet icon.

As the monsoon pours down on the city and water torrents search for lower ground, CogniCity OSS simultaneously detects and responds to thousands of messages in the digital torrent of information that follows. Every time CogniCity intercepts a message about flooding in the city, the resident is guided through the process of the microsurvey and then directed back to the map, where they see their own report appear as a water droplet icon, among hundreds of others. Each droplet contains a unique observation about flooding in the city, mapping the striated reappearance of the river in this complex urban environment.

One resident notices a water droplet close to her child's school. She checks the report and then rushes out to pick up her son early, referring repeatedly to the flood map along the way to ensure that inundated streets are avoided. Another resident notices a water droplet appear in an adjacent neighborhood and checks the report. He starts to move his furniture to the second floor, anticipating that the water will soon reach his own home.

In a control room deep inside the Jakarta government, the free public map is also monitored by a handful of disaster management professionals. Alerted by a cluster of water droplets that appear sequentially in close proximity, one operator calls a well-known neighborhood leader to confirm the situation. *"Yes, the water level is rapidly rising here. I have been helping residents evacuate, but we need more boats."* The operator immediately dispatches response teams and updates the map: almost instantly, the inundated neighborhood appears as a dangerous red zone on the public map, indicating that water levels have exceeded 1.5 meters. Thus, data enable rapid responses to the serious risks hydraulic torrents create throughout the city.

This proliferation of data continues throughout the monsoon, informing the decisions of residents in real time as they sense, share, and organize together. A parent on his way to pick up his children notices a red zone on the map; he decides to avoid a normal shortcut and reroutes, avoiding the inundated neighborhood, which operators flagged only seconds before in the control room.

As digital water droplets fill the map, the urban ecology of floods renders a public map. The river presents itself in this dimension as well, but through CogniCity, its presence is shared among all residents, and its dangers are avoided. The virtual envelope of the city responds to its dynamic temporalities in real time, as the aggregated actions of the city's heterogeneous human and nonhuman agents are rendered on the map. The residents reposition themselves in the city's shifting network of exchanges through the digital interface of the mobile phone. Through this interface, the residents are able to orient themselves in a city presented as the continuous reframing of urban programs.

The Architecture of Attention

The remarkable penetration of digital media into urban life has created a condition where most residents can no longer occupy a single dimension in the city, but instead tune into several space-times in multiple dimensions concurrently.[2] As urban residents spend more and more time caressing hand-held screens, participation in the city's programmatic and social exchanges becomes increasingly mediated by the digital interface. Fueled by a global apparatus of algorithmic media, the digital handset frames how users interact with their environments. This framing ensures that the transformation of the city follows a logic of inclusion and exclusion that exerts real influence on users' decisions, always inclining users toward certain ends and discouraging others. Recent global political events have demonstrated the extent to which the apparatuses of digital media can reshape perceptions and encourage the reorganization of society across various heterogeneous layers of the urban fabric. As the interface becomes an urban force in its own right—structuring new spatial and temporal contingencies, altering social subjectivities, and shifting programmatic contiguities in the city—the capacity for digital registers to affect urban transactions drives an increasingly competitive race to capture attention on digital platforms. As corporations hunt for this limited resource through ever more intrusive means, the injection of continuous psychic stimulation into media spheres diverts the attentive capacities of city inhabitants.

We must ask if our attention is being directed to the areas that are meaningful to our lived experiences, especially if we want to concentrate on addressing those concerns most pertinent to our societies. When urban interactions are increasingly controlled by the modulation of attention on digital interfaces, the contemporary city is effectively authored by profit-driven corporations. If architecture, through its capacity to coordinate and attenuate human attention, is a practice committed to organizing the social and material exchanges in the city, how can the discipline better attune the new sensibilities produced by the ecology of attention?[3] If residents are increasingly required to divide and multiply their attention, and thus, their social labor, between corporeal realities and simultaneous online presences, the architecture of the city must begin to engage the augmented dimensions of space-time introduced by the materials and technologies of the information age. How might architecture support alternative approaches to a *co-authorship* of the city by coordinating the collective space-time of our urban environments into *shared* forms of attention, collaboration, and care?

This applied urban design research in Indonesia experiments with the affordances of distributed computation to create collective visualizations of the city. Co-constructed in real time

Fig. 1
In 2013, an infrastructure failure inundated districts in Jakarta typically unexposed to flooding, including the central business district. In an age of climate change, where "overcapacity" of physical infrastructures is by now normal, flooding in the city is largely a result of unanticipated failures of embankments, levees, and canals.

by a variety of actors and agencies, they redirect attention toward mutual aid during disaster events. By repurposing the same platforms that attempt to program a behavioralist mode of economic submission, they aim to reorganize patterns of urban attention to foster the emergence of collective modes of enunciation and improvisational modes of social solidarity and humanitarian coordination. By repatterning practices of urban attention, residents can begin to co-create new multistable networks for mutual aid. By way of a considered redesign of the dispersed ecology of urban attention, strategic architectures that leverage the potentials of distributed computation can also help concentrate and coordinate offline spatial encounters and interactions.

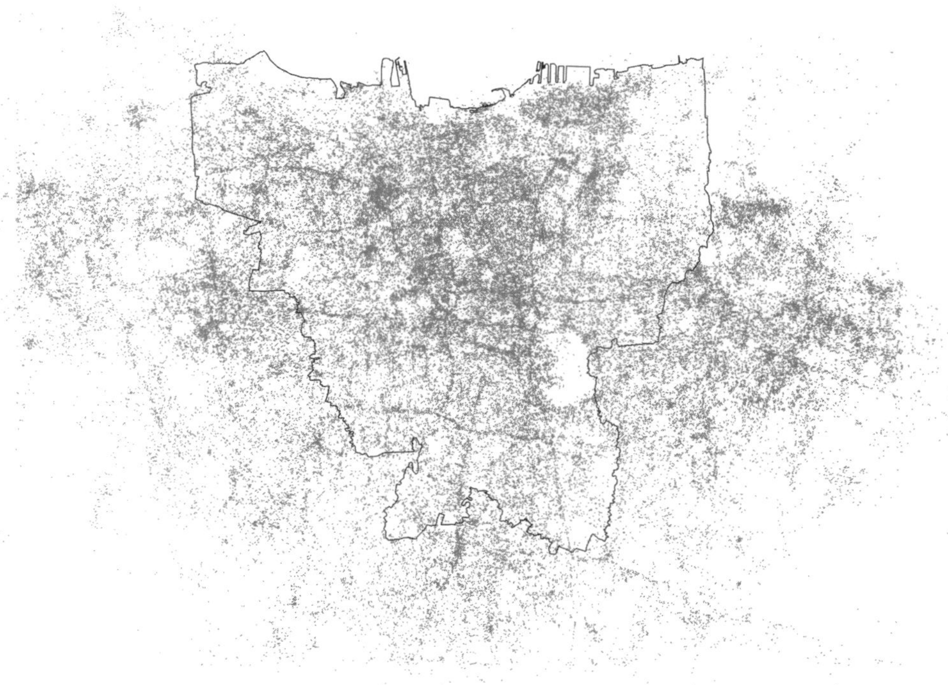

Fig. 2
A Twitter #DataGrant revealed that during the 2013–14 monsoon season, Jakarta's residents sent over 150,000 tweets about flooding in the city. The geospatial map of tweets renders visible the intersection of the city's informational infrastructures with its physical materiality; the mobile interface becomes a tool by which to narrate experiences of the city, navigate the city in real-time, and engage in informal networks of organization.

Learning with PetaBencana.id

> *"[W]hen referring to architecture, one can no longer only refer to the 'built things' with disregard for the anthropological reasons that led to the necessity of their appearance in reality."*
>
> —Xavier Wrona[4]

If architecture must engage with the multiplicity of space-times that the attentive registers of its inhabitants are drawn to, it must necessarily also consider the externalities of planetary scale media apparatuses; as the race to accumulate attention through the digital interface accelerates, the growing appetite for the earth's natural reserves place the city's infrastructures under increasing vulnerability to extreme weather events. When physical infrastructures are forced to operate far beyond the capacities they were originally designed to manage, the unexpected sudden rupture of concrete enclosures paralyze the city's flows of organization and information, amplifying confusion in already frenzied minds. As climatic forces infiltrate the urban environment, discordant barrages of information increasingly force attention to split into multiplying dimensions as residents seek to grasp on to modes of reorganization where built structures have failed in their operation. However, if the mediated city diverges resident attention into augmented space-times, then in the condition of *overcapacity urbanism*, it also invites urban infrastructures to extend into spaces with different limits and capacities.

This research began in Jakarta, a megacity where attention captivity via social media is especially visible—the city generates 2.4 percent of the world's tweets annually and has one of the highest rates of social media usage in the world.[5] The megacity of over thirty million residents is also situated on a coastal edge of the world's most disaster-prone region, rendering it especially susceptible to flooding.[6] Although Jakarta's residents have lived with seasonal flooding since the seventeenth century, unpredictable weather patterns caused by climate change have increasingly paralyzed the city due to the unanticipated failures of embankments, levees, and canals (fig 1). Despite five hundred years of infrastructure investment, Jakarta remained susceptible to severe flooding events in 1918, 1942, 1979, 1996, 1999, 2002, 2007, 2013, 2017, and 2018.

When the organizational capacities of built structures dissolve under heightened climatic stresses, we notice that residents actively use digital networks to coordinate informal networks of organization. A Twitter #DataGrant revealed that during the 2013–14 monsoon season, Jakarta's residents sent over 150,000 tweets about flooding in the city (fig. 2).[7] In the interlaced and interoperative digital and concrete layers of a megacity, we see that the excess of overcapacity urbanism is in fact not lost, but converted to another form—both through and as digital media. The torrent of the flood instigates its own virtual double. Real-time geotagged images, shared across ubiquitous networks of exchange, render a dynamic image of the city as it shifts in space and time. A careful and deliberate coordination of these active social and informational networks could relieve the inevitable confusion of a city under siege by cataclysmic water flows, by way of dynamic frameworks that support responsive, transparent, and aligned reprogrammings of urban transactions in real time.

In order to develop such a framework, with the capacity to filter through the torrential noise of social media, to help residents share their empirical observations more effectively, and to register resident participation into meaningful systems that support actionable response, we developed an open source software, CogniCity, that underpins a freely available web-based map called PetaBencana.id (Disaster Map Indonesia). The platform gathers confirmed on-the-ground situational reports from residents in real time, by engaging in AI-assisted conversations through humanitarian chatbots over social media. Upon detecting specific keywords on social media platforms (for the flood map, the OSS listens for "banjir" or "flood") in designated geographic areas, the software programmatically invites users to participate in community flood mapping (fig. 3). CogniCity's chatbots guide users to submit real-time flood reports through four sequential inputs; users verify their location, record flood heights, add photos and descriptions, and within milliseconds are able to view their contribution to the map (fig. 4).

Through curating software architectures to interact with residents by way of responsive programmatic framings of the city, CogniCity is not only able to filter through the noise of social media, but, by way of the four sequential inputs, begins to guide user observations of the city; directing attention to what we have understood to be the most critical and actionable pieces of information during a flood. Guiding sensory observations into categorical inputs not only makes residents more perceptibly aware of critical dimensions of the flood, but also grants scientific merit to subjective experiences, thereby transforming public noise into citizen science.[8] Through a framework that coordinates intentional observations of the city's dynamic fluctuations, the attentive participation of the city's inhabitants are made more readily

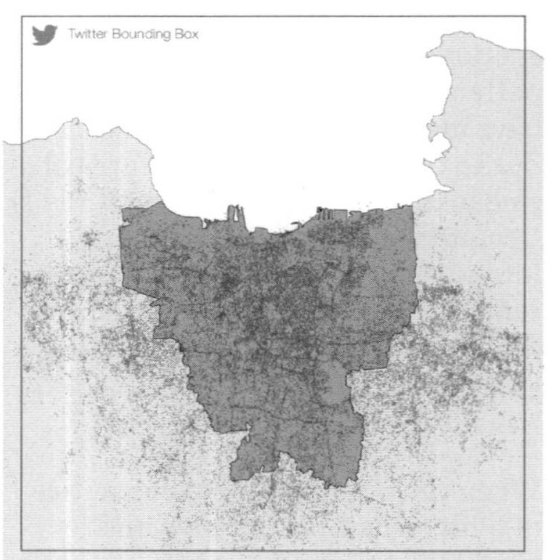

Fig. 3
PetaBencana.id gathers confirmed on-the-ground situational reports by engaging in conversations with residents through chat bots on social media. When the software detects a tweet with the key words *#flood* or *#banjir* within a specified geographic area (as illustrated here, the bounding box surrounding Jakarta), PetaBencana bots send a programmatic response inviting users to participate in community flood mapping.

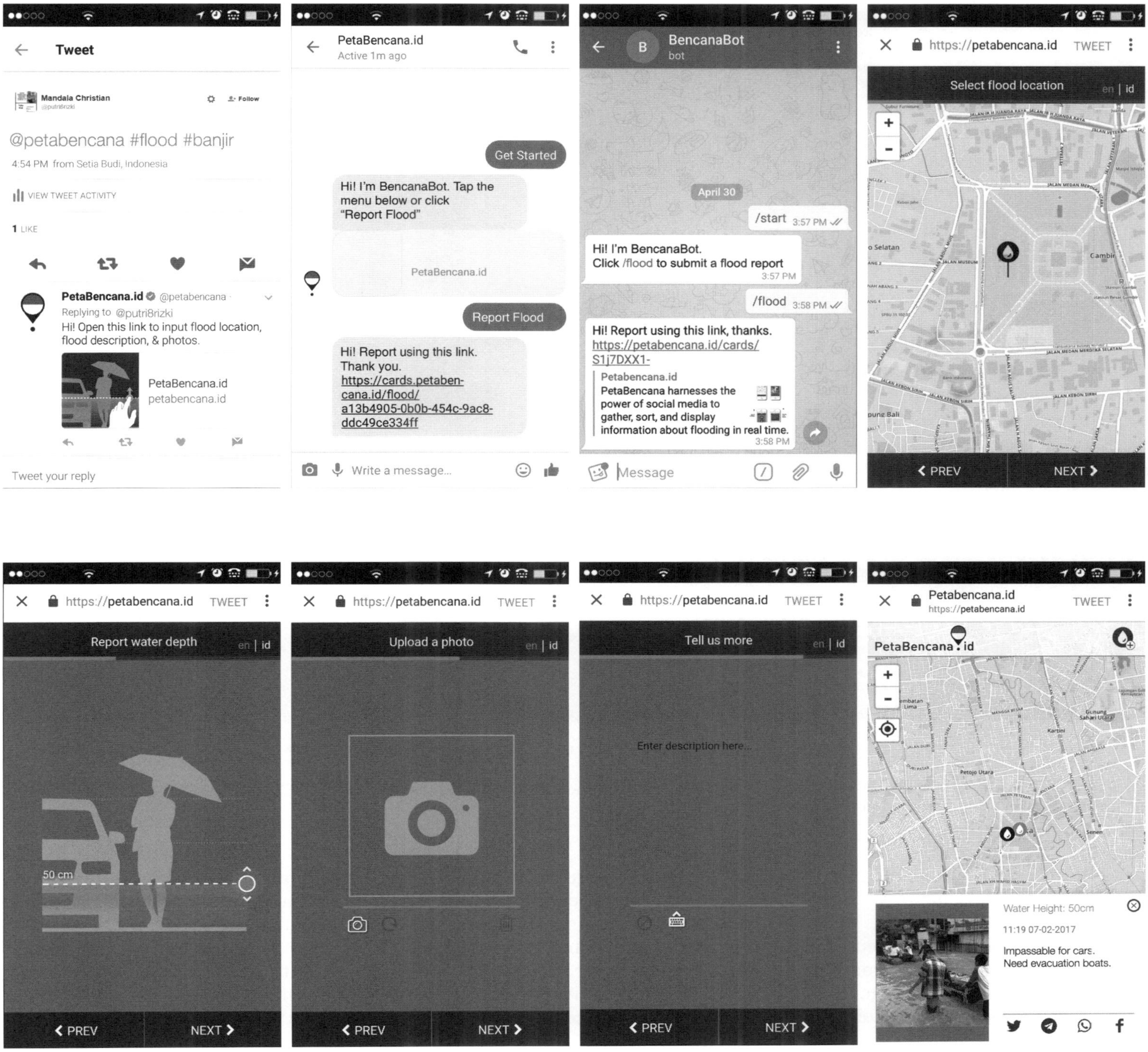

Fig. 4
Chat bots on social media respond to "*#flood* or *#banjir* @petabencana" on Twitter or Facebook, and "*/flood* or */banjir* @bencanabot" on the instant messaging service Telegram, with a unique link that guides users through submitting a flood report.

Fig. 5
The publicly accessible web-based map is monitored by emergency managers who are able to view real-time, on-the-ground situational updates of disaster events from resident reports.

available for integration into disaster management infrastructures.

In aggregating verified resident flood reports and emergency information from local and government agencies into a real-time visualization of flooding in the city, the platform enables residents to strategize personal efforts for resilience as they actively check the map to avoid flooded areas, organize for the safety of their families, minimize the loss of personal belongings, and plan collaborative efforts through the coordination of resources within and between local communities and emergency agencies. By repurposing the attentive seize of social media platforms into systems for mutual aid, the urban resident makes a more considered participation in the interlaced digital and concrete layers of the urban fabric. Emergency managers also actively monitor the map and are immediately alerted to incoming resident reports (fig. 5). The variety of textural descriptions of the city's rapidly fluctuating conditions contained within these reports—ranging from requests for help to warnings about impassable roads and the locations of infrastructure failures—supports timely response and helps emergency managers direct resources toward the city's most urgent needs (fig. 6). By realigning the city's divergent attentive capacities during disaster events into frameworks supporting attuned, coordinated, and collaborative exchange, the platform enables safe navigation and situational awareness for millions of residents while also supporting emergency response.
On February 21, 2017, PetaBencana.id received 1,061 reports in under twenty-four hours (fig. 7). As the web-based map was accessed 312,000 times by 252,449 unique users, this peak monsoon event clearly demonstrated that open source software can operate as a critical urban design medium to realign programmatic social functions in the city to respond to various urban contingencies in real time.

Becoming-Platform

By operating as media, architecture has the capacity to sustain the relationships that its frameworks orchestrate, through iterative interactions with its users. Such a platform must not only attune the attention of human agents, but as a critical actor of the city itself, it must ensure that its own attentive capacities respond to shifting social dynamics in the city. Flooding is a highly politicized disaster in Jakarta; the urgency of alleviating the paralysis of overflowing water is often employed as a pretext to justify the displacement of lower-income communities, to fuel the profits of disaster capitalism, and to conceal illicit funds through the construction of large-scale defense structures.[9] The disjunctive priorities of the city's various agents often impede abilities to recognize the interdependencies of diverse communities, infrastructures, and ecologies—resulting in ineffectual efforts to address the city's most pressing needs. In this context, the capacity of the mediated city to curate programmatic and social organizations within *topological* dimensions of space grants opportunities to engage physically segregated agents into coproduced environments that draw attention to less visible urban affinities. As residents navigate through the rapidly shifting temporalities of the flood equipped with the knowledge shared anonymously by their various counterparts, PetaBencana.id directs the attention of disparate agents toward the shared dimensions, temporalities, and spaces of the city. By granting eligibility to the multiplicity of voices that inhabit and compose the city, the architectures of software democratize decision making and enable access for creative practices of improvisation and opportunity, supporting the emergence of meaningful synergies for mutual aid (fig. 8).

The capacity of the platform to act as a political medium that enables

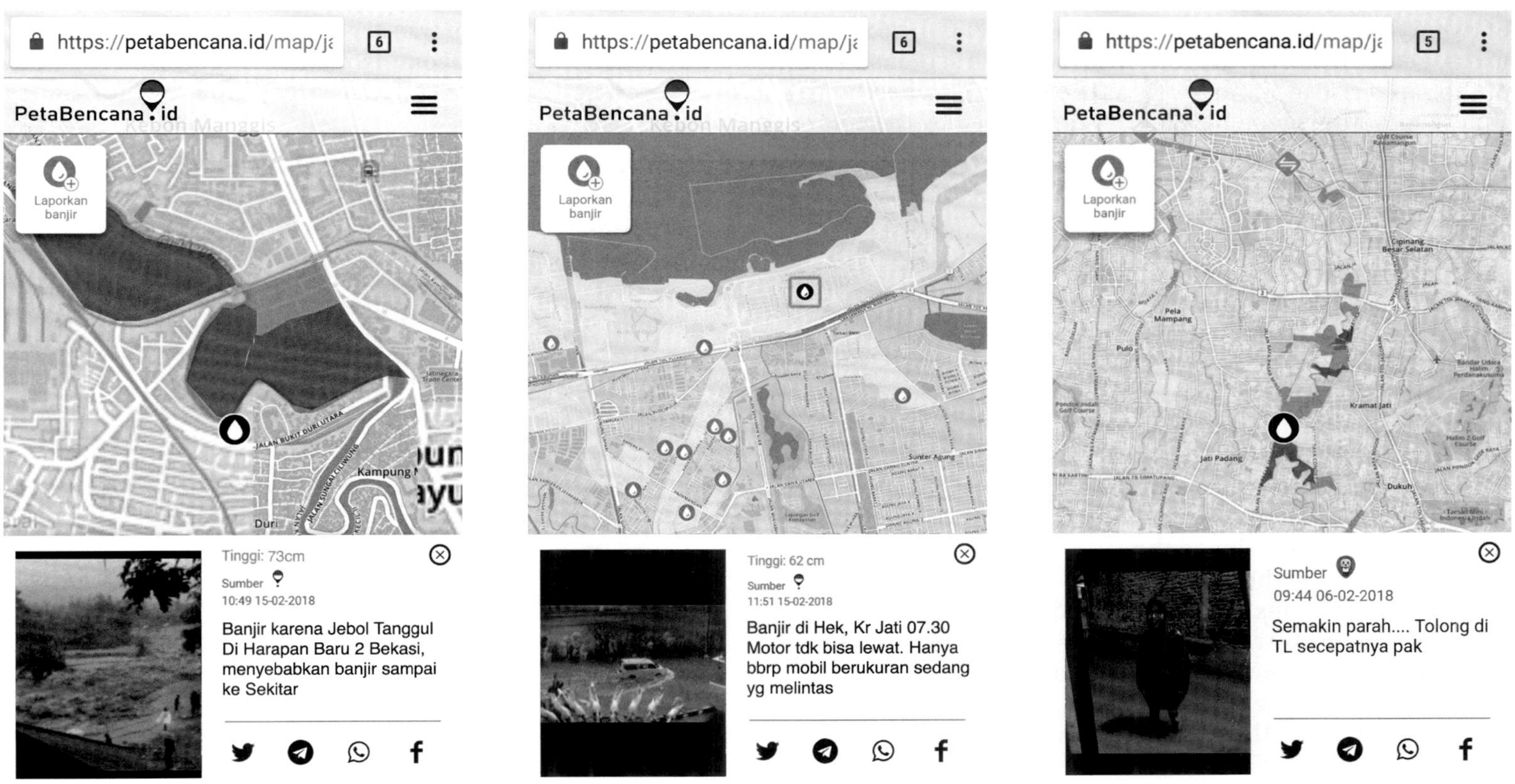

Fig. 6
A sample of the various descriptions of the city contained in resident reports; (a) a resident reports flooding caused by the failure of an embankment; (b) a resident warns about impassable roads; (c) a resident describes the flooding situation in their neighborhood and requests evacuation assistance. In creating a space that encourages greater public participation in infrastructure monitoring and flood event reporting, the platform develops a framework for *civic comanagement*. By activating millions of mobile phones into a network of sensors that can share real-time updates of the city, PetaBencana provides residents and emergency agencies with free access to time-critical information. The platform fosters *new architectures of social organization*, enabling safe navigation for residents while also supporting emergency agencies to better respond to emergency needs.

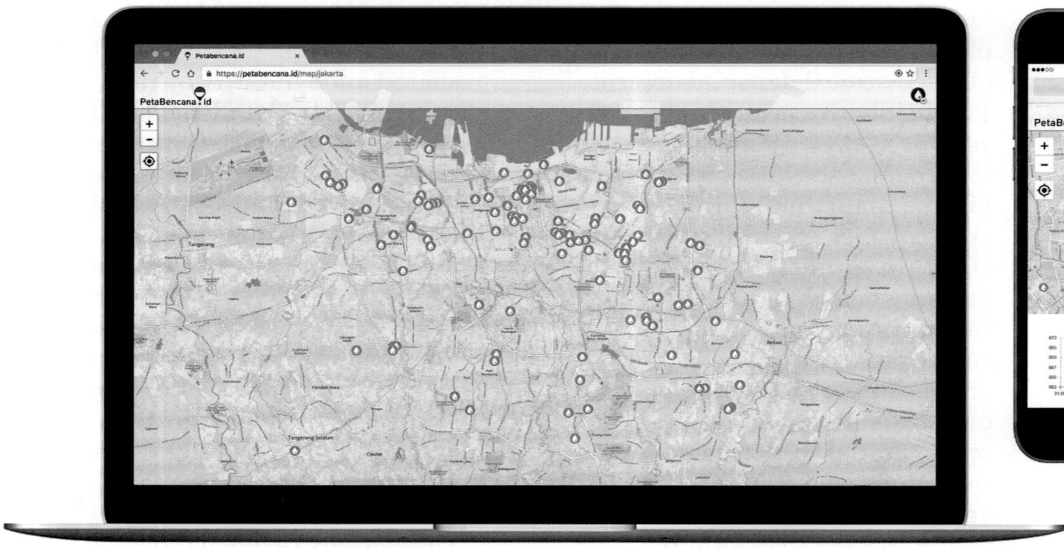

Fig. 7
On February 21, 2017, after heavy overnight rains, the city experienced its most severe flooding of the season. Over a period of twenty-four hours, PetaBencana.id received 1,061 resident reports and the platform was accessed by 252,449 unique users, generating over 312,000 sessions. The screenshots capture the spatial range of incoming resident reports, an example of the rapid rise of water levels as they were graphed hourly at flood gates, and the flood-affected areas input by the Jakarta Emergency Management Agency represented by the colored polygons.

partially segregated communities to pay attention to each other without having to necessarily agree on the variegated dimensions of a politicized disaster, has, in some instances, manifested new relationships in the physical spaces of the city. As an illustrative example, we have noticed meaningful shifts in synergies between the National Agency for Disaster Managementof Indonesia and the Provincial Disaster Management Agency of Jakarta. Prior to the implementation of the platform, pronounced frictions between the two agencies frequently resulted in ineffective communication, disjointed measures for emergency support, and, consequently, the misallocation of critical resources. These were often the result of protocols that were misaligned with the temporalities of the flood; although the provincial agency is operationally required to deliver updated pdf flood reports every six hours to the national agency, the severity of flooding in Jakarta often rises and falls on much shorter temporal cycles. The gaps in communication during these critical

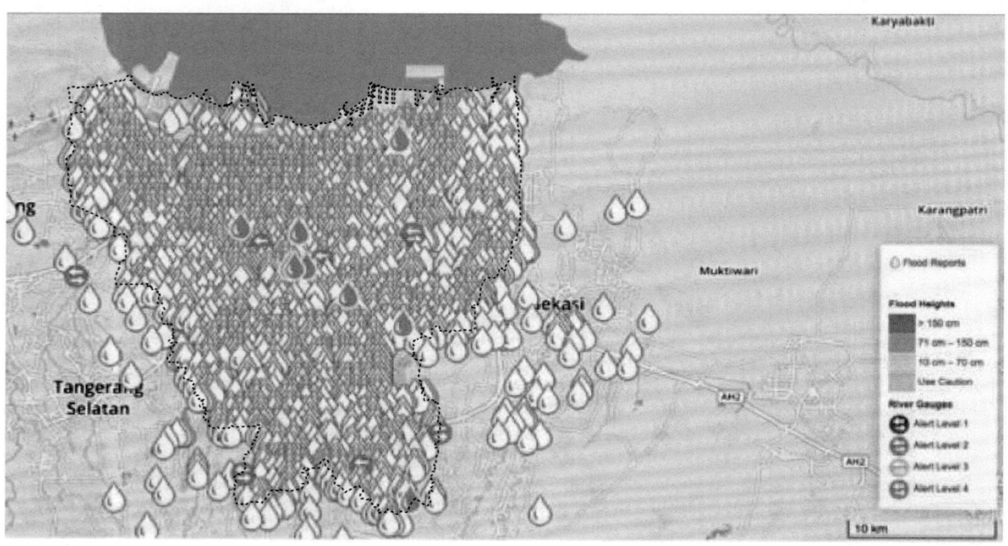

Fig. 8
A map of all resident reports received over a period of six months during the 2014–15 monsoon seasons reveals the inclusivity that software architectures are able to foster. The aggregated reports render the boundary of Jakarta itself, represented here by the dashed line, demonstrating both the extent to which flooding affects the city and the capacities for software architectures to undiscriminatingly enroll the city's diverse communities into a coproduced environment. Actors that may not collide physically in the material layers of the urban fabric begin to coalesce in the virtual layers of the city, through the platform as a political medium. (Note: On the publicly accessible flood map, reports only stay on the map for one hour before expiring, in order to maintain the representation of real-time information of the platform.)

time periods often exacerbate atmospheres of urgency and result in rising institutional tensions as the national agency finds itself without the necessary information to respond to the city and the media.[10]

Through careful ethnographic studies and collaborative research, the platform was designed to fill these critical information gaps in a manner that would avoid intrusive technological impositions. Using CogniCity OSS, PetaBencana.id provides a platform whereby the provincial agency is able to update the map with emergency information in real time, in an operational flow that is concurrent to the agency's practices of managing the physical flooding situation. PetaBencana.id thereby enables emergency responders to meaningfully participate in the city without requiring their attentions and resources to be completely diverted toward bureaucratic politics and protocols. As the emergency information input by the provincial agency is immediately made available on the public map, the platform not only enables the national agency to receive critical updates in real time, but also facilitates a transparent two-way communication system between residents and government agencies (fig. 9).[11] Through the public web-based map, emergency operators are able to receive and respond to real-time situational updates from the most widespread range of sensors in the city—primarily, residents equipped with smartphones—and with a user login to the same map are able to disseminate time-critical information back to residents, neighboring jurisdictional agencies, and first responders in an integrated operational flow. Despite inevitable political variables, the alignment of attention through and across multiple bodies, curated by the data flows designed into the software architecture that find expression through a transparent interface, reduces possibilities for confusion in the densely populated megacity, as everyone is accessing and acting on the same verified information in real time (fig. 10). By catalyzing the formation of relationships around a transparent two-way communication platform, we have begun to see that Jakarta's residents (typically unimpressed by the lack of attention devoted by government agencies to community concerns) have begun to express greater levels of trust. Reciprocally, we also notice that government agencies are increasingly turning to participatory information as valuable sources of granular, sensory data such as that provided by PetaBencana.id to supplement larger-scale overviews of the city issued by government agencies in planning and policy. In the interfacial city, coproduced representations of shared infrastructures foster generative social exchanges and relationships.

It is important to note, however, that in the capacity for platforms to act as integrated organizational structures of the city, the simplicity

Fig. 9
As a two-way transparent communication platform between residents and government agencies, PetaBencana.id supports individual and collective responses to emergency events by bridging critical information gaps. Government agencies are able to view real-time, on-the-ground situational updates of disaster events from resident reports, and simultaneously disseminate time-critical information to residents.

evoked by their interfaces seldom communicates the necessary iterative complexities of maintaining the relationships that underpin them. While the representation of our partnership with the emergency management agency on the public-facing platform has remained the same over the course of four years (the same logo represents the institution), the people behind that institution have changed four times in this period, two of these changeovers having occurred in 2017 alone. Entire reorganizations of institutional protocols, even during short interim periods, necessitate a reformulation of the platform's own protocols. The frequent changing of government counterparts directly drives design decisions about the reorganization of the platform itself. The attentive registers of the platform and its users, then, necessarily construct each other to contend to the shifting temporalities of both climatic and political environments.

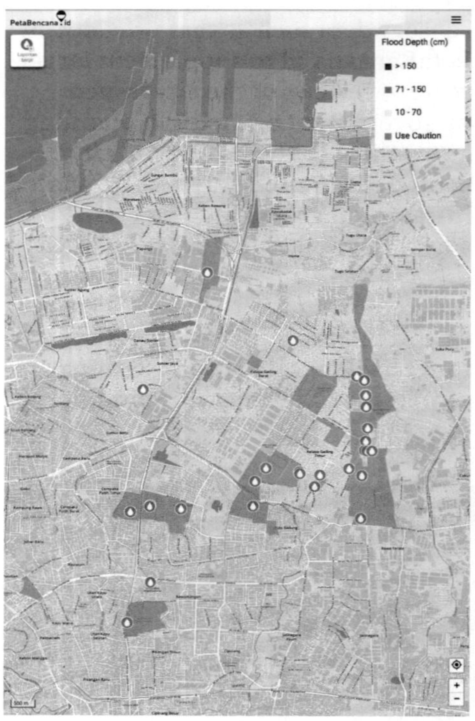

Fig. 10
A screenshot of PetaBencana.id from the afternoon of February 15, 2018, reveals the attentive alignments the platform fosters; the locations of crowd-sourced resident reports correspond directly with locations of flooded areas input into the platform by the emergency management agency (represented here as the shaded polygons). Among the torrential flows of information during disasters, software architectures attune the diverged attention of the city's actors in order to support the city in attending to its most urgent needs.

As a sociotechnical armature, PetaBencana.id reminds us that while platforms have the capacity to mediate urban relationships, the city is not, and should not be, governed by data management alone. In the fetishization of smart cities to optimize urban transactions by altering algorithms or expanding data sets, leaving the analysis of urban data to computational technologies alone foregoes critically significant dimensions of urban intelligence that are less easily codified.[12] The city is composed of multiple intelligences; it is only by enrolling these ways of seeing and thinking into a co-constitutive framework, and thus creating augmented models for thinking and sensing the city, that meaningful responses to disaster can emerge (fig. 11). In the mediated city, the digital interface grants unprecedented capacities to engage with the city's expanded geographies of variegated intelligences. PetaBencana.id has demonstrated how software architectures can harness the penetration of surface-oriented media in the contemporary megacity and repurpose profit-driven platforms to support shared forms of attention, collaboration, and care. Redirecting attention to the city's most pertinent needs through a choreographed interplay of the interlaced physical and digital layers of the urban fabric, the platform harnesses the capacities of the city's variegated dimensions, actors and agencies (fig. 12). Through a considered interweaving of the hard and soft layers of the city, architecture is invited to attune the various affinities and dissonances of diverse urban intelligences, infrastructures, and systems in order to foster creative reorientations to dynamic vicissitudes in the city of the Anthropocene.

1 Félix Guattari, *Soft Subversions: Texts and Interviews 1977–1985* (Los Angeles: Semiotext(e), 2007), 49.

2 For an especially compelling summary of this multiplicity of attention domains and its relation to cognitive labor, see Hito Steyerl, *Duty Free Art: Art in the Age of Planetary Civil War* (New York: Verso, 2017).

3 See especially Yves Citton, *The Ecology of Attention*, trans. Barnaby Norman (Cambridge, UK: Polity, 2017).

4 Xavier Wrona, "Beyond the 'Post' and Evil: Preliminary Considerations Regarding a Post-ethnographic Museum," *Oberon* 2 (April 2016): 94.

5 "Twitter Reaches Half a Billion Accounts," Semiocast, July 30, 2012, http://semiocast.com/en/publications/2012_07_30_Twitter_reaches_half_a_billion_accounts_140m_in_the_US/.

6 On Jakarta's proximity to disaster, see the United Nations Economic and Social Commission for Asia and the Pacific, *Disasters in Asia and the Pacific: 2015 Year in Review* (2015).

7 "Twitter #DataGrants selections," Twitter Engineering blog, April 17, 2014, https://blog.twitter.com/engineering/en_us/a/2014/twitter-datagrants-selections.html/.

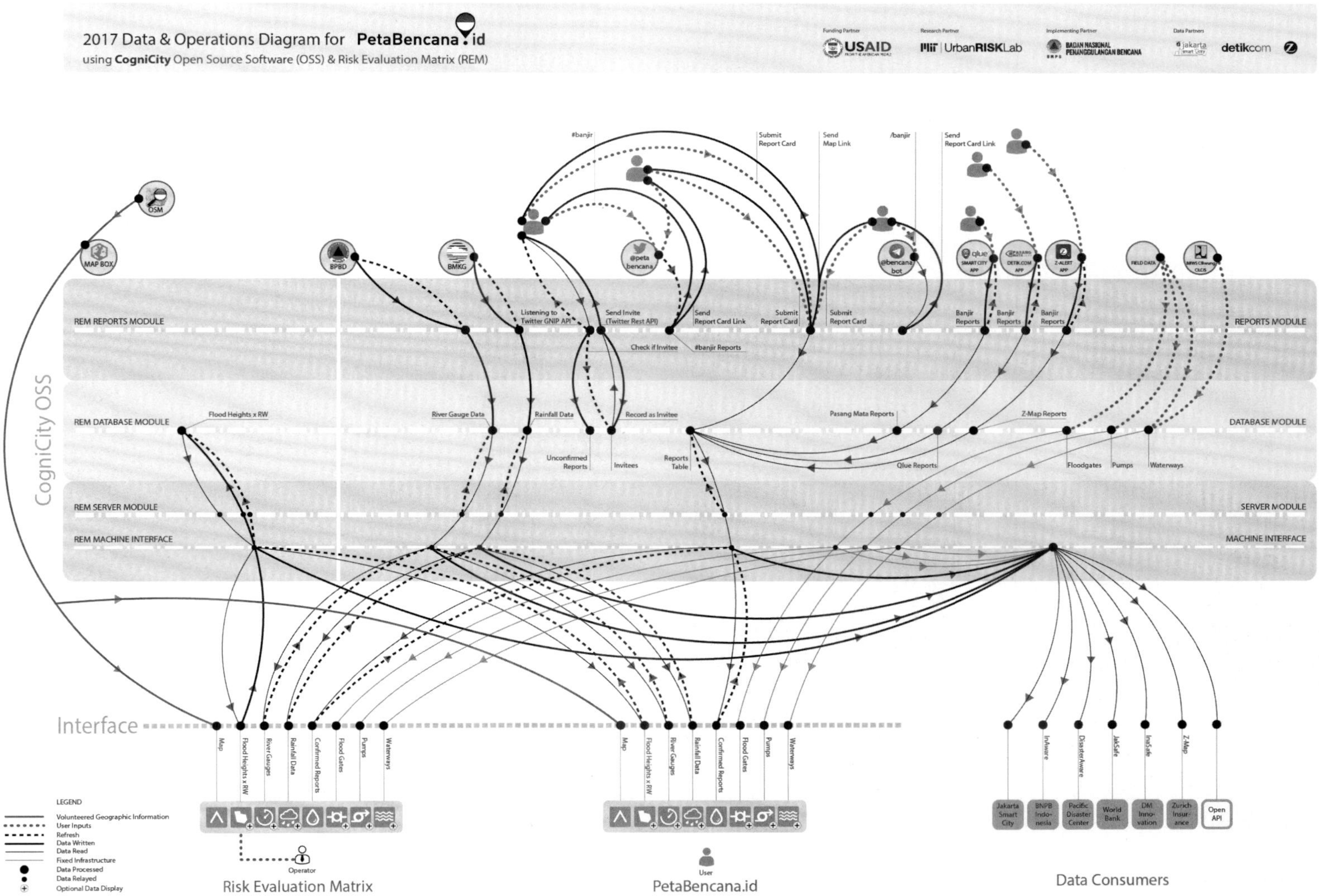

Fig. 11
2017 Data and Operations Diagram for PetaBencana.id using CogniCity Open Source Software. The platform develops as a sociotechnical armature, enrolling an array of existing urban agencies and intelligences into a framework that supports the emergence of productive relationships for mutual aid.

8 See Pietro Michelucci and Janice L. Dickinson, "The Power of Crowds: Combining Humans and Machines Can Help Tackle Increasingly Hard Problems," *Science* 351, no. 6286 (2016): 32–33.

9 On disaster capitalism, see Naomi Klein, *The Shock Doctrine: The Rise of Disaster Capitalism* (Toronto: Knopf, 2007).

10 On the other hand, the governor, to whom the provincial agency reports, did not find it necessary to send immediate updates to the national agency, with the reasoning that the severity of the flood was manageable on a provincial scale.

11 PetaBencana.id also allows emergency operators to input flood height data, derived from various sources including flood reports, government field officers, and NGOs.

12 Shannon Mattern, "A City Is Not a Computer," *Places*, February 2017, https://placesjournal.org/article/a-city-is-not-a-computer/.

Fig. 12
With the expanded brief of designing armatures that engage in the co-construction of the city through multiple dimensions—aligning the interweaving hard and soft interfaces of the city—our research is also now engaged in materializing the digital platform into urban images that act as physical interfaces into the virtual spaces of the city. By intervening in spaces of public gathering and alongside public infrastructures, these experimental interventions allow for the physical city to serve as a reminder that the city is also digital, and it is only through an aligned structuring of the co-constitutive layers of the city that we can hope to generate organizations of consequence.

Richard Vijgen

Spectrum Tapestry: Information as a Machine for Living In

Each time we use our cellphones or adjust our connected thermostat we briefly interact with the physical objects that link our bodies to the *infosphere*, a man-made technological ecosystem that we increasingly depend on to survive in the digital age. In most parts of world, we are completely surrounded by this invisible system of radio signals from cell towers, satellites, and wireless access points. We live, quite literally, in information.

Despite our total immersion in this technological environment, we are unable to perceive it directly; there is no visual confirmation of its existence. Instead we probe this environment using devices that bridge the gap between our embodied reality and the ethereal world of digital information. These are the "blind sticks" we depend on to navigate and survive in the new world.

What if we could experience this world more directly? Would it bring us closer to our digital reality?

Spectrum Tapestry is an electronic textile wall hanging that explores this question. The tapestry reveals the information density of a space by visualizing the activity of the Wi-Fi radio spectrum in real time. With its focus on the home, it emphasizes the immersive nature of the digital world. This is where we live, eat, and sleep, surrounded by information. By visualizing the fundaments of the infosphere (radio) rather than the front-end of the Stack,[1] Spectrum Tapestry hopes to provide a technological point of orientation and perhaps a starting point for alternate paths.

The project addresses questions such as:

How can we make a tactile imprint of the information surrounding us?

How can we measure and visualize the Wi-Fi radio spectrum?

How can reflective, ambient screens express an alternative information attitude?

1 The Stack is the term that describes a group of computer programs that work in tandem to produce a common goal or form a single system. It is also used by Benjamin Bratton to describe a total system of "planetary-scale computation."

Living in Information

Ever since the first radio broadcasts in the early twentieth century, radio technology has become part of everyday life. Initially the manifestation of radio in modern life was well defined. The large T-antennas that were used to extend the reach of the signal made radio a very visible medium. As the technology matured and radio became a key instrument for nation states, radio towers such as the Shukhov Tower in Moscow became not just monuments of technology, but public icons celebrating modernity. All this time, the model was clear: a centralized infrastructure, like a power plant or a water system, that spreads words, music, and images within a radius defined by the height of the antenna and the amount of power put into it.

Any structure within this radius would either allow the signals to pass through it, or would need a (roof-mounted) antenna to bring the signal inside. As a user you could either tune in or tune out.

Fig. 1
Cage T-antenna of amateur station in 1922
Photograph: Robert C. Higgy

While for most of the twentieth century analogue radio sent signals from one point to all, digital communications have allowed for a more targeted model. A digital signal could more easily be addressed to one specific receiver. With the popularization of digital mobile phones and their supporting infrastructure in the 1990s, radio gradually became a decentralized many-to-many system. Radio towers were first augmented, and later superseded, by smaller antennas distributed throughout the city. Meanwhile, Wi-Fi routers started replacing wired connections in large numbers in the early 2000s. Digital radio, instead of covering a circular area with a single signal, has become a dispersed habitat.

Rooftop antennas bringing a central signal in gave way to Wi-Fi antennas sending their service beacons out. Instead of tuning in or out, users now define the radio spectrum in a space just by being present. We take ownership of the spectrum through our mobile devices. Everywhere we go we send out signals: who we are, where we've been, and that we want to make a connection. The Wi-Fi routers and cell towers around us pick up these signals and direct their resources to fill our space with information.

The traditional notion of the space that surrounds us, shields us, and separates us from the outside has been augmented with the spatial properties of radio. We can occupy a space and extend beyond it; we can create bubbles of private space in public through mobile hotspots; and we can be watched, probed, and manipulated while being alone in a room with the doors and windows closed. Yet while the convergence of constructed spaces and radio might slowly change our notion of space, our direct perception of it remains unchanged.

Seeing Wi-Fi

Although most of the wireless signals that underpin digital life are based on radio, they are in fact different technologies that use different parts of the radio spectrum. Low frequencies allow us to go through, or around, obstacles and are used for long-range communication. Higher frequencies allow for more information to be transmitted but are easily blocked by obstacles. The spectrum ranges from 9 KHz for navigation applications to 30 GHz for satellite communication. Wi-Fi uses a slice of the radio spectrum around 2.4 GHz and another at 5 GHz.

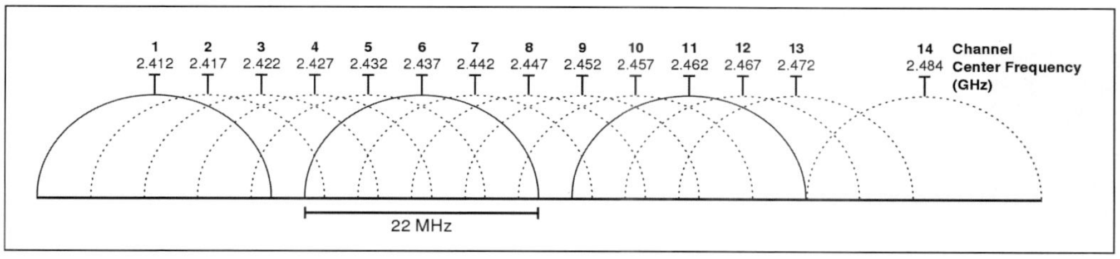

Fig. 2
The Wi-Fi spectrum (2.4 GHz) ranges from 2.412 to 2.472 GHz and is divided into 13 (14 in select areas) overlapping "channels." These channels can be thought of as traffic lanes. When there is too much traffic on one lane, the signal degrades and the connection speed drops. To keep traffic flowing, devices may choose a quiet channel. In very densely connected areas there is a constant change of activity on all the channels as devices try to find the one that is the least crowded.

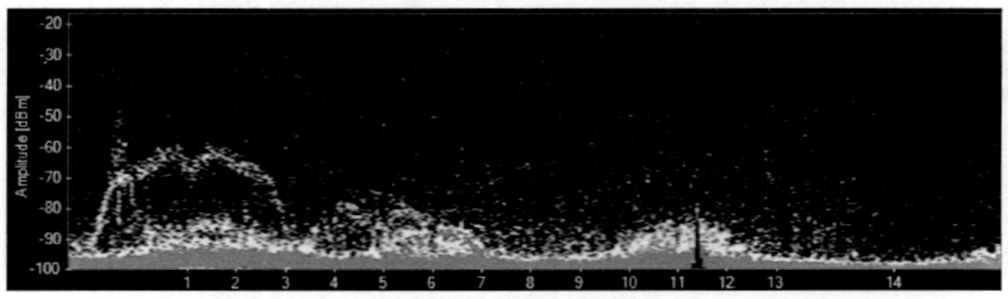

Fig. 3
A Wi-Fi spectrum analysis that shows traffic across channels.

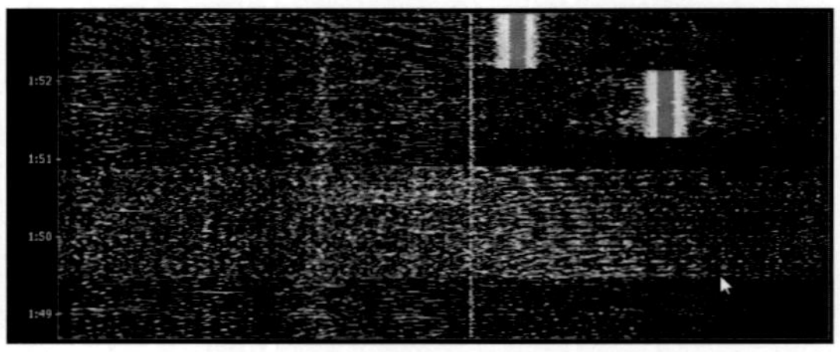

Fig. 4
A "waterfall" representation of the Wi-Fi spectrum. A waterfall visualization shows activity across the frequency spectrum over time.

Although radio is part of the same magnetic spectrum as visible light, we cannot see it directly. As radio is a nonvisual medium, any visualization is a matter of artistic interpretation. However, the seemingly simple question, what does radio look like? is surprisingly difficult to answer, even when looking at art for answers. The difficulty seems to be both technical and artistic.

For one, what are you visualizing? The term radio describes all applications across the spectrum. Capturing or even measuring radio as a whole would require a vast array of different equipment and antennas. Even if we could capture all this information, imagining it would still be difficult as it has no visual properties and would represent an enormous variety of functions and purposes.

EMF meters (electromagnetic field meters) are devices that can be used to measure the electromagnetic fields around you. Typically, these devices measure the amount of energy across a range of frequencies. This kind of measurement is too coarse to be suitable for visualization. It can tell you whether there is Wi-Fi activity somewhere, but not how much or of what kind.

In order to look at Wi-Fi in more detail we can use the Wi-Fi receiver itself. Typically, a Wi-Fi receiver is tuned to the channel it is connected to, but many Wi-Fi chips allow us to switch to monitor mode. In monitor mode, the receiver doesn't connect to any particular channel, but just listens to any traffic it can pick up, including traffic on different networks. By sampling each channel in succession, a script developed for Spectrum Tapestry loops through the channels, recording each packet that passes the receiver. The script then compares how many frames were received on each channel. By running the script continuously, it produces a semi-real-time stream of "traffic data" on the 2.4 GHz spectrum that can be used for visualization.

While Spectrum Tapestry uses a summary of activity on the thirteen channels of the Wi-Fi spectrum, this approach would allow for a more specific analysis of the frames, such as which devices are in communication with each other, whether the communication is encrypted, and in some cases the kind of communication.

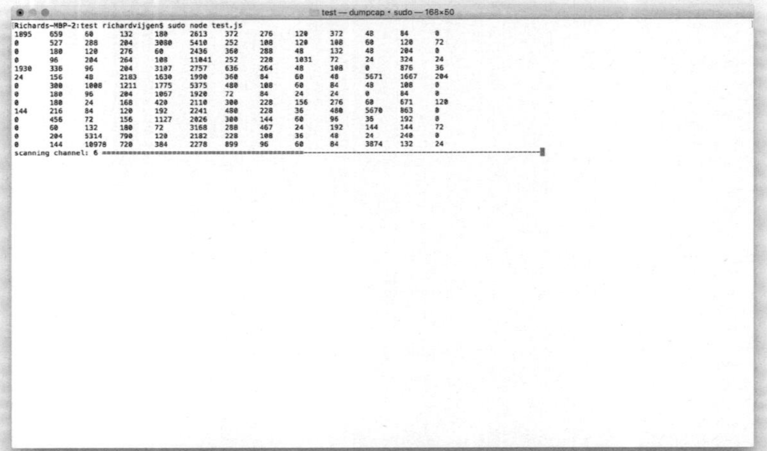

Fig. 5
Wi-Fi Scanner. A script developed for Spectrum Tapestry written in Node.js continually samples the 2.4 GHz range. At the end of each cycle it outputs the number of "frames" that were picked up at each channel. This information can be used to visualize the Wi-Fi spectrum.

Slow Data

Spectrum Tapestry is a research project that aims to develop new strategies for imagining and visualizing the daily reality of radio-augmented space. Apart from capturing the signals around us, it looks to visualize these signals in a way that emphasizes their immersive and ambient nature. As such, it seeks to integrate the display of dynamic information into the space it describes. Rather than using a large LCD screen or a projector, it explores the use of passive (reflective) surfaces. In contrast with an active surface, passive surface does not emit light but reflects it like a painting or a print. To integrate with the domestic space the display should not only be passive, but also be designed to function in the background and have a material quality.[2] In the project's current phase, we are exploring the tapestry as a potential medium for an ambient visualization, as a link between past and future, and a bridge between the abstraction of wireless data and the tactility of textile.

To use the tapestry as a dynamic surface, the material needs to be activated. This can be done mechanically, or as in this experiment, chemically, by using heat-activated, color-changing inks. When a small current is applied to a resistive thermal thread, a specific area can be heated to change the color of the ink. By working the thermal thread into the surface according to a specific design, lines and patterns can be created and controlled using a microcontroller. The result is a reflective, flexible textile surface that can display dynamic patterns based on digital signals.

The prototype uses a digital embroidery machine to sew the thermal thread into the surface and create a pattern.[3] Thirteen overlapping wave patterns represent the thirteen Wi-Fi channels. Each channel has three additional "layers" that represent different levels of activity on a channel. Each layer consists of a single electrically insulated thread that allows overlap without shorting the circuit. By switching layers on and off, the visualization ranges from very structured to very complex.

2 Most screens and interfaces are designed to function in the foreground. This conveys a sense of urgency. In contrast, a screen designed to function in the background should convey a sense of slow flux, like a window looking out on a landscape.

3 Future experiments might look at weaving and tufting of thermal thread.

test

```
Richards-MBP-2:test richardvijgen$ sudo node test.js
1895    659     60      132     180     2613    372     276     120     3
0       527     288     204     3080    5410    252     108     120     1
0       180     120     276     60      2436    360     288     48      1
0       96      204     264     108     11041   252     228     1031    7
1930    336     96      204     3107    2757    636     264     48      1
24      156     48      2183    1630    1990    360     84      60      4
0       300     1008    1211    1775    5375    480     108     60      8
0       180     96      204     1067    1920    72      84      24      2
0       180     24      168     420     2110    300     228     156     2
144     216     84      120     192     2241    480     228     36      4
0       456     72      156     1127    2026    300     144     60      9
0       60      132     180     72      3168    288     467     24      1
0       204     5314    790     120     2182    228     108     36      4
0       144     10978   720     384     2278    899     96      60      8
scanning channel: 6 ===============================================-------
```

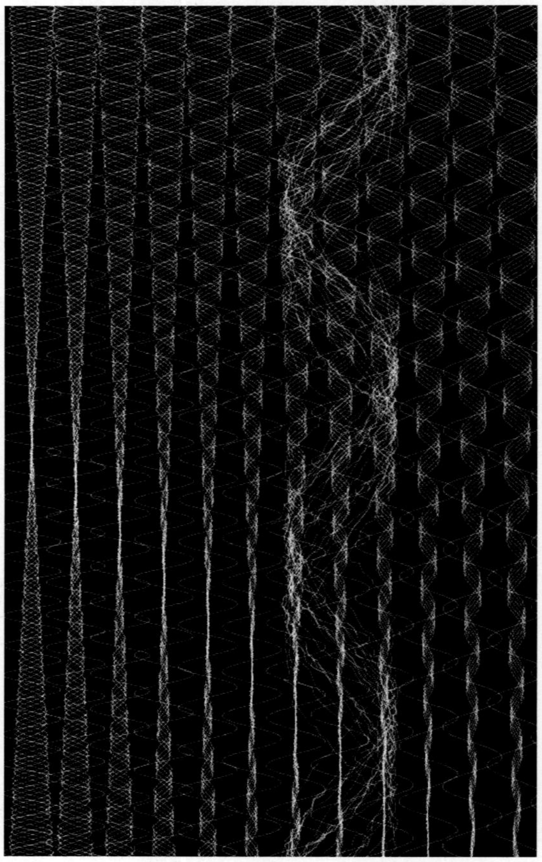

Figs. 6, 7
Simulated visualization of 13 overlapping channels with traffic on channels 2, 4, 5, 8, 9, and 13.

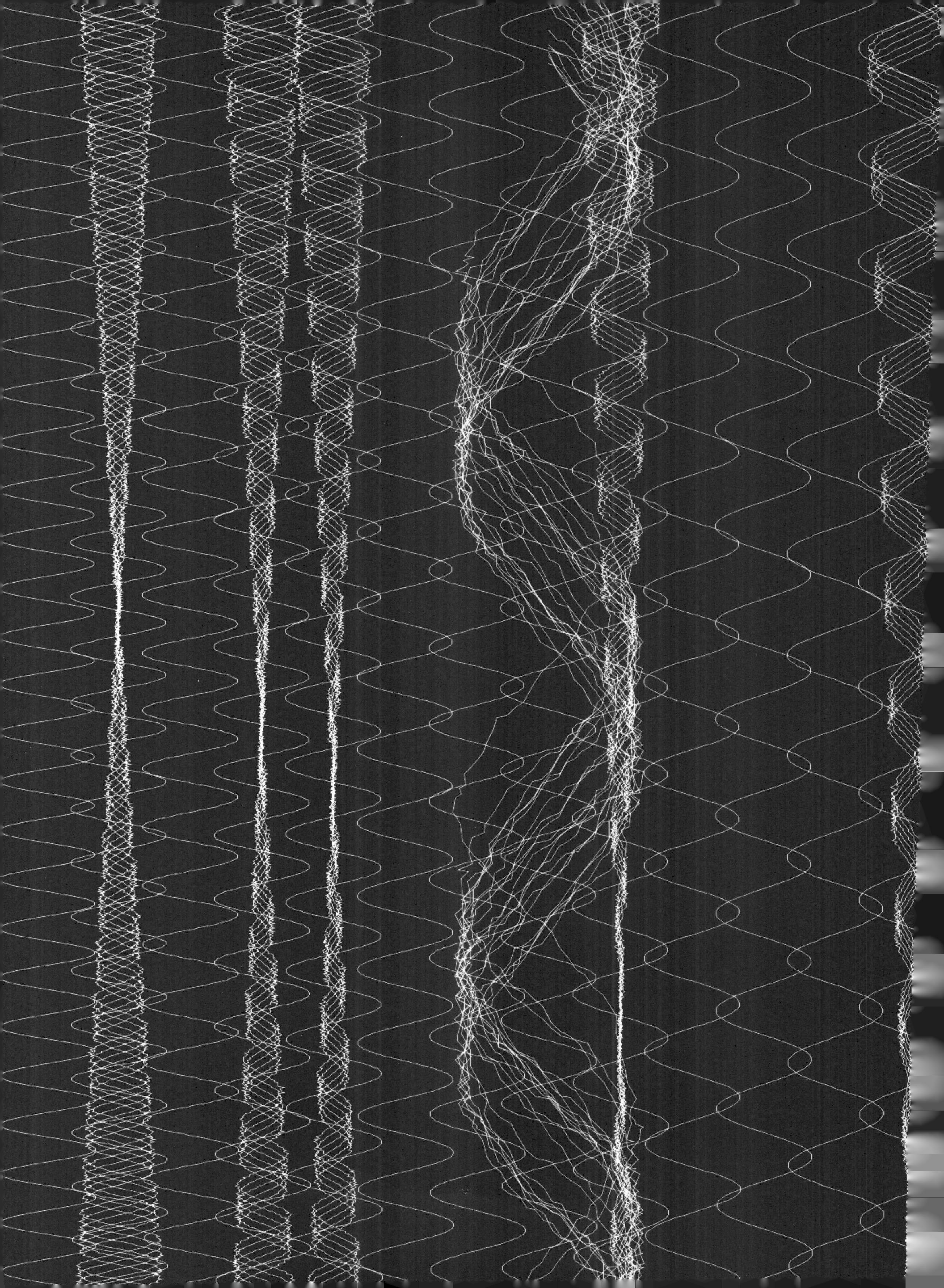

In its current state, the project's goal is to investigate different strategies and techniques to visualize Wi-Fi activity in a domestic space. The historic role of tapestry as a bridge between design and architecture, between environment and space makes it an interesting medium to explore and visualize the new role radio plays in defining, inhabiting and extending spaces.

However, visualizing Wi-Fi activity using a flat surface, no matter how coarse or detailed, is still an abstraction. Spectrum Tapestry translates the invisible signals into visible patterns. It helps us relate to the presence of Wi-Fi and perhaps some of its properties, but it does not reveal any of its spatial behavior.

Understanding radio as a property of the spaces we live in could help get us closer to the technological reality of our surroundings. The tapestry is a first attempt to give radio a visual presence in the domestic space. Once we are aware of radio as a property of space we can start to think about how to design with it.

Fig. 8
Embroidering thermal thread using a digital embroidery machine.

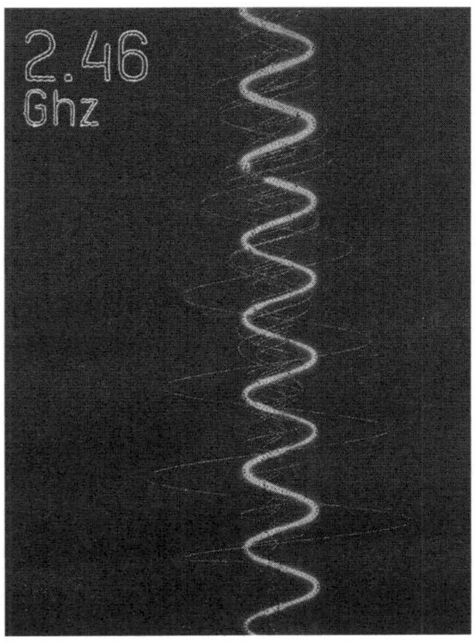

Fig. 9
Sample 2.46 GHz sheet

Fig. 10
Microscopic image of embroidered textile overlapping insulated thermal wire.

Shamsher Ali, Shveta Sarda & Prasad Shetty

Of Gheras, Goats, and Ghosts: Awkward Futurities of Incremental Settling

01

The make of a place is a palimpsest activated through the many ways in which it is used. The possibilities of use, in turn, give a place its form over time: they give a place its ease, its different gradients. What guides usage—the make of the place, or the acts that maintain the make?

When it began, the municipal survey moved at lightning speed through the neighborhood. Three teams of surveyors appeared, each bearing a register gridded with rows and columns, along with twenty to twenty-five years of experience. Documents tumbled out of trunks. The oldest acceptable document is the Lal Card, so called because the I.D. photo on it is taken against a red background. Ration cards, first issued in the 1980s, are not acceptable—they do not bear an address, just the name of the neighborhood. It was the Lal Card that marked the address of a plot with a name of the occupant. It tied people to their plot and produced a property type. So it can be said that the predemolition survey of 2009 is a reinforcing of the legal seizure that had started with the 1990 survey for the Lal Card.

The tenants always struggled to prove their presence. They rented their houses from earlier occupants with legal documents. The earlier houses were extended by adding a room or a floor for rent. The earlier occupants always seemed to be threatened by the tenants for fear they would make claims on the land and property as they themselves had done before. This relationship manifested itself in many things—use of toilets (tenants had to pay more than occupants), parking (tenants' vehicles were not allowed inside the neighborhood), committee meetings (tenants were not invited to participate), et cetera. The space of the neighborhood revealed itself differently to different persons, depending on whether one was an occupant or a tenant.

02

Ease of a place is the malleability of its common space—where children play, elders gather, boys and girls hang out, and women get together. Here a dance platform can be set up for a birthday or a wedding, a meeting can be held or fights can be fought. This is where after a destructive fire a temporary camp can be assembled, festivals can be celebrated, and prayer meetings held.

But just because the doors of many houses open into this space doesn't mean inclusion is easy or that departure is without strain.

What did the Lal Card do to the neighborhood from 1990 to 2009? It brought with it a form of tenurial stability. Now that there is a claim to one's space, one can grow, circulate the surplus, expand. The porous boundary of occupancy begins to reshape itself. The neighborhood applies deep administrative and cultural intelligence for this negotiation. There is a contested and intricate operation through which occupants enter administrative ledgers. The negotiation itself becomes a medium through which the confidence of occupants grows.

As people have built their houses without land titles and approvals, the legality of occupancy in the neighborhood has always been fuzzy, and there is generally a looming threat of eviction. Modest shrines or a statue of Babasaheb Dr. B. R. Ambedkar can often be found at neighborhood entrances. While the shrines and statues do not provide legal legitimacy to the houses, they nevertheless structure the way the settlement is organized. The houses are built such that, in case of eviction, one would have to demolish the shrine or the statue before demolishing houses.

03

Over time, one might come to realize that the make of a place and its entanglements aren't quite as complicated as they seemed at first glance. Yet there is no guarantee that just because one is looking at it closely today, a place will quickly uncoil and reveal itself.

Two friends shared a wall. When one left the neighborhood two decades ago, the other one took that space over, enfolding it into his own. Now when the survey is happening, he wants to repay this debt that he has carried with him from the time he entered the neighborhood. He partitions the house again, returning it to its dimensions of twenty years ago. He is vehement he must ensure his friend's entry into the survey ledger. He has kept and maintained his friend's documents all these years.

However, no god ever protected tenants and subtenants. They were often evicted by the earlier occupants. Whenever there was a survey for a subsidy or a new house, all tenants in the neighborhood were asked to leave, and their space was filled by a family member of the occupant. This ensured that the subsidy would be maximized within the family and not shared with the tenant. These evictions happened all the time—at a large scale, or as singular instances where the occupant needed the premises for some purpose. Since the whole neighborhood operated in an extralegal landscape, paper contracts did not exist, nor were they useful. These were silent evictions.

04

This entire place was once a camp of poles and canvas sheets, used for recycling waste. Few people lived here. Then a huge fire burned and everything turned to ash. Structures of brick and wood sprouted. Today there are houses that are twenty, even thirty, feet high.

Like puzzles made and unmade, places defy one's expectation of a steady count of time.

The neighborhood is known for the craftsmanship of artisans who make jewelry boxes in the *karkhanas*, or workshops. The first one was set up in the early 1990s. Parents sent their young sons here to develop a capacity to work with others, to learn concentration and acquire *hunar* (skill). *Laakh ka kaam* (lac work) needs application of heat, which is done in workshops, to make diaries, bracelets, and souvenirs. Young girls also picked up *thhappe ka kaam* (making envelopes) for multinational companies and banks. There are *karkhanas* with machines to bring metal to a shine. At the beginning, in the 1960s, this settlement was a *godaam*, a base for recycling goods. As it grew dense, the *godaam* shifted to one side. Those who worked at the *godaam*, the first settlers, continue to live here and work at the *godaam*. Recycling work continues within houses: soap is recycled, biscuits past their "best before" date are pulled out of packets to be resold in the market. The late 1990s saw phone booths, cable operators, and audio cassette and CD sellers thrive. Gift shops proliferated. Food joints, where people would eat before heading out for work, did good business. The young apprentices of the workshops grew into confident young men and started setting up their own *karkhanas*.

The legislated urban plan demarcates the city into distinct places of residence, work, and commerce. This partition is disregarded by neighborhoods in their form of living. The survey becomes a time when the plan reimposes its division onto the neighborhood. As soon as the survey began, workshops folded up, shops shut down, and services withdrew. The very things from which the neighborhood is made and for which it was known pulled back from view, came to a stop. The neighborhood shrunk to just houses—fixed residences of people with documents.

As most old neighborhoods were forced from incremental settlements into high-rise apartments, there were always heated discussions among occupants regarding whether their neighborhood should be identified as an old village, a resettlement colony, a slum, or a factory. Each identity had its own advantages and disadvantages. While in some cases occupants were entitled to bigger houses, in other cases they would be compensated with a sum of money.

05

Pointing to a cluster of houses he said, “Once, they were a single structure.” When the man who lived there sold it and left, it shape-shifted: it was shared, split, carved, built into six places to dwell. It made room for newcomers. Even when the coiling, knotted, turning, shifting insides of a place are not visible, thresholds can be internally marked, decorated, and expressed—through celebrations, accidents, decisions, and risks. Place thickens through changes, lived in its thresholds.

The neighborhood enmeshes the surveyors into its weave, slows them down. A survey is an administrative procedure with legal consequences. But the neighborhood pushes it toward a kind of juridical performance, where evidence and questions of justice and inequality are continuously performed and argued. The surveyor is made to perform as a judge—to weigh evidence. He mediates and intervenes. The better judgment of one surveyor over the others is lauded, publicly praised in his presence.

The neighborhood managed relationships between animals and humans. Both roamed freely on the streets and were clear about where to go and which places to enter. The relationship was neither of excessive affection nor of indifference. It appeared that all—goats, sheep, dogs, cats, and humans—knew each other, and everyone’s lives were fused together. Whenever there was talk of moving into high-rise apartments, everyone feared what might happen to the animals—where would the goats go?

06

Far-sightedness is an uneven count of time.

Not one door opened for the hand pumps. Homes were already cramped enough. What about common spaces? Houses need water, but the small pockets of shared space needed protecting too. A hand pump calls to itself a different kind of gathering, a different routine. "Come on, it's a great thing—one hand pump for every cluster of houses," the *pradhan*, or local leader, spent weeks trying to convince everyone to make room for something he thought all would have jumped at.

Finally some eight houses agreed. Maybe they understood the stakes most, or maybe they were the ones who best overcame their fear of perpetual slush and sludge. Still, flowing water changed things. It compressed time—the water to be used by each house had to be filled by households turn by turn. Unlike a clock, when a pump breaks, things actually stop flowing. The heads of the eight households earned praise and, in time, the streets they lived on began to be called by their names.

To build is to "build on" something and yet remain in dialogue with that which is approaching. Years passed. When running water arrived, most households welcomed it.

"See, we have a receipt from the 1980s. Son, we are poor. Please think about it." Only specific documents gained one entry into the survey ledger, but every document is a foot in the door to delay it from shutting. The neighborhood responds to the surveyor's questioning of the legibility or legality of a document with accounts of reputation, journeys, mutuality. Through silence, verbal support, evasion, and denials, the neighborhood mobilizes enormous cultural and intellectual resources to obstruct the eye of the state, to make it blurry. As surveyors advance from house to house, lane by lane, *ghera* after *ghera*, occupants resist the immense pressure of turning on each other by refusing to become eyes of the state.

When the neighborhood became an apartment block, its long maze-like streets were replaced by short, straight, and dark corridors between homes. Doors remained shut all day. While in the neighborhood problems and celebrations intensified or became diffused across many houses and the street, when they shifted into the apartments, people found these remained contained within houses, breaking out as conflict or violent events. Families did however manage to bring goats into their houses, where their bleats added to the soundscape.

07

A *ghera* is made up of a group of houses. It is both an occupancy and an encirclement. It pulls in slowly, as ties deepen and conversations condense—so that accepting, rejecting, sacrificing, withdrawing, encouraging, and refusing get drawn up in space as walls and extensions—over weeks, over months, over years. The *ghera* inhales, exhales, swells, ebbs, includes, excludes, and discards.

Just as houses link with one another in specific ways to make a *ghera*, the structure of each house is enlaced in the *ghera*. This is what gives a *ghera* its ambience, its mood, its capture.

Are there things, lives, people that refuse to come into the ledger? The survey requires relationships to be *pardarshi* (transparent). But the reality of an impending loss in the future does not displace the mutuality of *pardedaari*, or keeping in the veil, that the inhabitants of a neighborhood maintain over the years. Complicated relational and conjugal journeys, obligations, interdependences, and misadventures are not revealed to the surveyors, even under duress. This contest over veiling to maintain a degree of opacity produces an intensified realm of negotiated illegibility for the neighborhood.

The apartment was not like the earlier neighborhood. While every house had running water and toilets inside the houses, many things weren't possible. The warehouses, the shops, the recycling units, the factories were gone. There were no fires to burn down existing houses so larger ones could be built. No shifting of walls, no extensions, no swelling or contracting was possible. But everything was more or less legal. As the inhabitants of the apartments came to terms with the layout of a multistory building, they also started getting familiar with the idea of a cooperative housing society, an association of all inhabitants of the apartment building responsible for its upkeep. The legitimacy of this society had to be maintained through several legal-sounding practices—maintaining a society office, having regular meetings, keeping accounts, filing returns, et cetera.

08

A *ghera* may look like it is merely a structuring unit of a *basti*, or a neighborhood, but it is a density in which houses not only make a common space, but also share walls. It is a practice, which we could call "a practice of the wall." When a person builds his or her house using brick and cement, neighbors get the gift of a wall. When walls are shared, they are common. Houses in a *ghera* build up slowly in this way, over time, strengthened and reinforced by each other.

The making of a settlement is an act of incremental autodidacticism. The self-learning is of architectural modes, infrastructural procedures, relationships with welfare institutions, alignments in electoral processes, and skills and trades. It is entangled with contests of life, and cautious in its transactions with the formidable apparatus of enumeration and governance. These transactions are to maneuver away, to the furthest extent possible, from the demands for clarity, legibility, and readability. The apparatus could fall as a hard edge of the state, or it could come through soft, welfare-oriented schemes. The digital has entered at both these edges, and therefore needs to be understood as an internally unstable form that is being, and will be, contested everywhere.

Someone's slippers got stolen. As news spread, other stories of theft came to light. In the annual general body meeting of the society, the issue was discussed with great interest. One man suggested installing CCTV cameras on all eight floors of the building—three on each floor and eight on the outside—a total of thirty-two cameras. He made calculations and worked out a plan. The whole thing would cost nothing more than INR 5000 per month, and there were ninety-six houses that would share the cost. Everyone agreed. CCTV cameras were installed the very next week.

Screens showing feeds from the building's thirty-two CCTV cameras were installed in the society's ground-floor office. For six months, people visited the office and watched live feeds from various parts of the building for hours. Soon interest faded and people went back to their televisions. A year later, no one bothered looking at the feeds even when sitting in front of the screens. But one day a man came to the society's office and asked to be shown footage from the previous night. The young woman managing the accounts got the password from the society's secretary and unlocked footage from three cameras on the fourth floor. When she asked the man what he was looking for, he said he suspected a ghost had entered the building and was wandering the corridors at night.

09

The lives that are lived in a *ghera* are also a *ghera*'s force of life. These lives are lived in common in their celebrations, festivals, promotions, mobility, and successes. Their events—a child gone missing, a fluctuation in production cycles in the market, an illness, death, risk-taking gone wrong—shapes the *ghera*. This weave of joys and tribulations gives a *ghera* its slant and its swerve. It is what creates the confidence that a *ghera* can be leaned on to take risks and make decisions, like leaving the family behind and traveling to another city for work, taking in a tenant, investing all savings in a parcel of land at a far end of the city.

Just as a *ghera* keeps being built through awkward steps in occupancy, the balance between its dwellings keeps weaving a common ground. It is an unspoken yet tested faith that, even though a *ghera*'s houses don't all rise together, no house in a *ghera* will collapse alone from weakness. This is something a *ghera* will never allow.

The workshops have given way to a world of new techno-social objects. It builds from the earlier milieus of musical gatherings produced by audio cassettes and players in the shared space of a *ghera*. The collective life of viewing, copying and gifting, song and dance, call to prayer, and announcement of events wove the neighborhood's affective ambience. Public telephone booths of the 1990s pleated in far-flung towns and cities, videocassette players gathered economies of repair and recycling, video game parlors drew young adults into a dexterous gaming culture, and cable networks and TV sets raised home-grown technicians. It is within this autodidactic culture that mobile telephony–based internet connectivity has accelerated, with overflows of information, interruptions, accelerations, crashes, unpredictable encounters, and threats. Low-resource video lending stores set up through downloading BitTorrents and copying CDs have proliferated on street corners and found sustenance through lateral connections and informal economies. A new spatial and temporal rhythm enmeshes into unrecognizable and provocative zones, nurturing figures who re-engineer materials and modes by which technical knowledge is learned and mobilized. This is where the biometric state meets its street fighters.

Collisional, unpredictable, spectral are the ways of urban life.

Scott McQuire

The City as Media

The city as medium

In a well-known essay, German literary and media theorist Friedrich Kittler argued that the city constitutes a *medium*.[1] What is at stake in such a conception? Following the common observation that cities can no longer be defined in terms of traditional structures of fortification and enclosure, Kittler suggests that the contemporary city is better characterized by its intersecting networks.[2] He extends this argument by insisting that all networked systems, including water, electricity, highways, broadcasting, and telecommunications, can be understood as platforms that exist to record, process, and transmit information. In other words, they are *media*.

However, in a less celebrated moment in the same essay, Kittler observes that the city also informs our current understanding of media from another direction. Urban forms underpin key terminology we use to describe contemporary media: Claude Shannon's application of Boolean algebra to coupling telegraph relays introduced the logic of binary switching systems, in which simple elements are called "gates" and computer programs perform "routing."[3] One could equally point to the complex relationship between windows and screens that developed in relation to cinema and television throughout the twentieth century and persists in our description of computer displays.

Holding these two trajectories together—one concerning the transformation of urban infrastructure and the other the role of the city and urban space in processes of conceptualization—creates a complex relation. In one sense, naming new phenomena such as digital media by adopting terms derived from the history of the city belongs to the common practice of attempting to master novelty by defining it with reference to the familiar; in this instance, urban spaces, structures, and modes of circulation become metaphors for electronic and computational media. But, as Jacques Derrida reminds us, metaphor is never innocent, least of all in this domain.[4] Even as we attempt to use the city to describe thresholds of new media, we are forced to recognize that the spaces, structures, and modes of circulation to which we appeal are caught up in a process of profound change, due in no small part to the concerted action of the very media we are trying to describe.

This uncertain interplay, defined by complex feedback between material infrastructures and cultural imagination, delineates the paradoxical terrain for thinking about the contemporary relationship between media and city. If the function of media in the cybernetic tradition that Kittler invokes was merely to transmit information, communication theory has long recognized that media is less about transmission than *translation*, and that processes of mediation inevitably alter the space-time frames that condition lived human experience. This sets up a circuit or relay between what might be called a restricted and a general economy of media. If media have never been simply a specific set of devices and institutions that transmit content, today it is the entire history of opposing mediation to the immediacy of face-to-face interactions that is increasingly brought into question.

1. Friedrich Kittler, "The City Is a Medium," trans. Matthew Griffin, *New Literary History* 27, no. 4 (1996): 717–29.
2. "Since cities no longer lie within the panopticon of the cathedral or castle and can no longer be enclosed by walls or fortifications, a network made up of intersecting networks dissects and connects the city—in particular, its fringes, peripheries and tangents." Kittler, "The City Is a Medium," 718.
3. Claude Shannon, "Symbolic Analysis of Relay and Switching Circuits," *Transactions of the American Institute of Electrical Engineers* 57, no. 12 (December 1938): 713–23, doi:10.1109/T-AIEE.1938.5057767/.
4. Jacques Derrida, "White Mythology: Metaphor in the Text of Philosophy," trans. F.C.T Moore, *New Literary History* 6, no.1 (Autumn 1974): 5–74.

Media as environment

Kittler's move in describing the city as a medium takes the work of Marshall McLuhan as one of its (mostly implicit) points of departure. For McLuhan, any technology or medium that achieves dominance constitutes a "total space" for thinking and acting.[5] Distinguishing between "content," which was the primary concern of media analysis at the time he wrote, and what he called "environment," McLuhan argued that environmental effects tended to recede from view within the perceptual frame established by any dominant medium. Instead, the media environment becomes the taken-for-granted space of thought and social life.[6] From this perspective, McLuhan later argued that new media such as television "are not bridges between man and nature: they are nature."[7]

In McLuhan's account, the environmental effects of media relate principally to questions of scale, pattern, and rhythm.[8] This underpins his famous assertion that the impact of television is less a function of what is "on" the TV than the fact that the TV is "on" simultaneously in millions of homes spread across what was starting to become a global territory. In his work McLuhan drew inspiration from Harold Innis's account of the biases of different media, such as stone and paper, in terms of their differential capacities to enable the archiving (preservation over time) and transportation (movement across space) of information.[9] By updating Innis to the era of electric media, McLuhan established his key provocations concerning the new modes of subjectivity, territoriality, commerce, and governance that were emerging under the artificial light of television.

Given McLuhan's argument that the environmental effects of any dominant medium tend to be invisible to those living in it, how, then, does one become conscious of them? He suggests that thresholds of transition play a significant role in establishing social awareness, albeit in a belated fashion: "every new technology creates an environment that translates the old or preceding technology into an art form."[10] Perhaps in part to justify his own role as the oracle of the new electric environment, McLuhan also floated the possibility that the 1960s in fact ushered in a new stage of reflexivity. Observing, "We may be catching up with ourselves," McLuhan extolled the example of Pop Art "in taking the outer environment and putting it in the art gallery," arguing that this marked a new phase of human existence in which "we have begun to process the environment itself as an art form."[11]

Half a century later this once-novel idea of processing the environment as art has taken on new connotations. Technical media (to use Kittler's phrase) have helped to propel art out of traditional institutional settings such as the gallery and into the urban landscape at large. If this process necessarily affects our understanding of the relation between art and other forms of visual communication, it also foregrounds the extent to which contemporary media no longer simply represent the lived environment of the city in the manner of Pop Art. Instead, networked digital media have extended processes of recursive feedback into more and more domains of contemporary urban life.

McLuhan's sense of this future is ambiguous. On the one hand, his environmental understanding of electric media leads him to prophesy the wholesale dissolution of urban form:

> With instant electric technology, the globe itself can never again be more than a village, and the very nature of the city as a form of major dimensions must inevitably dissolve like a fading shot in a movie.[12]

This logic was shared by many contemporaries, including architect Charles Moore. In the same issue of *Perspecta* in which McLuhan published "The Invisible Environment," Moore argued, "In an electronic world where space and location have so little functional meaning, there seems little point in defining cities spatially."[13] While this kind of rhetoric proclaiming the looming irrelevance of physical space didn't gain significant purchase in the 1960s, it was revived with a vengeance in the 1990s, as cyberspace was persuasively imagined as a parallel world that could somehow be magically separated from the messy materialities of fleshy bodies and city streets.[14] McLuhan, posthumously adopted as the "patron-saint" of *Wired* magazine,[15] was frequently called on to justify this seeming irrelevance of bricks in favor of bytes. But it would be a mistake to regard this as the sole trajectory of McLuhan's thought. A different configuration emerges from his suggestion that electric media elevates pattern recognition over older forms of categorization:

> As data can be processed very rapidly we move literally into the world of pattern recognition, out of the world of mere data classification. One way of putting this is to say that our children today live in a world in which the environment itself is a teaching machine made of electric information.[16]

As urban space becomes saturated with information gathering, storing, and processing technologies, this idea of an environment "made of electric information" has gained new momentum. It is fast being naturalized in contemporary agendas for the smart city, in which the full implications of conceiving—and *equipping*—the city as media acquire new force and urgency.

5. Marshall McLuhan, "The Invisible Environment: The Future of an Erosion," *Perspecta* 11 (1967): 161–67.
6. McLuhan, "The Invisible Environment," 164.
7. Marshall McLuhan, *Counter Blast* (London: Rapp and Whiting, 1970), 14.
8. McLuhan argued, "For the 'message' of any medium or technology is the change of scale or pace or pattern that it introduces into human affairs." Marshall McLuhan, *Understanding Media: The Extensions of Man* (London, Abacus, 1974), 1.
9. Harold Innis, *The Bias of Communication* (Toronto: University of Toronto Press, 1951).
10. McLuhan, "The Invisible Environment," 163.
11. Ibid., 164.
12. McLuhan, *Understanding Media*, 366.
13. Charles Moore, "Plug It In, Rameses, and See if It Lights Up, Because We Aren't Going to Keep It Unless It Works," *Perspecta* 11 (1967): 38.
14. See, for example, John Perry Barlow, "A Declaration of the Independence of Cyberspace," February 8, 1996, accessed February 16, 2017, https://www.eff.org/cyberspace-independence/.
15. Paul Levinson, "Five Views of St. Marshall," *Wired* 1, no. 3 (July/August 1993), https://www.wired.com/1993/03/five-views-of-st-marshall/.
16. McLuhan, "The Invisible Environment," 164.

From media to geomedia

Despite the idealistic fantasies of cyberspace that fetishized the immateriality of the digital, networked digital media have always depended on specific material infrastructure such as fiber optic cables, computers, and servers. Moreover, far from creating a separate domain outside physical space, the digital has profoundly altered the social relations of inhabitants to city and territory.[17] The current transition to a networked digital milieu is now decisively changing the *place* that media occupy within the city. A range of new technologies, from smart phones capable of utilizing place-sensitive data, to LED screens embedded in central urban locations, have contributed to a new spatialization of media as an integral part of the contemporary city. In the process, media have become increasingly important to our experience and understanding of urban place and the city.

In order to demarcate this more recent digital media environment from the electric environment that McLuhan described in the 1960s, I have adopted the term "geomedia" to refer to both the new spatialization of media in the city and the way this supports the reconfiguration of urban spatial relations more generally.[18] Geomedia is a condition emerging at the intersection of three related trajectories driven by digital convergence: ubiquity, positionality, and real-time feedback. In comparison to a past defined by more restricted conditions of media access, mobile devices and embedded media platforms re-create the contemporary city as a media space in which content and connection is seemingly available anywhere, anytime. While access is still filtered in practical terms by a range of commercial, technical, and cultural pressures, connection has become the new default setting. This capacity works in concert with the enhanced role of location in framing media function and content. Location-aware devices using GPS tracking, in conjunction with widespread availability of geocoded data, make place and position central to a wide range of social practices, commercial strategies, and governmental logics enacted in contemporary urban space.

The third trajectory, which I refer to as "real-time," highlights the new capacities for rapid communication and coordination that define contemporary urban environments. These capacities need to be distinguished from the kinds of simultaneous experience that became a feature of modernity with the advent of live broadcasting in the twentieth century. The broadcast regime came to be implicated in the orchestration of what media scholars Daniel Dayan and Elihu Katz defined as "media events," referring to live broadcasts of major non-routine events such as John F. Kennedy's funeral in 1963 or Pope John Paul II's visit to Poland in 1979. These events were experienced primarily by millions of people watching them simultaneously on television in their own homes.[19] Such media events were themselves key exemplars of McLuhan's model of the "global village" proposed in the 1960s.

What is different in the present is the way the distributed architecture of digital networks opens up a potential for real-time feedback from many to many, enabling communication and coordination between diverse actors. This can include communication between those who are taking part in an event even as it unfolds. Such rapid mobilization and mobile coordination was once the prerogative of highly centralized institutions such as the military or the police, but this capacity is now increasingly available to other social actors. While this should not be hastily equated with a unilinear trajectory of democratization, distributed communication infrastructure has clearly altered some of the historical constraints on public assembly and is influencing the dynamics of urban social encounters more generally.

What happens to *place* and *locality* in this context? On the one hand, the capacity of digital media to span space and time continues to produce the experiences of spatial extension that Innis and McLuhan emphasized. If anything, the *disruptive* effects of media have been further intensified, both in terms of the global scale of connectivity and the range of situations in which networked digital media can now be deployed. However, alongside this *dislocative* trajectory, we can also see increasing integration of digital media platforms into particular urban spaces and lived social routines. This means that processes of media displacement now coexist with a heightened role for digital media in contemporary strategies of place-making. This tension between displacement and emplacement marks one of the key fault lines of the contemporary relation between media and the city.

17. Saskia Sassen, *Territory, Authority, Rights: From Medieval to Global Assemblages* (Princeton, NJ: Princeton University Press, 2006).
18. Scott McQuire, *Geomedia: Networked Cities and the Future of Public Space* (Cambridge, UK: Polity, 2016).
19. Daniel Dayan and Elihu Katz, *Media Events: The Live Broadcasting of History* (Cambridge, MA: Harvard University Press, 1992).

City as event

Growing penetration of the urban lifeworld by networked media has heightened the need to understand the city as a temporal entity. In fact, this endeavor has a long, if mixed, history in architecture. At least since Antonio Sant'Elia's famous "Manifesto of Futurist Architecture," published in 1914,[20] modern architecture has evinced an interest in the dynamic and ephemeral aspects of urban life.[21] For much of the twentieth century, the key media form catalyzing this interest was cinema. In this respect, we might recall Sigfried Giedion's contrast between the aesthetics of previous eras and the more fluid "space-time" of the modern city.[22] The latter was manifest in a range of phenomena, including glass architecture, but also the parkways built outside New York in the 1930s:

> As with many of the creations born out of the spirit of this age, the meaning and beauty of the parkway cannot be grasped from a single point of observation, as was possible from a window of the château at Versailles. It can be revealed only by movement, by going along in a steady flow, as the rules of traffic prescribe. The space-time feeling of our period can seldom be felt so keenly as when driving.[23]

The need to capture flow rather than structure situates a key challenge that Giedion perceived for representing modern design: "Still photography does not capture them clearly. One would have to accompany the eye as it moves: only film can make the new architecture intelligible."[24] Bernard Tschumi's stance, formulated almost half a century later, echoes this claim. In his *Manhattan Transcripts*, Tschumi argued, "Architecture is not simply about space and form, but also about event, action, and what happens in space."[25] While he replaced Giedion's formalism with a sharper political critique, Tschumi's framing of his ambition—to reinsert *time* into architecture—was also articulated by appealing to an explicitly cinematic conception of architecture:

> The temporality of the *Transcripts* inevitably suggests the analogy of film. In both, spaces are not only composed but also developed from shot to shot so that the final meaning of each shot depends on its context.[26]

While the filmic metaphor offered those such as Giedion and Tschumi rich resources for reconceptualizing architecture in terms of process and event, its constraints have become increasingly apparent in the present. Cinema is no longer what it then was: celluloid has vanished, while the dominant media environment is characterized by large-scale digital platforms that frequently eschew professional production in favor mass, user-generated content creation. Moreover, while film offered Giedion and Tschumi an image of process-based textuality, contemporary media is far less governed by the distribution of linear texts. In this respect, the directorial vision that appealed to many advocates of CAD systems in the 1990s, leading Michael Eleftheriades to argue that that "the world of architecture will merge imperceptibly with the world of cinema,"[27] seems increasingly nostalgic.

As much as film has changed, so has the nature of the media event. The capacity of the architect to function as a director who composes spatial experiences by controlling sequences and flows has been overtaken by the complexity of the ubiquitous, real-time information exchange that characterizes urban life in a digital milieu. This underlines the need to look elsewhere than cinema or broadcast television for models to understand the space-time of the contemporary city. One suggestive starting point can be found in the work of urban sociologist Henri Lefebvre.

20. Antonio Sant'Elia, "Manifesto of Futurist Architecture," in Umbro Appollonio, ed., *Futurist Manifestos*, trans. Robert Brain (London: Thames and Hudson, 1973).
21. Sanford Kwinter, *Architectures of Time: Toward a Theory of the Event in Modernist Culture* (Cambridge, MA: MIT Press, 2001).
22. Sigfried Giedion, *Space, Time and Architecture: The Growth of a New Tradition* (Cambridge, MA: Harvard University Press, 1967), 435.
23. Giedion, *Space, Time and Architecture*, 826, 831.
24. Giedion, cited in Andres Janser, "'Only Film Can Make the New Architecture Intelligible!' Hans Richter's *Die Neue Wohnung* and the Early Documentary Film on Modern Architecture," in François Penz and Maureen Thomas, eds., *Cinema and Architecture: Melies, Mallet-Stevens, Multimedia* (London: BFI, 1997), 34.
25. *The Manhattan Transcripts* (1976–1981), Bernard Tschumi Architects, accessed December 20, 2016, http://www.tschumi.com/projects/18/.
26. Bernard Tschumi, "Index of Architecture: Themes from The Manhattan Transcripts," *Questions of Space: Lectures on Architecture* (London: AA Publications, 1990), 107.
27. Michael Eleftheriades, "Architecture or Cinema: Digital 3D Design and the World of Multimedia," in Penz and Thomas, *Cinema and Architecture*, 143.
28. Henri Lefebvre, "The Right to the City," in *Writings on Cities*, ed. Eleonore Kofman and Elizabeth Lebas (Oxford: Blackwell, 1996).
29. Lefebvre, "The Right to the City," 179.
30. The urban media events described here were produced as part of the Large Screens and the Transnational Public Sphere Project (LP0989302) funded by the Australian Research Council. The project included my colleagues Nikos Papastergiadis, Audrey Yue, Sean Cubitt, and Ross Gibson and partners Fed Square Pty Ltd, Australia Council of the Arts and Nabi Art Centre (Seoul).
31. *SMS_Origins* was created by Australian artists Leon Cmielewski and Josephine Starrs, in collaboration with programmer Adam Hinshaw.
32. Guy Debord, "Report on the Construction of Situations," in *Situationist International Anthology*, ed. and trans. Ken Knabb (Berkeley, CA: Bureau of Public Secrets, 2006), 41.
33. Adam Greenfield, *Against the Smart City* (New York: Do Projects, 2013), 68.

The right to the networked city

Writing in the tumultuous year of 1968, Lefebvre famously posed the question of urban space in terms of "the right to the city."[28] Lefebvre's right to the city is not a formal rights agenda, but relates to the capacity of city dwellers to become inhabitants rather than to merely occupy the city as an indifferent habitat. Contrary to the top-down ethos that dominated modern urban planning, Lefebvre argued that the capacity for a city's inhabitants to actively appropriate the time and space of their surroundings was critical to any modern conception of citizenship and democracy.[29] While Lefebvre remained wonderfully vague about what appropriation might mean in practice, his conception of urban inhabitation is fundamentally concerned with processes of social encounter and public communication. This suggests that any consideration of the right to the city in the present needs to be re-posed in terms of the right to the networked city.

Such a transposition asks us to do several things. First, it demands that we think about architecture and media together, as differentiated but related elements that are constitutive of urban space in the present. Second, we need to acknowledge that the new capacities that networked digital media bring in terms of many-to-many communication, collective organization, and the recursive shaping of public events in real time creates a complex and historically distinctive situation. Distributed digital networks have contributed to fundamental reshaping of the space-time of contemporary social encounters in multiple ways, from specific behaviors such as the looser punctuality around meetings between friends or the new modes of being alone in public to broader logics concerning public assembly and social encounter. Distributed digital media offer distinctive capacities for altering urban ambiance, evidenced by numerous interventions using combinations of digital projection, interactive art, responsive architecture, computerized lighting, and geotagged data. In the nexus of new social practices and technological platforms, we can see intimations for developing a more open sense of urban encounter, one in which the creative entanglement of embodied and mediated interactions might enable inhabitants to rewrite the city from the ground up.

But this potential remains embryonic. If it is to develop into something more fully resembling Lefebvre's ambition for citizen-based appropriation of urban space-time, it will demand further work in thinking through the different affordances, modes of attention, and emotional intensity produced by specific instantiations of digital media platforms in urban space. The brief history of the urban screen offers a microcosm of the challenges this entails. Developed in the 1970s as a dynamic advertising medium, most urban screens around the world remain dominated by commercial and corporate messages. As a result, they tend to be located high up on skyscrapers so as to achieve maximum visibility, dwarfing the inhabitants in the streets below who have learned to routinely ignore them. Nevertheless, there are more recent examples where urban screens have successfully articulated traditional public spaces such as squares and plazas. As a result, they have been able to support new kinds of experimental social encounters.

A good example of this potential can be found at Federation Square in Melbourne. Opened at a prominent city center location in 2002, the new public square incorporated a large outdoor screen from an early stage in its design. Rather than an afterthought added to an existing space, the screen was conceived in relation to the operation of the space as a dynamic whole. Basic choices, such as siting the screen so it faces back toward a gently sloping plaza rather than onto the busy street, which would be the normal orientation for an advertising-based screen, broaden its potential. It means that the public is able to stop and gather in front of the screen, rather than simply glance at it as they drive past. As a result, the screen has become a key element of the site, supporting new forms of public display, including large-scale public spectating of live sporting and cultural events. More radically, the screen has also been used to stage several "urban media events," in which audiences located in different cities are able to collectively shape the content displayed on screens in each place.[30]

The first such event, *Come Join Us, Mr. Orwell*, was held in August 2009. The event linked the screen in Federation Square with one in the Tomorrow City complex in New Songdo City in Korea, using a combination of live camera crosses, screenings of artists' videos, and live performance. It also included two interactive artworks specifically commissioned for the occasion. Both used text messaging (popularly known as SMS at that time in Australia) as the interface to the large screens. For SMS_Origins, participants texted the details of their birthplace and that of their parents to a phone number displayed on the screen.[31] This information was automatically transcribed into vectors connecting the different cities on a world map, enabling audiences located in each city to see the dynamic evolution of a single image reflecting their collective input. A second work, Value@ Tomorrow City, created by Korean artist Seung Joon Choi, used the screen in the manner of a public bulletin board. Responses to a question concerning the values most important to the future city were displayed in both Korean and English, with their size and position changing in response to user input.

While small-scale, these events are suggestive of the potential for using the communication infrastructure of distributed digital media to support new geographies of urban encounter. In fact this kind of potential was perceived as early as 1957, when Guy Debord argued for alternative uses of telecommunications in order to construct new types of urban "situations":

> One can envisage for example, televised images of certain aspects of one situation being communicated live to people taking part in another situation somewhere else, thereby producing various modifications and interferences between the two.[32]

Subsequent history demonstrates a notable lag in exploring such creative opportunities.This underlines the extent to which social outcomes are not simply a function of technical capacity, but of the settings—imaginative, organizational, commercial, cultural, political—in which technologies operate. It also alerts us to critical challenges facing the deployment of networked digital technology in the contemporary city. To this point, technologies such as mobile devices have been predominantly deployed to serve individual, consumer-oriented needs. Development and support for forms of collective communication that might be more germane to active and inclusive citizenship—what Lefebvre glossed as "appropriation"—remain underdeveloped.

Accentuating this orientation is a further profound change that the digital threshold brings to urban life. This relates to the growing ease and decreasing cost of gathering, storing, analyzing, and retrieving large volumes of data in a digital environment. While the early internet was extolled as a space of untrammeled freedom, in practice it rapidly became a social space subject to unprecedented mass surveillance predicated on the aggressive settings and protocols normalized by dominant search and social media platforms. This level of scrutiny is now being extended throughout urban space under the rubric of the "smart city," according to the logic that a pervasively instrumented urban environment will provide multiple data streams capable of measuring urban processes and organizing the deployment of resources.

There are many reasons to be concerned with the narrowness of the current smart city agenda. As Adam Greenfield has observed, the lack of anything resembling a traditional public sphere in canonical smart city proposals is mirrored by a disturbing lack of public debate about the politics embedded in their architectural and informational design.[33] This silence suggests that mass surveillance has already become the new "invisible environment" of the digital urban milieu.

This context situates the urgent need to rethink the "city as media" in the present. How might we design and deploy urban media technology so as to shift default settings away from the dominance of spectacle and surveillance toward the modes of more open, bottom-up, citizen-based appropriation of the kind that Lefebvre and Debord imagined? Such a question asks us to collectively reimagine the uses of digital infrastructure such as screens, sensors, and mobile devices and rethink how they interface with some of the traditional affordances and functions of urban space.

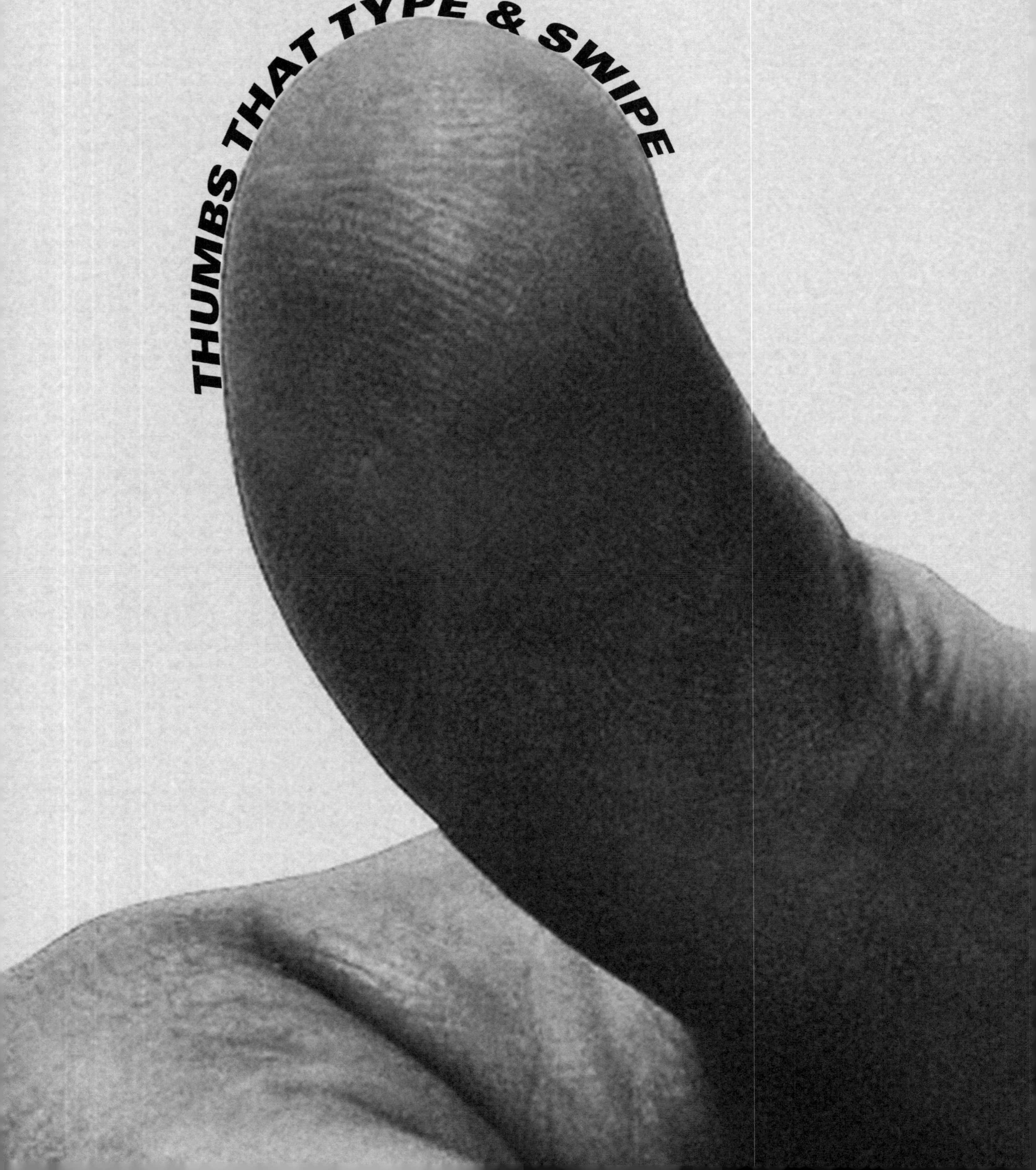
THUMBS THAT TYPE & SWIPE

In 2016, Rem Koolhaas took the stage for a keynote interview with Mohsen Mostafavi at the AIA Convention in Philadelphia, during which he grappled with the effects of tech industry development in Silicon Valley on the profession of architecture. "Architecture and the language of architecture–platform, blueprint, structure–became almost the preferred language for indicating a lot of phenomenon that we're facing from Silicon Valley," he told Mostafavi. "They took over our metaphors, and it made me think that regardless of our speed, which is too slow for Silicon Valley, we can perhaps think of the modern world maybe not always in the form of buildings, but in the form of knowledge or organization and structure and society that we can offer and provide."[1]

One wonders to what extent Koolhaas was complicit in these formulations of architectural metaphors in Silicon Valley, however. In 1998, he founded AMO, the research-based mirror image to his architectural practice OMA, shaping the intangibles of architectural research into a viable business in similar fashion to digital consultancies of the time. In 2003, *Wired* magazine's editor-in-chief anointed him "the world's most wired architect"—a fitting title considering he had more engagement with *Wired* than any other architect at the time.

In the late 1990s and early 2000s, a number of architects and architectural practices engaged with developing digital territories, casting the burgeoning internet as a space for architecture through either

1 Diana Budds, "Rem Koolhaas: 'Architecture Has a Serious Problem Today,'" *Fast Company; Co.Design*, May 22, 2016, http://www.fastcodesign.com/3060135/innovation-by-design/rem-kool haas-architecture-has-a-serious-problem-today/.

Molly Wright Steenson

Virtually Material: Architecture, Media, and the New Economy, 1997–2003

the nature of their projects or the situation of their practices in sync with digital consultancies. This phenomenon is specifically evident during a particular market moment—the "new economy"—that aligned with the first major internet boom and bust between 1995 and 2003. Distinguished by the explosion of information technology, networks, computation, and connectivity, the "new economy" shaped the architecture of cultural production. As Kevin Kelly wrote in *Wired* magazine in 1997, "This emerging new economy represents a tectonic upheaval in our commonwealth, a social shift that reorders our lives more than mere hardware or software ever can. It has its own distinct opportunities and its own new rules. Those who play by the new rules will prosper; those who ignore them will not."[2] Far from a fringe concern, architects and theorists participated enthusiastically in those "tectonic" shifts, claiming them for architectural projects and studio practices. The new economy and its new digital culture inspired high-profile architectural practices to cast their work in the mold of the management and innovation-focused approaches of dotcom consultancies, capitalize on the intangible knowledge products of research, design flows of capital into architectural design projects, and engage directly with pop-tech media outlets.

This article considers two examples of projects by such high-profile practices: the early explorations of "virtual architecture" by Hani Rashid and Lise Anne Couture with their studio, Asymptote Architecture, and the June 2003 issue of *Wired* magazine guest edited by Koolhaas and AMO. These projects occupy a pubescent period for investigations into digital technologies and media within architecture—particularly those enabled by the internet—a domain the discipline continues to probe and grapple with today.

2 Kevin Kelly, "New Rules for the New Economy: Twelve Dependable Principles for Thriving in a Turbulent World," *Wired* 5, no. 9 (1997): 140.

"Virtual Architecture"

Asymptote Architecture's projects in the second half of the 1990s explored the pixel-lit architecture of infographics and data visualization, while their texts adopted the language of the digerati expressed in *Wired* magazine and the work of dotcom consultancies. They were exercises in what principals Rashid and Couture called "virtual architecture": a critical stance toward digital technology and media that applied the spatiotemporal shifts they introduced to architecture. "Virtual architecture is an evolving discipline that results from the convergence of data mapping and simulation, digital form making, information 'architecture,' and virtual reality constructs and theory," they wrote in their 2002 book *Flux*.[3] In these early projects, Rashid and Couture equated the design of information architecture and data visualization with the primary tenets of architectural design, in which "spatial, informational, and temporal circumstances provoke experiences and create assemblies that are tangible and plastic."[4] Working from data visualization spaces on screens to the mediascape that contained the screens, Asymptote developed hybrid spaces that co-situated and co-created each other, in which information became architectural and architecture became information.

3 Hani Rashid and Lise Anne Couture, *Asymptote: Flux* (New York: Phaidon, 2002), 50.

4 Ibid.

Fig. 1 Rendering of the Three Dimensional Trading Floor, New York Stock Exchange, 1999–2000

The most trenchant examples of virtual architecture are two of their projects for the New York Stock Exchange (NYSE): the Advanced Command Center (known as "The Ramp") and the NYSE Three-Dimensional Trading Floor ("3DTF") between the years 1997 and 2000. The Ramp is a media control room on the floor of the NYSE. Comprising a curved blue glass backdrop supported by horizontal steel posts, the Ramp forms a physical infrastructure for information infrastructure. Sixty flat-screen monitors mounted to the glass backdrop show different news feeds, media channels, cable news anchors, stock tickers, and data visualizations, while behind the glass, a powerful network infrastructure of rendering engines fed by Ethernet cables connects mainframes and SGI servers to fiber-optic links. In tandem with this physical control center, Asymptote designed the 3DTF, a virtual data visualization environment to be displayed on the screens of the Ramp and used by operations management. The environment meshes a variety of information feeds, from individual stock activity to market performance, server outages, and news headlines, while providing visual and analytical tools for oversight of activity on the floor. The Ramp is still in operation on the floor of the NYSE today.

In the 3DTF virtual trading environment, the streams of data and other content are meant to reveal patterns in the operations of the exchange and the machinations of the market—an architecture of "correlations and exceptions," to use Couture's description of the exchange, revealing cause, effect, and, particularly, abnormalities.[5] Rendered using Virtual Reality Modeling Language (VRML), the twenty cyan conical stock market kiosks of the 3DTF look like knobs one could grasp and turn, each displaying facets of information relating to stocks. The order queue of the 3DTF advances like a conveyor belt, with a bar below each stock indicating performance. Striking rainbow-colored ribbons extend throughout a long, digital space, rendering the movements of stocks over what would seem to be a floor below, a black and gray field marked by yellow stripes reminiscent of yard lines on a televised football field. It seems like in the 3DTF all the lights are on, all the data are on, all the time, an experience of the movement of capital manifested in vectors and pixels.

While some of these elements correspond with the geography of the actual NYSE trading floor, others reflect the data that suffuses the environment. The NYSE 3DTF is a datascape and information system rendered as an architectural project, "allowing users to enter a parallel 'reality' and exist in an entirely different space," Rashid and Couture wrote.[6] It is the mediascape of the new economy circa 1999, viewed from a perspective that cannot and does not exist in physical space, but one that exists by means of the new digital, networked visualization of the time.

If the 3DTF was virtual architecture, it was not to be confused with "virtual buildings," Rashid and Couture wrote in *Flux*: these two ideas were fundamentally different.[7] Virtual buildings were "representations of buildings and built space as we already know them to be . . . especially if we can inhabit them in three-dimensional representations."[8] In other words, a virtual building version of the NYSE would not help with navigating its data, but the virtual architecture recast in data visualization and information flows would. Yet for as

5 Ibid., 35.

6 Ibid.

7 Ibid., 50.

8 Ibid., 50.

Fig. 2 Rendering of the Three Dimensional Trading Floor, New York Stock Exchange, 1999–2000

much as virtuality—and virtual architecture—might expose shifts in time and space brought about by digital technology and privilege visualization over realization, virtuality cannot exist without materiality. Following N. Katherine Hayles's "strategic definition of 'virtuality'" in her book *How We Became Posthuman*, "Virtuality is the cultural perception that material objects are interpenetrated by information patterns. The definition plays off the duality at the heart of the condition of virtuality—materiality on the one hand, information on the other."[9] As Hayles points out, "for information to exist, it must always be instantiated in a medium, whether that medium is the page from the Bell Laboratories Journal on which [Claude] Shannon's equations are printed, the computer-generated topological maps used by the Human Genome Project, or the cathode ray tube on which virtual worlds are imaged."[10] If the 3DTF was ultimately a virtual architecture—or perhaps a building—its medium was its material cousin, the Ramp. In the end, it is the screenscape of the Ramp that endures, alongside Asymptote's critique of technology and cultural practice that began with the digital as material for architecture in the first place.

"The world's most *Wired* architect"

"Rem Koolhaas: Architect, Iconoclast," read a caption introducing a black T-shirt-wearing Koolhaas set against the nuclear red background of the cover of his June 2003 guest-edited issue of *Wired* magazine titled "KOOLWORLD: The Ultimate Atlas for the 21st Century." It wasn't the first time the magazine had celebrated the architect. *Wired*'s coverage of Koolhaas and OMA included an interview in 1996 and a lengthy feature in 2000. Koolhaas had situated himself as the prototypical *Wired* subject. In the feature "Exploring the Unmaterial World" in 2000, he promoted his interest in "bits" over "atoms," borrowing Nicholas Negroponte's differentiation between the digital and the physical.[11] "AMO thus intends to test a basic proposition of the new economy: The fewer atoms you move, the more money you make. . . . Money for thoughts, rather than structures, represents virtual architecture in its purest and most lucrative form."[12] To put it another way, AMO could still charge for the ideation and research (bits) in which the firm engaged, whether or not it resulted in a constructed building (atoms).

AMO's tactic is exemplary of what architectural theorist Michael Speaks called the new "managerial disposition" of architectural

9 N. Katherine Hayles, *How We Became Posthuman: Virtual Bodies in Cybernetics, Literature, and Informatics* (Chicago: University of Chicago Press, 1999), 13–14.

10 Ibid.

11 Our notions of value, Negroponte writes in an issue of *Wired* in January 1995, derive not from atoms, but bits—the data carried in a digital medium like a floppy disk or videocassette—are often far more valuable than the medium on which it is carried. Nicholas Negroponte, "Bits and Atoms," *Wired* 3, no. 1 (1995): 176.

12 Gary Wolf, "Exploring the Unmaterial World," *Wired* 8, no. 6 (2000): 315. Ironically, this article was published right as the internet bubble deflated, though the cover announced, "Keep Cool: The New Economy Is Hotter Than Ever." By the time the issue hit the newsstand, the internet bubble had burst. Trading would be on a steady downturn for the next thirty months.

practice that differed from the concerns of twentieth-century modernist theory.[13] In the wake of the September 11th terrorist attacks and the stock market crash of 2001, Speaks wrote an article in *Architectural Record* that called for architecture to "develop forms of practice able to survive and prosper in the fiercely competitive global marketplace where intangible things like brands, experience, identity, terror, fear, and even access . . . are becoming increasingly important."[14] Speaks's words echoed Kelly's on the "new economy"—he also quoted him at the beginning of the article. Although Koolhaas used similar terms to Asymptote—"virtual architecture" or "architecture in virtual reality"—he was interested in the market-making potential of virtualization and the virtualization of architectural strategy, not in the representation of market machinations. Where Asymptote explored the digital media spaces of finance through data visualization, Koolhaas aligned his practice with the interests of the new economy, even in its waning days.

Koolhaas's atlas for *Wired*, "30 Spaces for the 21st Century," employed a variety of strategies, from mapping and infographics to interviews chronicling shifts from nano to macro, peaceful to war-torn, domestic to global.[15] The first page spread of the atlas featured a photo of Koolhaas in shadow, overlaid with his essay about the change in space introduced by the internet. "Our old ideas about

13 Michael Speaks, "Tales from the Avant-Garde: How the New Economy Is Transforming Theory and Practice," *Architectural Record* 188, no. 12: 74.

14 Michael Speaks, "Design Intelligence and the New Economy," *Architectural Record* 190, no. 1 (2002): 79.

space have exploded," he wrote. With the vast amount of change that occurred within just one generation, "entirely new spatial conditions, demanding new definitions, have emerged. Where space was considered permanent, it now feels transitory—on its way to becoming."[16] He and his contributors then unfolded a narrative of these emerging spaces. They started with a piece called "Atlas Space," which showed the scale of global change through a set of maps and visualizations, while "Nano Space" explored architecture that merged atoms and bits. "Space Space" introduced Koolhaas and Hans-Ulrich Obrist's "Mission to Mars, Utah"—a piece that may have been more appropriately titled "Simulation Space" for its enactment of a Mars mission in the Utah desert.

Some of the essays were prescient. Anticipating the swell in social media, Duncan Watts wrote about "Relationship Space," introducing the now-familiar notion that everybody lives in a set of interconnected networks. "Secure Space" by Bruce Schneier illustrated the insecurity of cyberspace, Luc Steels's "Robo Space" presented robots that were learning cognition, and "Bush Space" by Sanford Kwinter highlighted the digital application of the tracking skills of the

15 The editorial team included the Office for Metropolitan Architecture (OMA) and AMO with collaborators including Hans-Ulrich Obrist, Jeffrey Inaba, and Lucia Allais. Other modalities that the atlas traced included "Home Space," an interview of Martha Stewart by architectural historian Beatriz Colomina, Miuccia Prada's "Body Space," a piece titled "Tight Space" that put the reader in the claustrophobia of a gas mask, and Bruno Latour's "Research Space."

16 Rem Koolhaas, "The New World," *Wired* 11, no. 6 (2003): 117.

YOU TO THE VIRTUAL
NYSE

NEW YORK STOCK EXCHANGE AND
ARCHITECTURE WELCOME YOU TO THE VIRTUAL VORTEX
NYSE Software Release Schedule
NYSE Seat Sales
NYSE

San Bushmen in southern Africa. Less optimistic was Silicon Valley chronicler Po Bronson, who offered an elegy of "Boom Space"—the experience of post-crash Silicon Valley. "When the tech economy recovers, will the area regain its stature in the national consciousness?" he asked.[17] "I don't think so. As a regional economy, Silicon Valley will steam ahead splendidly; as an icon, however, it's over. ... I doubt startups will ever become commonplace again."[18] His predictions, of course, turned out not to be true, as from 2005 onward the practices known as "Web 2.0" emerged: they expanded the Web's capability as a digital platform as smartphones became the computers in everyone's pockets and venture capitalists dreamt of 10x and 100x exit returns.[19]

17 Po Bronson, "Boom Space: What's Left after the Thrill is Gone: Life in the Bust Belt," *Wired* 11, no. 6 (2003): 138.

18 Bronson, "Boom Space," 138–39.

19 "Web 2.0," a term popularized in late 2004, refers to programming practices and digital content structures that frame contemporary digital use in which the Web browser has more functionality, including social media, advertising models, and Web applications (interactivity on the surface of a Web page without a server call). It was initially coined in 1999 by Darcy Dinucci. See Darcy Dinucci, "Fragmented Future," *Print* 53, no. 4 (1999): 32; and Tim O'Reilly, "What Is Web 2.0? Design Patterns and Business Models for the Next Generation of Software," O'Reilly Media, September 30, 2005, http://www.oreillynet.com/pub/a/oreilly/tim/news/2005/09/30/what-is-web-20.html/.

Fig. 4 Cover of *Wired* magazine, June 2003

Other pieces seem strikingly familiar when read today. Farouk El-Baz explained the importance of accuracy when calculating crowd sizes at political demonstrations in his essay "Crowd Space," today evoking the controversy over the crowds at the 2016 US presidential inauguration. "Limbo Space" advocated for neutral humanitarian spaces for refugees, and "Border Space" mapped the conflicts in six contested regions. "Protest Space" by Sarah Whiting offered an idea about the erosion of public: "What we call public is being radically compressed into, at best, mere megabytes."[20] Today, we might say gigabytes. Koolhaas's essay, "Waning Space," offered a pessimistic perspective of New York from the vantage point of 9/11. The final article, "Public Space," also by Koolhaas, looked darkly upon the public sphere. It featured an image of an empty plaza in Chandigarh designed by Le Corbusier, its stone ramp stained black. Although the plaza in the image is devoid of people, it is in fact a teeming, busy market by day. "When the space is vacated ... all that's left from the Western imagination's most radical attempt to organize public space is a lesson in the sublime."[21]

As ads for Hewlett-Packard color inkjet printers snaked throughout the atlas—perhaps a comment on the nature of the virtual versus the physical, the bits versus the atoms—the relationship between architecture and the digital remained at odds. Returning to Koolhaas's introduction to the atlas, "The words and ideas of architecture, once the official language of space, no longer seem capable of describing this proliferation of new conditions. But even as its utility is questioned in the real world, architectural language survives, its repertoire of concepts and metaphors resurrected to create clarity and definition in new, unfamiliar domains (think chat *rooms*, Web *sites*, and *firewalls*)."[22] Thirteen years later, he would question this architectural clarity and definition from his white leather chair on a stage in Philadelphia.

Taking place

As the geographer Yi-Fu Tuan writes, "Place is an organized world of meaning."[23] It is a means of containing, organizing, and creating boundaries that make spaces comprehensible. Just as Asymptote and OMA/AMO turned to the internet and narratives of architecture to bring grounding to virtuality, designers and writers turned to architectural language and metaphors as a way to think about digital spaces. "The Internet is a place," Doc Searls and David Weinberger wrote in their collaboratively authored bestseller *The Cluetrain Manifesto* in 1999.[24] "We buy books and tickets *on* the Web. Not *over*, *through*, or *beside* it."[25] More importantly, these notions of place underscored the reality and materiality of burgeoning digital spaces. "The Net is a *real* place where people can go to learn, to talk to each other, and to do business together. It is a bazaar where customers look for wares, vendors spread goods for display, and people gather around topics that interest them. It is a conversation. At last and again."[26]

In addition to writers like Searls and Weinberger, information architects also adopted architectural metaphors to lend a sense of place to the Web. For them, these metaphors were vital in developing taxonomies and categorizations to make the Web more navigable and usable. As Louis Rosenfeld and Peter Morville wrote in their 1999 book *Information Architecture for the World Wide Web*, "Like web sites, buildings have architectures that cause us to react. Buildings and their architectures therefore provide us with great opportunities to make analogies about web sites and their architectures."[27] Architectural language offered a way to move between scale and scope, to consider the effects of digital technologies on the people who used them—even if they wrote about architecture in a way that no traditional architect would.

Asymptote and Koolhaas understood these analogies, but in different terms: for Asymptote, the stakes were plastic and representational; for Koolhaas and AMO, they were about investigating new spaces of global capital. For both offices, designing new mediascapes materialized the stakes of virtuality. Both practices were invested—literally and figuratively—in the tropes of the new economy. Architects played a role in the new economy by using data streams as a material for architectural design and approaching the visualization of data as an architectural project, adopting the strategies of dotcom consultancies to solve architectural problems, and rebirthing both through the rhetoric of new media. While the NYSE and KOOLWORLD projects mark a particular moment in the late 1990s and early 2000s when architecture became a technovisionary tool for the new economy, the projects point forward to the continued exuberance and cycles of hype around artificial intelligence at the scale of our cities—and in the societal tendency to turn to architects for narratives both virtual and material.

---

20 Sarah Whiting, "Protest Space: When Speech Is Zoned, Is It Free? Quiet Riot," *Wired* 11, no. 6 (2003): 145.

21 Rem Koolhaas, "Public Space: Somewhere Between Success and Failure: Best-Laid Plan," *Wired* 11, no. 6 (2003): 169.

22 Koolhaas, "The New World," 117.

23 Yi-Fu Tuan, *Space and Place: The Perspective of Experience* (Minneapolis: University of Minnesota Press, 2001), 179.

24 Rick Levine, Christopher Locke, Doc Searls, and David Weinberger, *The Cluetrain Manifesto: The End of Business as Usual* (Cambridge, MA: Perseus, 2000), 82. In March 1999, *Cluetrain*'s authors published ninety-five theses on the Web about how the internet was changing business, starting with "Markets are conversations," and including "Hyperlinks subvert authority," "You want us to pay? We want you to pay attention," and "We are waking up and linking to each other. We are watching. But we are not waiting." In 2000 , they published the theses as a book, *The Cluetrain Manifesto*. The manifesto outlined many tenets of social media, half a decade before it would become a dominant mode of conducting business. A central imperative of the book was the idea that business needed to be conversational, community-oriented, and networked.

25 Levine, Locke, Searls, and Weinberger, *Cluetrain Manifesto*, 82.

26 Rick Levine, Christopher Locke, Doc Searls, and David Weinberger, *The Cluetrain Manifesto: The End of Business as Usual: 10th Anniversary Edition* (New York: Basic Books, 2011), 154.

27 Louis Rosenfeld and Peter Morville, *Information Architecture for the World Wide Web* (Sebastopol, CA: O'Reilly, 1998), 1–2.

Khoon&Carr

There is a recent book by Jacques Ellul. It is called **Propaganda**. Ellul's book has as a theme that propaganda is not ideology. It is rather the hidden, but complete, image of a social way of life that is imbedded in the social technologies and social patterns just as it is imbedded in, say, the English language. Ellul would say that the action of the English language or the action of the French language—**that** is propaganda. That presents a total psychic and environmental image to men, whereas the ideologies, explicit verbalized messages, are relatively insignificant compared to this overall image. Ellul's theme in a word is this: Propaganda consists in using all the available means of one's society to create a way of life. Whatever that way may be, is propaganda—that is action that is total and invisible, and invincible.

This is another mysterious feature about the new and potent electronic environment we now live in. The really total and saturating environments are invisible. The ones we notice are quite fragmentary and insignificant compared to the ones we don't see. The English language, for example, as it shapes our perceptions and all our habits of thought and feeling, is little perceived by the users of the English language. It becomes much more perceptible if we switch suddenly to French. But in the case of environments that are created by new technologies, while they are quite invisible in themselves, they do tend to make visible the old environments. We can always see the Emperor's old clothes, but not his new ones.

I want to use this theme a little bit for my purposes here. If the new environment is invisible, it does serve to make very visible the preceding environment. The obvious and simple illustration of that is the late show. On the late show on television we see old movies. They are very visible; they are very noticeable. Since television, the movie form has been re-processed. The form of movie which once was environment and invisible has been re-processed into an art form, and, indeed, a highly valued art form. Indirectly, the new art films of our time have received an enormous amount of encouragement and impact from the television form. The television form has remained quite invisible—will only become visible the moment that television itself becomes the content of a new medium. The next medium, whatever it is—it may be the satellite environment or the extension of consciousness—will include television as its content, not as its environment, and will transform television into an art form; but this process whereby every new technology creates an environment that translates the old or preceding technology into an art form, or into something exceedingly noticeable, affords so many fascinating examples I can only mention a few.

In 1963 Eric Havelock published a study called **Preface to Plato**. It is a study of what happened in Greece before Plato. "Preface" means how did the Greeks educate each other before writing? What were the processes by which they educated their young people before Plato? He calls this process that preceded Plato the "tribal encyclopedia." The young memorized the poets. The poets were operative purveyors of practical wisdom and counsel. Homer, Hesiod, and the rest actually provided the young people with models of perception and models of behavior and strategies for overcoming all sorts of difficulties and obstacles. The great Odysseus was above all a Greek hero because of his resourcefulness—his unfailing initiative and skill in every type of opaque and threatening situation. Havelock first describes this education that went on through the poets, and then describes the advent of writing and the complete change that came over education as a result of that. With the coming of writing, education shifted from the memorizing of the tribal encyclopedia that made education a sort of "singing commercial." With writing came the classification of knowledge, the ideas, the categories. Plato's detestation of the poets was mainly a rivalry between the new and the old educational establishments. The poets had naturally failed to come to grips with the new technology of the written word.

Havelock's book has a fascinating quality, because it really tells the story of what we are going through right now. We are playing that tape (the situation he describes) backwards—the change from tribal man to individual man. As we move into the world of integral, computerized knowledge, mere classification becomes secondary and inadequate to the speeds with which data can now be processed. As data can be processed very rapidly we move literally into the world of pattern recognition, out of the world of mere data classification. One way of putting this is to say that our children today live in a world in which the environment itself is a teaching machine made of electric information. The young person today is a data processor on a very large scale. Some people have estimated that the young person, the infant and the small child, growing up in our world today works harder than any child ever did in any previous human environment—only the work he has to perform is that of data processing. The small child in 20th Century America does more data processing—more—work than any child in any previous culture in the history of the world, according to Jacques Ellul, among others. We haven't really cottoned to the fact that our children work furiously, processing data in an electrically structured information world; and when these children enter a classroom—elementary school—they encounter a situation which is very bewildering to them. The youngster today, stepping out of his nursery or TV environment, goes to school and enters a world where the information is scarce but is ordered and structured by fragmented, classified patterns, subjects, schedules. He is utterly bewildered because he comes out of this intricate and complex integral world of electric information and goes into this 19th Century world of classified information which still characterizes the educational establishment. The educational establishment is a 19th Century world of classified data much like any factory set up with its inventories and assembly lines. The young today are baffled because of this extraordinary gap between these two worlds. Perhaps we feel now a confusion similar to that which preliterates used to experience on making contact with the mechanized societies of the West.

Paul Goodman has a book recording one aspect of the situation. It is titled **Growing Up Absurd**. To grow up today is to be absurd, because we live in two worlds, and neither one of them inclines you to grow up. I have a friend who once pointed out to me something that struck me with great force. He said, "You know, the only work that royalty has to do is to grow up, and for a young prince or princess growing up and acquiring all the types of knowledge and language necessary for survival is a fantastically difficult job." It would seem that we have paradoxically created on a democratic scale a situation of education for royalty. Our youngsters today are mainly confronted with the problem of just growing up—that is our new work—and it is total. That is why it is not a job; it is a role. Growing up has become, in the age of electrically processed information, the major task of mankind. We still have our eyes fixed on the rear-view mirror looking firmly and squarely at the job that is receding into the 19th Century past. The job, which we feel we should have by rights, belongs to the old mechanical technology of classified data and of fragmented tasks. Yet we are now surrounded by a new environment, of integrated tasks, integrated knowledge, and that demands pattern recognition. The kind of contrast between those two situations creates an absurdity that has launched the theatre of the absurd. The theatre of the absurd itself is postulated on this kind of dichotomy between these two cultures that never seem to get any closer together.

I have started then with the theme of the imperceptibility of new environments, and that what is perceptible in typical human situations is the old environment. It is plain that the content of Plato's work, of his new written form, was the old oral dialogue. The content of the print technology of the Renaissance was medieval writing. For 200 years after printing there was hardly anything printed except medieval texts—think of poor Don Quixote! Don Quixote was the victim of the current Renaissance craze for medieval comic books or medieval romances. This went on for another century. What got printed in the main, for two centuries and more after the printing press, was the medieval tale, medieval Books of Hours, medieval liturgies, and medieval philosophy. Shakespeare lived in the Renaissance world, and the content of Shakespeare's plays, as Tolstoy complained, is medieval. His politics, his world picture—the Elizabethan world picture. The Elizabethans looked back firmly and squarely at the receding medieval forms. But the middle ages were the late show for the Renaissance. By the 19th Century the Renaissance had come into full view in the rear-view mirror. As the industrial environment formed, this progressive time firmly and squarely confronted the Renaissance. The content of the 19th Century mind was the Renaissance; the content of the 20th Century mind is the 19th Century. We are obsessed with it. It is not as easy to banish that mirage as one might wish. But one of the most bizarre growths in this development occurred when railways and factories came in. The content of this new industrial, mechanical environment was the old agrarian world, and there was this upsurge of awareness and delight in the old agrarian environment of arts and crafts—the pastoral world. This discovery of the receding age was called the "romantic movement."

The sudden discovery of nature was made possible by the railway and the factories which were so very different from nature. The romantic movement was a product of the mechanical age by way of a contrapuntal environment. It was not a repeat of the mechanical age; rather it was the content of the mechanical age, and the artists and poets turned to processing the old agrarian world into delightful landscapes and delightful pastoral poems. This was in turn altered by the rise of electric technology which went around the old mechanical world of a few decades ago. When the electric technology jacketed the machine world, when circuitry took over from the wheel, and the circuit went around the old factory, the machine became an art form. Abstract art, for example, is very much a result of the electric age going around the mechanical one.

In our time we can see that pop art consists in taking the outer environment and putting it in the art gallery, or indoors somewhere, suggesting that we have reached the stage where we have begun to process the environment itself as an art form. We may be catching up with ourselves. When we begin to deal with our actually existing new environment as an art form, we may be reaching that stage the planet itself seems to have reached. With satellite and electronic antennae as probes, the planet ceases in a way to be the human environment and becomes an old nose-cone satellite itself—a probe into space, creating new space and environments for the planet. If the planet itself has thus become the content of a new space created by its satellites, and its electronic extensions, if the planet has become the content and not the environment, then we can confidently expect to see the next few decades devoted to turning the planet into an art form. We will caress and shape and pattern every facet, every contour of this planet as if it were a work of art, just as surely as we have put a new environment around it.

I think the computer is admirably suited to the artistic programming of such an environment, of taking over the task of programming the environment itself as a work of art, instead of programming the content as a work of art. This situation suggests some considerable changes in the human state. It suggests that the role of art in the past has been not so much the making of environments as making of counter-environments or anti-environments. Flaubert, a hundred years ago, said: "Style is a way of seeing." Ever since that time the painters and artists have been quite conscious of their jobs as teaching people how to perceive the world they live in. "It is above all that you may see," said Conrad, apropos the meaning of his work. The training of perception upon the otherwise unheeded environment became the basis of experimentation in what is called modern art and poetry. The artist, instead of expressing himself in various patterns and packages of message, turned his senses and the work of art to the business of probing the environment. The symbolists, for example, broke up the old romantic landscape into fragments which they used as probes to explore the urban and metropolitan environments. Then they turned to probing the inner life of man with the same verbal instruments in hand. Instead of using the verbal as a way of expression, they turned it inward for the purpose of exploring and discovering the contours of the inner life. The psychiatrist took over in the same pattern and began to erode the unconscious. If the unconscious has an important and irreplaceable function in human affairs, we had best look to it—it is being eroded at a furious pace; it is being invaded by dazzling investigations and insights, and we could quickly reach a stage in which we had no unconscious. This would be like dreaming awake. Such may well be the prophetic meaning of **Finnegans Wake** by James Joyce. His idea being in that book, among may others, that tribal man lived a dream and modern man is "back again Finnegan" into the cycle of the tribal involvement; but this time awake. This possibility that we are actively engaged in liquidating the unconscious for the first time in history, behooves us to pay some attention to how it is structured and to what function it serves in human affairs. It may prove to be indispensable to sanity.

One overall consideration for our time is to consider how, in the past, the environment was invisible in its operation upon us. Environments are not just containers, but are processes that change the content totally. New media are new environments. That is why the media are the message. One related consideration is that anti-environments, or counter-environments created by the artist, are indispensable means of becoming aware of the environment, in which we live and of the environments we create for ourselves technically. John Cage has a book called **Silence** in which, very early in the book, he explains that silence consists of all of the unintended noises of the environment. All the things that are going on all the time in any environment, but things that were never programmed or intended—that is silence. The unheeded world is silence. That is what James Joyce calls thunder in the "Wake." In the "Wake" all the consequences of social change—all of the disturbances and metamorphoses resulting from technological change create a vast environmental roar or thunder that is yet completely inaudible. It is like heat that in organic or other systems creates "noise."

If the environment or process of change gets going at a clip consistent with electronic information movement, it becomes very easy to perceive social patterns for the first time in human history. In the pre-electric age patterns were imperceptible because change occurred just slowly enough to be invisible. Was it Bertrand Russell who asked if we were in a bath whose temperature rose half a degree an hour, how would we know when to scream? The pattern recognition that is quite impossible during processes of slow change, becomes quite easy when the same changes are speeded up even to movie or cinematic levels. So, the artist, as a creator of anti-environments or counter-environments, created to permit perception of environments, has a very peculiar role in our society.

The artist as a maker of anti-environments becomes the enemy in society. He doesn't seem to be very well adjusted. He does not accept the environment with all its brainwashing functions with any passivity whatever; he just turns upon it and reflects his anti-environmental perceptions upon it. The artist, for the past century, has increasingly fused or merged with the criminal in popular estimation, as he has become anti-environment. Since Baudelaire, the artist, the sleuth—the Sherlock Holmes type, the James Bond type, the Raymond Chandler-Marlowe type—these men have turned a vision onto society that is very anti-environmental, very self-conscious, and the artist has mysteriously been hybridized with the criminal or the anti-social figure. By the same token, crime has become obsessional in our society as a form of artistic expression. This is not lost on children. The delinquent child is often a very bright and keenly perceptive person. It is not lost on him that the kind of overwhelming, brainwashing forces of his environment really call for a little anti-social or artistic and exploratory activity. The child, by delinquent behavior, is aping the exploratory artist. Dostoevski was aware of this in **Crime and Punishment**. He saw the criminal as a sort of cross between the saint and the artist.

Our newspapers create an information environment, yet without crime as content we would not be able to perceive the environment. The newspapers have to have bad news, otherwise there would not be any newspapers, but only ads, or good news. Without bad news we could not discern the ground-rules of the environment. This does not necessarily mean the environment is bad, but it means its operation upon us is total and ruthless. The environment is always the brainwasher, so that the well-adjusted person, by definition, has been brainwashed. He is adjusted. He's had it. There is a book by Erwin Strauss recently which throws new light on Pavlov's operations (the Russian psychologist). He didn't get his conditioning effects by means of stimuli or signals to his experimental subjects. Rather he did it by environmental controls. He put his subjects in environments in which there was no sound, in which the heat and other sensory controls were very carefully adjusted and maintained steadily. Pavlov discovered that if you tried to condition animals in an ordinary environment, it did not work. The environment is the real conditioner, not the stimulus or the content. So the Pavlov story needs to be turned around in order to be observed; but the role of crime as a way of perceiving society is a mysterious one. I am not going to make any moral observations on it whatever. It has increasingly pushed the artist and the scientist into the role of being an enemy.

Let me resume a moment. We have, in the Electric Age, come suddenly to the end of the Neolothic Age. After several thousands of years of specialized habits and technology and fragmentary tool-making, we discovered the electric circuit. It is the circuit that has ended the Neolithic Age. The Neolithic Age, just like its ultimate phase, the factory age in the 1 9th Century, was dedicated to specialism, fragmentation, and extensions of this or that limb of man. With circuitry we have, instead of extensions of hand or foot, or back, or arm, a kind of involvement of the whole nervous system, an extension of the nervous system itself, a most profoundly involving operation. The form and function of the telegraph press can help our observations here. One of the mysterious things about newspapers is that the items in them have no connection except the dateline. The only connecting factor in any newspaper is the dateline, and it is this dateline that enables us to enter the world of the news, as it were, by going through the looking glass. Just as Alice in Wonderland went through the looking glass, when you enter the world of the telegraph or of the circuit, you really become involved in the information process. When you enter through the dateline, when you enter your newspaper, you begin to put together the news—you are producer. And this is a most important fact to understand about the electric time, for it is an age of decentralism. It is hard to face this. We still like to look in the rear-view mirror. We still tend to think of the electric age as a mechanical age. It is in effect organic, and decentralist. But the reader of the news, when he goes through his dateline apertures, enters the new world as a maker. There is no "meaning" in the news except what we make—there is no connection between any of the items except the instant dimension of electric circuitry. News items are like the parts of the symbolist structure. The reader is the co-creator. In a newspaper as in a detective story in which the reader has to make the plot as he goes. The detective story was one of the very first anticipations of electric technology. Edgar Allen Poe was a considerable innovator in the matter of anti-environments for the electric age. The newspaper is also very much like the world of the delightful films of Stan Vanderbeek; the world of multi-screen projection is the world of the newspaper where umpteen news stories come at you without any connection and without connected themes. So, what the new film is doing is stripping off the story line in favor of this mosaic pattern of simultaneous projections, which is very much in accordance with electric technology. It is the film world receiving its baptism by electricity. This hybridizing, this crossing of one technology with another, goes on all the time. The internal combustion engine was a wedding of the old machine and the electric circuit. Perhaps the most startling and most upsetting electric innovation is coming in the matter of xerox and xerography.

Xerography is bringing a reign of terror into the world of publishing because it means that every reader can become both author and publisher. It decentralizes the long-centralized publishing process. Authorship and readership alike can become production-oriented under xerography. Anybody can take any book apart, insert parts of other books and other materials of his own interest, and make his own book in a relatively fast time. Any teacher can take any ten textbooks on any subject and custom-make a different one by simply xeroxing a chapter from this one and a chapter from that one. The problem is copyrighting, and Congress is now pondering these problems—how to protect the old technology from the new technology by legislation. They will not succeed. There is no possible protection from technology except by technology. When you create a new environment with one phase of a technology, you have to create an anti-environment with the next. But xerography is electricity invading the world of typography and it means a total revolution in this old sphere, or this old technology, a revolution which is being felt in the classroom itself.

I invite you to consider that perhaps the best way of estimating the impact of any new environmental technology is to notice what happens to the older technologies. You can never perceive the impact of any new technology directly; but it can be done in the manner of Perseus looking at the Gorgon in the mirror of art. You have to perceive the consequences of the new environment on the old environment before you know what the new environment is. You cannot tell what it is until you have seen it do things to the old one. The need, however, to understand the processes and changes brought about by the new technology gets stronger as the technology does.

We are engaged in Toronto in carrying out a unique experiment—it is far too big for us—we need a lot of help and a lot of collaboration. We are carrying out an experiment to establish what are the sensory thresholds of the entire population of Toronto. That is, we are attempting to measure, quantitatively, the levels at which the entire population prefers to set its visual, auditory, tactile, visceral, and other senses as a matter of daily use and preference—how much light, how much heat, how much sound, how much movement—as a threshold level. Anything that alters a sensory threshold alters the outlook and experience of a whole society. The sensory thresholds change without warning or indications to the users thereof, for it is new technological environments that shift these levels. We are concerned with what shifts occur in a sensory threshold when some new form comes in. What happens to our sensory lives with the advent of television, the motor car, or radio? If we can establish this sort of knowledge quantitatively, we will have something which the computer can really bite into. A child is a genius till he is five because all his senses are in active interrelation. Then his senses specialize. The computer will be in a position to carry out orchestrated programming for the sensory life of entire populations. It can be programmed in terms of their total needs, not just in terms of the messages they should be hearing, but in terms of the total experience as picked up and patterned by all the senses at once. For example, if you were to write an ideal sensory program for Indonesia or some area of the world in which you wanted to leap-frog across a lot of old technology, this would be possible if you knew in the first place its present sensory thresholds and, second, if you had established what kind of sensory effect a given technology like radio or literacy had upon sensory life as a whole.

On this continent the sensory levels have changed drastically since television. The visual component in our lives has been dropped dramatically and the visceral, the kinetic, the auditory modes of response have shot up to compensate for the drop in the visual component of our culture. This sensory shift has changed the taste in design, in packaging, in every form of entertainment, as well as in every form of vehicle, food, and in clothing.

The "Beatles" stare at us with eloquent messages of changed sensory modes for our whole population, and yet people merely think how whimsical, how bizarre, how grotesque. The Beatles are trying to tell us by the anti-environment they present just how we have changed and in what ways.

To repeat, and to make toward a conclusion, every new technology creates a new environment just as a motor car does, as the railway did, or as radio and airplanes do—any new technology changes the whole human environment, and envelops and includes the old environments. It turns these old environments into "art forms": — old Model T's become precious art objects, as do old coach lamps, old anything. The world of Camp, for example, is the world of the nursery of thirty years ago being turned into a conscious art form. By simply taking into the shop window old toys, old ornaments, and the things Mom used to wear thirty years ago, you turn them into art forms and you have CAMP, this mysterious new archetype. The new environment is always creating new archetypes, new art forms, out of the old environment. This process can provide invaluable information for those who want to have some autonomy in controlling their destinies and their environments. I think we are rapidly moving toward a time when we might say, with full awareness of cause and effects: "In our present sensory condition I don't think we could properly accommodate 200 more lines on T.V." Colored T.V. will considerably change the whole sensory life of the public. It is a much more tactile form than black and white. For the latter is seen only with the periphery of the eye. But what would happen to the North American world if we did as the French and Germans have done; if instead of 450 lines on our television, we were to put 800? The results might be most gratifying to the educational establishment. If we raised the visual intensity or the visual component of the T.V. image, it might serve enormously to ease the transition from the old mechanical age to the electronic age. What would be the chances of getting an experimental study of such a change in our time? I don't know. Lindegren would say the chances were not good. Anything that is serious is out of bounds. I think it was David Riesman who said no social scientist would ever study anything important. To be scientific you must study the fragmental, the insignificant. How else can you give assurance of your precision and concentration? Perhaps this attitude explains why, in our world, we tend to substitute moral indignation for observation. Moral vehemence is proof positive of superior perception. For example, we now experience simultaneously the drop-out and the teach-in. The two forms are correlative. They belong together. The teach-in represents an attempt to shift education from instruction to discovery, from brainwashing students to brainwashing instructors. It is a big dramatic reversal. Viet Nam, as the content of the teach-in, is a very small, misleading Red Herring. It really has nothing to do with the teach-in as such anymore than with the drop-out. The drop-out represents a rejection of 19th Century technology as manifested in our educational establishments. The teach-in represents a creative effort to switch the educational process to discovery, from package to probe. As with the Hawthorne experiment, its strategy is to use the audience and the student body as work force—one of the great things that is happening under electric conditions. As the audience becomes participant, involved in the total electric drama, it can become a major work force; and the classroom, as much as any other place, can become a scene in which the audience can perform an enormous amount of exciting discovery. The audience as work force has unlimited possibilities.

Suppose we were to brief 50,000,000 people on some extremely difficult problems facing top-level scientists. Inevitably, some dozens, hundreds, of the 50,000,000 audience would see instantly through any type of opaque problem, even on the highest scientific levels. Robert Oppenheimer is fond of saying that "there are children playing here in the street who could solve some of my top problems in physics, because they have modes of sensory perception that I lost long ago." There are enormous possibilities for using an audience as work force in scientific research, or any other type of research. It is simply that we insist on beaming instruction at them instead of allowing them to participate in the action of discovery.

For example, when printing was new, it created what was known as the Public. In the 16th Century and after. Montaigne's phrase "le publique," came into use. The 16th Century created the public as a new environment. This completely altered politics and altered all social arrangements in education, in work, and in every other area. Electric circuitry did not create the public; it created the mass, meaning an environment of information that involved everybody in everybody. Now, to a man brought up in the environment of the public, the mass audience is a horror—it is a mess. In the same way, the public was a many-headed monster to a feudal aristocrat. He never bothered to study its structure any more than we study the mass. Circuitry brings people into relation with each other in total involvement which creates the possibility of dialogue and discovery on an enormous scale. The structure of the public had less of such possibility. The public consisted of fragmented separate individuals with separate points of view. The public was an additive structure. The mass audience is a quite different structure, enormously richer—enormously more capable of integrated creative activity than the old public was. All the old public could do was to enunciate private points of view which they clashed into each other furiously. At the present moment in Canada, if you want a DEW line warning, we are having an election in which no one is interested. There is no involvement because the old political forms do not permit participation. You simply register a fragmented, unrelated-to-anything vote. The population has dropped out of the political setup. Yet when these changing structures are studied they yield enormous meaning.

Let me suggest that it may be possible to write programs for changes, not only in consciousness but in the unconscious in the future. One could write a kind of science fiction story of the future of consciousness, the future of the unconscious, "the future of an erosion." The future of consciousness is already assuming a very different pattern, a very different character. The future of the child is changing beneath our gaze. The child as a separate social fact was an invention of the 17th Century, according to the historian Philippe Ariès; historically the child came out of the 17th Century and did not exist, so to speak, in Shakespeare's day. The child had, up until that time, been so completely merged in the adult world that there was nothing that could be called childhood in our sense at all. And so it is with the family, another 17th Century discovery. Suddenly today the child is merging with the total adult environment under electric information processing and is disappearing from the scene as child. The future of child may resemble the future of city. The city—under conditions of very rapid movement—takes on a totally new meaning. The motor car has served to destroy the city as it existed under the railway conditions. The future of city may be very much like a world's fair—a place to show off new technology—rather than a place of work or residence. It is also fascinating to consider the future of language. We know right now some very important structural things about language that are new. The future of language will not be as a system of classified data or meanings. The future of language, as a complex structure which can be learned without learning the words at all, is a possibility that the computer presents increasingly. A child does not learn language as a series of classified meanings. He learns language as he learns to walk, or to hear, or to see. He learns language as a way of feeling and exploring his environment. Therefore, he is totally involved. He learns very fast because of this enormous sensuous involvement and the resulting depth of motivation. It will be possible in this generation, I hope, to program the environment in such a way that we can learn a second language as we learned our mother tongue, rapidly and totally, as a means of perception and of discovery. The future of language presents the possibility of a world without words, a wordless, intuitive world, like a technological expression of the action of consciousness. E.S.P.

I had a friend visiting from Harvard the other day who said: "You see, my generation does not have goals." (He was a young architect.) "We are not goal-oriented. We just want to know what is going on." Now that means not a point of view but total ecological awareness. I was reading aloud from **Finnegans Wake** for a moment, and he said: "When you take LSD, the whole world takes on a multi-dimensional and multi-sensuous character of discovery, and when I listened to **Finnegans Wake** I got the same experience as LSD." (Perhaps **Finnegan** would be safer, and also more rewarding.)

The point this person was making was that it is absurd to ask us to pursue fragmentary goals in an electric world which is organized integrally and totally. The young today reject goals—they want roles—ROLES—that is, involvement. They want total involvement. They don't want fragmented, specialized goals or jobs. Now that is not easy to explain nor to prescribe for. I have touched upon the future of language, the future of consciousness, the future of the city, the future, perhaps finally, of work.

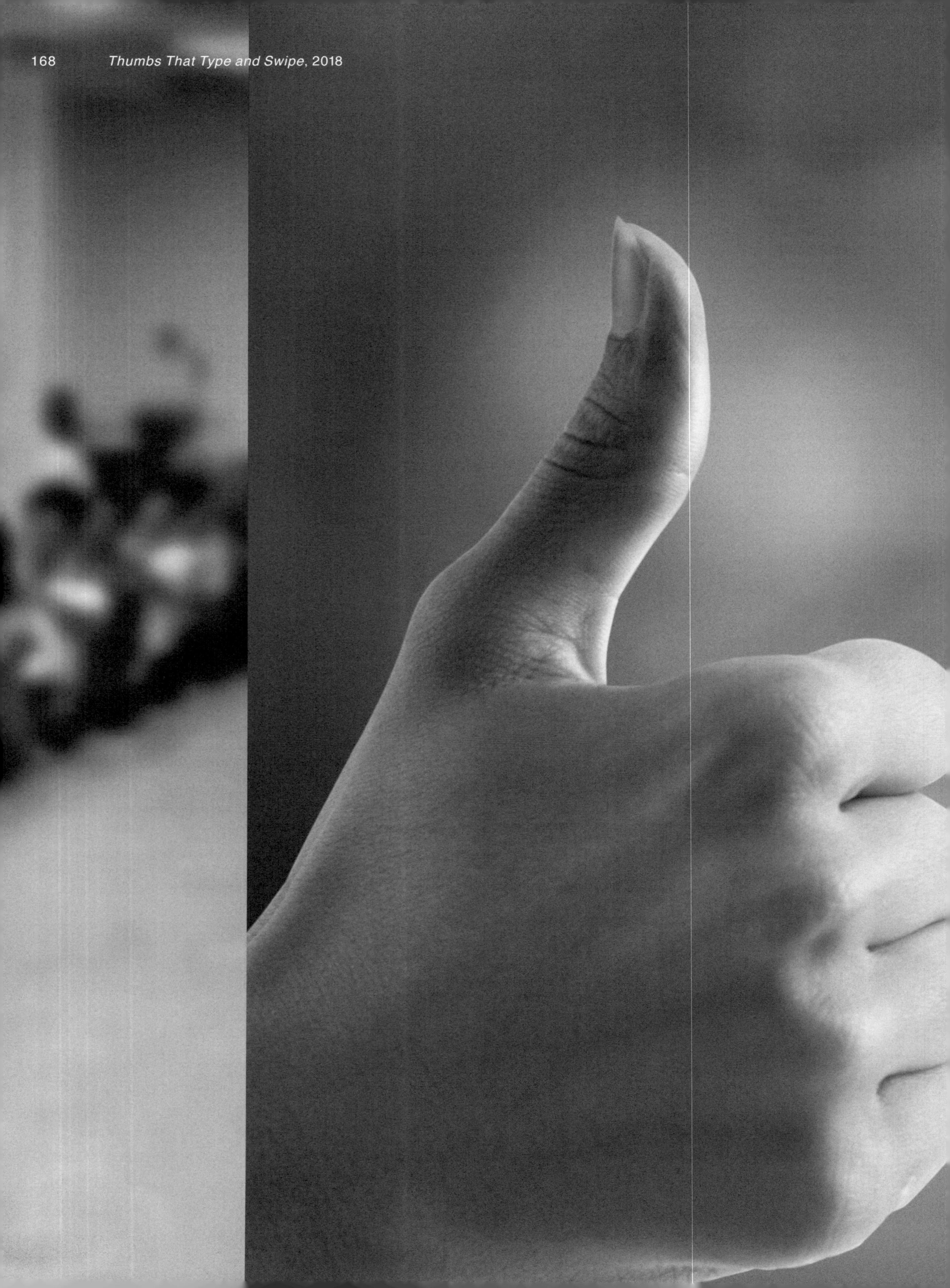

Nick Axel

Architectures of Behavior

I

A couple in their mid-fifties drives down a country road in silence. A young man in his early twenties stands in front of a train shelter with his rucksack, dressed in military uniform, facing the road. The car, a silver BMW X3, pulls up to the shelter area and slows to a stop. The boyish figure has disappeared. The couple, confused, dial a number on their phone yet receive no answer. It's a brisk winter day. Leaves have fallen off the trees, revealing traditional, mid-twentieth century, white German houses with pitched roofs in the distance. The older man steps out of the car. Looking around, he wanders up to the shelter. Back to the car with a look of confusion, when the young man jumps out from behind the shelter's full-height aluminum walls and onto the back of the older man, surprising him. They embrace. The older man, gesturing to the woman in the car, asks about the boy's bag. Pausing, with his eyes suspiciously darting across the frame, the young man replies: "I must have lost it." "Did it have anything valuable in it?" the older man asks. "Just my ID," he responds. Grabbing his crotch, he continues: "I have all my valuables right here." The two walk back to the car, where the woman steps out to take the young man into her arms. Cut.

At home, the older man welcomes the boy into the bedroom of a teenager, with black-light posters on the wall and unsmoked joints on the desk. "Just as you left it." Walking in with a gleaming smile, the older man asks whether the young man has been taking care of himself. Continuing to smile, the older man raises his hand up to the boy's mouth and begins to touch his teeth. With his gaze fixed, the older man inspects the inside of the boy's mouth. He stops and he tells the boy to clean himself up. Cut.

The three sit around a long wooden dinner table with a gold-rimmed porcelain table setting. Night has fallen. The boy, having changed clothes, jovially recounts a story from his time in Afghanistan in which two members from a bedouin family are killed after running into a fellow soldier urinating in the bush and how the situation was redressed by giving the family two goats and an Audi. The three laugh. Sitting back, the man takes a sip of his wine, the woman gets up to go into the kitchen, and the boy takes another bite of food. Brussels sprouts, spätzle, and pork. On her way back in, she sits down next to the young man. Turning towards him, the woman presses her body firmly up against his and moves her mouth, eyes closed, towards his neck. Cut.

The couple drives down a country road in silence. The woman glances over toward the older man driving. A young man, a different young man, stands in front of a train shelter with his rucksack, dressed in military uniform, facing the road. As the car pulls up, both the man and woman get out of the car and begin walking toward the boy. He appears more frail, less confident and slightly more troubled than the previous person who occupied this place. The man walks up to the boy to hug him. The woman follows suit. Holding the young man in her arms, they both start to cry. Arriving back home, the older man leaves the boy in the bedroom. Sitting down on the bed, he looks around and picks up a sketchpad. Flipping through it animates a man's arm ripping off a woman's burka, only to find another one beneath it. The arm keeps trying to unveil the woman, only to reveal more burkas. The background moves as the scenes repeat, giving the impression that the two figures are moving. The three sit around the dinner table. They eat, talk, and drink. The spätzle starts moving, turning into maggots; the Brussels sprouts into eyeballs. "Don't you like it?" the woman asks. The conversation continues with a sorrowful overtone. The couple moves to seduce the boy. Cut.

The couple drives down the country road in silence. A camel appears ahead blocking the way. The car stops. They stare, confused. A young man, a different young man, stands in front of a train shelter with his rucksack, dressed in military uniform, facing the road. The car pulls up to the shelter area and comes to a stop. The couple gets out. They embrace. They return home, eat, talk, and drink. The couple gets into a disagreement. Nonetheless, seduction ensues. Cut.

Omer Fast's *Continuity* (2016)[1] is a film without beginning or end. If you watch it for long enough, you will eventually see something you've already seen. The film itself is a series of repetitions. The characters stay the same. Two of the people are the same. The car, the train shelter, the bedroom, the dinner table, are the same. The sequence of events repeat, yet the performance is different every time. The single foreign element—the young man—triggers a chain reaction, unleashing a dynamic set of forces and unknown variables. Repetition is never simply repetition. Repetition is always, in the words of Tom McCarthy, one of Fast's closest interlocutors, *reenactment*.[2] As part of the architecture for Fast's 2016 exhibition at Martin-Gropius-Bau, Berlin, *Talking is not always the solution*, Studio Miessen designed a series of three waiting rooms to punctuate black box screening rooms at regular intervals. Each was designed to mimic a distinct and recognizable space of control, from an immigration office in Berlin to an economy-class airport lounge and a doctor's office, and in so doing give form to a corresponding existential condition of discomfort.

Studio Miessen collaborated with the scenographer Heike Schuppelius to exhaustively detail each waiting room typology with their respective accoutrements, from broken vending machines to empty chip bags, tacky plants, strewn newspapers, cheap reading material, and children's play areas. The phenomenological blurring of architecture and scenography, between exhibition space and the referent, results in a disjunctive, at times disturbing, experience. Yet the space of disjunction produced by the waiting rooms is not simply predicated on identity, but also, perhaps more importantly, difference and distinction. Through its relationship with the ideal, the idea of a perfect copy, reenactment opens a space for critical positions to be taken and pronounced. We should thus understand the concept of *repetition* to be categorically distinct from that of *reenactment*. Repetition is deceptive not for its appearance of similitude, but rather for its impression of ease. While reenactment allows for intent and agency to be read, repetition, as a Platonic ideal, attempts to erase any trace of difference.

Repetition is thus predicated on control, for which we can understand the laboratory to be the spatial type, or architectural apparatus, for engendering such conditions. From the white coats to the ventilation systems and airlock chambers, everything in the lab is designed to minimize irregularity and difference in the space of the experiment, be it a petri dish or hadron collider, so as to allow for its repetition. Taken one step further, we could say that the design of a laboratory is married to the material being experimented with, whether bacteria, particles, or currents. Toward these ends, domestic architecture has not only been implicated within but is a determining factor of experiments in behavioral science that endeavor to study the human animal. Infamously, the Milgram experiment of 1961 was constituted by the figure of authority, but perhaps more importantly by the wall of glass that physically—though not visually or aurally—separated the subject administering the electrical shocks from the one supposedly receiving them.

From modulating each room's light, temperature, and humidity, to calibrating every object's frame and intended viewing position, the museum is predicated on control. This architectural mediation is, so it seems, essential for the production and legitimation of knowledge. Yet unlike the architectural death drive of science, one that seeks to negate its existence as much as is technically possible, contemporary art institutions use the relationship between architectural form and artistic content as a source for curatorial experimentation. The gallery walls that Willem Sandberg first painted white were constitutive of artistic intent, such as with the raw affect of abstract expressionism, and a source of artistic material, such as with the work of institutional critique. The work of Studio Miessen not only reflects on this understanding of architecture as a historically burdened device of sociopolitical mediation, but rehearses new systems of relation and forms of behavior.

1 Omer Fast, *Continuity* (2012, video, 40 mins.), originally commissioned for Documenta 13, Kassel, Germany, 2012.
2 Tom McCarthy, *Remainder* (New York: Vintage, 2005).

Fig. 1 Omer Fast, *Talking is not always the solution* at Marin-Gropius-Bau, Berlin, Gemany, in 2016.

BURGER
KING

Fig. 2 Omer Fast, *Talking is not always the solution* at Marin-Gropius-Bau, Berlin, Gemany, in 2016.

AIRBOX

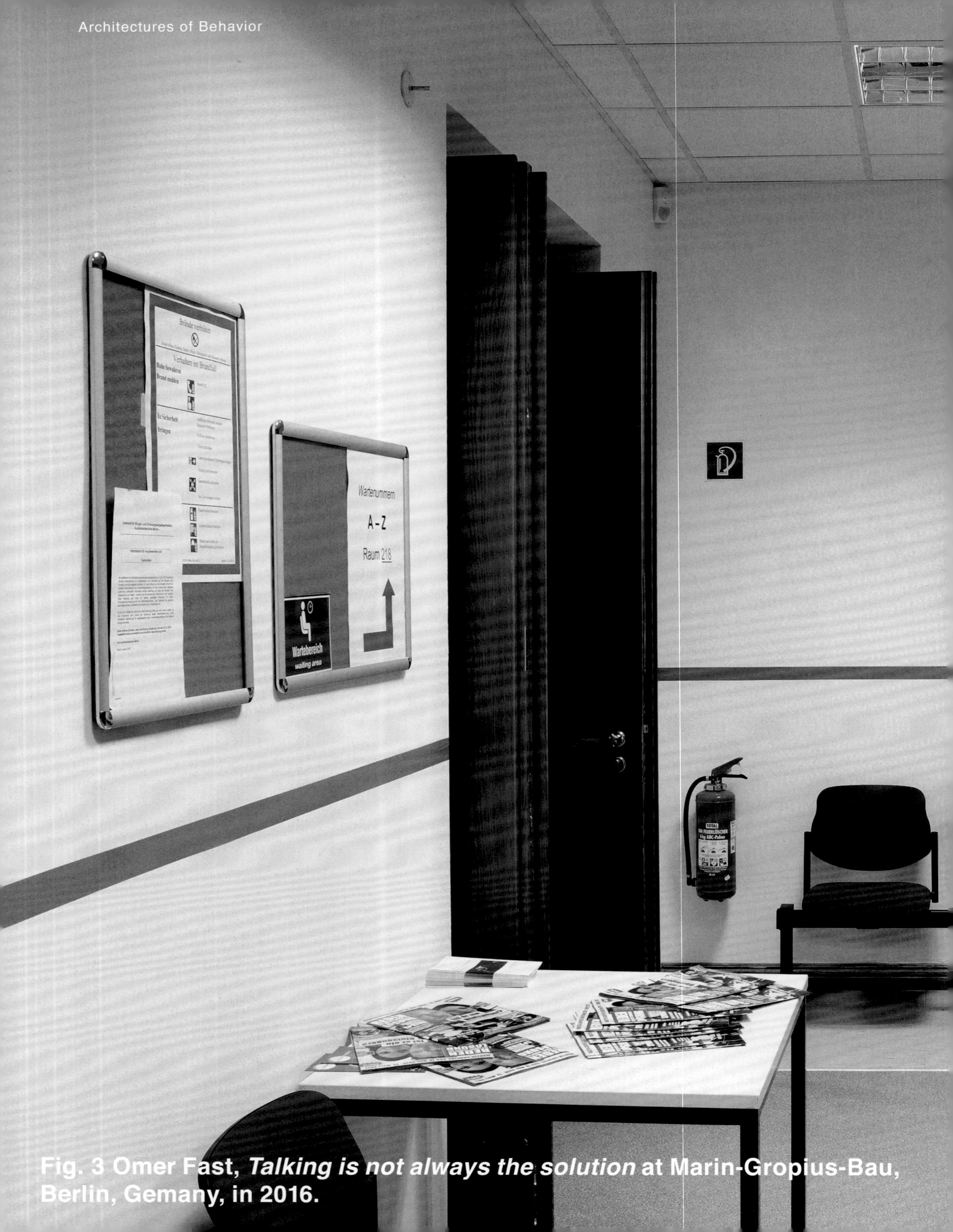

Fig. 3 Omer Fast, *Talking is not always the solution* at Marin-Gropius-Bau, Berlin, Gemany, in 2016.

Lycamobile
NIE MEHR
OHNE DATEN –
UNSCHLAGBAR
GÜNSTIG!
5GB
19.99€
1GB
3GB
10GB
REDEN IST NICHT
IMMER DIE LÖSUNG
WC

Fig. 4 Omer Fast, *Talking is not always the solution* at Marin-Gropius-Bau, Berlin, Gemany, in 2016.

II

Since 2007, Studio Miessen has produced a series of architectural works that reconfigure familiar institutional environments to engender a space of intensified perception, reflection, and action. Miessen's interventions collapse the distinction between observer and observed and create an anarchic laboratory where the architecture of social relations and personal identity is revealed through the understanding of habitual behavior as cultured performance. Designed to the scale of the human body, these spaces intervene in individual and collective habits of spatial occupation and interpersonal relation. In *The Violence of Participation* (2007), for instance, six vertical partitions divide a table's circular shape to constrain the field of view of whoever sits down. Sized so that only one person can occupy each section at a time, peripheral distraction is minimized, and focus is forced on what is directly in front: either the contents on the table or whoever sits directly across. This puts the ability to maintain dialogue—not just verbal, but also more subtle forms of sustained communication such as mental concentration, eye contact, and body language—to the test. Similarly, the "inverted pyramid" of *Archive Kabinett* (2009–11), designed in collaboration with architects Magnus Nilsson and Ralf Pflugfelder, draws out the metaphysical implications of sharing space. With an area of no more than eighteen square meters, the room played host to discursive events such as book launches, presentations and exhibitions. The steps surrounding its perimeter were capable of holding forty-five people; this incredible proximity and density of bodies transforms even the most mundane movements or gestures into highly reflective and performative acts. The configuration forces an intimate understanding that any act, from entering the room to looking around, deciding where to go to actually getting there, sitting down to shifting seated positions, gazing off into space to taking notes, conversing to standing up to leave, affects others' states of being. All are forced to confront their egos and reflect upon private desires, becoming hyper-aware of their positions as individuals within an organized group of people, that thing that might have once been referred to as society. Studio Miessen's work presents architecture as that which organizes, as that which indiscriminately subjects, as that which both creates common conditions and the conditions of the commons.

Both the *Violence* table and the *Kabinett* room are "secret" architectures. They operate without the consent or awareness of those who inhabit them. They appropriate and displace performative intention, be it to read something or attend an event. Form confronts the norm. While in these two instances behavior is understood in perhaps its most literal manner—the minute gestures and movements of the body—social and behavioral norms also play out in less immediate, more drawn-out fashion. Museums, for instance, bring together and mediate the relations between a diverse and multi-tiered set of stakeholders, each with distinct and at times conflicting agendas, toward a common goal: the exhibition itself. As the moment in which these sets of relations and layers of mediation effectively collapse, artists are both privileged and constrained by the institution they enter. Studio Miessen's contribution to the 2016 exhibition titled *Conditions of Political Choreography* at the Center for Contemporary Art (CCA), Tel Aviv, does not so much deconstruct the institutional framework of the collective exhibition as it embeds architectural form within its constitutive process in order to shape it, to mold it.

A group exhibition is a spatial problem. With nine other artists situated in a single double-height space, Studio Miessen shrouded the room with a continuous plywood surface, a tight quarter-pipe structure fit to the dimensions of the space. Acting as a new common datum, architecture became the intermediary device around (and on top of) which collective negotiations over the use of the space took place. Who is to use what, when, and where? The performance work, as a result, came to be defined by the architecture it occupied, from the structural support of the 90-degree upturn to the floor, the balcony, the stairs, the bleachers off to the sides, or even the tables out front, thus extending the performative consciousness of architecture beyond the limits of the installation itself.

Not unlike the inclined planes of Claude Parent and Paul Virilio's *Oblique Function* (1970), the quarter-pipe is a deceptively simple architectural form that displaces the normative relationship of the body to the ground—bound by gravity and the upright nature of the human skeleton—and forces a new, temporary equilibrium. While at the CCA the radius of the quarter-pipe was compact, leaving plenty of horizontal space for (gravitationally normative) performance and the monumental presence of a plywood wall, when the form was first deployed two years earlier as a part of Hito Steyerl's 2014–15 mid-career retrospective tour, it was articulated with a significantly larger radius to draw out the geometry's destabilizing potential. The quarter-pipe was originally designed as the architecture of *Liquidity Inc.* (2014), a video work that treated the instability of labor, value, and desire by tracing the journey of an orphan from the Vietnam War from his job as a high-frequency stock trader to a mixed martial arts (MMA) fighter. At *Artists Space*, New York, in 2015, the architecture stood at an oblique as a discrete object in the center of a large, square room. Enlarged to the height of the space and surfaced with a padded vinyl-covered foam typically used on the walls of gyms, the fillet radius served as the designated area, common amongst lengthy video installations, for people who do not want to stand to sit and watch. Beanbags scattered on top became islands of precarious balance in a sea of gravitational instability, where even the slightest of movements or subtlest of waves might offset the equilibrium found between body and architecture and give it reason to be sought again.

The potential for architecture to mediate the relation between a body and its immediate environment can extend beyond the scale of the anthropological figure to society more widely, through its institutions and the city. *European Kunsthalle* (2007) was a project for a new art institution in Cologne, Germany, that sought to re-conceive the form of the museum as a spatial construct. The Kunsthalle existed as intent. As a typology, the Kunsthalle is an archetypal European art institution that is pure exhibition space. It differs from a museum in that it does not own and have built space for the maintenance of an archive or permanent collection, but instead depends on the circulation of artworks for a perpetuity of temporary exhibitions. The *European Kunsthalle* had yet to manifest itself in Cologne or any other city; as a project, it existed solely as intent. The question thus became what spatial or architectural form is most suitable for such an institution?

With a 2007 research project entitled *Spaces of Production*, undertaken in collaboration with Nikolaus Hirsch, Philipp Misselwitz, and

Matthias Görlich, the project held the idea of a building was held in abeyance and its program instead distributed throughout the city in a choreographed route. At the same time, the project sought to explore the abstract nature of the Kunsthalle as an architectural typology, a space for the exhibition of unknown artworks. By critically examining the relationship between artwork (content) and its architecture (the container), the institution building was designed as an endless interior of disjointed and fragmented volumes, offering a near infinite potential for the artistic and curatorial territorialization of space.

While speculative, *Spaces of Production* signified a delicate and creative attunement to both the conditions and constraints of the art institution. Ever since, Studio Miessen has been commissioned to rethink and redesign the performative logic of these institutions—museums, galleries, foundations, -ennials, and other cultural initiatives—by way of their architectural form and spatial manifestations. For Witte de With Center for Contemporary Art, Rotterdam, in 2014, for instance, Miessen "punched holes onto the street" with windows four-and-a-half-meters tall (nearly fifteen feet), granting its ground-floor exhibition space a public, pedestrian presence. *Discursive Sauna* (2014), a project for Art Sonje Center, Seoul, was designed to allow the institution's public program to continue while the building was under construction. By severing the traditional socio-spatial relations between the audience of an event and its speakers—relegating the former to a lecture hall underneath the museum, the latter to an inverted pyramid reenactment placed out front, and connecting the two via video link—the respectively alienating conditions of spectator and performer were pushed toward their logical extreme. Even further behind the scenes, Miessen was commissioned to write policy and reenvision one Pristina's most important and politically contested public spaces, the Kosova National Art Gallery, for which he brought local experts together with foreign agents to frame the institution within narratives both local and international.

THE VIOLENCE OF PARTICIPATION
§1 SIT DOWN
§2 TAKE PEN
§3 A)TAKE BLANK PAPER (OR)
B)TAKE EXISTING DRAWING
§4 A)DRAW YOUR SPATIAL PERCEPTION OF EUROPE (OR)
B)CORRUPT DRAWING BY SUPERIMPOSING YOUR OPINION
§5 GO TO WALL
PIN UP CONTRIBUTION
TODAY, USA JOINS EUROPE

Fig. 6 *The Violence of Participation* at the 2007 Lyon Biennale of Contemporary Art, Lyon, France.

Fig. 7 *Archive Kabinett* with Magnus Nilsson and Ralf Pflugfelder (nOffice). Completed in 2011 at Archive Books in Berlin, Germany.

Fig. 8 *Archive Kabinett* with Magnus Nilsson and Ralf Pflugfelder (nOffice). Completed in 2011 at Archive Books in Berlin, Germany.

Fig. 9 ***Conditions of Political Choreography*** **at the Center for Contemporary Art (CCA) in Tel Aviv, Israel, 2016.**

Lloyd's pamphlet[edit]
In 1833, the English economist William Forster Lloyd published a
pamphlet which included a hypothetical example of over-use of a
common resource. This was the situation of
sharing a common parcel of land on which t
to let their cows graze, as was the custom i
postulated that if a herder put more than his
cattle on the common, overgrazing could re
additional animal, a herder could receive ad
the whole group shared damage to the com
made this individually rational economic dec
could be depleted or even destroyed, to the

Fig. 10 Hito Steyerl, *Retrospective Exhibition* at Artists Space, New York, 2015.

4:39
Friday, May 17

Fig. 11 Witte de With Center for Contemporary Art, Rotterdam, the Netherlands, 2014.

III

It is not expertise that has granted Miessen permission to occupy the infrastructural position he has, but rather a sensitivity to institutional context. Yet Miessen's immersion within such contexts is not one of subjugation and subsumption, but instead performs the adversarial position Chantal Mouffe advocates for as "agonism," a philosophy that understands conflict and the discrimination between friend and enemy as essential and ineradicable to politics. Agonism is a curious political philosophy in that its rejection of consensus (as an ideal) and acceptance of antagonism (as social nature) allows for a form of democracy to be envisioned that is both more accepting of and less violent toward difference.[3] Furthermore, Miessen has drawn from the political architecture of the British House of Lords and the presence of the "crossbenchers," members of Parliament who sit between and perpendicular to the government and opposition benches, not aligning themselves to any particular party.[4] Since its foundation in 2004, Miessen's practice has firmly come to occupy the position of an outsider within a widely expanded (and expanding) field of spatial practice. As an outsider, Miessen is invited to see what cannot be seen from within, to look beyond vested interests, and is charged with defining the horizons of commonality. One could argue that the site of Miessen's practice is the brief itself: opening the project up to a wider set of stakeholders, processes, actors, agents, interests, and concerns, and revealing previously unimaginable relations and techniques for their performative enactment.

Miessen's practice recursively operates on a set of concepts and principles that actively constitute the performance, our understanding, and our position in relation to contemporary society and its institutions, such as consensus, conflict, participation, boundaries, the archive, assembly, and agency. His work moves fluidly between spatial proposition, formal intervention, and theoretical observation, a dynamic that can be seen even in its earliest projects, such as *Substitune* (2004), his diploma project at the Architectural Association in London under Carlos Villanueva Brandt, and *Did Someone Say Participate?* (2006), a book published with Shumon Basar as the result of his master's degree at the London Consortium. The former was an experimental participatory project on the health providence system for recovering heroin addicts in Kings Cross, London. Miessen mediated the divergent interests and conflicting concerns of the system's agents and stakeholders—from users to the local governing authority—to rearticulate the infrastructure of methadone's distribution, and in so doing make it available to more citizens who were hitherto excluded and disenfranchised by governance mechanisms such as municipal registration. The latter was an edited volume of texts that sought to expand architecture's disciplinary understanding of participation. Instead of focusing on inclusive, bottom-up or grassroots initiatives, contributions focused largely on mechanisms of exclusion and obstruction. Participation was thus framed not as a design project to be invented or willed, but rather as a way to see the always already preexisting political conditions of society and space, which are inherently contingent and insecure as such.

While a vanguard in the contemporary debate on the architect's political agency, the architectural practice of Studio Miessen can be situated within a much longer disciplinary history on the critical agency of form, and in particular what Beatriz Colomina and Mark Wigley—with reference to one of Bernard Tschumi's later *Advertisements for Architecture* (1977)—have recently termed "Perverse Design."[5] Underneath a photograph of a woman in bondage, Tschumi writes, "The game of architecture is an intricate play with rules that you may break or accept. These rules ... have [an] erotic significance." Where Tschumi identified architecture as being bound by "so many knots that cannot be untied,"[6] Miessen demonstrates that architecture and spatial practice more widely can be the very means by which they can. Beyond this, Miessen's installation work provides context for the transgressive pleasure Tschumi saw in the liminal space between form and program.

Whereas Tschumi inherited both the idealism and formalism of his generation, Miessen is a pragmatist, and radically so. While there are no pole-vaulters in his catacombs, Miessen's architecture nonetheless reveals the performativity—the limits, the norms, the potential, the essentiality—of bodies in space: how we see, how we think, how we move, how we speak, how we act, how we want, how we do, how

we don't. The architecture of Studio Miessen can be seen to interrogate the normative architectures of behavior and reflect upon the metaphysical performance of everyday sociality. If, in the words of Colomina and Wigley, "design is always the design of the human," Miessen's architecture potentiates the redesign of the human; it positions us as the scientists in control of that unruly substance of ours called life. It is reflective in that it reveals ourselves as we have been designed, and critical in that it points toward what, if not how, we want to be. Provoking the self out of its slumber of complacent habit, this experience of existential disjunction ultimately constitutes the present as a historic moment, allowing for a distinction to be made—if made by the agency of the individual—between everything that came before and whatever we want to come after.

3 Chantal Mouffe and Markus Miessen, *The Space of Agonism*, ed. Nikolaus Hirsch and Markus Miessen, *Critical Spatial Practice* 2 (Berlin: Sternberg Press, 2012).

4 Miessen has transformed the crossbenchers and their theoretical position of participatory non-allegiance into a figure of spatial practice with doctoral research at the Centre for Research Architecture, Goldsmiths, and a book: Markus Miessen, *Crossbenching* (Berlin: Sternberg Press, 2016).

5 Beatriz Colomina and Mark Wigley, *Are We Human? Notes on an Archaeology of Design* (Zurich: Lars Müller Publishers, 2016).

6 Bernard Tschumi, *Advertisements for Architecture*, 1976–77, postcard-sized images. http://www.tschumi.com/projects/19/.

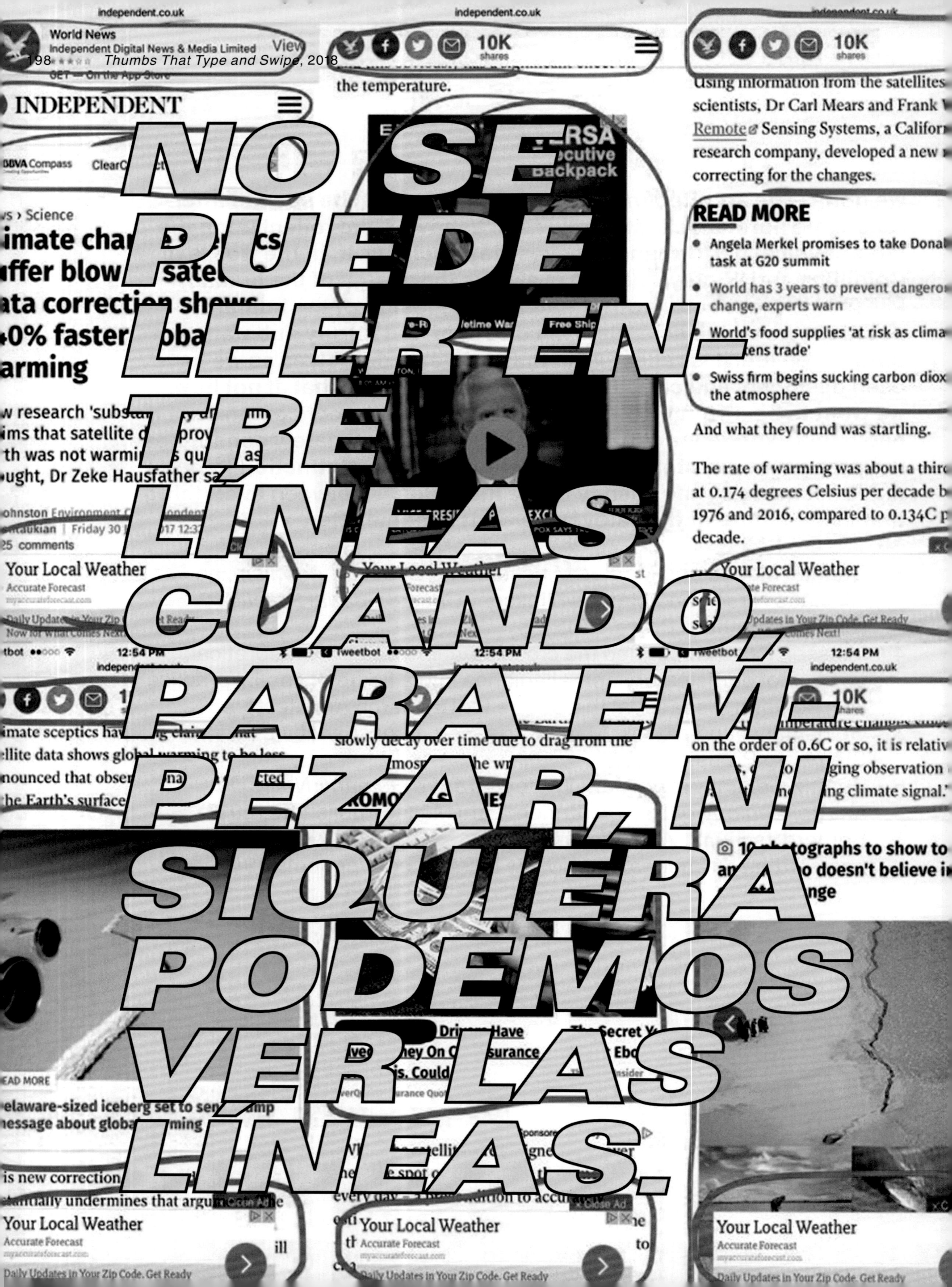

Thumbs That Type and Swipe, 2018

From Storage to Transmission: Architecture and the Communication of Heat

Architectural stories have a way of beginning around the campfire. In the case of Vitruvius, it was the accidental discovery of fire that prompted the first gatherings and, as a result, dwellings of men; for Gottfried Semper the hearth was the most moral and significant of the four elements of architecture, around which the protecting "negations" of the roof, enclosure, and mound group themselves.[1] Prior to any consideration of the aesthetic and symbolic dimensions of the built, architectural history has, in this sense, always presented itself as the history of communication, as the narration of the roots of congregation and common understanding between people. The current text sets out to demonstrate how this perception underwent a fundamental shift in the late eighteenth and early nineteenth centuries. During these years, architecture became not only an object of the history of communication, but of media history. That is, architecture's role transformed from a singular locus and framework of interpersonal exchange to one in which it enacts generally understood processes of mediation. Significantly, this account of medial thinking in architecture can start from fire too, but its origins lie less in the firesides of the mists of primeval times and for more in the historically datable flames harnessed to serve technology and science.

Concerning a pile of charcoal in a laboratory in Uppsala, Sweden, the German-Swedish apothecary Carl Wilhelm Scheele published the results of his 1777 research in a laboratory in his influential *Chemical Observations and Experiments on Air and Fire*. He thus describes the heat of the fire:

> Represent to yourself a little hillock of burning coals; in this case the heat darting from this hillock all around is that which may be reflected by a metallic polished plate; that on the contrary which rises upwards, and may be driven by winds to and fro, unites with Air. I will call the first kind, for distinction sake, radiant heat.[2]

Scheele's finding epitomizes the understanding of distinct modes of heat transmission that emerged in the second half of the eighteenth century. In this case, he clearly formulated the two phenomena known today as thermal radiation and convection. According to this understanding, warmth does not emanate diffusely from a source, but can be divided into the proportion that is reflected and that which dissipates into the air.

This insight is based on a comprehensive epistemological and technological development that can be described, using Peter Sloterdijk's concept of the "revealing inclusion of latencies and background data in manifest operations."[3] In other words, at the beginning of the eighteenth century, in numerous scientific and technological experiments, a distinction was made between thermal processes, until then barely discussed. These concepts start to be incorporated into concrete practices.

The aspect that attracted prime consideration was the combination of warmth with seemingly ephemeral air. Scientists such as the American statesman, Benjamin Franklin, recognized that it was the key factor in the functioning of stoves and fireplaces. In his *Observations on Smoky Chimneys*, published in 1793, Franklin described the manifold attempts to exploit this moment of transmission. His aim was to diminish the loss of warmth caused by the emission of smoke, thereby increasing the warmth emitted by both radiation and convection into a room—

1
Cf. Vitruvius, *The Ten Books on Architecture*, trans. Morris Hicky Morgan (Cambridge, MA: Harvard University Press, 1914), 38–39; Gottfried Semper, *The Four Elements of Architecture and Other Writings*, trans. Harry F. Mallgrave and Wolfgang Herrmann (Cambridge, UK: Cambridge University Press, 1989), 102.

2
Carl Wilhelm Scheele, *Chemical Observations and Experiments on Air and Fire* (London: J. Johnson, 1780), 74.

3
Peter Sloterdijk, "Airquakes," *Environment and Planning D: Society and Space* 27 (2009), 41–57, here 41. Sloterdijk introduces the concept of explication using an atmospheric phenomenon that is comparable to that of heat transmission, namely the first use of poison gas during the First World War.

a technique that would be variously picked up upon and refined over the succeeding decades.[4] However, this understanding of the thermal capacities of air did not only inspire new (heating) techniques and scientific research, it also had profound consequences for the construction and above all for the discursive conceptualization of buildings, consequences that to date have gone largely unnoticed.[5] The moment air was understood as a factor in heat transmission and a variable susceptible to manipulation, a multitude of architectural developments were triggered, with significant ramifications for our understanding of building and dwelling. Last but by no means least, as will be shown over the following pages, the knowledge of the convective qualities of air would lead to a fundamentally new medial and operational understanding of architecture.

Air as a Vehicle

One of the first figures to successfully exploit the phenomenon of convection at an architectural level was the inventor and factory owner William Strutt, the son of a rich business family that operated a number of cotton mills in county Derbyshire in the English East Midlands. William Strutt was in charge of the mechanical and technical activities of W. G. & J. Strutt Ltd., one of the key aspects of which was the planning and construction of the factory buildings. In order to confront the specific spatial requirements and the high risk of fires in cotton mills, between 1792 and 1793 he designed the Derby Cotton Mill, a factory that would go down in the history of structural design as the first integrated frame construction and the first multi-story fire-resistant building.[6]

In the same period, motivated by various considerations including fire protection, William Strutt also developed the new type of heating technology. From the beginning, this development was relevant beyond the context of industrial architecture. As with many of Strutt's inventions, it found applications in family owned cotton mills as well as in their own residences. Unlike Benjamin Franklin and his followers, Strutt's innovation did not simply use the convective potential of air to improve the heat output in the immediate vicinity of a heat source. Fundamentally, he used this potential to distribute the warmth beyond the location of that heat source.[7] The heating system he developed to produce this effect was in essence based on an ordinary domestic iron stove. With his attention focused more on the exterior of the device, Strutt wrote that "the great object is to bring the greatest possible quantity of air in contact with the stove, and that contact … be contained and renewed the longest, and this often also as possible."[8] To this end, he experimented with two basal elements: with a casing to control the circulation of the air around the stove, and with a channel to induce its further flow. Eventually, he enclosed the stove in a closely fitting honeycomb-like perforated brick mantle creating a sort of oven-building. He connected this structure, independent of the flue pipe, with an incoming and an outgoing "air tube" (fig 1). The result is a heating mechanism that emits practically no heat radiation but that provides a "continual stream" of warm air.[9] This invention is significant not only as a component of early central heating systems, but also because its architectural application is comparatively well documented.

4

Cf. Barry Donaldson and Bernard Nagengast, *Heat & Cold: Mastering the Great Indoors* (Atlanta: American Society of Heating, Refrigerating and Air-Conditioning Engineers, 1994), 25–29.

5

One of the few sound accounts of the results of new heating technologies on architectural designs in the eighteenth and nineteenth centuries is to be found in Robert Bruegmann, "Central Heating and Forced Ventilation: Origins and Effects on Architectural Design," *Journal of the Society of Architectural Historians* 37, no. 3 (1978), 143–160. Bruegmann, however, similarly concentrates on technical-constructional developments, leaving discursive and conceptual aspects largely aside.

6

Cf. H. R. Johnson and A. W. Skempton, "William Strutt's Cotton Mills, 1793–1812," *Transactions of the Newcomen Society* 30, no. 1 (1955), 179–205, here 180–184; and, regarding William Strutt's biography, C. L. Hacker, "William Strutt of Derby (1756–1830)," *Journal of the Derbyshire Archaeological and Natural History Society* 80 (1960), 49–70.

7

For a detailed description cf. Michael C. Egerton, "William Strutt and the Application of Convection to the Heating of Buildings," *Annals of Science* 24, no. 1 (1968), 73–87.

8

Ibid., 81, citing from a letter from William Strutt to Richard Lovell Edgeworth, January 21, 1817.

9

Ibid., 78.

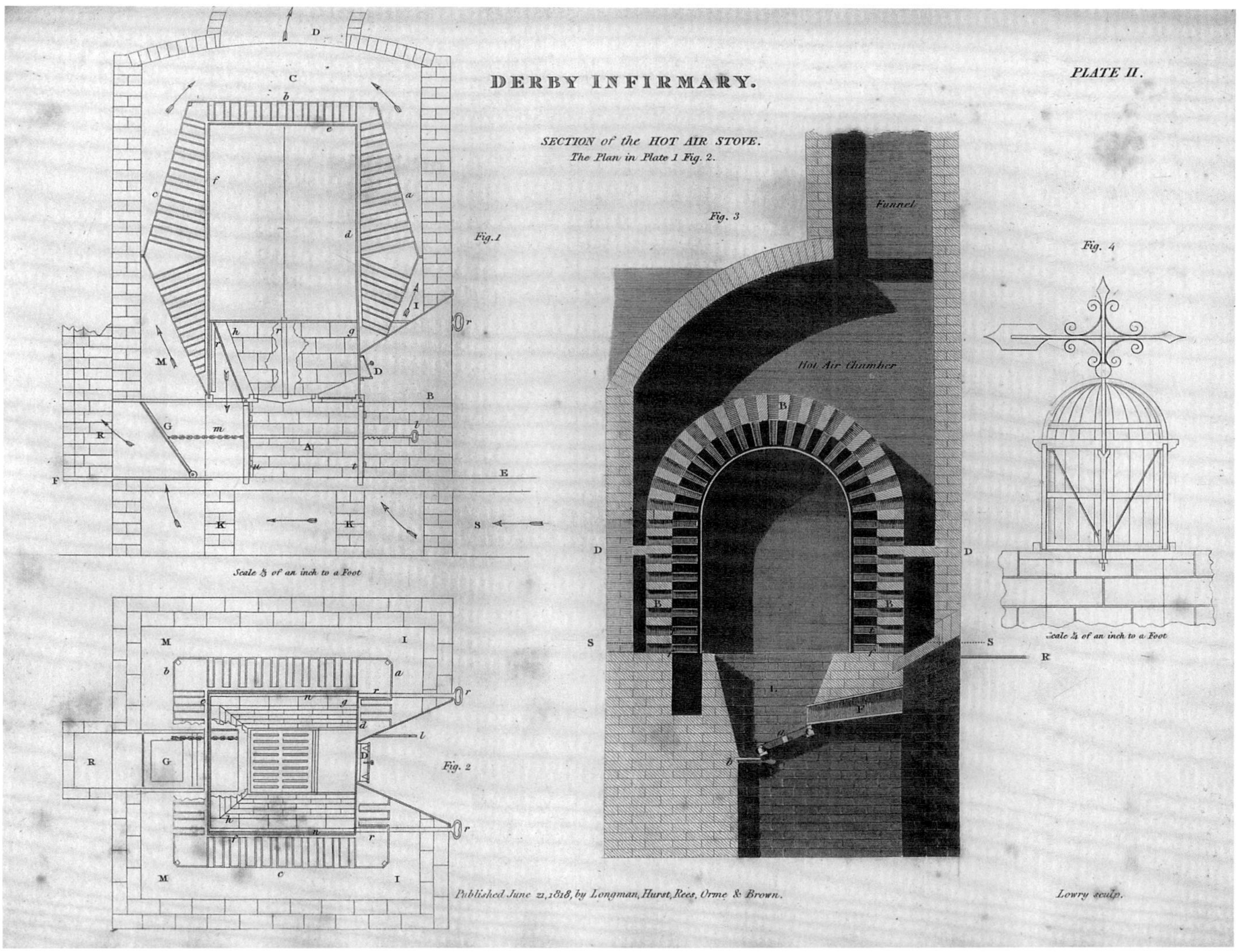

Fig. 1
Charles Sylvester, Derby Infirmary hot air stove, 1819.

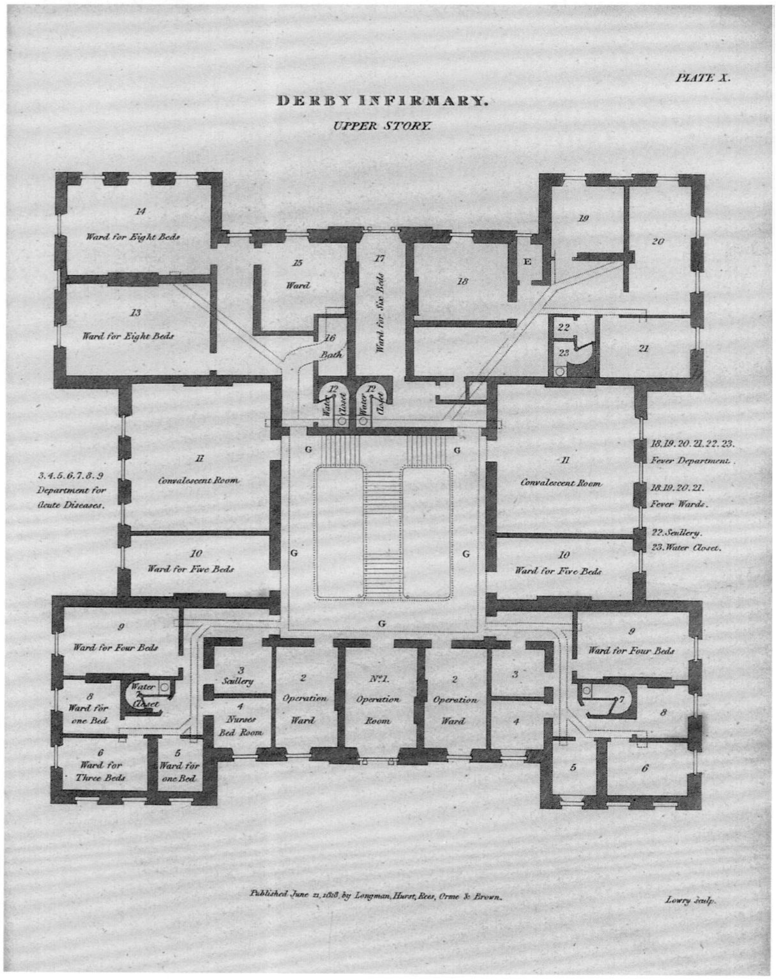

Fig. 2
Charles Sylvester, View of the Derbyshire General Infirmary, 1819.

Fig. 3
Charles Sylvester, Derby Infirmary floor plan, 1819.

Strutt himself never published on his inventions, but the implementation of his system was extensively recorded in a treatise by friend and engineer Charles Sylvester. Printed in 1819 under the title *The Philosophy of Domestic Economy*, this eponymous science, which would later become the umbrella term for numerous emerging findings and specifications about household management, was defined by Sylvester as "[t]hat branch of natural philosophy which has for its object the improvement of domestic life, as far as relates to our food, clothing, and local habitation." In his book, however, the scope is restricted almost entirely to the technology of central heating and ventilation.[10] He uses as an example the Derbyshire Infirmary, a hospital built outside Derby between 1804 and 1810 planned and sponsored by Strutt, to demonstrate the principles and functioning of such systems in their interplay with an architectural structure.

Sylvester begins with the description of a channel system. It starts with an air inlet situated 70 yards away from the hospital, connected via underground shaft. The shaft enters the cellar of the three-story hospital building, then proceeds vertically to the second floor where it merges with a cavity, from which a series of horizontal flues branch out to the individual hospital rooms. Sylvester marks the progression of these conduits using dotted lines on the ground plan. The infirmary rooms, for their part, are equipped with additional flues with different locations. These lead to the roof and terminate with an air outlet situated above the ridge (figs. 2–3). By means of two cowls mounted on the inlet and outlet, the system ensures a continuous air exchange within the building. In addition, the whole scheme is attached to a furnace in the cellar based on Strutt's design, placed at an optimal distance from the second floor. Once activated, cold air is sucked into the building via the underground conduit, fed from the floor of the furnace into and around it, and then collected in a "hot air chamber." "Here it has attained its full degree of heat," explains Sylvester, "and is now transmitted through different flues to the apartments to be warmed."[11]

Therefore, commencing from a specific understanding of the convective properties of air Strutt conceived an elaborate heating and ventilation system based on the principle of physical transmission. This technique does have solitary, partially apocryphal predecessors, as do warm-water and steam heating, the other two other central heating systems that emerged more or less contemporaneously. In the Roman hypocaust, the fumes from a fire flow through floor or wall cavities and heated air was sometimes channeled into the living spaces. The castles of the High and Late Middle Ages also possessed rudimentary forms of hot-air heating. Similarly, the use of warm water, as propagated starting in the late 1770s by Frenchman Bonnemain, can be traced back to Ancient Rome; and steam heating, as unequivocally realized by Matthew Boulton and James Watt in the 1780s, had already been proposed at least forty years earlier.

Nevertheless, it is only the late eighteenth century that marks the beginning of a concerted technological and architectural development of these systems based on scientific findings concerning the thermal properties and the controlled dispersal of the respective heat-carriers. During this period, related practices and knowledge entered into a discourse. In the words of a representative of what would later become the German-speaking professional association of the discipline's practitioners: "the fact is that it was only later that it was learnt how to distribute the heat-transferring

10
Charles Sylvester, *The Philosophy of Domestic Economy* (London: Longman, Hurst, Rees, Orme, and Brown 1819), 1. Sylvester's book enjoyed a large public following and was published in a French translation in 1824 in the journal *Annales de l'Industrie*. For a compendium of household practices under the heading "domestic economy" see for example Thomas Webster and Frances Parkes, *An Encyclopædia of Domestic Economy* (London: Longman, Brown, Green, and Longmans, 1844).

11
Ibid.

12
Hermann Vetter, "Aus der Geschichte der Zentralheizungstechnik bis zum Jahre 1870," *Gesundheits-Ingenieur: Festnummer zur 6. Versammlung der Heizungs- und Lüftungsfachmänner* (1907), 10–25, esp. 10 (italics in the original). Vetter presents a collection of the predecessors of the individual techniques and systems. Bruegmann also locates the emergence of the three central-heating systems to the late eighteenth and early nineteenth centuries, likewise based on their concentrated thematic currency. Cf. Bruegmann: "Central Heating and Forced Ventilation," 143.

medium across *multiple* rooms."[12] As with the Derbyshire Infirmary, this act of distribution was coupled with a consequential penetration of architectural spaces lacking an existing circulation structure. Channel systems began, to interlink floors, rooms, apparatuses, and inside to outside. This was added to in the nineteenth century in the form of water, gas, and electricity conduits.

Thus, the technology of central heating is a core element in a series of architectural developments that originated around 1800 connecting distinct social realms. The technology began as a response to particular safety requirements in the manufacturing sites of early industrial capitalism, yet at the same time it was a mainstay for both the increasing compartmentalization of comfortable living from external influences as well as the ever-more stringent partitioning of modern disciplinary institutions into isolated and centrally controllable cells. In other words, central-heating channels allow rooms to be heated without the need for the servants entering or the delinquents exiting. Meanwhile, the second function of Strutt's system, artificial ventilation, had already advanced to become an architectural objective in the mid-eighteenth century, against the backdrop of emerging theories of miasmas and contagion. Independent of respective assumptions about the origins of pestilent or cleansing effects of air and how it caused, promoted, or spread diseases, it was increasingly recognized that fans or special window constructions were desirable to propel, mix, and substitute air within enclosed spaces. Due to the fact that this was particularly relevant to facilities that spatially isolate large numbers of people, such as hospitals, prisons, or ships, Sylvester's infirmary is therefore paradigmatic.[13] However, in the case of the Derbyshire Infirmary, air becomes more than a protean substance, malleable component of improved mechanical and construction processes; instead, air become an architectural instrument itself. It serves as the qualifiable and quantifiable material carrier of what was understood, following the thinking of Joseph Black and Antoine Lavoisier, as "caloric" or the "substance of heat," and which, with its help, was to be distributed systematically throughout the building. "In this method of warming rooms," wrote Charles Sylvester, "air is made the medium of vehicle for supplying caloric."[14]

Becoming-media

Both the term "medium" and the term "vehicle" indicate that Strutt's system is eminently qualified to be viewed from the perspective of media history. A prerequisite for this undertaking is a definition of media techniques, which as Friedrich Kittler has proposed, lending from Marshall McLuhan and Harold Innis, does not restrict these techniques to information systems for the storage, processing, and transmission of messages, but instead also takes communication systems into account that beyond regulating messages, also regulate the traffic of people and objects. Taken from this perspective, communication systems encompass completely disparate media, ranging from language to road schemes, but are nevertheless open to an analysis using the terms of information systems.[15] The underlying concept of communication, which includes symbolic, physical, and social processes, is not a theoretical positing, rather it is etymologically rooted, as applied in the context developed here. Prior to its prevailing meaning established during the course of the nineteenth century as the transmission of immaterial goods such as thoughts, ideas, and values, communication designated forms of transportation, interconnection, exchange, and conveyance. It follows, in particular from a historical perspective, that a broad definition of communication should be assumed and that special attention should be paid to the parallels, divergences, and transitions between its various different uses.[16]

13
Cf. Jeanne Kisacky, "Breathing Room: Calculating an Architecture of Air," in Anthony Gerbino (ed.), *Geometrical Objects: Architecture and the Mathematical Sciences 1400–1800* (Cham, Switzerland: Springer, 2014), 247–279. Specifically referring to the Derbyshire Infirmary see also Christine Stevenson, *Medicine and Magnificence: British Hospital and Asylum Architecture, 1660–1815* (New Haven, CT: Yale University Press, 2000), 218–33.

14
Sylvester, *Domestic Economy*, 13.

15
Cf. Friedrich Kittler, "The History of Communication Media," in "Global Algorithm," ed. Arthur and Marilouise Kroker, *CTheory*, special issue (1996), http://ctheory.net/ctheory_wp/global-algorithm-the-history-of-communication-media/.

Based on this supposition, the technical-architectural innovations embodied in the Derbyshire Infirmary can indeed be understood in the framework of a media-technological differentiation process and can be tied to two crucial transitional moments useful for a description of information systems. The first of these transitions is functional and concerns the shift between the two media procedures of storage and transmission. According to this, a building such as the Derbyshire Infirmary, explicitly designed as a transportation system, no longer simply stores the warmth generated by a chimney or furnace, but instead starts to furthermore transmit it. The basis for this is nothing more than the introduction of a channel, in this case William Strutt's "air tube" and the distribution network attached to it. The second, concomitant transition is historical and concerns—if not in its meaning, all the more so in principle—one of the epochal shifts in the history of media: the transition between speaking and writing. Therefore, as a parallel, in the same sense that the written word freed spoken communication from the presence of a speaker, central heating dissolves the heat source and heat from one another and makes the distribution of warmth and the presence of a fire independent of each other. Furthermore, just as these transitions demonstrate seminal repercussions for social and cultural systems in general terms, so they would equally suggest fundamental ramifications for the social and cultural system of architecture.

In the context of his call for a media history of architecture, Kittler himself has, on repeated occasions, presented such an information-theoretical reading of built structures. Yet his analysis was limited the media-conditionality of the architectural design process and the permeation of built spaces with communication infrastructures such as street, electricity, or water-supply networks.[17] Rather than ascribing and reducing the medial character of architecture to other media techniques and practices, the intention here is to utilize Kittler's concept of media and the transitions outlined above as a starting point to focus on the operative aspects of architecture itself. Thus, the emergence of central-heating techniques does not simply endow architecture with a further communication system; but rather, it triggers an explication process that pertains to its own mediality. In other words, the specific prerequisites and procedures of these techniques expose the building and its elements in their material characteristics as operative units.

Of the three rival central-heating methods developed in around 1800, the water-, steam-, and air-based systems, the latter plays a special role. As a way of heating buildings the hot-air system was overtaken, in terms of energy efficiency and practicality, in the second half of the nineteenth century by steam and warm-water systems; by the beginning of the twentieth century, however, it reasserted itself as an integral part of the expanded cooling, humidifying, and purification functions of air conditioning, advancing to become the cornerstone of a technology that continues to govern the construction of built space in numerous regions and spheres up until the present day. In addition, in terms of the history of knowledge there are two reasons why, from its origins onward, air-based systems have acquired a singular significance: on the one hand because they have always existed in tandem with the practice of artificial ventilation, and as such—as well as through temperature—have established a second direct connection to the health and activities of man; on the other because air-based systems, at least in part, have always involved the visible sides of a building. Once they have been transported to their destination, the convective flows of a hot-air system do not diffuse themselves in hidden pipes and radiators but instead in the room being occupied itself. Their delineation

16
Cf. Jonathan Sterne, "Transportation and Communication: Together as You've Always Wanted Them," in *Thinking with James Carey: Essays on Communications, Transportation, History* (New York: Peter Lang, 2006), 117–135; and as an a further contribution Gabriele Schabacher, "Mobilizing Transport: Media, Actor-Worlds, and Infrastructures," in Media and Mobility, ed. Dorit Müller and Heike Weber, *Transfers: International Journal of Mobility Studies* 3, no. 1, special issue (Spring 2013), 75–95.

17
Cf. Friedrich Kittler, "The City Is a Medium," trans. Matthew Griffin, New Literary History, 27, no. 4 (Autumn 1996), 717–729; Friedrich Kittler, "Die Zukunft auf Siliziumbasis / A Silicon-Based Future," in *Die Zukunft des Raums The Future of Space*, ed. Bernd Meurer (Frankfurt/Main and New York: Campus, 1994), 129–144; Friedrich Kittler, "Stuttgarter Rede über Architektur," *Zeitschrift für Medien- und Kulturforschung*, 1 (2012), 97–104.

becomes congruent with occupied space that becomes a direct component of the system.

Therefore, central heating and air-conditioning techniques impact the conception of architecture on at least two levels. First, they provide an infrastructure for the distribution of warmth and air on the basis of which new spatial distributions and connections can be undertaken. Second, they are a contring factor in a shift in the notion of built space itself. Built space is no longer only seen as a location in which the residents meet and interchange with each other, but increasingly also as a system of distribution.

With this the appearance of central (hot-air) heating marks a decisive moment in the becoming-media of architecture.[18] The advent of an architectural transmission concept signals the locally and historically situated emergence of an elementary media function while simultaneously challenging versions tied to other technical media and those that are substantial or supra-historical of architectural mediality.[19] It is the combination of a series of heterogeneous conditions—new thermodynamic and aerodynamic learning, the development of building types such as factories and hospitals, the demand for early living comforts, and above all the discursive reflection upon these developments and their relationships—that first creates the situation in England in around 1800 in which a transformation in architecture from a pure storage structure into a genuine storage and transmission structure can be observed. What makes this medial metamorphosis so fundamental is that it does not simply concern individual built elements but rather the architectural construction as a whole.

Central heating transforms the entire building into an operational assemblage, addressing a wide range of different elements and entities in the process. This relationship is initially evident in the Derbyshire Infirmary in the form of a special safety precaution: in order to prevent a potential overheating of the centrally heated upper rooms, Strutt's system is equipped with a type of emergency valve, situated not, however, at the technical level of the furnace, but instead at the architectural level of the building. A vertical shaft connects one of the horizontal air flues on the second floor with a small sliding door that can be opened onto the central hall of the hospital on the first floor.[20] By this means excess warm air can be forced downward and distributed across the rooms on the first floor. Similarly to the way Strutt transforms the stove into a type of house by surrounding it with a brick shell, so he transforms the actual house into a type of stove in which the warm airflows circulate through the interior rooms in the same planned manner as patients and hospital workers.

Set against this backdrop, it hardly comes as a surprise that Sylvester's book also contains an early reference to the revolving door, that very architectural element that was designed like no other to combine the control of artificial atmospheres and people. All of the entrances to the toilets in the Derbyshire Infirmary are equipped with centrally hinged double-winged doors placed in a cylindrical cavity space, resembling the installation that American Theophilus van Kannel would patent in 1888 under the description "storm door structure" (fig. 4).[21] According to Sylvester, the use of these doors in the Derbyshire Infirmary activated a whole series of processes:

> They are so contrived that the person who enters them, by the action of the door, and without any attention on his part, expels all the foul air; which is, at the same time, replaced by the warm fresh air of the house: and, in returning, leaves this fresh air in its place; whilst by the same action of the door, the basin is washed in the usual manner.[22]

18
Cf. Joseph Vogl, "Becoming-media: Galileo's Telescope," trans. Brian Hanrahan, in "New German Media Theory," ed. Eva Horn, *Grey Room*, 29, special issue (Fall 2007), 14–25.

19
Schäffner, for instance, would appear to be proposing such a supra-historical perspective in his call for a "fundamental reconstruction of architecture as a media technique". Cf. Wolfgang Schäffner, "Elemente architektonischer Medien," *Zeitschrift für Medien- und Kulturforschung*, 1 (2010), 137–150, here 138.

20
Cf. Sylvester, *Domestic Economy*, 45–46.

21
Theophilus van Kannel. Storm door structure. US Patent 387,571, filed August 7, 1888.

Fig. 4
Charles Sylvester, Derby Infirmary door to water closet, 1819.

This represents a dynamic threshold technique. Simultaneously open and closed, it not only guarantees the differential passage of air and people, but serves as a ventilator and transfers the act rinsing from the forgetful patient to a reliable mechanism. Thus, the development of this elaborated door device is based on a conception of architecture as a regulator of generally understood transmission processes. Sylvester describes the basic principle for this construction explaining that "[d]uring the returning motion one of the panels of the door is made a valve."[23] This means that the doors in the Derbyshire Infirmary are conceived as control devices; they can be seen as elements of an operational architectural system that has begun to process the atmospheric conditions and the actions of the residents alike.

Operational Systematization

The repercussions of central heating do not simply concern constructions and doors, but also involve a far-reaching discursive aspect. Along with the spread of new heating systems in Europe and North America in the first decades of the nineteenth century, a deluge of books, articles, and patent documents appeared on the topic. At the same time as the application and effects of these new techniques are discussed in these publications, a new treatment on the architectural implications emerges. In 1837 the Englishman Charles James Richardson, a former assistant to the famous neo-classicist John Soane, published a successful volume with the title *A Popular Treatise on the Warming and Ventilation of Buildings*. The book stands out amongst the mass of publications as the first work on the subject to be written by a trained architect. Written in plain English, the book provides a comprehensive overview of the developments of the preceding decades, clearly demonstrating the extent to which the implementation of central-heating and ventilation techniques transformed architecture into a complex operational arrangement transcending established constructional and symbolic systems.

Even more than Charles Sylvester, Richardson applies medial terminology throughout his writing, whether referring to a substance as a "circulating medium for transmitting heat," to the need for a "formal medium" to induce such circulation flows, or indeed at another level to the "medium of the plates" used in the book to visually present the respective arrangements.[24] Unlike earlier architectural discourse designating direct connections, such as a door between adjacent rooms or a corridor between distant ones, Richardson employs a notion of communication that designates physical transmissions.[25] Even though these expressions are not to be understood in the sense of today's technical media, but rather need to be set against the physical-mechanical understanding current at the time and originating with Newton of a medium or a milieu as an intermediary agent that is capable of transmitting forces and effects, these expressions reveal a fundamental thinking in architectural transmission processes. This is nowhere more clear than when Richardson describes the actual heating systems, for instance a certain "Calorifere Fumivore" that is able "to send" any amount of warmed air to every room of a moderately sized manor house.[26]

Richardson's treatise provides three central moments of an operational systematization of architecture. First, the architectural object and its constituent elements enter a new systemic context. Flawed heating systems illustrate the mutual dependency of the house's individual components and their corresponding configuration. They demonstrate, in Richardson's words, "that the openings for the purpose of ventilation must be placed with reference to the system introduced in the rooms in order to become

22
Sylvester, *Domestic Economy*, vi.

23
Ibid., 49.

24
Charles James Richardson, *A Popular Treatise on the Warming and Ventilation of Buildings* (London: J. Weale, 1837), 26, 57, iv.

25
Ibid., viii. For the contemporary architectural-theoretical use of "communication" in the sense of a connection cf. e.g. Sir William Chambers, *A Treatise on the Decorative Part of Civil Architecture*, vol. 2 (London: Priestley and Weale, 1825), 347, 412.

26
Richardson, *Warming and Ventilation*, 62. For Newton's notion of media and its dissemination cf. Leo Spitzer, "Milieu and Ambiance: An Essay in Historical Semantics," *Philosophy and Phenomenological Research* 3, no. 1 (1942), 1–42, here 36–37.

efficient."[27] In particular, this makes the positioning of doors and windows a focus: "Serious professional attention should always be given, not only to the form of the flue, but the position of the chimney breast, with the relative situations of doors and windows."[28] Second, the architectural structure undergoes a process of literal and figurative "operational closure." This entails on the one hand the actual hermetical sealing of the interior rooms vis-à-vis the outside, and on the other the attribution of multifunctional elements to precisely specified "proper uses." "With the warming and ventilation of a dwelling, managed by this apparatus," writes Richardson about an installation described in his book, "we should not depend for the supply of pure air in our rooms on the action of doors and windows. Let them remain as tightly closed as the skill of a modern joiner can make them,"[29] or further, "[t]he doors are meant to admit the occupants to the chambers, and the windows to give the light."[30] Finally, Richardson explains that the inputs and outputs of a closed system must be balanced, taking into account the amount of air entering and exiting a building:

> In admitting a regular quantity of pure air, warmed to an agreeable temperature, it becomes necessary that a corresponding proportion of air should be displaced. Unless this is attended to, no system of warming in a private building will be found successful and satisfactory.[31] (fig. 5)

The consequence of this systematization extends far beyond the problems of heating and ventilation and the context in which they emerged; it goes beyond the immediate environment and everyday activities of residents establishing general terms for the formulation of architectural transmission processes. Thus, the operational principle of central-heating methods was not confined to the limits of the technical installations, but instead encompassed both the internal atmosphere and the use of elements such as doors and windows. The resulting experiments with habitation can be taken as a decisive moment in the socio-technical connectivity between people and their built environment. It simultaneously constitutes the beginning of an ambient technical and climatic knowledge that only reached its full scope in the course of the widespread establishment of building services in the late nineteenth century, and, based on the former, would still later inform ideas of architecture as a controlled environment. In tandem with myriad technical and socio-cultural effects—concepts of hygiene, rationalities governing working and production organization, disciplinary control practices, (self-) techniques of comfort, as well as other architectural distribution systems[32]—efforts to regulate the transient movement of well-tempered air represent a significant origins of the modern idea of the house as a regulator and distributor of diverse flows of energy, substances, and people. Nevertheless, the profound conceptual consequences of this thinking were by no means first manifested in the buildings of classic modernism or with the advent of electronic media, but made their initial appearance in the early phase of the spread of this new technology.

The architectural inferences of building using central-heating and ventilation technologies, and in particular William Strutt's inventions, were drawn as early as 1820 by a young man named John Vallance. In that year, Vallance registered a patent for the concept of a hermetically sealed building. With the exception of a mechanically operated intake for warmed or cooled air, the building was furnished with only two other openings. "To free rooms from distressing heat and cold, Mr. Vallance made his

27 Richardson, *Warming and Ventilation*, 63.

28 Ibid., 12.

29 Ibid., 71.

30 Ibid., 74.

31 Ibid., 58.

32 For an overview of the developments that affected house building in this regard during the "long" nineteenth century cf. Georges Teyssot, "The Disease of the Domicile," *Assemblage* 6, (June 1988), 72–97; Renzo Dubbini, "Birth of the Idea of Comfort," in History of Industrial Design, 1750–1850: The Age of the Industrial Revolution, ed. Enrico Castelnuovo (Milan: Electa, 1990), 86–107.

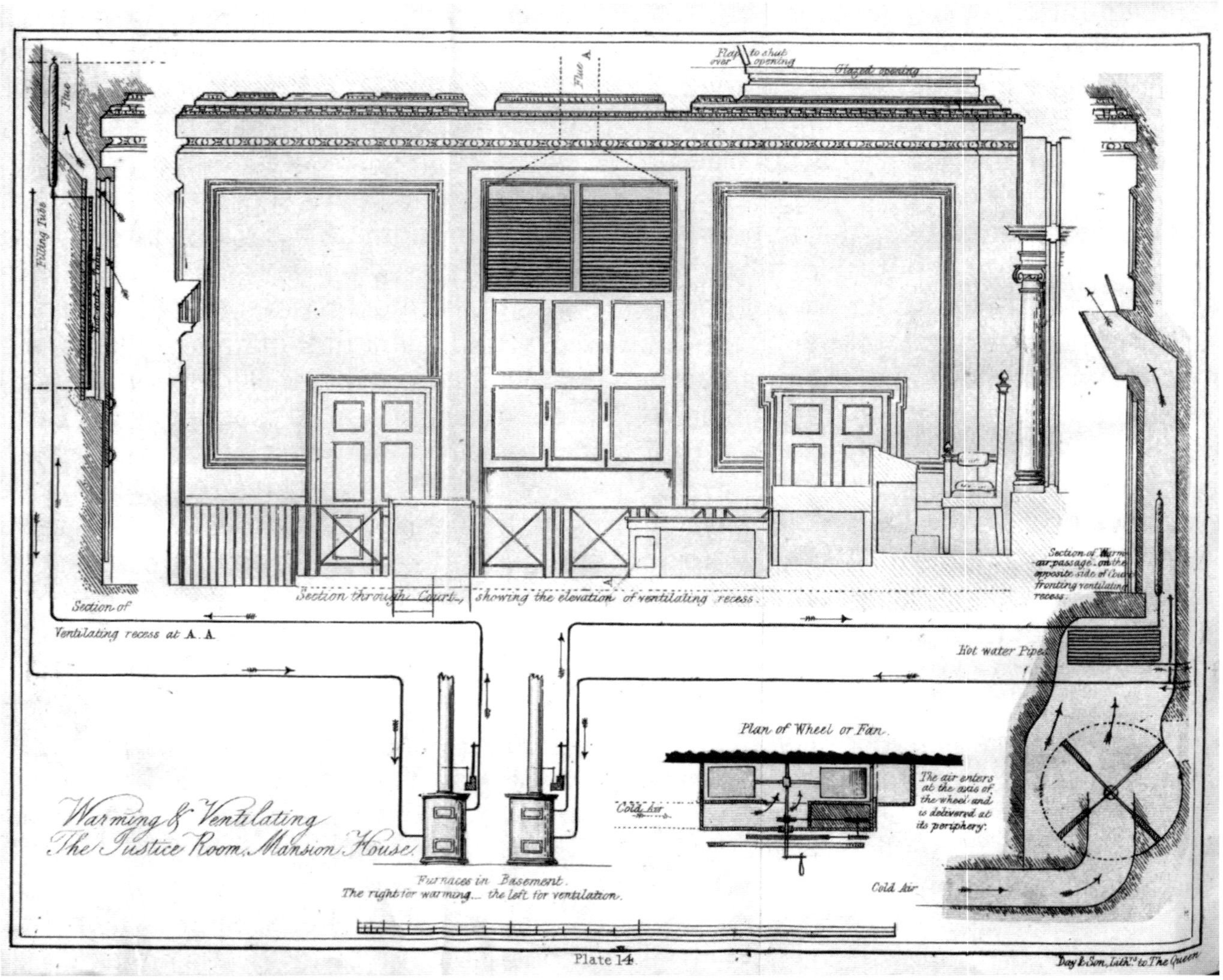

Fig. 5
Charles James Richardson, Warming & ventilating arrangement, 1837.

windows and room air-tight, and left one aperture only in the ceiling and one for the door," ran a later description of the idiosyncratic design.[33] The entrance was equipped with a revolving door hidden in a pillared portico, like a winnowing machine to separate the person stepping in from the outside air, while an aperture in the ceiling was equipped with a water valve designed to allow the external release of air only when a certain atmospheric pressure was reached inside the building. The upshot of this construction, which was presumably never realized in this form, would have been an ideal climatic architecture, the sustained and controlled exclusion of an inhabitable space from the surrounding environment (figs. 6–7). Whilst the editors of the *London Journal of Arts and Sciences* rated the project to be "impracticable and ridiculous,"[34] it nevertheless embodies the basic version of an emerging spatial thinking, namely the conception of architecture as a thermodynamic system.

Twenty years later, the physician and chemist David Boswell Reid, formulated the corresponding discursive inferences. In the course of a protracted dispute with Charles Barry, the architect of the Houses of Parliament in London, Reid, who had been commissioned to execute the building's heating and ventilation system, published a treatise in 1844 that contained a definition of architecture that was as elementary as it was radical:

> After all, though the invisible air is too apt to be forgotten amidst the more obvious attractions of architectural art, still, in a practical point of view, the visible structure is only the shell or body of that interior atmosphere without which existence could not be supported, while it is also the medium of intellectual communication, and the channel through which heat, light and electricity convey their influence upon the human frame. It is no exaggeration to say, that along with those means of defence and seclusion which they naturally present, the great and primary object of architecture is to afford the power of sustaining an artificial atmosphere, such as the constitution under each variety of local circumstances may require.[35]

Therefore, long before Frank Lloyd Wright would talk of a new architectural reality that was space instead of matter, long before Le Corbusier would adopt the term *machine-à-habiter*, and long before Reyner Banham radicalized this approach in the concept of an "un-house" or "environment-bubble" representing a home devoid of all claims to monumentality. Already here in the 1840s the visible constructions of architecture were being stripped of all their aesthetic values and described as mere shells for an enclosed atmosphere. The determining factors of this artificial atmosphere with which the house frees itself of external influences and provides a surroundings for its dwellers are transmitted via the "medium" or the "channel" of air, thereby definitively bestowing an architectural precedence upon it. For David Boswell Reid the Vitruvian *initium topos* of the campfire, the ideal of congregating warmth and direct conversation, has been transformed into an structurally controllable physical and intellectual communication processes and architecture has become describable as a medium.

Translated from the German
by Thomas Skelton-Robinson

33
Walter Bernan, *On the History and Art of Warming and Ventilating Rooms and Buildings*, vol. 2 (London: G. Bell, 1845), 95.

34
"Recent Patents, Vallance's, for Heating and Cooling Rooms," *The London Journal of Arts and Sciences* 7, no. 2 (1821), 26–28, here 28.

35
David Boswell Reid, *Illustrations of the Theory and Practice of Ventilation* (London: Longman, Brown, Green & Longmans, 1844), 71. The grammatical structure of Reid's definition does not permit a clear determination of whether he is referring to air or the architectural structure as the medium and the channel, but the physical understanding current at the time would suggest the likelihood that it is the former. For Reid and Barry and the Houses of Parliament cf. Moritz Gleich, "Architect and Service Architect: The Quarrel between Charles Barry and David Boswell Reid," *Interdisciplinary Science Reviews* 37, no. 4 (2012), 333–45.

Fig. 6
John Vallance, Air-Tight House, 1823.

Fig. 7
John Vallance, Door-way cylinder, 1823.

Image credits

Figs. 1–4
Charles Sylvester, *The Philosophy of Domestic Economy* (London: Longman, Hurst, Rees, Orme, and Brown, 1819), frontispiece, plate II, V, X.

Fig. 5
Charles James Richardson, *Popular Treatise on the Warming and Ventilating of Buildings*, (London: John Weale, 1837), plate 14.

Figs. 6, 7
John Vallance, *A Letter to the Right Honourable the Earl of Chichester*, (London: W. Baynes & Son, 1823), 98, 101.

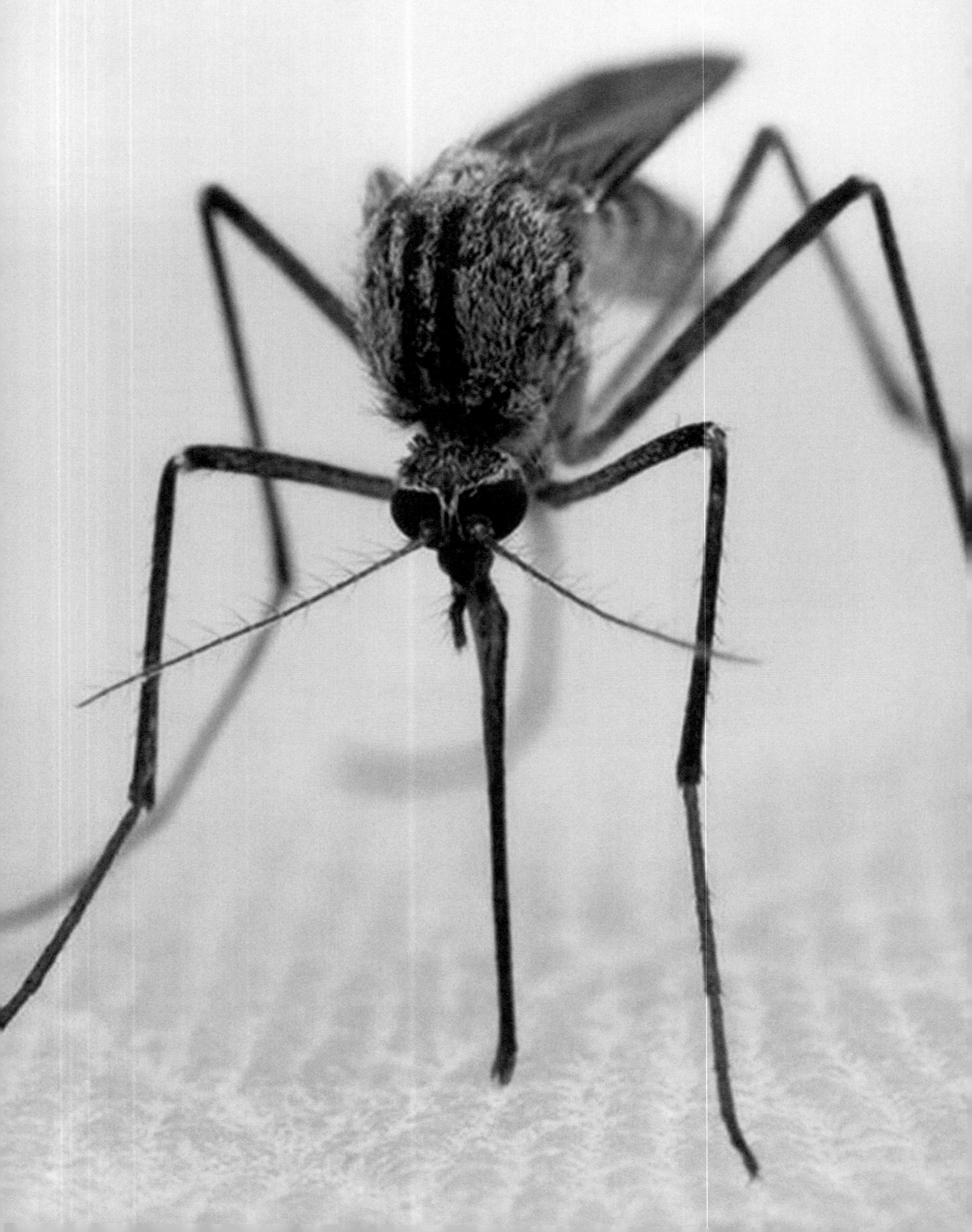

Fig. 1 Pratt & Whitney Aircraft Company Engine Test House, East Hartford, Connecticut. From George Nelson, *The Industrial Architecture of Albert Kahn, Inc.* (New York, 1939), p. 74.

r Bierig

Albert Kahn, Famous Bureaucrat

I. Corporate Architecture Without Architects

Albert Kahn was an exceedingly famous human being. During his lifetime, he was well known and well publicized, not just in architectural journals and magazines, but also in mainstream press profiles, where his "rags-to-riches" story was told repeatedly.[1] This became particularly true through the late 1930s and early 1940s, as coverage tracked his firm's prolific work designing factories for a rapidly industrializing American military. The August 1938 issue of *Architectural Forum* claimed that the work of Kahn's office measured "by sheer bulk" amounted to nineteen percent of all industrial building in the United States at the time. "To reduce this accomplishment to the basis of a formula," the text continued, "would be to miss the essential genius of the man."[2]

Today, in histories of modern architecture, Kahn appears—if he appears at all—not as a genius, but as a symbol of corporate architectural practice. He is remembered as the founder and leader of an immense architectural firm that employed as many as 450 people.[3] The growing scale of operations in Kahn's office necessitated organizational transformations: construction, management, operations, engineering, and the coordination of these multiplying fields. Both contemporaries and subsequent historians interpreted these changes as a reflection, within architectural practice, of the rapidly intensifying methods of industrial production seen in early-twentieth-century America.[4] Some of the seminal examples of those industrial methods were housed in structures designed by Kahn's firm.[5]

This version of Albert Kahn has enjoyed a revival in recent years, most notably in the *OfficeUS* exhibition at the United States Pavilion for the 2014 Venice Biennale of Architecture. In short, Kahn has come to serve as the taproot of a certain kind of world-spanning architectural office. His firm's apparently modern, replicable methods turned it into a crucial antecedent of the kind of extensive design practice that projects oases of rationalized space throughout the world as an accomplice to global capitalism. But in the process of becoming a standard ancestor to the corporate offices of today, Kahn himself disappeared.[6] The image most associated with this Kahn is not his face or any of the buildings designed in his firm, but rather a diagram of the branching corporate hierarchy that organized the work of his office. Kahn became less a historical figure than an emblem of an architectural practice shaped by the dispersed, diffuse, and elusive effects of modern industries and economies.

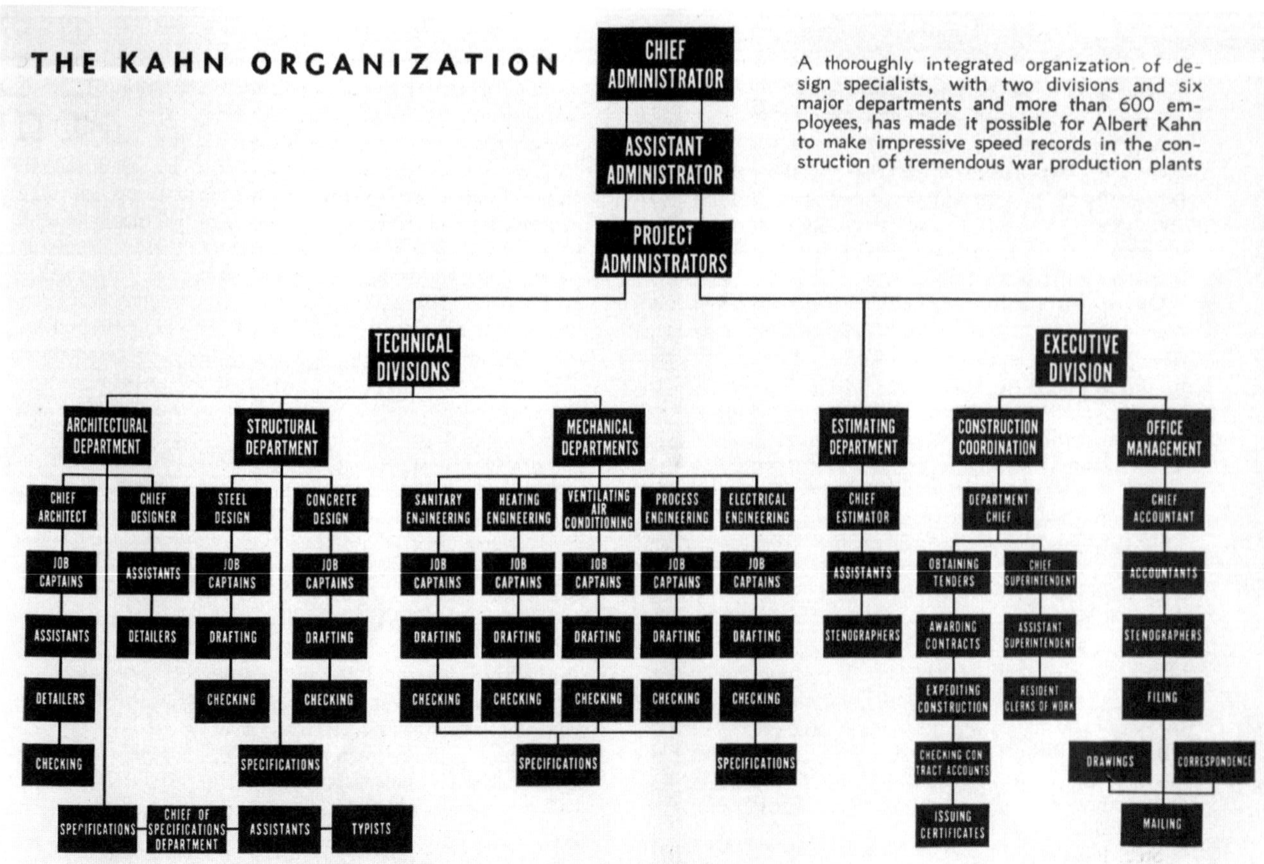

Fig. 2 Office organization diagram. From *The Industrial Architecture of Albert Kahn, Inc.*, 21.

Despite its apparent timeliness, this role for Kahn in the historiography of modern architecture is at least seventy years old. It extends back at least to Henry-Russell Hitchcock's seminal 1947 article, "The Architecture of Bureaucracy and the Architecture of Genius."[7] In the essay, Hitchcock bisected architectural authorship into two types. The architecture of "genius"—exemplified for him by Frank Lloyd Wright—emerged from the artistic will of an individual. The architecture of "bureaucracy" depended instead on a robust, large-scale organization able to seamlessly integrate the myriad concerns of contemporary building: structural engineering, mechanical services, functional space planning, construction management, and so on.

Hitchcock assigned Kahn to embody this second category—even five years after his death he was famous enough to shoulder the weight of "bureaucracy." The choice also indicates something about the deathless status of bureaucracy, which owes its existence to no single human, but rather a ceaselessly shifting and potentially indestructible conglomeration of participants.[8] Thus, Kahn's ghostly appearance in Hitchcock's essay reveals his role in architectural history as non-authorial author. As Hitchcock claimed, the "anonymity" of the work of the office "is the more obvious now that Albert Kahn, the founder, is dead."[9]

But how is anonymity constructed? Who is allowed to become anonymous, how do they perform this disappearing act, and what price must they pay? This essay proceeds from these questions and others that follow: what kind of image did Kahn himself create? In what ways does this image persist, and what does it say about modern architecture and its history? Kahn's particular story involved the collision of his considerable fame and his position at the head of an exceptionally large office. The result was that Kahn became a famous bureaucrat. Which is to say he became a contradiction in terms, since there is no such thing as a famous bureaucrat. This personal transfiguration muddles the pristine rationality with which corporate architectural practice and its histories have often been portrayed. Becoming the image of corporate practice pushed Kahn to perform peculiar acts of dissimulation and self-erasure. Recounting these authorial anxieties, in turn, illuminates certain tensions within the disciplinary self-perception of architecture and the relationship of architects to the economic, social, and public demands they accommodate.

Within many architectural histories that followed Hitchcock's, Kahn's body of work violated a presiding principle of architectural authorship (and perhaps authorship in general). It was inconsistent. The primary evidence for this inconsistency were the historicist, Beaux-Arts-inflected designs he produced in parallel to the concrete, steel, and glass factories for Packard, Ford, and many other industrial concerns. Kahn's office took up residential and institutional projects, often commissioned by the same clients for whom they built factories. These were carried out with eclectic ornamentation; notable examples included the palazzo-like Detroit Athletic Club (1915), a neoclassical office block for General Motors (1919), an Italian Renaissance library for the University of Michigan (1923), as well as houses in varied styles for the Detroit business elite.[10] For historians looking for the development of a coherent authorial voice evident in the visible language of architecture, these inconsistencies put into question the integrity of all Kahn's work.

Fig. 3 Advertisement for American Blower Company, featuring Albert Kahn's 1915 Detroit Athletic Club. From *The American Architect*, July 14, 1915, 15.

Architectural historians John Burchard and Albert Bush-Brown concisely rehearse this position in their 1961 book *Architecture in America*:

> Buildings such as [the reinforced concrete Packard and Ford factories] commanded great respect in Europe, encouraging men like Gropius and Neutra to develop a consistent theory of modern architectural design. Kahn's achievements in [industrial architecture] were in the end genuinely colossal. But he could not universalize them. Suffering the ambivalence of his colleagues, he hardly thought of his best works as architecture at all. He confined realistic design to the lower echelons of the building hierarchy. Thus when he was later asked to design an administrative building for Ford, or the Detroit Public Library, or large office buildings in Detroit for Fisher and General Motors, he and his clients rejected the factory experience and ventured into eclectic dress and ornament. Thus the buildings he wanted most to be fine were least fine.[11]

Like most straw men this stance is an easy target, but it is also lucid. Burchard and Bush-Brown search for a "consistent theory of modern architectural design." As detailed below, Kahn held a theory of modern architecture emphasizing the technical demands of modernity and the organizational processes of the office over an identifiable visual style. The universalization Buchard and Bush-Brown speak of is an aesthetic one.[12]

When other historians looked at Kahn, they hinted that his legacy was not quite as straightforward. Reyner Banham reassessed Kahn's work as part of his 1986 *A Concrete Atlantis.* The book situated late nineteenth- and early twentieth-century American architecture within a broader historical context and argued for the importance of figures like Kahn and pioneering architect-engineer of reinforced concrete, Ernest Ransome. "European modernists," Banham writes, "looking across the full width of the Atlantic and in almost complete ignorance of the former tradition, might have believed that what they saw was radical, unprecedented, and revolutionary; but on its territory and in context, it looks no more radical, no more innovative, than was needed to ensure, step by step, competitive economies for the clients."[13] While this position threatened to minimize the role of designers in negotiating these new "competitive economies," Banham emphasized the newly ruthless conditions under which they had to operate.

Looking closer at Kahn, Banham seemed at once appalled and fascinated by the extent to which his designs were able to accommodate these economizing forces. Images of Kahn's factories that circulated as models of rationality among European modernists were, in Banham's judgment, "cheap and nasty in real life." These represented "the null-value condition, the zero-term of architecture, and hardly any other architect or builder with a professional conscience could have done it. Few could have brought themselves down (or up?) to this level of cheese-paring economy—or ruthless rationality, if you prefer."[14] In his brilliant set of rhetorical oppositions, Banham struggled with the meaning of a "zero-term" architecture. He left open whether the building emerged from an impeccable economy or bleak austerity—Kahn had both risen to the challenge and submitted to external pressures. While there is a sense of disdain in his "cheap and nasty" evaluation, it is evident elsewhere that Banham believed that Kahn, through his embrace of the constraints of modern industry, had produced something undeniably new.

Manfredo Tafuri and Francesco Dal Co's *Modern Architecture* made a similarly ambivalent reference to the originality of Kahn's work. On one hand, they claimed Kahn as one of the figures who had "renewed the American architectural language and equipped it to cope with the new demands" of an intensified industrial capitalism. However, they also highlighted Kahn's divergent stylistic tendencies, his Beaux-Arts projects next to his "logical and meaningful functionalist" work for industry. Based on this divide, Tafuri and Dal Co delivered a diagnosis: Kahn's work presented him as an "oddly split personality."[15] In producing different styles for different buildings, he betrayed himself as incoherent. Kahn, like his firm—and perhaps like America, itself—is legion; an unruly, unformed historical force.[16] But the full meaning of this "split personality" was left open.

In his essay "What Is an Author?" Michel Foucault outlined what he names the "author function": the organization of works that is allowed into the oeuvre of the author. This retrospectively constructed author "serves to neutralize the contradictions that may emerge in a series of texts: there must be—at a certain level of his thought or desire, of his consciousness or unconscious—a point where contradictions are resolved, where incompatible elements are at last tied together."[17] Foucault's author is willful distillation, an editing out of inconsistencies in order to fashion a convincing, fabricated whole. Though he presents this analysis as a way to question fundamental assumptions of authorship, the exercise points toward what he names a "historical analysis of discourse," which, to repeat his terms, might interrogate the conditions under which certain discourses are circulated, valorized, attributed, and appropriated.

We might submit Kahn's persona to the same interrogation. In what follows, I explore a set of crucial episodes in Kahn's self-fashioning. Through them, I want to suggest that Kahn occupies a limit condition of architectural authorship, a case which complicates certain assumptions regarding the discipline of architecture and the conditions of its production.

II. I Have No Dignity to Be Impaired

Albert Kahn was the subject of newspaper profiles, magazine essays, and architectural journal articles that traced the ascent of his firm. The culmination of this trend was the August 1938 issue of *Architectural Forum* dedicated entirely to "The One Man Building Boom."[18] Yet long before that late-career celebration, he balanced his personality between artist and technician, architect and bureaucrat. His "oddly split personality" was a deliberate strategy from the beginning.

As evidence, look thirty years earlier to 1908, when the *Detroit News Tribune* published the first profile of Kahn, alongside his brother, the structural engineer Julius Kahn. Its heroic title: "The Romantic Rise of Two Brothers Whose Achievements Have Worked a Revolution in the Constructive World." The reporter begins in mythic terms: "A man had two sons. One was a dreamer, the other a doer. One saw poetry in life, the embellishments and the beauties; the other saw the structural backbone, the practical relations of concrete things. … One was an artist; the other a builder. One was an architect; the other an engineer."[19]

The architect was Albert; the engineer was his younger brother, Julius.[20] The "revolution" was the brothers' use of reinforced concrete, which began to receive attention for its combination of multistory functionality and resistance to fire, qualities that improved upon traditional heavy timber construction or iron-framed factory buildings.[21] The Packard plant, then under construction, helped establish both Kahns as pioneers in the field.[22]

While this simplified narrative depicted their success arising from a set of fortunate coincidences, historian Chris Meister has shown that the brothers' adoption of reinforced concrete involved at least a decade of painstaking experimentation to develop, patent, fund, and produce a proprietary system of construction. Meister provides circumstantial evidence that the Kahns may have even used a 1901 apartment building to secretly test Julius's designs, perhaps using the structure as a covert way to gather information to apply for a patent.[23] Soon, Julius created his own company—the Trussed Concrete Steel Company—to sell his system to other architects and engineers. Albert was one of his primary investors.

By contrast, the 1908 profile depicted this new system of reinforced concrete as emerging spontaneously from the relationship between artist and engineer. While Albert provided the artistic half of this equation, the profile insisted that he was not too much of an artist. "He left school in Germany when he was eleven. He is self-taught, or, better, office-taught. He learned to design by designing and build by building." Following this hardworking ethic, Albert's instinctive mode was deferral: "To induce him to talk of himself for publication was well-nigh impossible. He would willingly talk for hours of his brother, and of that brother's achievements." The author credited Julius for calculating and testing the substance of the brothers' innovation (he "deals in tangible things, as distinguished from merely perceptible things"), while Albert provided a statement on its visual qualities. "It is a trying problem. Concrete presents many discouragements to the architect. Its ugly surfaces and its lack of fine edge make it a difficult material. … But it is a great deal more interesting to study artistic uses for concrete than to follow along in some old beaten paths. It is difficult, that is why it interests us."

In the course of the article, Albert deferred to his clients and his brother, and even to the material, itself. He discussed how concrete should not be used as "an imitation of stone," and how the "lines of the building" should "indicate that there is behind them a sustaining skeleton." Following a nineteenth-century trope of "truth to materials" that can be extended back at least to Eugène Viollet-le-Duc and Auguste Choisy, he portrays himself as guiding this unfamiliar substance toward a supposedly natural form.

If it was heavy-handed, this self-presentation was also prescient. It anticipated many of the qualities later associated with Albert Kahn: the suspension of contradiction; the delicate balance of being a skillful artist, without being prepossessed; the public figure that shies away from publicity; and the servant of industry who exudes a vague moral compass. Kahn's split personality was already formed at the moment of his arrival.

Seventeen years later, in 1925, an article in *Pencil Points* followed a similar storyline. The magazine included Kahn as part of its "Master Draftsmen" series alongside such eminent designers as Paul Cret, Cass Gilbert, and Charles McKim.[24] By this date, Kahn's name was closely associated with his work in industrial architecture. Consequently, the article begins with a near-apology for his inclusion in the series, arguing that Kahn proves that "being an artist, skilled draftsman, and traveling scholar are not necessarily impediments to remarkable success as a business man, organizer, producer and salesman of his product." Kahn's travel sketches, published in this issue, suggested a further reversal of his persona: "Much as Mr. Kahn has done in raising the standard of intelligence in the design of industrial buildings," the article continues, "his reputation would have been greater, rather than less, had he been limited by different circumstances to the designing of residences and such buildings of the more intimate natures, which call forth the powers to charm."[25]

As narrated by *Pencil Points*, Kahn's "powers to charm" were honed as an "office boy" in Detroit architecture firms after emigrating from Germany in 1880 at the age of eleven. By nineteen, he was made head of residential projects at the office Mason and Rice. One of the partners later recalled Kahn's extraordinary work ethic, stating, "I have never known anyone with such an enormous capacity for concentration and study."[26] Kahn, however, never studied architecture in the academy. The closest he came was on a

European traveling fellowship from *The American Architect and Building News*, which he received when he was twenty. On his journey, he encountered Henry Bacon, a student with extensive Beaux-Arts pedigree.[27] The cultivated Bacon tutored Kahn, who later referred to the period as his "real education in architecture."[28] At the same time, Bacon had rapidly exhausted his considerable funds. Kahn took control of the pair's finances, sustaining them through the trip. Even in his origin myth, that is, Kahn traded his economy for artistry.

Within a few years of his return to Detroit, Kahn established his own office. The commission for Packard (the subject of the 1908 profile) proved to be the turning point. Kahn was soon after hired by Henry Ford to design his new plant at Highland Park, again using reinforced concrete to create spaces of remarkable flexibility. By 1913, the constant improvements at Highland Park led to the development of what many historians consider the first moving assembly line.[29]

This launched the other Kahn, the Kahn of business. *Pencil Points* reported that by 1925 his firm had work "by volume, probably as great as any in the United States." However, the article tried to temper this financial success. Kahn was an artist exploiting business for architecture's benefit: "he is a human being who can do something besides turn the handle of a money-making machine. Business with him is a matter incidental to a more interesting purpose."[30]

What that purpose was, exactly, was a question that hovered over this and later histories. An article from 1929 in the popular publication *The American Magazine* pointed to a fuller erasure of Kahn's authorship. Titled "You Can't Build Skyscrapers with Your Head in the Sky," it focused on Kahn's ability to transform the desires of others into built form.

Kahn's legendary work ethic was again crucial to this narrative. One former client, the article recorded, called Kahn "the human steam engine."[31] Another stock story, published repeatedly—including in an article in *Time* from the same year—was that Kahn supposedly belonged to six country clubs but "has never held a golf club in his hand."[32] *The American Magazine* described Kahn buzzing around his office as a "coatless, acrobatic figure, with its upstanding hair, moving with almost incredible celerity from one group to another."[33] This constant movement was paired with a distinct lack of introspection. "I find that most men worry all through their work about which is to come—the thing they are going to do, the money they are going to get," Kahn tried to explain. "*I worry only about the thing I am doing.* The rest will take care of itself."

As in the 1908 profile, in 1929 Kahn displaced his authorship to almost entirely to others. "Nine tenths of my success," he claimed, "has come because *I listened to what people said they wanted and gave it to them.*" This delegation to the desires of others extended to the nature of the work itself. "When I began, the real architects would design only museums, cathedrals, capitols, and monuments. The office boy was considered good enough to design the factory buildings." This, of course, was a complete fabrication: as mentioned above, Kahn and his brother had spent years developing their system of concrete construction, leading to his prominence in industrial work. But the Albert Kahn in *The American Magazine* had no such pretensions. "I am still that office boy designing factories. I have no dignity to be impaired."[34]

Kahn allowed himself to be portrayed as a hard worker, a "human steam engine," but his authorship was a mere conduit for the desires of others. This was Kahn's second violation of the myth of architectural authorship. Historian Andrew Saint, in his thematic *The Image of the Architect*, looked to Kahn's alter ego Frank Lloyd Wright to outline the conventional myth of the architectural author. Wright's

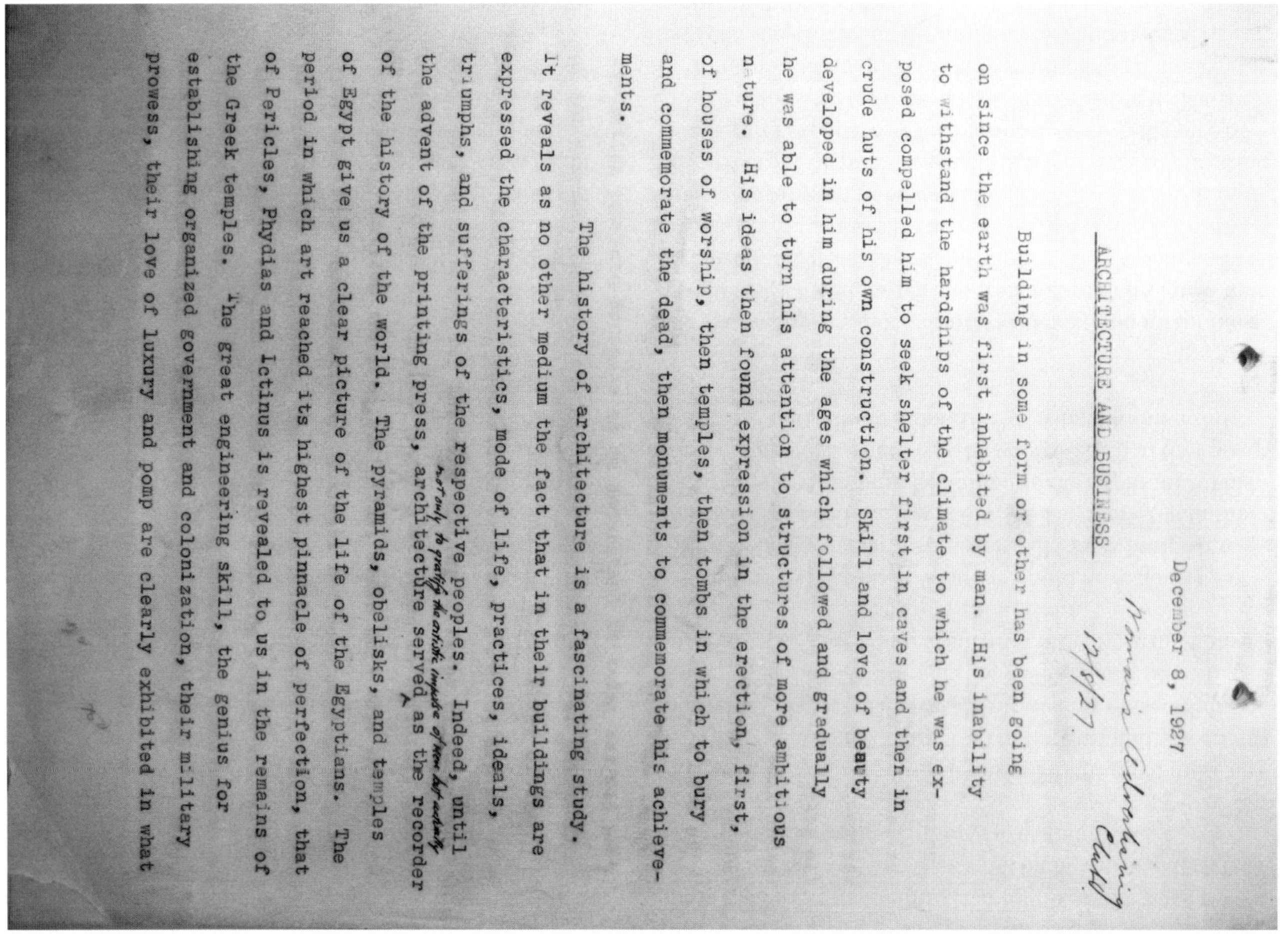

December 8, 1927

Woman's Advertising Club 12/8/27.

ARCHITECTURE AND BUSINESS

Building in some form or other has been going on since the earth was first inhabited by man. His inability to withstand the hardships of the climate to which he was exposed compelled him to seek shelter first in caves and then in crude huts of his own construction. Skill and love of beauty developed in him during the ages which followed and gradually he was able to turn his attention to structures of more ambitious nature. His ideas then found expression in the erection, first, of houses of worship, then temples, then tombs in which to bury and commemorate the dead, then monuments to commemorate his achievements.

The history of architecture is a fascinating study. It reveals as no other medium the fact that in their buildings are expressed the characteristics, mode of life, practices, ideals, triumphs, and sufferings of the respective peoples. Indeed, until the advent of the printing press, architecture served not only to gratify the artistic impulse of man but actually as the recorder of the history of the world. The pyramids, obelisks, and temples of Egypt give us a clear picture of the life of the Egyptians. The period in which art reached its highest pinnacle of perfection, that of Pericles, Phydias and Ictinus is revealed to us in the remains of the Greek temples. The great engineering skill, the genius for establishing organized government and colonization, their military prowess, their love of luxury and pomp are clearly exhibited in what

Fig. 4 "Architecture and Business," speech by Albert Kahn, delivered December 8, 1927, box 1, Albert Kahn Papers, Bentley Historical Library, University of Michigan.

guiding principle, in the words of a contemporary, was to "treat the client rough," reforming their wishes to fit the architect's vision.[35] Saint's book has a single mention of Albert Kahn, which serves as another counterpoint to this unleashed artistic approach. He notes that Kahn refused to hire anyone who had studied architecture at a university, concerned that such employees might "place self-expression over team co-operation."[36] But Kahn's relationship with the academy, architectural discourse, and tensions between an emergent modernism and the Beaux-Arts tradition he had absorbed would be more complicated than a simple rejection.

III. An Era of Misunderstanding

In his 1943 obituary of Kahn, architect and educator Paul Cret wrote, "Albert Kahn was not a theorist: the 'architecture of tomorrow' had little interest for one so engrossed in creating the architecture of today."[37] As opposed to other well-known architects of his time, Kahn seemed to have little interest in affecting architectural discourse within the academy—in addition to turning away architectural school graduates from his firm, he never taught or lectured at a school of architecture.[38] Yet, by the early 1920s Kahn was a regular speaker in many venues, addressing clubs of businessmen and societies of engineers. He also began publishing articles reflecting on design and practice. These essays and speeches cut against the image of invisibility and complicity he tried to convey elsewhere. In them, Kahn grappled with the rapidly changing material conditions of modern architecture, over and against what he saw as a facile aesthetic certitude promoted by some European modernists. In short, Kahn began to formulate a theory of modern practice and its multiplying complications. He believed that modern architecture should not be understood as an aesthetic formula, but rather as the result of the array of material and organizational changes that had transformed practice over the course of his career.

However, the primary theme extracted by others from these statements—both during his life and since—were Kahn's attacks on the aesthetics of what he sometimes called the "ultra-modern" style. During a 1924 speech at the American Concrete Institute, Kahn indicted the Art Nouveau movement as having a "deleterious influence upon design in general and particularly reinforced concrete which permitted the use of such extraordinary forms."[39] In a 1931 speech titled "Architectural Trend," he implored: "Is all that has proven of merit in the past to be abandoned and replaced with crude vagaries? Must the grotesque be substituted for the beautiful? To the dyed-in-the-wool modernist, the work of the past is a closed book to be forgotten and never to be referred to." Later in the speech, he lamented that the "expression of contemporary life and thought need not mean ugly buildings entirely of steel and glass."[40]

Kahn, meanwhile, had become synonymous with steel and glass, most decisively in the August 1938 issue of *Architectural Forum*—which was so popular that the volume was republished as a book the following year, entitled *The Industrial Architecture of Albert Kahn, Inc.*[41] George Nelson was its credited author. A designer and writer, Nelson had graduated in 1928 from Yale University with a degree in architecture. Soon after, he traveled through Europe, visiting modernist buildings and their architects, which he promoted on his return to America. Later he became an editor at both *Architectural Forum* and *Fortune* magazines.[42] In other words, Nelson was a peculiar figure to contend with the stylistically varied work of Kahn. He was as embedded within elite academic and theoretical discourse as Kahn was separated from it.

This tension is palpable throughout *The Industrial Architecture of Albert Kahn*. Nelson began with a simplified history of industrial building, culminating in the influence of industry on daily life, culture, and artistic production.[43] He disparaged nineteenth-century eclecticism as a tradition that had produced "Roman baths for railroad stations" and "pseudo-Gothic" religious buildings. Accordingly, Nelson dismissed much of Kahn's output:

> In addition to factories, the firm has done a large amount of non-industrial work, hospitals—where they are rated as specialists—schools, banks, clubs, hotels, theaters, and office buildings. ... It might be of some interest to note that, unlike the factories, it exhibits the eclectic tendencies which have long been characteristic of American architecture. ... Kahn will speak of "the re-use of well-tried forms" or state that "evolution is preferable to revolution." Coming from one who has played no insignificant part in bringing about an architectural revolution, such statements present a striking contradiction. Perhaps the best explanation is that Kahn, precisely as his contemporaries in 1900, still divides building into factories and architecture.[44]

Nelson split Kahn's personality. He correctly cast Kahn as an architect of the nineteenth century, attempting to preserve the aesthetic ambit of his discipline. In a broader sense, Nelson and Kahn were—like each of us—products of their moment. Just as Nelson's dismissal found traction in the histories and theories that followed, the recently revived interest in Kahn's entanglement with modern technical demands must be, in some way, telling.

In between, however, a subtler understanding of these debates was obscured. Opposed to the ambiguity seen in the articles discussed above, Nelson cleanly erased Kahn's agency; it is the machine age, not Kahn, that produced Kahn's work. "One could argue that industry would have found its new architecture without Kahn," he wrote, "or conversely, that Kahn's career would have flourished without this particular inspiration. All that is beside the point. It happened the way it did."[45] The final step in this argument was to submerge Kahn into the apparatus of his 450-person office. There was, he wrote, "truth in the statement that Albert Kahn, Inc., is Albert Kahn—and vice versa."[46]

The statement was more accurate than Nelson might have recognized. Though he tried to transfigure Kahn into a mute organizational head, the recollection of one former employee reveals how much Kahn, Inc. was, in fact, Kahn himself. Unlike the large architectural offices that took up his legacy—diffuse corporate practices made efficient by the delegation of tasks and expertise—the organizational intelligence of Kahn's office was, to some extent, embodied in its leader. In this sense, Kahn quite literally spanned the distance between the nineteenth-century atelier and twentieth-century corporate firm.

An article from 2001 provides an anecdotal glimpse into the everyday operations of the office. In "Working for a Genius: My Time with Albert Kahn," Henry Jonas Magaziner recounted his experiences from the early 1940s.[47] Magaziner had been employed at a small Philadelphia office when he read the August 1938 issue of *Architectural Forum*, inspiring him to apply for work at Kahn's office. Eventually hired in January 1942, he joined the office during an intense period of work, propelled by the accelerating war effort. As he recounted, the only time the production slowed was on Friday nights, when every drawing made that week was sent to the blueprinter. On Saturday morning, Kahn met with each job captain.

In these meetings, Magaziner recalled, Kahn was able to instantly register inconsistencies within a drawing set—he seemed to hold a comprehensive image of each project in his head.[48] This was also true across the historical breadth of his firm's output. As Magaziner recounted, Kahn would sometimes register a problem with a detail and reference another project: "He seemed to remember every detail on every plant the office had designed."[49]

While these recollections are filled with questionably reconstructed dialogue and characterized by an awestruck tone, they provide evidence showing how Kahn, Inc. was inseparable from Kahn himself. While elsewhere Kahn portrayed his role as mere conduit for the desires of others, here he appears as the irreplaceable center of a vast organization, delegating while also holding an encompassing knowledge. He was the titular head of the firm, but also the gravitational center around which its operations orbited.

It was perhaps because he held such intimate knowledge of the conditions of modern practice that Kahn became so irritated by a doctrinaire, formulaic version of architectural modernism. In a 1932 article he wrote on "The Approach to Design," Kahn ridiculed the recipe of certain architects for whom, to be modern, a building must be "box-like," must have "whether needed or not, vast glass surfaces, in horizontal bands and these preferably carried around the corners; must have flat roofs with pipe rails, no cornices, cantilevered slabs supporting themselves in most baffling manner." This is, he continued, the "formula which the new cult would apply to all types of buildings ... and what is still more amazing the new style is suited not only for one particular country or climate but is proclaimed an 'international style,' applicable as well in China as in Europe and the United States."[50]

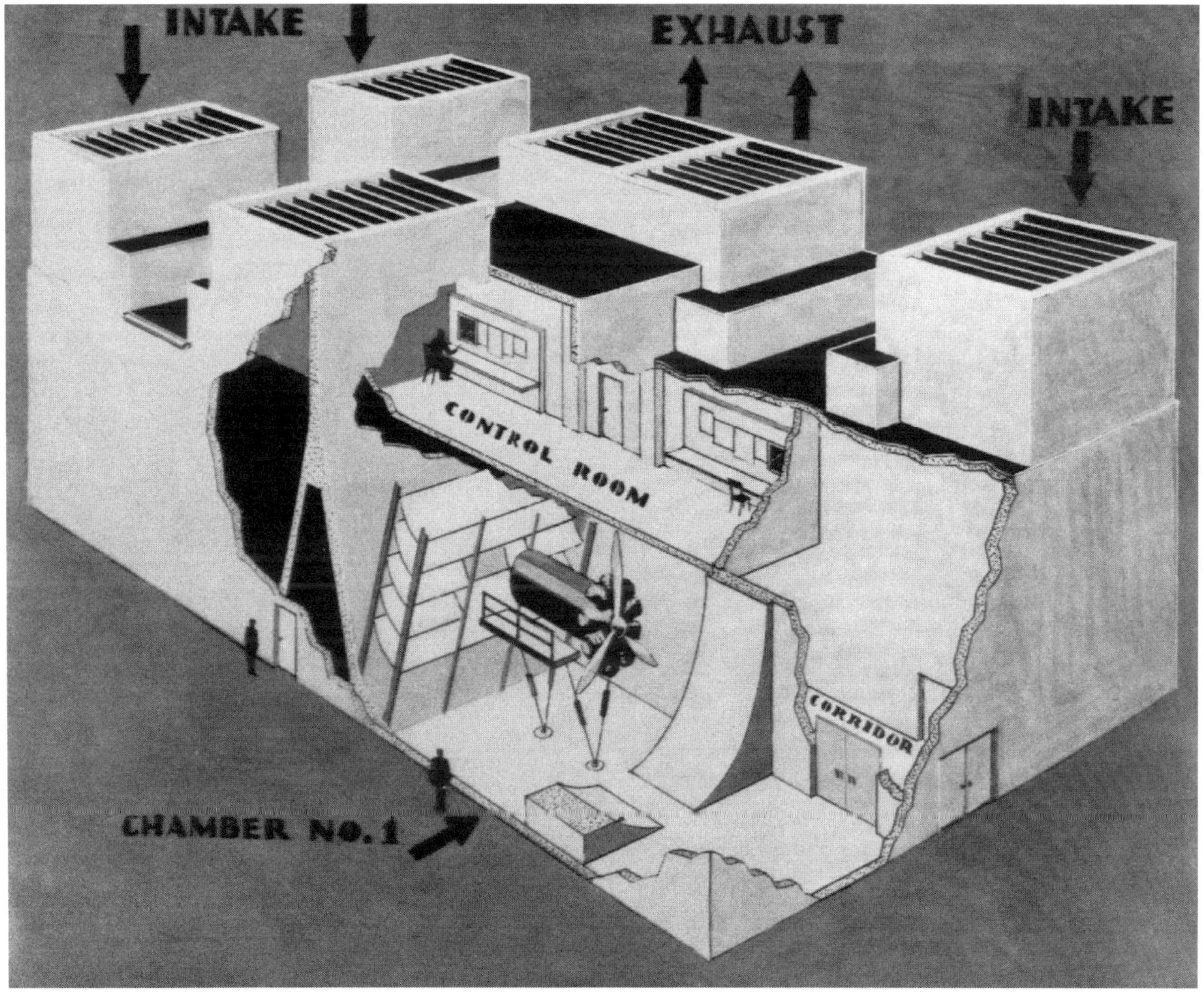

Fig. 5 Pratt & Whitney Aircraft Company Engine Test House, East Hartford, Connecticut. From *The Industrial Architecture of Albert Kahn, Inc.*, 76.

It is striking that Kahn—perhaps the first architect who worked on a worldwide scale—placed "international style" in scare quotes in 1932. He contrasted this placeless image with what he saw as the abandoned principles of building—solidity, consistency, and truth to materials—holding particular disdain for structures "in which all is made to look alike and the cheapest of all materials, stucco, is employed as *the* ideal material." Beyond his opposition to these formulas, Kahn also offered a discerning interpretation of a range of European architects. He expressed admiration for the Dutch architects J. J. P. Oud and Willem Marinus Dudok, and the Van Nelle tobacco factory, all of which, he wrote "are altogether admirable and clearly indicate what modern architecture at its best may be."[51] What he opposed was rigid doctrine, and he identified one culprit above others for this crime:

> Probably no one has done more injury than Le Corbusier and his followers. Only those who have actually seen the finished results can appreciate the difference between their theories and their accomplishments. But for the writers who too often laud their abortive attempts to the skies, form wrong public opinions and cause an era of misunderstanding, their sad creations would probably receive but little notice. It is certainly remarkable what the press agent and the science of advertising may accomplish even in the field of architecture.[52]

Kahn thus criticized what he saw as a perversion of the physical material of architecture through its rhetorical, mediated transformation. Words and theories had come to stand in for material conditions.

Kahn's exception to modernism was acutely architectural and specifically disciplinary. It was a fear of architecture as just another modern object. He resisted what he saw as an ongoing transformation of architecture from a heavy historical and material expression of an improved world into a weightless aesthetic ideology. Inseparable from this was Kahn's critique of architectural authorship. Modern architecture had become the result of multiple concerns and multiple actors:

> In former days, the architect was called upon to merely plan, design and supervise construction. The artistic result was the chief end of his efforts. Building, as compared to today, was a simple matter. Plumbing pipes, ventilating ducts, elevator shafts, electric conduits, acoustics, artificial lighting, refrigeration, air condition and all other adjuncts of building today were unknown, therefore required none of the architect's consideration. These are only a small portion of what must now be properly provided in a structure. Needless to say, no one person could possibly be efficient in all fields, wherefore the day of the individualist, temperamental artist has passed.[53]

In relation to the singular role he held within his own office, this statement becomes more complicated. But it is here that Kahn authors his own authorial absence.

In the late 1920s, Kahn first used an axiom that seemed to typify his approach and was repeated in articles and histories long after: "You will no doubt be surprised to learn that architecture is about 90% business today and 10% art." Rarely, however, are the next sentences included: "And this not only in those operations which serve commercial ends but in those which serve more purely artistic ones, for even in these, business methods must govern. This explains to a large degree why the ancients built more beautifully than we. Theirs was a totally different problem."[54]

Kahn had to account for new structural techniques, new materials, and new functions. Ventilation ducts and insulation batting and heating pipes kept washing into the interstices of his walls, no matter what expression was elected for the outside. Kahn, in other words, provided an alternate approach to architecture and modernity, one in which a split personality constituted the integral center of a reformed discipline.

IV. So-Called Architecture and So-Called Architects

One of the most indelible photographs in *The Industrial Architecture of Albert Kahn* is a forbidding concrete building for Pratt & Whitney Aircraft, an image which opens this essay. Its caption and subsequent drawings cut open and illuminate its initial opacity, explaining that the building was designed to test aircraft engines. It held four isolated chambers, each with its own intake and exhaust system. To sonically dampen the loud engines, the design used a material called calistone, in addition to 18-inch-thick reinforced concrete walls. The building, Nelson wrote, exemplified the idea that a "form taken by a purely functional design has frequently more architectural quality than much so-called architecture."[55]

An architect—as figure or as corporate body—must collaborate with society's most powerful members, those who have a fundamental interest in maintaining the same social structures that afforded their influence. This was certainly the case with Albert Kahn. What was unusual around the turn of the twentieth century was that the form of power itself changed.[56] Much has been written about the ascent of Taylorism and Fordism, of the new techniques of production that characterized the second industrial revolution that Kahn's buildings housed. The shocking unfamiliarity of twentieth-century industrial architecture emerged from this background.

But it also emerged from a unique figure, one caught between multiple worlds. Because of historical circumstance and perhaps disposition, Kahn chose caution and humility in the face of overwhelming transformation.[57] His split personality, as we have seen, was an intentional strategy. The result was a flexibility and openness to defining modern architecture that emerged alongside the methodological flexibility of the modern businesses that his office emulated and defined. Kahn's image, as he presented himself—this seeming contradiction, this famous bureaucrat—indicates some of the unresolved tensions at work in the practice of any architect who must collaborate with the interests of modern economies, industries, and bureaucracies.[58] This is not to lessen the importance of Kahn in the organizational advances highlighted by many of the scholars mentioned above. But corporate architecture was also made by architects. The particular requirements of architecture necessitated personal contortions that were unneeded in fields less reliant upon public reception, or in those calculating disciplines in which authority was less tethered to the inspiration of a single author. In the contexts in which he found himself it was left to Kahn to perform the hard work of mediation.

In other words, Kahn was caught between different worlds. He was an immigrant and an American. He was self-taught, and he received an initiation through his European fellowship and his encounter with the educated Henry Bacon. He had embraced a Beaux-Arts approach, while refusing graduates of Beaux-Arts architecture schools. He was a famous individual who argued that the age of the individualist had passed. He was a nineteenth-century architect who believed in sampling the vast storehouse of history to find an appropriate expression for the march of civilization, as well as a twentieth-century architect reckoning with the wave of technical and social change that upended the shape and scale of the built environment. He was an architect of process, not form, and he saw no other way but to comply with architecture's new technical conditions—its bureaucracy and its multiplying, unavoidable building systems. These were, for him, the churning, cold substance of modern architecture. Kahn was relentlessly opportunistic, but he was also aware of these changes. His position between worlds allowed him to consider and theorize the technical and organizational demands that were transforming the discipline. Kahn did not make a new architecture despite his split personality, but rather because of it.

Research for this essay was carried out thanks to a research grant from the Center for Arts and Cultural Policy Studies at Princeton University. For their patient reading and suggestions, thanks to Matthew Allen, Samaa Elimam, Lisa Haber-Thomson, Andrew Kovacs, Bryan Norwood, and the *Perspecta* editors.

1 For example, see the profile "Poor as a Boy; Rich and Famous at 54," *Detroit Sunday Times*, March 11, 1923, box 7, Albert Kahn Papers, Bentley Historical Library, University of Michigan.

2 George Nelson, *The Industrial Architecture of Albert Kahn, Inc.* (New York: Architectural Book Publishing Co., 1939), 15.

3 This represents an organizational scale unique to Kahn's firm. For comparisons to other late nineteenth- and early twentieth-century practice, see the essential history of American architectural practice: Mary Woods, *From Craft to Profession: The Practice of Architecture in Nineteenth-Century America* (Berkeley: University of California Press, 1999). The size of Kahn's office can be seen as an intensification of the process identified by Jay Wickersham of, in Louis Sullivan's words, "bigness, organization, delegation, and intense commercialism" that transformed architectural practices in Chicago in the late nineteenth century, particularly in the office of Daniel Burnham. Wickersham records that, at his death in 1912, Burnham's office had 180 employees; a successor firm, Graham, Anderson, Probst, and White, employed between 175 and 250 in the 1930s. Jay Wickersham, "Learning from Burnham: The Origins of Modern Architectural Practice," *Harvard Design Magazine* 32 (Spring/Summer 2010): 18–27.

4 Histories focusing primarily on Kahn include Grant Hildebrand, *Designing for Industry: The Architecture of Albert Kahn* (Cambridge, MA: MIT Press, 1974); Federico Bucci, *Albert Kahn: Architect of Ford* (New York: Princeton Architectural Press, 1993); Brian Carter, ed., *Albert Kahn: Inspiration for the Modern* (Ann Arbor: University of Michigan Museum of Art, 1991); Lindy Biggs, *The Rational Factory: Architecture, Technology, and Work in America's Age of Mass Production* (Baltimore, MD: Johns Hopkins University Press, 1996), chaps. 4–7; Terry Smith, *Making the Modern* (Chicago: University of Chicago Press, 1994), chaps. 2–4. More recently, Claire Zimmerman has critically reassessed the work of Albert Kahn Associates within the history of industrial techniques and capitalist development in the early twentieth century. See Claire Zimmerman, "Albert Kahn in the Second Industrial Revolution," *AA Files* 75 (2017): 28–44.

5 See Hildebrand, *Designing for Industry*, 55–61, 126–27, 153–56; Federico Bucci, *Il metodo Kahn/The Kahn Method* (Milan: FrancoAngeli, s.r.l., 2017), 74–82; Claire Zimmerman, "Albert Kahn's Territories," in Eva Franch i Gilabert, et al., eds., *OfficeUS Agenda* (Zürich: Lars Müller Publishers, 2014), 127.

6 See Franch i Gilabert, *OfficeUS Agenda*; Jana Venee Cephas, "Beyond the Factory Gates: Detroit and the Aesthetics of Fordism, 1903–1941" (Ph.D. diss., Harvard University, 2014); Mauro F. Guillén, *The Taylorized Beauty of the Mechanical: Scientific Management and the Rise of Modernist Architecture* (Princeton, NJ: Princeton University Press, 2006).

7 Henry-Russell Hitchcock, "The Architecture of Bureaucracy and the Architecture of Genius," *Architectural Review* (January 1947): 3–6. For interpretations of Hitchcock's text, see Hyun Jung, "Organization and Abstraction: The Architecture of Skidmore, Owings & Merrill from 1936 to 1956" (Ph.D. diss., Columbia University, 2011), 209–12; Michael Kubo, "The Concept of the Architectural Corporation," in Franch i Gilabert, *OfficeUS Agenda*, 37–45. As Jung explains, Hitchcock draws heavily on Max Weber's concept of the two types of authority in the modern world: bureaucratic and charismatic. See Max Weber, *From Max Weber: Essays in Sociology*, ed. H. H. Gerth and C. Wright Mills (New York: Oxford University Press, 1958), 196–252. Daniel Bell (also following Weber) identified this friction between bureaucracy and charisma as crucial to what he called the "cultural contradiction of capitalism": "the radical disjunction between the social structure (the techno-economic order) and the culture. The former is ruled by an economic principle defined in terms of efficiency and functional rationality. ... The latter is prodigal, promiscuous, dominated by an anti-rational, anti-intellectual temper in which the self is taken as the touchstone of cultural judgments." Daniel Bell, *The Cultural Contradictions of Capitalism* (New York: Basic Books, 1976), 37. For another, less polemical interpretation of these issues from around this same period, see John Summerson, "Bread & Butter and Architecture," *Horizon* 6, no. 34 (October 1942): 233–43.

8 On this problem in relation to architecture, see John Harwood, "Corporate Abstraction," in Joseph Clarke and Emma Bloomfield, eds., *Perspecta: Error*, 46 (2013): 218–47.

9 Hitchcock, "The Architecture of Bureaucracy and the Architecture of Genius," 4.

10 Bucci, *Albert Kahn*, 141–63.

11 John Burchard and Albert Bush-Brown, *Architecture of America: A Social and Cultural History* (Boston: Little, Brown, 1961), 242.

12 See Albert Bush-Brown, "The Architectural Polemic," *The Journal of Aesthetics and Art Criticism* 18, no. 2 (December 1959): 148.

13 Reyner Banham, *A Concrete Atlantis: U.S. Industrial Building and European Modern Architecture, 1900–1925* (Cambridge, MA: MIT Press, 1986), 53–54.

14 Ibid., 86.

15 Manfredo Tafuri and Francesco Dal Co, *Modern Architecture*, trans. Robert Erich Wolf (New York: Harry N. Abrams, 1979 [1976]), 238.

16 Here, Tafuri and Dal Co follow a long line of trans-Atlantic appropriations. Its earliest example was offered by Walter Gropius, who, in the 1913 *Jahrbuch des Deutsches Werkbund*, displaced American industrial building in both space and time, writing that structures like Kahn's were "in the force of their monumental impression ... almost comparable to the buildings of ancient Egypt." Walter Gropius, "Die Entwicklung moderner Industriebaukunst," *Jahrbuch des Deutschen Werkbundes* (1913): 21.

17 Michel Foucault, "What Is an Author?," in *Aesthetics, Method, and Epistemology*, ed. James D. Faubion, vol. 2 of *Essential Works of Foucault, 1954–1984* (New York: The New Press, 1998), 215.

18 "One Man Building Boom," *Architectural Forum*, July 1938, box 8, Albert Kahn Papers.

19 "The Romantic Rise of Two Brothers Whose Achievements Have Worked a Revolution in the Constructive World," *Detroit News Tribune*, September 20, 1908, box 7, Albert Kahn Papers. This self-presentation was not unique, even at his early stage. In a 1915 profile in *The Brickbuilder*, the author explained, "Mr. Kahn is not alone endowed with a very keen sense of what is best in art ... but has combined with this rare gift, in an unusual degree, commercial ability of a very high order." "As He Is Known, Being Brief Sketches of Contemporary Members of the Architectural Profession," *The Brickbuilder* 24, no. 5 (May 1915), box 8, Albert Kahn Papers.

20 It is with good reason that the brothers merited a case study in Andrew Saint's of the "sibling rivalry" between architects and engineers. See Andrew Saint, *Architect and Engineer: A Study in Sibling Rivalry* (New Haven, CT: Yale University Press, 2007), 242–49.

21 For a broader discussion of this history, see Peter Collins, *Concrete: The Vision of a New Architecture* (New York: Faber and Faber, 1959), 56–75; Hildebrand, *Designing for Industry*, 28–34.

22 Hildebrand, *Designing for Industry*, 30–34; Collins, *Concrete*, 81–82.

23 Chris Meister, "Albert Kahn's Partners in Industrial Architecture," *Journal of the Society of Architectural Historians* 72, no. 1 (March 1, 2013): 78–95.

24 George E. Hartman and Jan Cigliano, eds., *Pencil Points Reader: A Journal for the Drafting Room, 1920–1943* (New York: Princeton Architectural Press, 2004), 87.

25 "Master Draftsmen XII: Albert Kahn," *Pencil Points* 6, no. 6 (June 1925), 43.

26 Quoted in Hildebrand, *Designing for Industry*, 8.

27 Bacon was then travelling on the MIT Rotch Fellowship. He would go on to design the Lincoln Memorial. See Christopher A. Thomas, *The Lincoln Memorial and American Life* (Princeton, NJ: Princeton University Press, 2002). Hildebrand, *Designing for Industry*, 9–14.

28 Hildebrand, *Designing for Industry*, 9–14.

29 Narrow floor plates (the first were 865 feet long and 75 feet wide) filled the factory with daylight. A sky-lit craneway running the entire length of the building created an arcade-like passage that served as a kind of internal pipeline, allowing all the plant's materials to be transferred throughout the four-story structure. Biggs, *The Rational Factory*, chap. 4; David A. Hounshell, *From the American System to Mass Production, 1800–1932: The Development of Manufacturing Technology in the United States*, (Baltimore, MD: Johns Hopkins University Press, 1985), 223–24.

30 "Master Draftsmen XII."

31 Helen Christine Bennett, "You Can't Build Skyscrapers with Your Head in the Sky," *The American Magazine* 58, no. 6 (December 1929): 121 Also quoted in Meister, "Albert Kahn's Partners in Industrial Architecture," 80.

32 "Great Kahn," *Time* 13, no. 20 (May 20, 1929): 59. See also Donald M. Davies, "Million Dollar Office Boy," *Detroit News*, May 5, 1940. "His work is still his chief recreation. He belongs to six golf clubs but never plays golf. He has never learned to play bridge well—says he is world's worst player. ... A. K. is a queer mixture of smart practicality and sensitive artist. The combination has made him probably the finest industrial architect of our time."

33 Bennett, "You Can't Build Skyscrapers with Your Head in the Sky," 121.

34 Ibid., 124. This was true, Kahn claimed, in his experience with Henry Ford. "A great deal of my knowledge grew from the Fords, father and son," he told *The American Magazine*. "They always have many ideas. Every new building they build has distinctive features. When Henry Ford took me to the old race course where the Highland Park plant stands and told me what he wanted, I was amazed. I had never known of buildings such as he said he wanted. But I designed them, according to his ideas."

35 Andrew Saint, *The Image of the Architect* (New Haven, CT: Yale University Press, 1983), 17.

36 Ibid., 80. Saint's reference is to Hildebrand, *Designing for Industry*, 127, 132.

37 Paul Cret, "Albert Kahn," *Michigan Society of Architects Bulletin*, special issue (March 1943), 25, box 8, Albert Kahn Papers.

38 Kahn's lack of academic training might also have contributed to the persistent resistance to seeing his work and legacy as part of the architectural discipline. For a brilliant and ambiguous statement on these boundaries, see Reyner Banham's final essay, "A Black Box: The Secret Profession of Architecture," in *A Critic Writes: Essays by Reyner Banham*, ed. Mary Banham, et al. (Berkeley: University of California Press, 1996), 292–99.

39 Albert Kahn, "Reinforced Concrete these past 20 years," 1924, 6, box 1, Albert Kahn Papers.

40 Albert Kahn, "Architectural Trend," speech given to Maryland Academy of Sciences, April 15, 1931, box 4, Albert Kahn Papers.

41 My own interest in Kahn emerged from an assignment in 2010 architectural design studio at the Princeton School of Architecture taught by Stan Allen, which used Mies van der Rohe's famous 1942 *Project for a Concert Hall* as its prompt. As I looked into the history of this image, I soon found that Mies (and later, his students) placed a collage on top of an image of an airplane factory from the book *The Industrial Architecture of Albert Kahn, Inc.* See Jean-Louis Cohen, Mies van der Rohe, trans. Maggie Rosengarten (London: E & FN Spon, 1996), 84; Neil Levine, "'The Significance of Facts': Mies's Collages Up Close and Personal," *Assemblage* 37 (December 1998): 70–101.

42 *George Nelson: Architect, Writer, Designer, Teacher* (Weil am Rhein, Germany: Vitra Design Museum, 2008), 340.

43 Nelson, *The Industrial Architecture of Albert Kahn*, 7.

44 Ibid., 18. Nelson's attitude toward authorship became more complicated. Many years later, in 1973, he wrote: "Wherever there is an artifact, whether a small object or an entire synthetic environment, there has to be a designer. It does not matter whether the 'designer' is an individual or a group, and it matters even less what the designer calls himself." Quoted in John Harwood, "The Wound Man: George Nelson and the 'End of Architecture,'" *Grey Room* 31 (Spring 2008): 93.

45 Nelson, *The Industrial Architecture of Albert Kahn*, 16.

46 Ibid., 15.

47 Henry Jonas Magaziner, "Working for a Genius: My Time with Albert Kahn," *APT Bulletin* 32, no. 2/3 (2001): 59–64.

48 Ibid., 62. "Saturdays, when I went down with 25 or 30 large blueprints, I was always amazed. Kahn would spend a minute or two studying a sheet with a dozen details on it, and then he would turn to the next sheet. Typically, when he got to, say, sheet 21, he would comment, 'The detail your man put on the lower right-hand corner of this sheet does not agree with what is shown on the top left of sheet 9.' Kahn had a complete mental picture of each sheet! When I got back to my desk, I would compare the two details. He was correct!"

49 Ibid.

50 Albert Kahn, "The Approach to Design," *Pencil Points* 13, no. 5 (May 1932): 299.

51 Ibid, 300. Elsewhere in the article he pointed to the "excellent work" of German architects Peter Behrens, Paul Bonatz, and Wilhelm Kreis, and "even" Erich Mendelsohn (who had used pictures of Kahn's work in his 1926 book *Amerika: Bilderbuch eines Architekten*).

52 Kahn, "The Approach to Design," 300. As Claire Zimmerman has recently noted, "Compare Kahn, with his nearly 2,000 completed job numbers, and Le Corbusier's 78 constructed buildings; then compare their footprint in architectural history." Zimmerman, "Albert Kahn in the Second Industrial Revolution," 30.

53 Kahn, "Architectural Trend," 25.

54 Albert Kahn, "Architecture and Business," 1927, 3–4, box 1, Albert Kahn Papers.

55 Nelson, *The Industrial Architecture of Albert Kahn*, 74.

56 For a historical overview of these changes, see Glenn Porter, *The Rise of Big Business: 1860–1920* (Wheeling, IL: Harlan Davidson, 1992), 91–120.

57 Others have noted this quality. Chris Meister writes: "Few architectural careers match Albert Kahn's rags-to-riches extreme and few architects received as much attention by the American popular press in the first half of the twentieth century. His rise from poverty to heading his own expansive architectural firm with a long list of international clients is the stuff of a legend drawn from selected reminiscences, drenched with humility, that he fed over the years to journalists, who took it from there." Meister, "Albert Kahn's Partners in Industrial Architecture," 79. Despite his extensive research into the early career of Kahn, Meister does not speculate, as I have tried to here, on why a persona "drenched with humility" would have served Kahn's purposes.

58 The ethics of this position are another matter beyond the scope of this inquiry. Perhaps their most unsettling accommodation was that Kahn, the son of an itinerant rabbi, worked for and tirelessly defended Henry Ford at the height of Ford's paranoid anti-Semitism. See David Lewis, "Ford and Kahn," *Michigan History*, September/October 1982, box 9, Albert Kahn Papers; Edmund Wilson, "The Despot of Dearborn," *Scribner's Magazine*, July 1931, 24–35.

Evangelos Kotsioris

Our daily interaction with architecture is mediated through a vast universe of sensors and controlling devices: the photoelectric sensors of super-market doors, the infrared eye of a touchless toilet flush, the load cell of a high-rise elevator, the ionization chamber of a smoke detector, the night-vision cameras and microphones of a home alarm system, the temperature sensor of a “smart home” thermostat. Our day-to-day engagement with the built environment is a constant negotiation with vast numbers of interconnected electronics that can sense human presence, tell how heavy something is, smell a fire, see in the dark, hear noises, and feel the temperature of a room. All of these sensors monitor and modulate our surroundings for us on a continuous basis. The operation of our houses, offices, factories, cars, airplanes, and satellites are no longer imaginable without them. Sensing architecture is literally all around us.

If this is the case, why don’t architects ever talk about it? Why have serious investigations into the origins of this technology been avoided in disciplinary discussions? In fact, the history of how architecture became sensate is not to be found in the annals and monographs of modern masters. It is an anonymous story that must be pieced together from evidence at the fringes of or even outside the discipline. The media landscape of sensor control systems has slowly but steadily constructed itself in front of architects’ eyes for more than a century. This landscape has taken the shape of patented inventions, trademarked devices, and branded products that promised to develop intimate feedback loops between us and our surroundings. Sensor control systems do not constitute a separate form or media to be studied in isolation, but rather they are one among multiple forms of material media, a material complex that surrounds us. In that respect, these systems cannot simply be relegated to a building-systems appendix. Instead, we must recognize that sensor control systems constitute architecture in their own right. Sensor control systems constitute part of an architecture we already inhabit.

How did we get here?

SENSORS

In 1948, Norbert Wiener defined the science of cybernetics as “the scientific study of control and communication in the animal and the machine.”[1] Cybernetics, the neologism used to define the burgeoning field of control and communication theory, originated in the Greek word *kyvernētēs*, meaning steersman or governor.[2] In his 1950 book *The Human Use of Human Beings*, Wiener explained the main points of his cybernetic theory in simple language. There, he describesd feedback as the “control of a machine on the basis of its *actual* performance rather than its *expected* performance.”[3] Feedback is a corrective mechanism interested in action, rather than theory. To elucidate this interpretation of the term, Wiener provided an architectural example: “The automatic photoelectric door opener is known to every person who has passed through the Pennsylvania Station in New York,” he wrote. “When a message consisting of the interception of a beam of light is sent to the

Sensing Architecture

apparatus, this message actuates the door, and opens it so that the passenger may go through."[4] Although it was a recent invention, the motion-activated door was found in familiar settings, allowing Wiener to make a point for a general audience: feedback systems comprising sensors and controlling devices were already part of everyday life. In other words, a technological revolution had taken place unannounced: the cybernetization of architecture was well underway, and architects had clearly missed it.

Less than two decades later, in 1967, Marshall McLuhan famously posited that media are extensions of our senses and "work as environments."[5] But in the age of "electric drama," he argued, these "really total and saturating environments are invisible. The ones we notice are quite fragmentary and insignificant compared to the ones we don't see."[6] Sensor control systems as architectural media have similarly been with us for quite a while, but almost never to be seen. Despite their omnipresence, sensors have evaded the scrutiny of architectural historians, who have left historians of technology to narrate the development of sensor control systems as a subtopic related to building services or mechanical engineering. Sensor control systems have consistently been brushed aside as just another mechanical system to have crept into the bodies of buildings over the last century and a half. Electricity, plumbing, heating, and telephony have received their fair share of recent historicization, paved largely by seminal accounts such as Sigfried Giedion's 1948 *Mechanization Takes Command* (published in the same year as Wiener's *Cybernetics*) and Reyner Banham's 1969 *The Architecture of the Well-Tempered Environment*.[7] Despite the permeation of sensor control systems in architecture before both of these two books were written, the words "sensor" and "feedback" are glaringly absent.

MAGIC

Wiener's example of the motion-activated door is one of the first examples of how sensor control systems began infiltrating American architecture *en masse*. Developed and patented by General Electric (GE) between 1930 and 1934, motion-activated doors made use of photoelectric cells to detect approaching users.[8] Produced and promoted at an industrial scale by the Stanley Company, Magic Doors became an immediate commercial success in restaurants, office buildings, hotels, and department stores (fig. 1).[9] For unsuspecting users, the doors induced reactions ranging from bewilderment to sheer horror. "It was weird, uncanny!" a local man reported to the *Boston Sunday Post*, after entering for the first time the Stanley doors installed at the Atlantic National Bank in Boston.[10]

The first users of this architecture wondered: How could architectural motion be a response to a seemingly

1 Norbert Wiener, *Cybernetics, or Control and Communication in the Animal and the Machine* (New York: John Wiley & Sons, 1948).

2 Ibid., 19.

3 Norbert Wiener, *The Human Use of Human Beings: Cybernetics and Society* (London: Free Association Books, 1989), 24.

4 Ibid., 23.

5 Marshall McLuhan and Quentin Fiore, *The Medium Is the Massage* (Berkeley, CA: Gingko Press, 2001), 26.

6 Marshall McLuhan, "The Invisible Environment: The Future of an Erosion," *Perspecta* 11 (1967): 164.

7 Sigfried Giedion, *Mechanization Takes Command: A Contribution to Anonymous History* (New York: Oxford University Press, 1948); Reyner Banham, *The Architecture of the Well-Tempered Environment*, 2nd ed., (Chicago: University of Chicago Press, 1984).

Fig. 1
Page from Stanley Company's brochure on the applications of "magic doors," ca. 1937. *Stanley Magic Door Controls*, brochure, ca. 1937. ID:89-B5028, Franklin Institute Trade Catalogue Collection, Canadian Centre for Architecture, Montreal, Quebec.

dissociated human trigger? When Magic Doors were installed in the dining room of the Stevens Hotel in Chicago in 1931, the *Daily Tribune* went as far as to report that they responded to the "shadows" of waitresses.[11] Many of these articles cite the folk tale of "Ali Baba and the Forty Thieves" as an allegory of the responsive architecture performed by Stanley's invention. However, as the *Boston Sunday Post* noted, in Ali Baba's tale there existed a clear connection between verbal command—"Sesame, open!"—and the opening of the treasure cave.[12, 13] How was this new kind of electric magic enacted?

Stanley's stunt relied on architectural mystery. The amount of design effort that went into concealing the sensors and control mechanisms of its Magic Doors attests to the paramount importance of this imperative. At train stations and movie theaters, Stanley's photoelectric cells were embedded in queue line poles right before thresholds.[14] In retail stores, like Neiman-Marcus in Dallas, they were embedded in the sides of the shopping windows framing each entrance.[15] In GE's official journal, Stanley's sophisticated electron tubes even appear hidden inside a pair of planters flanking the doorway of the Wilcox's Pier Restaurant in Savin Rock, Connecticut.[16]

While the GE and Stanley patent drawings exposed the individual components of the complex contraption, their architectural integration was deliberately veiled (fig. 3). Through meticulous concealment, the motion-triggered "electric eye" and the hydraulic mechanism that opened the door were made indiscernible to the unsuspecting eye. Popular magazines were keen to expose the fact that the workings of the trigger mechanism were kept out of sight: "the secret of the door's remarkable behavior is an inconspicuous ray of light crossing the path of approach"[17] (fig. 4). When a photograph of the installation at Pennsylvania Station in New York, was published in *Popular Science* it was annotated with two arrows identifying the unexpected location of Stanley's light- sensitive cells[18] (fig. 5). These and countless similar exposés, vignettes, and diagrams reveal the concealed power behind the magic.

Reyner Banham made a distinction between architecture's "concealed" and "exposed power" to theorize the introverted and exhibitionist treatment of mechanical services in the articulation of buildings.[19] But this dichotomy could have not been theorized outside the philosophical lineage of Cartesian duality between mind and body. It was precisely this mysterious rift between sensory input and physical reaction that René Descartes

Fig. 2
Louis de La Forge, engraving of stimulus–reflex action, from the French translation of René Descartes's *Treatise on Man*, 1664.

René Descartes. *Tractatus de Homine*. (Amsterdam: Apud Danielem Elsevirium, 1677), 58. Originally published in René Descartes. *L'Homme de René Descartes*. (Paris: T. Girard, 1664), 27.

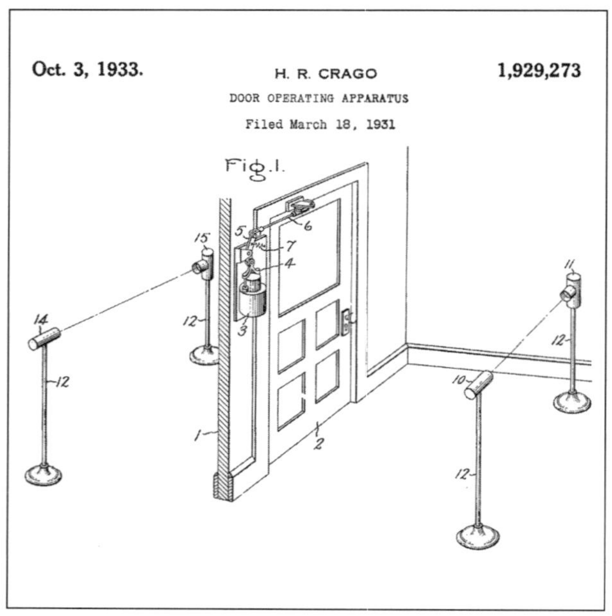

Fig. 3
Patent drawing from General Electric's "Door Operating Apparatus," 1933.

H. R. Crago, Door operating apparatus. US Patent 1,929,273, filed March 18, 1931, and issued October 3, 1933.

had attempted to reconcile in *De Homine*, his 1662 treatise on the human body and its workings [20] Descartes famously proposed a mechanical understanding of embodied cognition. To interpret the reflexive response, in *De Homine* he uses the example of a human limb retracting when approaching too close to an open fire (fig. 2). According to this schema, an external stimulus sensed by the body travels through the nerves to the pineal gland, which plays the role of the governor. In turn, the pineal gland sends a signal back to muscles in the foot, causing it to retract. Despite the fact that Descartes's theory has known medical inconsistencies today, his mechanical model is significant for its combination of sense organ, message channel, and governor. It formed the conceptual basis and explanatory diagram for nearly all modern sensor control systems.

Door That Is Opened by Electric Eye When Approached, and Apparatus Which Operates It

Fig. 4
Illustration of an early automatic door and the electric eye apparatus that opens it.

"Door That Opens Itself Is Boon To Waitresses," *Popular Mechanics* (Feb. 1931), 199.

ALARMS

If Magic Doors were designed to facilitate the influx of people into spaces, inventors and engineers went to similar lengths designing devices that would keep them out. Some of the first motion-detecting burglar alarms to make a sensation in American press were developed and patented in the early 1950s by electrical engineer and prolific inventor Samuel M. Bagno.[21] An early example of his, which was immediately featured in *Time* magazine, could detect movement by sensing variations in the sound waves bouncing off walls and furniture in confined spaces.[22] "The air of the room to be protected is filled with ultrasonic waves," Bagno writes in an article on alarm system design.[23] If the exteriors of churches and tombs were once adorned with apotropaic symbols to deter intruders, in the age of cyber-physical architecture, electronic sensors protecting buildings were tactfully hidden. Virtual environments became the new site of architecture.

In one of Bagno's patent drawings demonstrating the installation of his alarm (fig. 6), protected space is represented as a generic cube, punctured only by a conventional, double-hung window and a half-light door. The true architecture in this drawing, though, is not to be found in the solid lines but in the array of concentric arcs that represent signal emissions. It is a new kind of architecture, produced by the vigorous sound waves of the alarm system emitted at an ultrasonic frequency, inaudible to the human ear. Bango's later designs for an "Optical Space Alarm"[24] (fig. 7) go as far as to question the age-old function of architecture as fortification. Solid walls are drawn paper-thin, rendering massive masonry with the flatness of an insubstantial surface. A bundle of deflecting lines in plan represents the alarm's infrared light beams, emitted from a light source

---

8 Crago, Door Operating Apparatus; A. S. Fitz Gerald, Automatic Door Opening Mechanism, US Patent Office 1,972,682, filed June 12, 1930, and issued September 4, 1934.

9 For Stanley's own patent and a brochure with its extensive applications see S. S. Roby et al. Apparatus for Operating Doors, US Patent 1,978,093, filed November 23, 1931, and issued October 23, 1934; *Stanley Magic Door Controls* (New Britain, CT: The Stanley Works, 1937), ID:89-B5028, Franklin Institute Trade Catalogue Collection, Canadian Centre for Architecture, Montreal.

10 John T. Brady, "Don't Even Use Magic Words to Open Untouched Doors," *Boston Sunday Post*, June 7, 1936, A4.

11 "'Shadow' Opens Door to Dining Room at Hotel," *Chicago Daily Tribune*, June 24, 1931.

12 Brady, A4

13 The phrase appears for the first time in *Les Mille et une nuits, contes arabes; traduits en français par M. Galland,* vol. 11 (Lyon: Briasson, 1717).

14 "Self-Opening Station Doors Worked by 'Electric Eye,'" *Popular Mechanics* 62, no. 2 (August 1934): 234.

15 *Stanley Magic Door Controls*, 12.

16 See "magic doors" installation by the Stanley Co. in B. S. Havens, "Industry Adopts the Electron Tube," *General Electric Review* 34, no. 12 (December 1931): 718.

17 "Electric Eye Opens Automatic Door," *Popular Science Monthly*, October 1930, 34; see also "Door That Opens Itself Is Boon to Waitresses," *Popular Mechanics*, February 1931, 199.

18 "Electric Eye Opens Railway Station Doors," *Popular Science* 124, no. 3 (March 1934): 21.

19 Banham, *The Architecture of the Well-Tempered Environment*, 195ff.

20 Appeared first in Latin as *Renatus Des Cartes, De figuris et latinitate donatus a Florentio Schuyl* (Lugduni Batavorum: Petrum Leffen & Franciscum Moyardum, 1662).

21 For a rare, if short, biographical note see: "Bagno, Samuel Meyer," in *Encyclopedia of American Biography: New Series*, vol. XL (West Palm Beach, FL: The American Historical Company, Inc., 1970), 280–81.

22 Samuel M. Bagno, Method and Apparatus for Detecting Motion in a Confined Space, US Patent 2,655,645, filed September 26, 1947, and issued October 13, 1953; "Science: Ultrasonic Alarm," *Time* 62, no. 17 (October 26, 1953): 91.

23 Samuel M. Bagno, "Designing Ultrasonic Alarm Systems," *Electronics*, August 1955, 106.

24 S. M. Bagno, Optical Space Alarm, US Patent 3,370,284, filed January 21, 1965, and issued February 20, 1968.

At left, passenger transport plane making a landing in a small field with the aid of its air brakes. Below diagram shows how air brakes decrease required landing space by cutting the speed at which a big plane can come down to the earth

AIR BRAKES ON PASSENGER PLANES CUT LANDING SPACE

Air brakes, already tried out successfully on a few private aircraft, enter the field of passenger transport for the first time with their installation in a fleet of new transcontinental air liners. The brakes consist of special flaps, mounted on the trailing edge of an airplane wing. They are depressed in landing and reduce the machine's speed so much as to decrease the required landing space by two-thirds. Thus they end a dilemma of aviation engineers, whose problem was to design faster airplanes without increasing their landing speed or extending the space required for a safe landing. As shown in the accompanying diagram, a plane equipped with the brakes can roar up to an airport at cruising speed and then abruptly sit down.

SPIN OIL AT HIGH SPEED TO TEST IT

This machine spins oil at high speed to test its efficiency as a lubricant

Outstanding problems of lubrication may be solved by a new machine, first of its kind, that tests and grades oil by whirling it on metal bands at speed up to 22,000 revolutions a minute. By weighing the bands before and after the test, as shown at left, engineers can gage the ability of the oil to penetrate and cling to metal. The first research task of the machine will be to solve lubrication problems involved in the operation of railway transportation.

Above, subway car insulated to keep out all noise. In ceiling are ventilation ducts. In oval, chains between cars covered with rubber to deaden the noise

ELECTRIC EYE OPENS RAILWAY STATION DOORS

Following successful tests of a single installation, six main doorways of the Pennsylvania railroad terminal in New York City are to be equipped with magic doors that open without the touch of a human hand when anyone approaches them. Operated by a light-sensitive electric eye, the new type of door has proved a boon, during its initial trial, to elderly persons and porters laden with bundles. This is believed to be the first application in a railway station of doors opened by the operation of photo-electric cells, although similar installations have been made elsewhere.

Railway station door opens itself at pedestrian's approach

SOUNDPROOF CAR MAKES NOISY SUBWAY QUIET

Subway riders in New York City recently enjoyed the novelty of silent travel when a soundproof car of new design received its first service tests. Insulation shuts out the roar, while five air-conditioning ducts in the ceiling take the place of open windows to bring fresh air to passengers. Even the clank of hanging chains between the cars is suppressed by encasing them in rubber tubing. To demonstrate the efficiency of the car the windows were opened during the trials and the familiar deafening noise was heard.

MARCH, 1934 21

Fig. 5
Photograph of "magic doors" at New York's Penn Station with arrows indicating the location of the "electric eye" ray, *Popular Science*, March 1934.

"Electric Eye Opens Railway Station Doors." *Popular Science* 124, no. 3 (March 1934): 21.

toward a "photosensor," which saturate the interior space. The function of the wall is here reduced to that of a reflector of photons, emitted at a frequency imperceptible to the human eye. The filtering of bodies, once relegated to doors, windows, and locks, is singlehandedly made obsolete. Sensors and controllers defeat bricks and mortar. The rulebook of architecture as a defensive device is effectively rewritten.

NERVES

Sensor control systems promised to provide a new level of awareness for architecture's users. Motion sensing alarms, like those devised by Bagno, would provide peace of mind by becoming a remote pair of watchful ears and eyes; a spatially distributed sensorium. In his 1967 book, *The Medium Is the Massage*, Marshall McLuhan argued that electric circuitry was an "extension of the central nervous system."[25] Long before the invention of artificial neural networks, McLuhan further contended that "the extension of any one sense alters the way we think and act—the way we perceive the world"[26] (fig. 8). Similarly, sensor control systems have radically changed not only the way we understand our own expanded sensorium, but also the ways in which we oversee and regulate architectural environments.

For modern architects, analogies related to sensory perception and the nervous system played a central role in the conception and understanding of the modern subject.[27] Yet, far less attention has been paid to the fact that the nervous system also served as a metaphor for the networks of information meandering through buildings. During his 1934 visit to New York, Le Corbusier was utterly shocked by the glass-encased, building

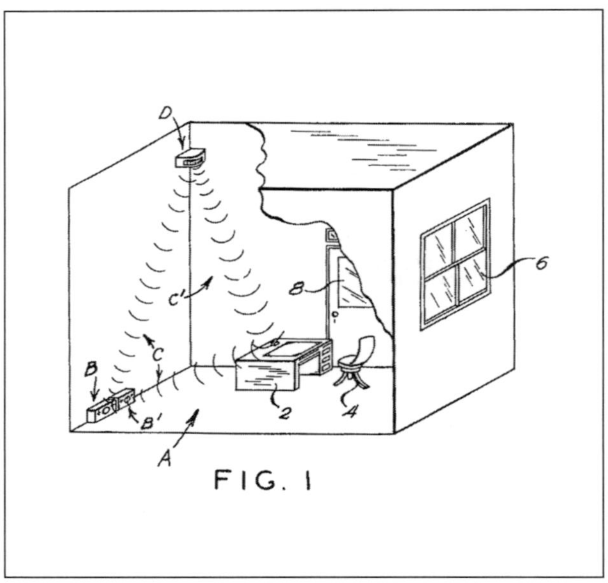

Fig. 6
Patent drawing from Samuel M. Bagno's "Method and Apparatus for Detecting Motion in a Confined Space," 1947–53.

US Patent 2,655,645 filed September 26, 1947, and issued October 13, 1953.

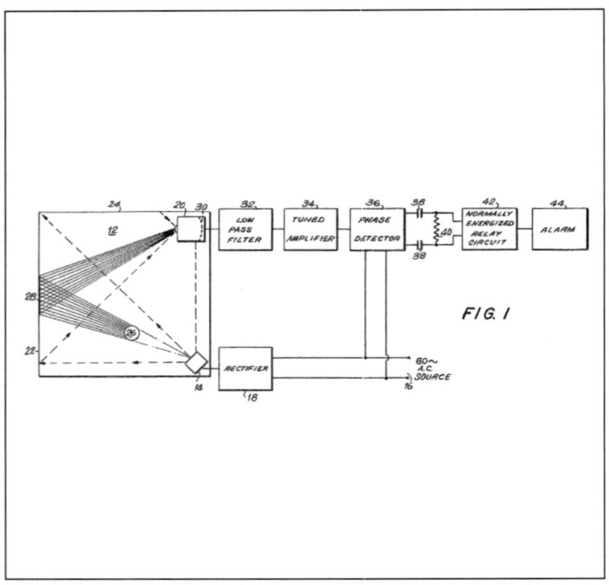

Fig. 7
Patent drawing from Samuel M. Bagno's "Optical Space Alarm," 1965–68.

US Patent 3,370,284, filed January 21, 1965, and issued February 20, 1968.

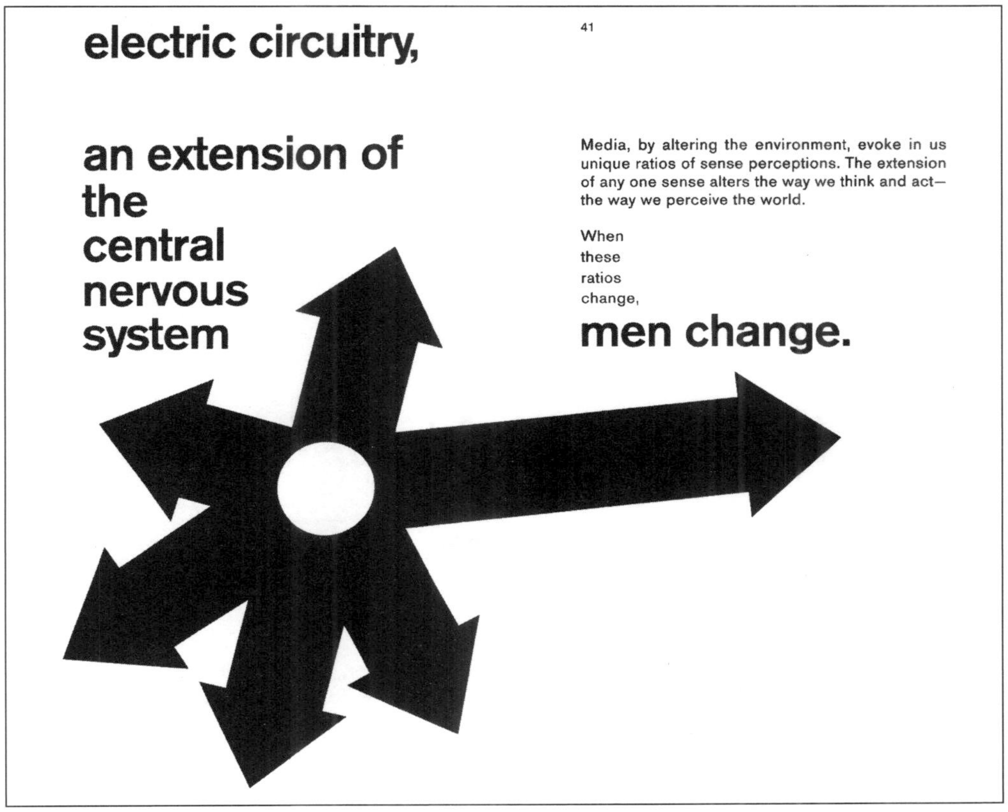

Fig. 8
Quentin Fiore, spread from McLuhan and Fiore's *The Medium Is the Massage*, 1967.

Marshall McLuhan and Quentin Fiore. *The Medium Is the Massage*. Berkeley, California: Gingko Press, 2001 [1967] 40–41.

services control room at the newly completed headquarters of the Radio Corporation of America, the RCA Building (fig. 9). For Le Corbusier, this "nerve center" was "the eye that sees everything, the brain that perceives everything."[28] For someone as fascinated with the human nervous system as Le Corbusier (fig. 10), the control room of the RCA Building embodied a new type of architectural brain: a singular space that had the ability to telescopically gather in a single location the input of myriad temperature sensors dispersed throughout Rockefeller Center. Reminiscing of his visit he later wrote, "everywhere in the skyscrapers there are thin 'guardian' tubes equipped with temperature recording instruments. When the temperature rises several degrees above normal, a bulb lights up on the panel. A bell rings. The place is known immediately."[29]

Le Corbusier considered himself at the forefront of the development of architecture aimed at controlling physical comfort. He authored the *brise soleil* (sun screen) intended for buildings in sun-drenched geographies, the principle of *respiration exacte* (exact respiration), and the *murs neutralisants* (neutralizing walls) initially proposed for the Tsentrosoiuz Building in Moscow.[30] However, when compared to early American sensor and

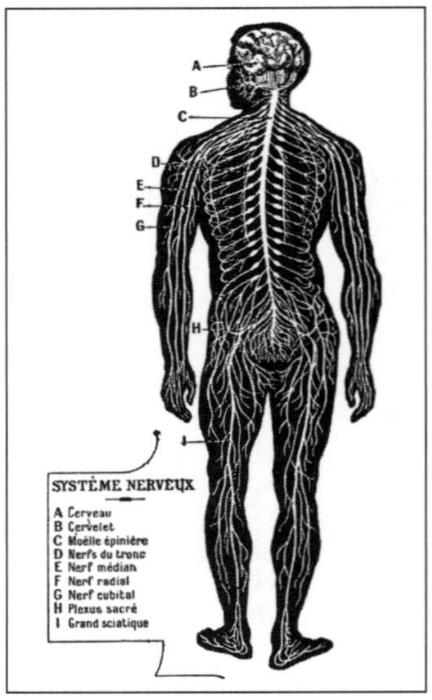

Fig. 9
"Système nerveux," illustration from *Petit Larousse illustré* (1906) included by Le Corbusier in *L'Art Decoratif d'Aujourd'hui*, 1925.

Original included in dictionary entry for the word "homme" in Pierre Larousse, *Petit Larousse illustré: Nouveau dictionaire encyclopédique* (Librairie Larousse, 1906), 474; republished in Le Corbusier, *L'Art Décoratif d'Aujourd'hui: Collection de "L'Esprit Nouveau,"* (Paris: G. Cr es et cie, 1925).

Fig. 10
"Nerve center," remote central control board, main control room, NBC studios, RCA Building, Rockefeller Center, *Architectural Record*, January 1934.

"The Radio City Broadcasting Studios of the National Broadcasting Company." *The Architectural Record*, January 1934, 73–92.

control systems, such as that implemented at the RCA Building in New York, Le Corbusier's inventions appear to fully belong to Banham's "first machine age" of architecture. It is rather telling that in his report of his visit to the RCA Building, Le Corbusier does not appear to grasp the fact that the air-conditioning temperature of all individual studios and nearly one hundred other individual spaces was automatically regulated by means of a network of centrally controlled thermostats.[31] Instead, Le Corbusier writes about workers he assumed would have to physically visit each of the spaces to manually adjust their corresponding temperatures. Baffled by the true climate-controlling potency of the glazed control room, he ultimately concludes: "The glass cage is diabolical."[32]

THERMOSTAT

The history of sensing architecture throughout the twentieth century could be told entirely through the thermostat. While the invention stretches back to at least the nineteenth century, it was in post–World War II America that the thermostat crept under the skin of every house, retail space, and office tower. As closed-loop regulating devices, thermostats are continuously seeking to restore temperature to a predefined setting. For Wiener, on the one hand, thermostats were paradigmatic of widely implemented "feedback chains in which no human element intervenes."[33] As electromechanical devices that emulated the biological function of homeostasis, thermostats presented a familiar example of cybernetic principles in everyday life. From McLuhan's standpoint, on the other hand, the thermostat presented another embarrassing defeat for architecture. As he explained in *Understanding Media*, "electric technology, extended to the job of providing global thermostatic controls, points to the obsolescence of housing as an extension of the heat-control mechanisms of the body."[34] In McLuhan's eyes the house lost its status as an interstitial layer between the human and the environment. The thermostat short-circuited this relationship by operating as an intermediary, as a medium in his sense of the term. The thermostat become an extension of our own homeostatic mechanism, making the primordial understanding of architecture as a climate-regulating shelter appear painfully outdated.

In the late 1930s, the Minneapolis Honeywell Regulator Company introduced a series of affordable thermostats that promised to automate the heat regulation of the American house. As a "revolutionary addition to human comfort," Honeywell's Acratherm thermostats were meant to eradicate heat fluctuations by dynamically controlling not merely the switching on and off but also the intensity of operation of domestic heating and cooling systems. The language employed by Honeywell for the advertisement of the Acratherm series is clearly rooted in a cybernetic understanding of the thermostat's function as a component of a feedback mechanism. As one print advertisement from this period explained, Honeywell's "automatic heating and air-conditioning" is made possible through the device's "controls, which *govern* the operation of the burner."[35] According to a vast marketing campaign launched in popular magazines such as *Life*, what set Honeywell's new thermostats apart from those of its competitors was their capacity that "actually *sense* temperature changes before they occur and speeds up the heating system to meet them."[36]

In 1944, Honeywell introduced an updated thermostat system branded as Moduflow Sectional Heating. Beyond simply switching the heating supply on and off, Moduflow promised to deliver "even, continuously distributed heat."[37] Instead of one, multiple thermostats distributed across all spaces of the house determined a syncopated pattern of operation for the house burner. A technology reserved for complexes as large as Rockefeller Center a mere decade earlier was suddenly made accessible to the average American house.

---

25 McLuhan and Fiore, *The Medium Is the Massage*, 40.

26 Ibid., 41.

27 Beatriz Colomina and Mark Wigley, "Good Design Is an Anesthetic," in *Are We Human?: Notes on an Archaeology of Design* (Zurich: Lars Müller Publishers, 2016), 89–101.

28 Le Corbusier, *When the Cathedrals Were White*, trans. Francis E. Hyslop, Jr. (New York: McGraw-Hill, 1964), 61.

29 Ibid.

30 On the latter, in particular, see Jean-Louis Cohen, *Le Corbusier et la mystique de l'URSS: Théories et projets pour Moscou*, 1928–1936 (Paris: Pierre Mardaga Éditeur, n.d.), 116–20.

31 "The Radio City Broadcasting Studios," *Architectural Record* 75 (January 1934): 86–88, 27.

32 Le Corbusier, *When the Cathedrals Were White*, 61.

33 Wiener, *Cybernetics*, 115.

34 Marshall McLuhan, *Understanding Media: The Extensions of Man* (Cambridge, MA: MIT Press, 1994), 130.

35 Minneapolis Honeywell Regulator Company, "What Makes Automatic Heating Automatic?" *Life* 9, no. 19 (November 4, 1940): 19. Emphasis mine.

36 Minneapolis Honeywell Regulator Company, "Now Acratherm Brings the Blessing of Stabilized Heat to Every Home," *Life* 3, no. 8 (August 23, 1937): 67. Emphasis mine.

37 Minneapolis Honeywell Regulator Company, "'Tailored Heat' for Postwar Homes," *Life* 16, no. 17 (April 24, 1944): 111.

"[B]y the simple addition of a few ingenious controls," Honeywell claimed, each individual space would be heated consistently.[38] In a print advertisement from 1944, a comparative illustration demonstrates the effects of heating controlled by the "ordinary method" versus Moduflow in a typical living room. Adopting a pseudoscientific visual language, this comparison was presented as proof of the system's efficacy in the even distribution of heat across the vertical dimension of a room (fig. 11).[39] If Bagno's burglar alarms suggested a new definition of security constructed by an invisible architecture of sound and light waves, Honeywell's Moduflow sensor system implied a new mastery over the invisible thermodynamics of interiors. By automatically regulating the climatic conditions of the house, Moduflow was imbued with its own kind of magic; the comfort it offered was invisible, but felt (fig. 12).

DRAG

Honeywell's early thermostats bore all sorts of architectural drag. Their naked presence was to be avoided at all costs. As early as 1929, industrial designer Henry Dreyfuss had created a speculative design for a thermostat disguised as a nineteenth-century banjo clock (fig. 13). Some of Honeywell's later models of the 1930s were decorated with Art Deco–style housings.[40] In 1937, Dreyfuss offered, yet again, to revamp the company's wall-mounted line of thermostats as a series of compact, circular dials.[41] Despite having filed three separate patents for similar "control instruments" in June 1942, his ideas were met with little enthusiasm by Honeywell at the time (fig. 14).[42] It was only in 1953, long after World War II had ended, that Dreyfuss's design for Honeywell's T-86 thermostat—later nicknamed the Round—went into production becoming "perhaps the most ubiquitous piece of domestic hardware in the United States."[43] Curved and flattened in section, the streamlined form of the Round looked less like a block stuck on a wall and more like an elegant, sewed-on button. Neither a bulky protrusion nor a threatening puncture, its design did not threaten to disturb the integrity of the wall. In its subtle presence, the Round was at once a thermostat and a charming interface, connecting physical space with the immaterial architecture it controlled.

The Round was branded as a highly appealing gadget. In Honeywell's own words, its "pleasing round lines lend themselves to any decorating plan."[44] Thus, the major selling point of the Round was not performance-related. Rather, it was centered on its detachable ring cover that could be painted to match the color scheme of

---

38 Ibid.

39 Ibid.

40 Russell Flinchum, *Henry Dreyfuss, Industrial Designer: The Man in the Brown Suit* (New York: Rizzoli, 1997), 51.

41 Arthur J. Pulos, *The American Design Adventure, 1940–1975* (Cambridge, MA: MIT Press, 1988), 338.

42 Henry Dreyfuss, Control Instrument, US Patent 136,848–50, filed June 19, 1942, and issued December 14, 1943.

43 Flinchum, *Henry Dreyfuss, Industrial Designer*, 124. In a time when digital programmable thermostats have saturated the market, a number of variations of the original Round thermostat are still in production by Honeywell today.

44 The Minneapolis-Honeywell Regulator Co., "A New Improved Thermostat," *Life* 35, no. 19 (November 9, 1953): 86–87.

45 Ibid

46 George Nelson, cited in Flinchum, *Henry Dreyfuss, Industrial Designer*, 138.

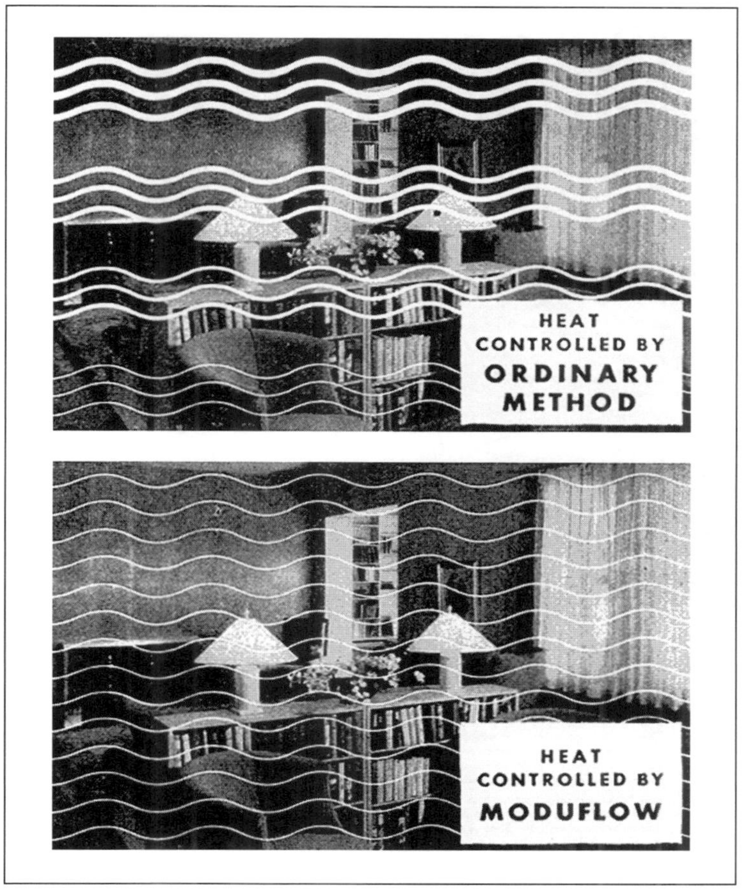

Fig. 11
"Heat controlled by ordinary method" versus "Heat controlled by Moduflow," ad for the Honeywell Moduflow Sectional Control system, *Life*, 1944.

Life 16, no. 17 (April 24, 1944), 111.

the wall on which it was affixed. Not by chance, Honeywell's first color print advertisement coincided with the 1953 commercial release of the Round demonstrating this feature (figs. 15–16). Contrary to all previous advertisements, no word on the actual functioning of the thermostat or its technologies was mentioned. Instead, a palette of colorful schemes promoted the Round as a "beautifully styled," customizable product able to "blend with any wall."[45]

The Round's magic was a disappearing act. Its design was an exercise in camouflage. Dreyfuss's ultimate goal was to make the thermostat an inconspicuous part of the interior, for it to dissolve into the architecture. Or, as fellow industrial designer George Nelson once pointed out, to render it "almost invisible."[46] Against modern architecture's highest moral imperative, to honestly express separate functions, sensor control systems were neurotically suppressed out of view. While imbricated with almost every single aspect of daily life, the presence of these systems was consistently elusive. How to explain this insistence on cover-up and masking?

Fig. 12
Minneapolis-Honeywell Regulator Company, "No! It's your morning to turn up the thermostat!," ad for the Honeywell Electric Clock Thermostat, *Life*, 1951.

Life 31, no. 19 (November 5, 1951), 63.

NAUSEA

Around the same time Wiener was writing *Cybernetics*, in 1947, French philosopher of science Georges Canguilhem was proposing a provocative inversion of the mechanistic understanding of biological organisms that dominated modern Western philosophy, largely cemented by figures like Descartes.[47] He advocated a break from the iatromechanical interpretation of life, an interpretation that privileged the laws of physics as an exegetic framework for all physiological and pathological phenomena. What if mechanical models for living organisms were merely rationalized reconstructions of the very organisms they represent? Canguilhem argued, "The construction of a mechanical model presupposes a living original," and by extension "the model for the living machine is that body itself."[48]

47 Canguilhem, whose works on biological "normalcy" would later greatly influence Michel Foucault, first presented these ideas in a lecture at the Collège philosophique in Paris titled "Machine et Organisme," a version of which was first published as Georges Canguilhem, "Machine et Organisme," in *La Connaissance de la vie* (Paris: Hachette, 1952), 124–59.

48 Georges Canguilhem, "Machine and Organism," in *Incorporations*, ed. Jonathan Crary and Sanford Kwinter, trans. Mark Cohen and Randall Cherry (New York: Zone, 1992), 53.

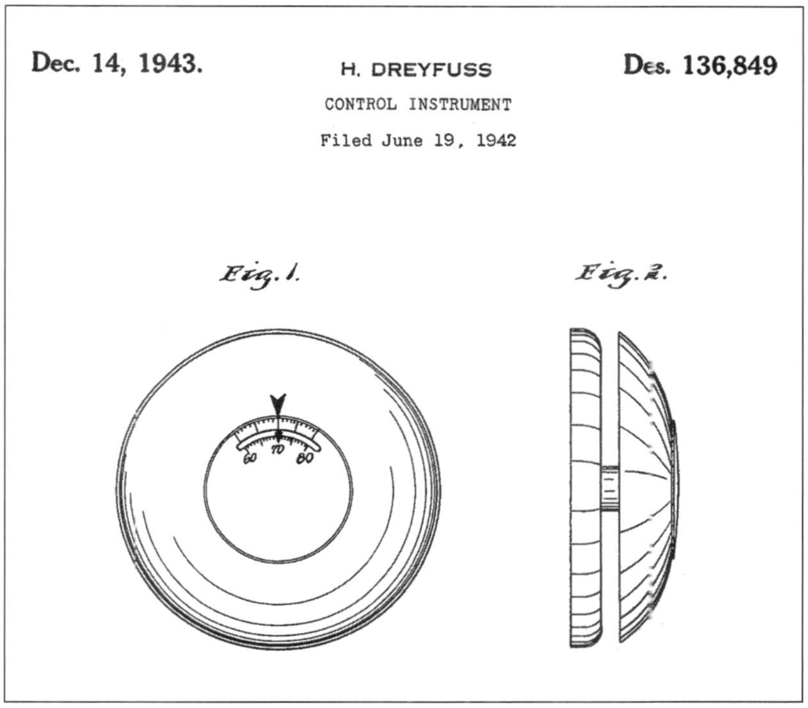

Fig. 13
Henry Dreyfuss, speculative design for a Honeywell thermostat disguised as a 19th c. banjo clock, 1929.

Flinchum, Russell. *Henry Dreyfuss, Industrial Designer: The Man in the Brown Suit*. New York: Rizzoli, 1997. Page 51.

Fig. 14
Patent drawings from Henry Dreyfuss' "Control Instrument," 1942–43.

US Patent 136,849, filed June 19, 1942, and granted December 14, 1943.

Following Canguilhem's syllogism, Wiener's rationalization of the nervous system as an analogue to the automatic machine should actually be inverted; a mechanical model for a sensate architecture presupposes the human sensorium itself. Conceiving sensor-regulated environments would have been impossible outside our own embodied experience. The very idea of architecture as a sensate automaton is inseparable from the mechanical theory of reflex—the theory that dominated Western medicine until the early nineteenth century.[49] And if the perverse idea of a sentient inanimate building was not unsettling enough, displaying the inner workings (the guts) of the sensor control systems would be as nauseating as exposing real organs, nerves, and brains in plain sight. Therefore, preventing the innards of these systems from surfacing into architectural space would be as crucial as ensuring the continuity of one's own skin.[50] If architecture was to be re-engineered as a sensing and responsive machine, the viscera of the "ghost" in this machine would have to be prevented at all costs from manifesting itself in the space of the humans.[51]

49 Canguilhem, Georges. "Machine and organism." *Incorporations*. (New York: Zone Books, 1992), 54.

50 Frank Lloyd Wright himself was equally appalled by the prospect of exposing the circulatory media that snake through buildings when he wrote: "Wiring for lights, as piping for plumbing and heating, should not show. . . unless by special design—any more than you would have organs of your body on the outside of your skin." Frank Lloyd Wright, *The Natural House* (New York: Horizon Press, 1954), 155; cited in Mark Wigley, *Buckminster Fuller Inc.: Architecture in the Age of Radio* (Zurich: Lars Müller Publishers, 2015), 77.

51 The term "ghost in the machine" was coined by philosopher Gilbert Ryle in his 1949 book *The Concept of Mind* to challenge the Cartesian dualism of body and mind. Gilbert Ryle, *The Concept of Mind* (London: Hutchinson's University Library, 1949).

FEEDBACK

"We look at the present through a rear-view mirror," McLuhan argued.[52] It is only when media produce new environments that previous environments suddenly come into focus.

> [I]n the case of environments that are created by new technologies, while they are quite invisible in themselves, they do tend to make visible the old environments... If the new environment is invisible, it does serve to make very visible the preceding environment... every new technology creates an environment that translates the old or preceding technology into ... something exceedingly noticeable.[53]

In their 1960 short film for IBM, titled An *Introduction to Feedback*, Charles and Ray Eames sought to induce a similar moment of awakening for their viewers when they emphatically proclaim: "All our lives we have made use of feedback, usually without being aware of it. We use it unconsciously"[54] (figs. 17–19). Thus, the current discourse on "home automation," "smart cities," and "ubiquitous computing" is one of today's sharpest rear-view mirrors. From smart refrigerators and biometric locks to home alarm systems and AI–powered voice-controlled assistants, our private spaces are increasingly populated by paraphernalia outfitted with multiple

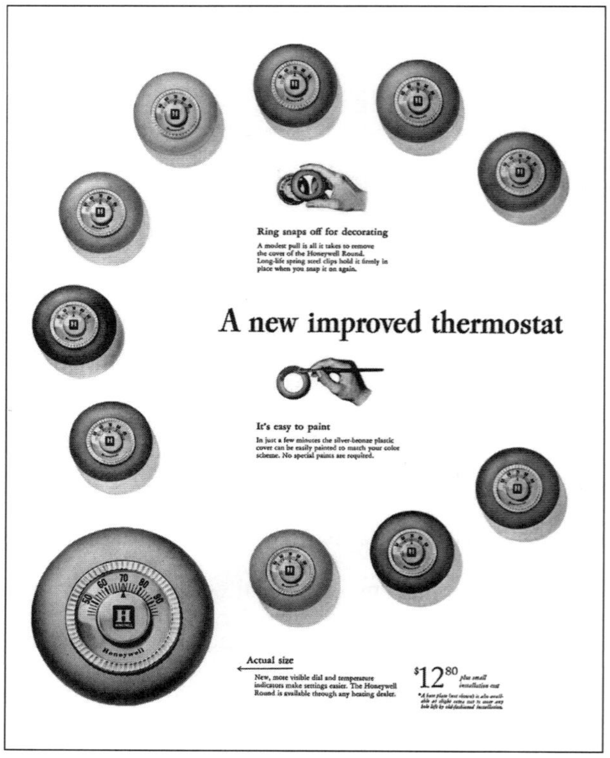

Figs. 15–16
Minneapolis-Honeywell Regulator Company, "A new improved thermostat that matches any color scheme," ad for the Honeywell Round thermostat designed by Henry Dreyfuss, *Life*, 1953.

Life 35, no. 19 (November 9, 1953), 87–88.

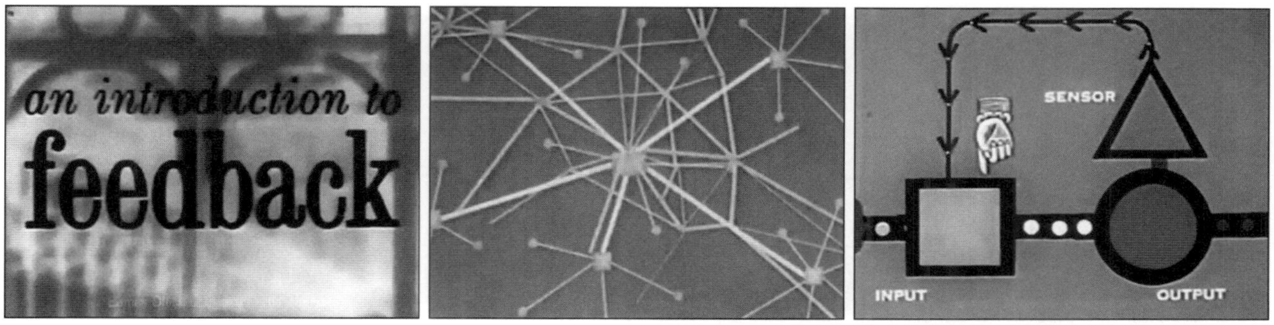

Fig. 17–19
Stills from Charles and Ray Eames, *An Introduction to Feedback*, film, The Eames Office, LLC, 1960.

sensor control systems. Comprising of an increasing number of interlinked feedback loops, today's environments enable us to discern the preceding paradigm of early sensor control systems in architecture, which we navigate unconsciously on a daily basis.

What becomes clear is that a comprehensive account of what one might call "the sensitization of architecture" has yet to be written. The more decision-making power we relinquish to sensor control systems, the more pressing the need for this history will be. Such an account is not intended to be a sensory history of architecture, but rather an architectural history of sensing. Unlike familiar modes of architectural historiography, such an endeavor will not revolve around the usual suspects: the twentieth century's heroic figures and canonical buildings. On the contrary, such an account will rely on closely weaving scattered evidence in documents produced primarily outside the architectural office. Patent applications, product brochures, building codes and technical reports the registers of this enduring process.

The idea that the material complex we occupy is a result of architecture's integration with other media, such as electricity, is no longer quite as hard to stomach.[55] At the same time, contemporary interpretations of our increasingly linked universe of devices, encapsulated in terms like "the Internet of Things," only bring to the fore the interplay among a variety of interlaced media. Like myriad data signals that permeate our rooms, media are impossible to unscramble. Their only mode of existence is that of interconnectedness, or intermediality. And it is only through this mode of investigation that the agency of traditional architecture be considered anew. Through the lens of intermediality, architecture can be understood not as superseded by seemingly immaterial and perceptually elusive technologies—in this case, sensor control systems—but rather as the indispensable medium for their spatial propagation.

---

52 McLuhan and Fiore, *The Medium Is the Massage*, 75.

53 McLuhan, "The Invisible Environment," 164.

54 Charles and Ray Eames, *An Introduction to Feedback*, film, 1960.

55 On this discussion see Christa Kamleithner, Roland Meyer, and Julia Weber (ZfM) in discussion with Reinhold Martin and Meredith TenHoor, "Feedback Loops: An Email-Interview about Media, Architecture, and the Aesthetics of Organization," web extra, translated as Reinhold Martin et al., *Zeitschrift Für Medienwissenschaft* 12, no. 1 (2015), http://www.zfmedienwissenschaft.de/online/feedback-loops/.

"1,500 People, 2 Elevators, and 500 Tons of Luggage," reads the headline of a news article describing the contents of a recent nine-day travel of Saudi Arabia's King Salman bin Abdulaziz to Indonesia.[1] Beyond the ludicrous extremity of the details—from the grandiose scale of accumulation and the logistical nightmare to the particularity of the lifestyle choices of a specific political leader—at a more general level, it makes visible and brings forth the phenomenon of "stuff," our exponentially growing cabinet of curiosities, our constant collecting, accumulating, and trashing of goods, artifacts, and material.

The exponential growth of this material accumulation is both about the ridiculous amounts we collect and also about the sums we trash. To illustrate these phenomena, consider two depictions. First is a scene from the remote Henderson Island, located in the Pacific Ocean at the western side of the South Pacific garbage patch, halfway between New Zealand and Chile. The island was named a UNESCO World Heritage site in 1988 for its exceptional "ecology that has been practically untouched by human presence" and was later designated as part of one of the world's largest protected marine wildlife reserves in the Pacific Ocean.[2] When examined in 2015, however, researchers found more than 55,000 pieces of trash, largely made of plastic deposited by ocean currents—fishing gear, water bottles, toys, et cetera—and currently estimate 17.6 tons of debris existent in the island, the peak density of plastic debris recorded anywhere in the world.[3] The image of an immense collection of a wide array of plastic objects in an "untouched" remote

1 Juliet Perry, "1,500 People, 2 Elevators and 500 Tons of Luggage—Here's How the Saudi King Travels," *CNN*, March 1, 2017, http://www.cnn.com/travel/article/saudi-visit-indonesia/.

2 "Henderson Island" (1988), UNESCO World Heritage Convention, ref. 487, http://whc.unesco.org/en/list/487/, accessed June 5, 2017. Adam Vaughan, "Pitcairn Islands to Get World's Largest Single Marine Reserve," *Guardian*, March 18, 2015, https://www.theguardian.com/environment/2015/mar/18/pitcairn-islands-marine-reserve-budget-2015/.

island not only stages confrontations between our value systems and material politics of accumulation at an almost post-natural moment, but also points to a puzzling fact. The trash scene at the Henderson Island depicts the quotidian and the planetary as the very same category.

Second is the 3D Warehouse, an online open source digital library in which more than two million 3D models of all kinds of objects, including buildings, geographic features, toys, tools, and machinery, are accumulated. Some with high and some with lousy detail and articulation, some truthfully built as perfect replicas for a specific project while others disregard precision, these digital ready-mades are the material ruins and debris of media accumulation. Similar to Hito Steyerl's articulation of "poor images" that carry the formal residues of their digital circulation such as low resolution or degradation, these models are equally poor, and since they are disposable and mutable, they complicate their own originality.[4] By existing in the 3D Warehouse, they disengage themselves from their original purposes and settings, and become a backdrop for other models and contexts. They remind us of David Joselit's articulation of "aggregators" that "make hyper-accumulation eloquent by causing asynchronous objects to occupy a common space."[5] They are the very stuff of the digital.

When positioned next to one another, the plastic piles accumulating on Henderson Island and the digital models piling within the 3D Warehouse present an important dilemma regarding human debris. First is their

3 For more on the expedition on the Henderson Island, see Jennifer Levis and Alexander Bond, "Exceptional and Rapid Accumulation of Anthropogenic Debris on One of the World's Most Remote and Pristine Islands," *Proceedings of the National Academy of Sciences of the United States of America* 114, no. 23 (April 2017). It is estimated that 8 million tons of plastic trash flow into the ocean every year. For more on the material politics around plastics, see Jennifer Gabrys, et al., *Accumulation: The Material Politics of Plastic* (New York: Routledge, 2014).

4 Hito Steyerl, "In Defense of the Poor Image," *e-flux journal* 10 (November 2009), http://www.e-flux.com/journal/10/61362/in-defense-of-the-poor-image/.

resemblance in relation to the equivocal categories they contain. They portray, after all, odd lists of collections. There is no logic to the grouping of these items (other than the fact that the Henderson Island pile is mostly plastic), putting them somewhere between a surrealist collection of magical, unique but strange objects found at a Parisian flea market and the profuse pile of a hoarder. Recalling the famous strange list of extraordinary animals that Michel Foucault borrows from Jorge Luis Borges, or the list of the debris ingredients in artist Vik Muniz's *Mounds*, the grouping is additive, accumulative and non-hierarchical, indifferent to both preciousness and category.[6]

In addition to their odd groupings, the second salient aspect regarding considering the piles of plastic debris and digital readymades together is the conceptual relationship between the geological and the digital accumulation as human ruin and rubbish. Consider Jennifer Gabrys's book ***Digital Rubbish: A Natural History of Electronics***, which provides us with an intellectual framework to understand the material, political and spatial infrastructures of electronic trash, or media theorist Jussi Parikka's geological studies of media, which build an alternative theoretical lineage between geology, media, and waste by providing a far more stretched temporal archeology of media. Could we think of a similar intellectual shift in our understanding of the relationship between digital and material accumulation for architecture, where their interaction is not reduced to a finished state nor a fixed medium, but to an elongated temporality of media archeology?[7] Can the creation and circulation of digital images conflate yet extend these kinds of

5 David Joselit, "On Aggregators," *October* 146 (Fall 2013): 18.

6 Michel Foucault, *The Order of Things* (New York: Pantheon, 1970), xv. Some ingredients mentioned in the list of Muniz's *Mounds* would give the right flavor: Rat Poison, Jade Buddhas, Pectin Drops Meteorites, Taylor Pins, Aspirin, Granola, Silver Glitter, Killer Bees, Dinosaur Dung, Shredded Ezra Pound Canto (XIX), Dice, AZT, Plastic Babies, Cat Hair, Beetles, Brillo Pads, Gold Scrap, Jelly Beans, Curry Powder, Metal Screws, Edible Worms, California Rolls, Headless Army Men, Coke Caps, Marijuana, Poison Scorpions, Feathers, Wristwatch Parts, Desyrel, etc. The relationship between architecture and additive tendency of accumulation is pointed out by Rem Koolhaas (as "junkspace") and Sylvia Lavin as a conceptual relationship between architecture and hoarding. See Rem Koolhaas, "Junkspace," *October* 100 (Spring 2002) and Slyvia Lavin, "Architecture in Extremis," *Log* 22 (Spring/Summer 2001): 51–61.

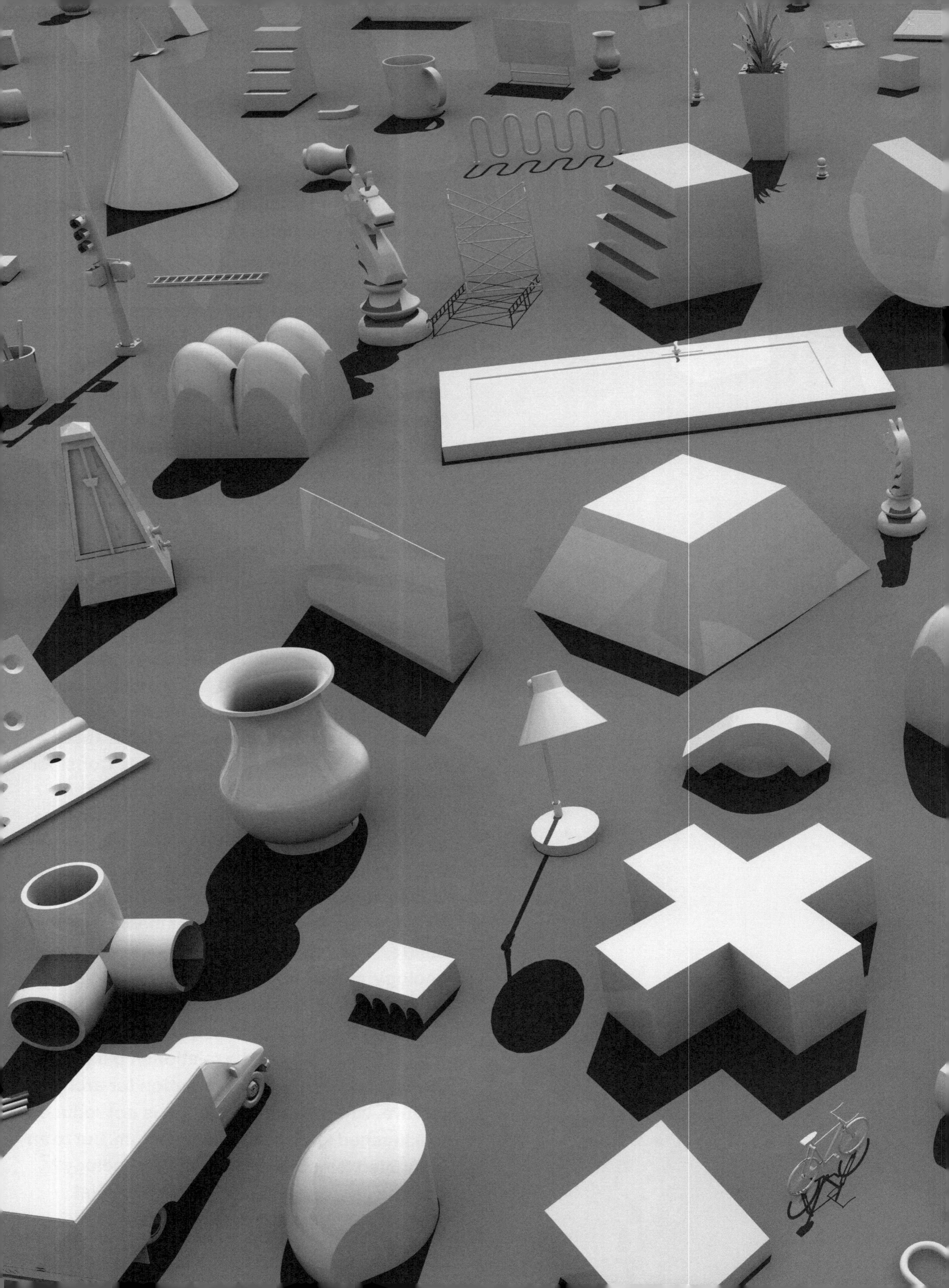

alternative discussions on architecture's materiality, both in terms of its temporal long-span and its representation?

***New Cadavre Exquis*, a recent project by NEMESTUDIO, speculates on the question of architectural materiality in the context of digital accumulation. The project consists of four architectural assemblies in which forms are created via a sampling process of digital readymade objects as an almost new surrealist *cadavre exquis*, investigating questions of assembly, ruination and waste. By depicting the formation of an architectural project from the accumulation of digital debris to material debris, *New Cadavre Exquis* builds alternative linkages between architecture, digital media, and geology, and opens up a range of aesthetic and political concerns for public imagination.**

In the project, each architectural assembly is composed of models from the 3D Warehouse, ranging from everyday objects and building elements to primitive forms and geographic features, all constituting an odd family of elements. To characterize these original 3D digital models strictly as found objects or readymades would be inadequate as they carry characteristics of both. As found objects, there is an element of encounter with these models, a selection, and a recognition of a singularity in that they are both lost and found (no model is the same even if they are replicating the same phenomena). As readymades, they are indifferent to the cause; they are multiple and not precious.[8] When compiled together, they are a Sample Collection from the Earth (fig. 1), a grouping of discrete objects deprived of their original category, purpose,

7 For more on the elongated temporality of architectural materiality, see Neyran Turan, "Nine Islands: Matters Around Architecture," *New Geographies* 08: Island (2016): 132–37.

8 For more on the distinction between the concept of readymade and found object, see: Margaret Iversen, "Found Object, Readymade, Photograph" in *Art Journal* 63, no. 2 (Summer 2004): 44–57. For the architectural relevance of the "as-found" idea especially during the 1950s and 1960s in the work of Alison and Peter Smithson, see: Dirk van den Heuvel, "As Found: The Metamorphosis of the Everyday," *OASE* 59 (2002): 52–67. For an excellent comparison of between Smithson's and Venturi Scott Brown's work in terms of their articulation of the everyday, the banal and the ordinary, see Martino Stierli, "Taking on Mies: Mimicry and Parody of Modernism in the Architecture of Alison and Peter Smithson and Venturi/Scott Brown," in *Neo-avant-garde and Postmodern: Postwar Architecture in Britain and Beyond*, ed. M.Crinson and C. Zimmerman (New Haven, CT: Yale University Press, 2010), 151–74.

Fig. 1
Digital readymades as a Sample Collection from the Earth.

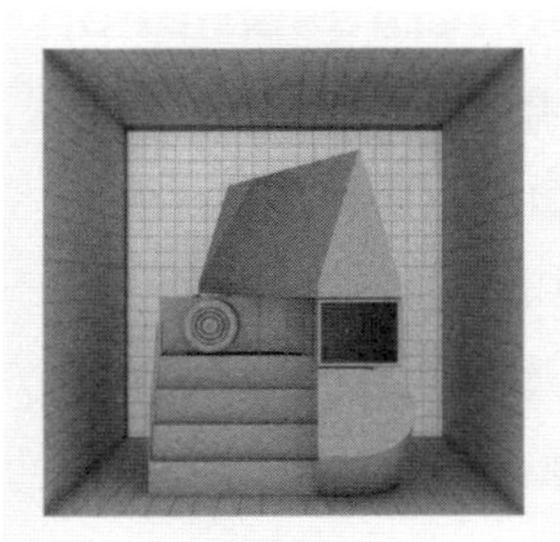

Fig. 2
Re-Assembly Archetype-1. Primitive forms, stair and an HVAC unit.

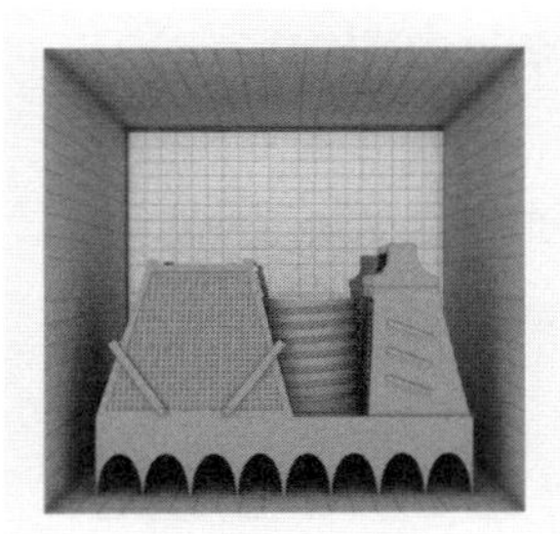

Fig. 3
Re-Assembly Archetype-2. Picnic basket, drainage pipe, and a grater on top of an arcade.

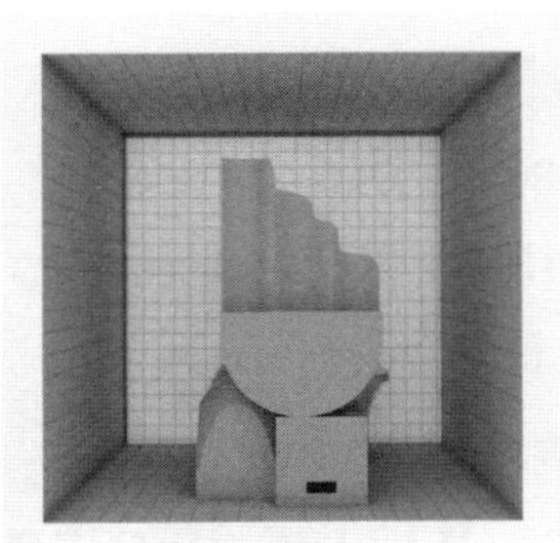

Fig. 4
Re-Assembly Archetype-3. Curtain, primitive forms, mailing box, and a chess piece.

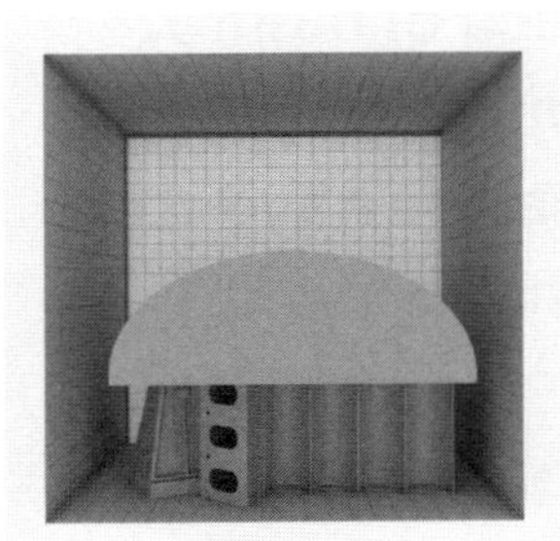

Fig. 5
Re-Assembly Archetype-4. CMU, primitive forms, and a metronome.

material and scale.

As a Re-Assembly Archetype, each assembly is initially a scale-less compositional pile where the miniscule and the giant are flattened, creating loose joints and shared edges and creating slightly unfamiliar compositional arrangements (fig. 2, fig. 3, fig. 4, fig. 5). Upon gaining a material definition, however, each Re-Assembly Archetype obtains architectural properties such as scale, program, and further material specificity as a "Re-Assembly as ___": "Re-Assembly as Copper," "Re-Assembly as Terrazzo," "Re-Assembly as Marble," and "Re-Assembly as Stucco" (fig. 6, fig. 7, fig. 8, fig. 9). Ranging from a small retail shop and a house to a housing structure and a large-scale infrastructural building, each Re-Assembly Archetype stages and exploits the potentials of its archetypal composition as a building, which eventually is destabilized by time and the materiality of its mass. The project tackles the elongated temporality of architecture's materiality by presenting each architectural Re-Assembly Archetype within a time span from composition to maintenance, ruination, demolition, and waste (fig. 10, fig. 11, fig. 12, fig. 13). From the extraction of as found digital models, to material and waste, each Re-Assembly Archteype alludes to the kinds of ordinary activities that take place around the material practice of architecture.

The drawings of *New Cadavre Exquis* allude to this by presenting each Re-Assembly Archetype as a scaled physical model that is being photographed. While the entourage in the foreground of each drawing depicts the particular activity presented (maintenance,

Fig. 6
Re-Assembly as Copper as a housing building.

Fig. 7
Re-Assembly as Terrazzo as a train station.

Fig. 8
Re-Assembly as Marble as a house.

Fig. 9
Re-Assembly as Stucco as a retail store.

Fig. 10
Re-Assembly as Copper going through maintenance.

demolition), the entourage that is placed in the background of each image gives hints about the scale of the photographed physical model. As the digital objects gain physical characteristics this way, *New Cadavre Exquis* restages the making of digital images as part of architecture's materiality. As self-aware images—images that acknowledge their representational imperative explicitly while presenting themselves as non-illusionistic depictions of reality—they juxtapose the two very contrasting techniques of representation on the same picture plane—scenery from everyday life around the building in the foreground and the rendering of a physical architectural model scene in the background. In this way, the drawings make possible for the two vantage points of the same reality to coexist on the space of representation.

In his recent book titled *After Nature*, law professor Jedediah Purdy writes:

> **"Environment needed to be invented before it could be saved during the 1960s and 1970s. ... The idea of Anthropocene is useful, but it needs to be seen in the right light. Despite its scientific trappings, it is mainly a cultural idea, and its potential is political and ethical. ... It is the starting place for a new politics of nature, a politics more encompassing and imaginative than what we have come to know as environmentalism."[9]**

If environment is at once a conceptual invention with ties to different forms of environmentalisms, and a source for alternative

Fig. 11
Re-Assembly as Copper as ruin waiting to be demolished.

Fig. 12
Re-Assembly as Terrazzo as waste.

Fig. 13
Re-Assembly as Marble during demolition.

cultural imaginations of the Anthropocene and its politics of nature, one may ask, can architecture contribute to a new imaginary of our contemporary environment beyond environmentalism?

New Cadavre Exquis **proposes another kind of environmental imagination for architecture. Similar to the close relationships that exist between legal regimes of environmental law and imagination, which is presented thoroughly in Purdy's work for instance, an alternative focus on the politics and nuances within our disciplinary inner workings can also have profound effects in triggering unconventional environmental imaginations. In other words, similar to the trash scene at the Henderson Island, architecture's familiar interior is the very image of its planetary outside. By speculating on the temporality of architecture's digital and material accumulation, ruination and waste as questions of representation and image making,** ***New Cadavre Exquis*** **is a call for a re-boost of our cosmic effect from within.**

The author would like to thank the Center for New Media at the University of California, Berkeley, for their support for the ***New Cadavre Exquis*** **project.**

New Cadavre Exquis **Project Team: Neyran Turan, Isabella Warren-Mohr, Keenan Gravier, Zhifei Xu.**

6 Jedediah Purdy, *After Nature: A Politics for the Anthropocene* (Cambridge, MA: Harvard University Press, 2015), 16–17. A familiar term by now, Anthropocene is the proposed name for our geologic era, in which humans have become the major force determining the continuing livability of the earth, an era in which our plastic trash gyres in our oceans accelerate while our rainforests and coral reefs diminish.

SI EL ÉXITO ES LA MEDIDA EN LA QUE ENCAJAS EN LA CATEGORÍA...

Fig. 4

Still from *Fun Palace Film*, ca.1964, Cedric Price Archive (Montreal: CCA)

15. Fun Palace Project Meeting: Joan Littlewood, Cedric Price (Architect) and Tom Driberg (Publicity), January 10, 1964, Fun Palace, DR1995:0188:525:002:002, Cedric Price Archive, Canadian Centre for Architecture, Montreal.

16. Letter, 30 April 1965, Fun Palace, DR1995:0188:525:002, Cedric Price Archive, Canadian Centre for Architecture, Montreal.

17. Report on Meeting, 2, Fun Palace, DR1995:0188:525:002, Cedric Price Archive (Montreal: CCA).

18. Cedric Price Notes, Fun Palace, DR1995:0188:525:002:001.0017, Cedric Price Archive, Canadian Centre for Architecure, Montreal.

an act of curation with the aim of stimulating and concentrating potential supporters for the successful realization of the project. During a 1964 team meeting, Price argued that the booklet of the Fun Palace "should be designed so that parts can be removed according to the type of person receiving it."[15] In other words, it should also be flexible.

This marketing approach was accentuated further by a 1964 collaboration with Melville Mark, the head of an international public relations agency based in Geneva and London, who was hired by Littlewood and Price to administer and promote the Fun Palace in the United Kingdom and abroad.[16] Contrary to the masquerading methodology employed until that time, the crux of Mark's proposal was to sell the project on a serious basis. In particular, he emphasized that "the government and the industry should be made aware of the use of this project," without hiding its educational and sociological objectives.[17] To accomplish this, the public relations expert diverted from the previous "bread and circuses" communication of the project and outlined a set of principles, phases to follow, goals to be achieved, and the economic structure and revenues for the entire venture. By doing so, Mark stressed the project's true potential and promoted a presentation of the Fun Palace to the media that relied on the linguistic capacity of flexibility. Consequently, he was able to communicate—to ordinary people, as well as to government and industry—two conflicting readings of the project: its unique potential as an appropriative and as an exploitative space.

This twofold reading of the Fun Palace reveals an alternative reading of flexibility. The proposal established flexibility as a notion of ambiguity and, for the first time in the architectural realm, transformed it into a polysemous technique of exploitation and rhetoric.[18] Flexibility mutated from a naive concept of modernization into a strategic disguise capable of mediating any finance capital needs. With the support of material and immaterial tools, design, and technologies, it constructed, contrary to common understandings of "free space," a space of absolute hierarchy and control. Flexibility capitalized on latent paradoxes within The Fun Palace—the contradiction between the permitted and the restricted—and proposed an alternative form of governing which, rather than imposing and confronting, would steer and conduct its subjects. In this way, the Fun Palace sought to subtly choreograph its users and create a set of fictional relationships with unaware participants. The employment of flexibility could be read as a pacifier: instead of encouraging the working class to take control of its own labor power, it outlined a sophisticated solution for the real concerns of the 1960s British establishment.

At the same time, the flexible use of flexibility allowed the Fun Palace proposal to sustain itself and transfigure into both a timeless and a "just-in-time" project. It became an exemplary design, by means of the constant reconstruction of its relevance. Within a context where change began to no longer constitute the exception but the rule, the Fun Palace constructed a stable ground within an unstable context. It not only absorbed any future crisis, but made crisis essential for its operation and survival. Therefore, the project anticipated the new economic doctrine of neoliberalism—unfolded in the midst of a crisis in 1970s—that used, and continues to use, the permanent state of crisis as the principal tool for its constant optimization and reestablishment. As a system that is nowadays fully manifested and once again in crisis, it could be argued, like Hans Urlich Obrist does, that the Fun Palace remains today more contemporary than ever before. Yet this is not because of the pseudo-liberating qualities for which the project became known, but rather due to its ability to suggest an ethos of flexibility that has transformed into a life-defining concept. Parallel to presenting life as a whole—the dissolution of the distinction between leisure and work—it became the project of subjugation *par excellence,* where economic wills and competition progressively colonized and replaced any moment of freetime with work. The Fun Palace, by positioning its agency at the level of free time and conceptualizing the project through flexibility, made work seem as natural as fun.

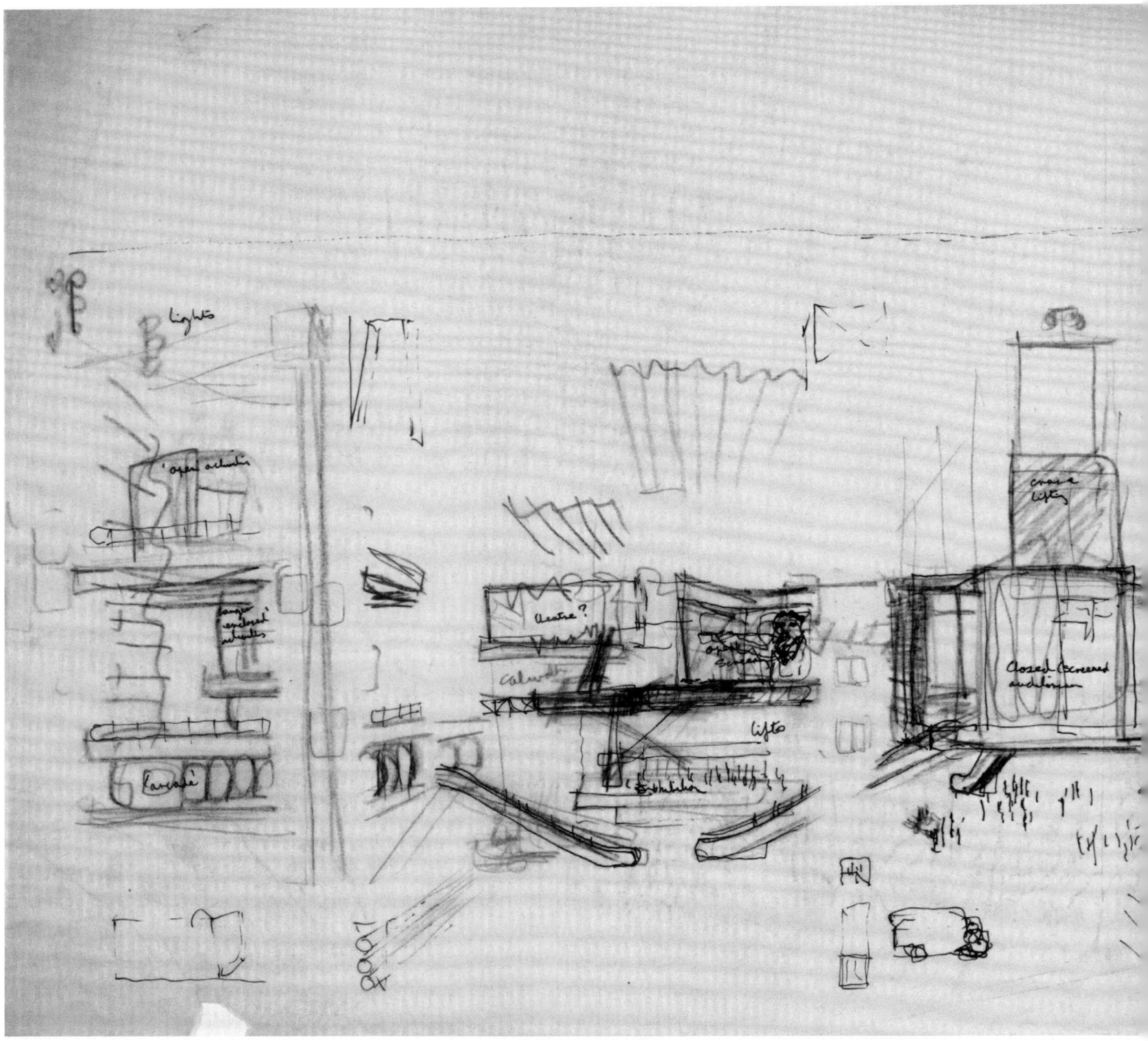

Fig. 3

Theater, restaurant, cafeteria and auditorium where some of the enclosures that communicated how much "fun" people might have when visiting the Fun Palace. Conceptual Perspectival Section, Fun Palace, ca. 1963, DR1995:0188:100, Cedric Price Archive (Montreal: CCA)

8. Fun Palace—Architectural Approach, June 1965, Fun Palace, DR1995:0188:525:004:009, Cedric Price Archive, Canadian Centre for Architecture, Montreal.

9. Gordon Pask was a friend of Joan Littlewood. During a meeting in 1964, Littlewood, Price, and Pask agreed on the formation of a cybernetic group in order to improve the project's flexibility. It was officially named "Cybernetics Committee of the Fun Palace" and consisted of twenty-six members, with Pask at the role of the director. As Pask explained in the committee's introductory text, the context of constant change—inscribed by the "increasing degree of automation and a society presented with the problems of maintaining stability and using leisure"—the use of control was "peculiarly apt." Meeting of Joan Littlewood, Cedric Price, and Gordon Pask, September 30, 1964, Fun Palace, DR1995:0188:525:002:003, Cedric Price Archive; Cybernetics Committee: Introductory Document, Circulation List and Basic Plans, January 27, 1965, 2, Fun Palace, DR1995:0188:525:004:009, Cedric Price Archive. See also Gordon Pask, *An Approach to Cybernetics* (New York: Harper, 1961).

10. *Cedric Price Notes*, Fun Palace, DR1995:0188:525:002:001.0017, Cedric Price Archive, Canadian Centre for Architecture, Montreal.

11. *Fun Palace Project Report*, 1, Fun Palace, DR1995:0188:525:005:010, Cedric Price Archive, Canadian Centre for Architecture, Montreal.

12. "Appendix 1: Programme Outline—The day's rhythm will follow a simple pattern", *Fun Palace: What Is the Fun Palace?*, Fun Palace, DR1995:0188:525:005:010, Cedric Price Archive, Canadian Centre for Architecture, Montreal.

13. As the team argued, "it is right, in a project of this kind, to advance beyond the bounds of respectably accredited fact into the hinterland of things we know how to do although we do not know the precise mechanics of our accomplishment. If you will think in these terms then a great deal is known about how to control people and how to make them happy." *Cybernetic Aspects*, Fun Palace, DR1995:0188:525:002:001:030, Cedric Price Archive, Canadian Centre for Architecture.

14. In a letter to Jim Richards, editor of the *Architectural Review* at the time, Cedric Price expressed his worries about the "major mistakes" made by Richards in "the first reasonably comprehensive expose of the scheme" (Cedric Price, "Fun Palace Project," *Architectural Review* 137, no. 815 (January 1965)). The architect stated that the team of the Fun Palace had until that time avoided publishing any "details of this building, due largely to its complexity," and described the situation as "desperate," requesting the insertion of an errata as the article was "incorrect in a major way." *Letter from Cedric Price to Jim Richards*, December 24, 1964, Fun Palace, DR1995:0188:525:005, Cedric Price Archive, Canadian Centre for Architecture, Montreal.

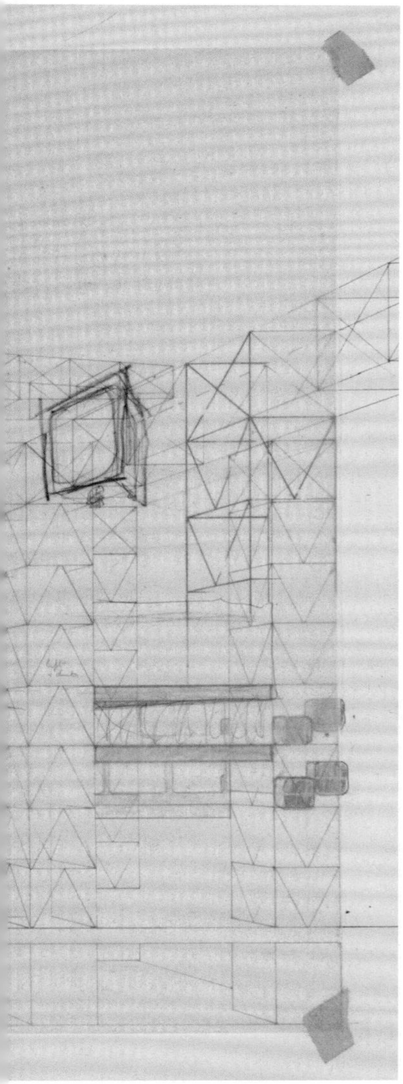

from drudgery. Thus, their project developed into a "laboratory of fun"[7] where the masses could simultaneously enjoy their freetime and become aware of their own capabilities. Human skill became central to the project, which organized working class enjoyment through a new condition: the dissolution of the dichotomy between leisure and work. As the duo was unable to predict whether free time or skilled labor would dominate in the future, the "university of the streets,"[8] as they imagined it, was an indeterminate setting where participants could freely stroll or educate themselves. Choice and freedom of movement were embraced within a permanently flexible, open platform free of predetermined programs.

To promote this environment of nonstop flexibility, Price and Littlewood made use of cutting-edge fields like information technology, game theory, and cybernetics. It was specifically this last field—a new science in which the principal objective was to govern and maintain control—that the architect employed, oddly enough, to promote constant dexterity and diverse configurations. Cybernetic concepts were incorporated into the project with the support of an expert in the field, Gordon Pask, and it became explicit across the entire design via the proposed installation of a sophisticated system of sensory apparatuses.[9] The devices would accumulate a variety of information with varying levels of accuracy, recording the participants' movements and engagement with the enclosures. They would collect intelligence and create an index of data. This data would then be organized and displayed as statistics to drive the continuous reorganization and programmatic variability of the enclosures. This way, the Fun Palace sought to construct an atmosphere of indeterminacy that demanded that participants constantly adapt to new triggers and encounters. As Price argued during the design process, "flexibility within the complex [was] not confined to the variation of the form and disposition of the enclosures and areas provided, but also by the ability to vary the public movement patterns."[10]

In other words, by claiming the utter flexibility of the object, the project capitalized on the flexibility of the subject. It relied on the wellspring of talent inherent in every individual and took advantage of this natural resource by staying open twenty-four hours a day. Not by chance, mentions of the "release of the human genius" and "the self" recur throughout Price's notes.[11] Nevertheless, concepts such as self-awareness, self-control, self-education, self-indulgence, and self-organization that emerged frequently within his writing about the design did not refer to human agency or free will as concepts in themselves, but rather as the inevitable results of the subject's interaction with the space.

Far from proposing an atmosphere of real self-determination, the project grew into a relentless mechanism of exploitation, where the implementation of subliminal restrictions explored the use of uncharted talents and creativity within a context of games and controlled euphoria. In reality, a rigorous surveillance system replaced the physical supervision of the factory, turning a random choice into a regimented one.[12] To play would be to employ oneself in the development of human potential. Subsequently, the Fun Palace could have fostered an endless physical and mental exhaustion within a space that supposedly knew "how to make [people] happy."[13]

It was precisely this blurriness between autonomy and control, enabling and constraining, that the project was able to camouflage under the rhetoric of flexibility. Already from their earliest publications, Littlewood and Price built upon the term's positive aura and constructed a very specific narrative.[14] Their strategy avoided communicating particular details of the project's complexity—like the use of technology or the elaboration of the structure's details—and, instead, presented solely the aspect of fun. In a sense, the presentation material became the output of a sophisticated process of filtering in which any layers of the project's mechanistic and supporting framework disappeared, leaving only the overlay of fun (fig. 3). The playful enclosures were presented with minimal reference to the rigid structure that served to initiate the project—just a few line traces of the steel frame columns—while the opacity of the cartridge paper took over the transparency of the initial representation. The project neglected its synthetic origin, becoming an autonomous product—the fun—that was meant to be viewed on its own. This way, the description of the Fun Palace not only remained abstract, but it also transformed into

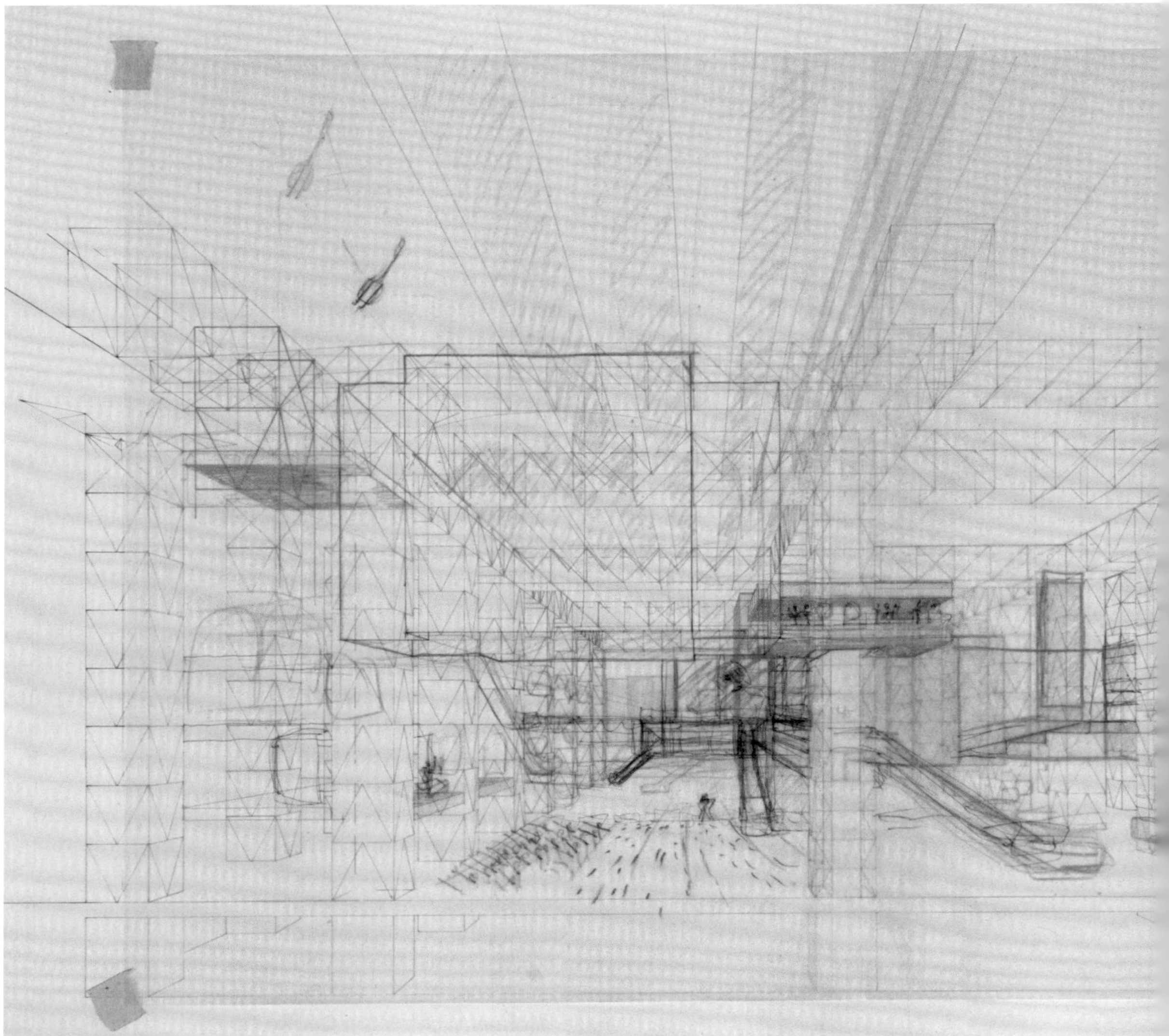

Fig. 2

The various enclosures obeyed the hierarchical organization of the frame. Small utilitarian volumes, were located in the flanking aisles, whereas large educational volumes were located in the grandiose central space. Perspective of the Structure and Units, Fun Palace, DR1995:0188: 081–103, Cedric Price Archive (Montreal: CCA)

1. Reyner Banham, "People's Palaces," *New Statesman*, August 7, 1964, 192.

2. Marcus Fairs, "Cedric Price Is "Like Marcel Duchamp" Says Hans Ulrich Obrist," Dezeen, June 12, 2014, https://www.dezeen.com/2014/06/12/cedric-price-is-like-marcel-duchamp-says-hans-ulrich-obrist/.

3. The two met at Lady Illingworth's house in Grosvenor Square, London, one afternoon in 1961, following an invitation by a mutual friend, Tom Driberg, a journalist and prominent member of the Labour Party. After a brief introduction, Littlewood and Price began discussing the present socioeconomic dilemmas and future alternatives. Littlewood revealed to the young architect her thoughts for a Palace of Leisure, an idea that they would later develop together and call the Fun Palace. Joan Littlewood, *Joan's Book: Joan Littlewood's Peculiar History as She Tells It* (London: Methuen, 1994), 582.

4. The movement and positioning of the enclosures was to be done by two overhead gantry cranes spanning the entire structure. See *Design*, Fun Palace, DR1995:0188:525:005, Cedric Price Archive, Canadian Centre for Architecture, Montreal.

5. According to Price, the demand for a space able to cope with its constant reconfiguration required a "three dimensional activity framework [which] must enable maximum flexibility and charge in individual volumes and the whole." Architectural brief, October 1962, Fun Palace DR1995:0188:525:002:001.005, Cedric Price Archive, Canadian Centre for Architecture, Montreal.

6. This "problematic matter" led members of Parliament to propose the formation of a "Ministry of Leisure." See John Smith, "Buildings for Pleasure and Leisure," *Architectural Association Journal* (London: 1964), 63; Fun Palace, DR1995:0188:525:002:003, Cedric Price Archive, Cancadian Centre for Architecture, Montreal.

7. Joan Littlewood, "A Laboratory of Fun," *New Scientist* 22, No. 391, May 14, 1964, 432–33.

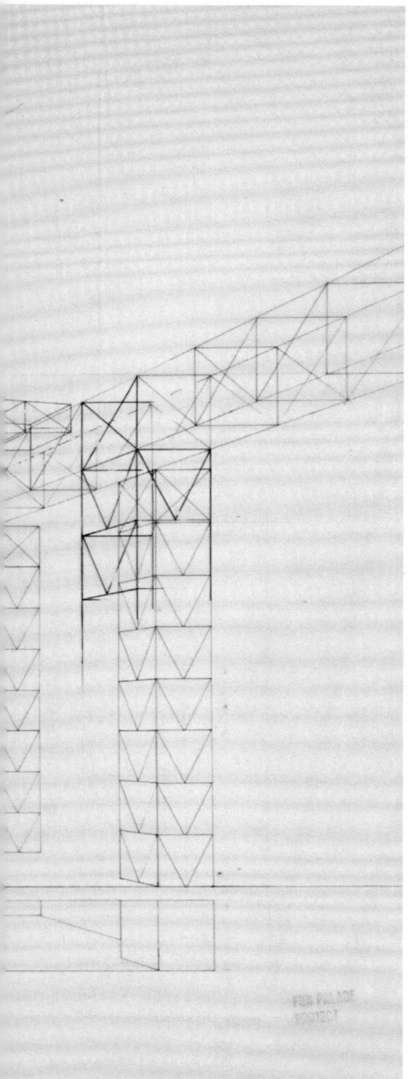

The Fun Palace was architect Cedric Price's visionary 1961–64 proposal for a cultural center in London. Since its inception, the unrealized project has garnered praise as ground-breaking and revolutionary. Reyner Banham, in his 1964 article "People's Palaces," described the proposal as "a breakout (not a breakthrough) ... an unprecedented situation which we cannot afford to pass up."[1] In the following decades, this celebratory aura transformed the project into the de facto paradigm of architecture's post war avant-garde. Theoretical works, like Archigram's 1964 Plug-in City, as well as realized buildings, like Richard Rogers and Renzo Piano's 1977 Centre Georges Pompidou, Paris, used the Fun Palace as a key reference. Even today, the project continues to be read with the same enthusiasm as in the 1960s. Samantha Hardingham's 2016 anthology, *Cedric Price Works, 1952–2003: A Forward-Minded Retrospective*, was launched at the Architectural Association, London, with a parallel symposium, exhibition, and lecture series, safeguarding this legacy. Curator Hans Ulrich Obrist used the Fun Palace as the main object of his intervention at the Swiss Pavilion at the 14th International Architecture Exhibition, Venice Biennial, "it is so contemporary."[2] Yet, the essence of the project lies beyond its sustained popular appeal, and within architectural culture.

The Fun Palace was the product of a three-year collaboration between the theatrical director Joan Littlewood and the young architect, Cedric Price.[3] Unlike Michael Webb's Sin Centre (1961) or Constant Nieuwenhuys' New Babylon (1959), two contemporary projects that also believed in the power of architecture to shape societal ambitions and foster economic growth—the proposal set forward a more carefully detailed design expressed through a highly defined and engineered framework able to accommodate any possible activity from theaters and dancing to museums and learning. The project was meant to be an open framework for any and all of these activities. Price delineated a three-dimensional mesh, 256.2 meters long by 109.8 meters wide and almost 38 meters high, composed of a modular system of steel lattice girders and towers, rendered on cartridge paper with thin rapidograph lines as a slightly asymmetrical single-point interior perspective view (fig. 1). Resembling a Roman basilica in its arrangement, the design formed a rigid hierarchical space with a central nave framed by two flanking aisles. Fifteen parallel strips of columns and beams provided order and, together with its concrete plinth, housed all the servicing networks and areas necessary for operation.

This precise structure was perceived as the permanent background upon which space could reinvent itself, while the programmatic content or foreground was conceived as an ephemeral infill. This transience was expressed in the overlay of enclosures that Price laid out on a sheet of tracing paper with colorful freehand shapes drawn with thick pencil and marker lines (fig. 2). The different programmatic enclosures were to be constantly purged and renewed, becoming part of the building's bimonthly shuffle.[4] In this sense, the project acknowledged change as a normal condition through an infinite number of layers and possible distributions overlaid on a static frame. Specifically, it was the desire for a perpetually changeable space that the Fun Palace achieved through the appropriation of a single—and celebrated—notion: flexibility.[5]

Derived from the Latin verb *flectere*, meaning "to bend" or "to curve," the term *flexibility* first appeared in fourteenth-century medical literature, to describe something as elastic. Two centuries later, its meaning expanded to a more abstract notion as a technique of persuasion, establishing a relationship to docility. Yet, it was during the eighteenth century that flexibility became part of mercantilist and architectural vocabulary as a way to manage the uncertainty, risk, and unpredictability of the future. Precisely due to this capacity, Littlewood and Price employed the concept of flexibility to respond to the economic crisis experienced in Britain during the late 1950s and early 1960s. It was a period of stagnation and local industrialists sought growth through the integration of automation. This transition towards a skilled production model made unskilled and low-skilled laborers redundant, increasing their freetime. The period was thus marked by the democratization of leisure, shaping a condition that soon transformed into a real threat, with the upper-middle class and institutions fearing the rise of an idle working class.[6]

Yet Littlewood and Price saw true potential in this crisis. They interpreted the proliferation of leisure as an opportunity to free the workers

Georgios Eftaxiopoulos

Fig. 1

During the design process of the Fun Palace's frame, Cedric Price was advised by the engineer Frank Newby, who not only corrected any initial malfunctions but also improved its structural and operational performance. Interior perspective. Rapidograph on cartridge paper. Fun Palace, DR1995:0188:081–103, Cedric Price Archive, The Canadian Centre for Architecture, Montreal.

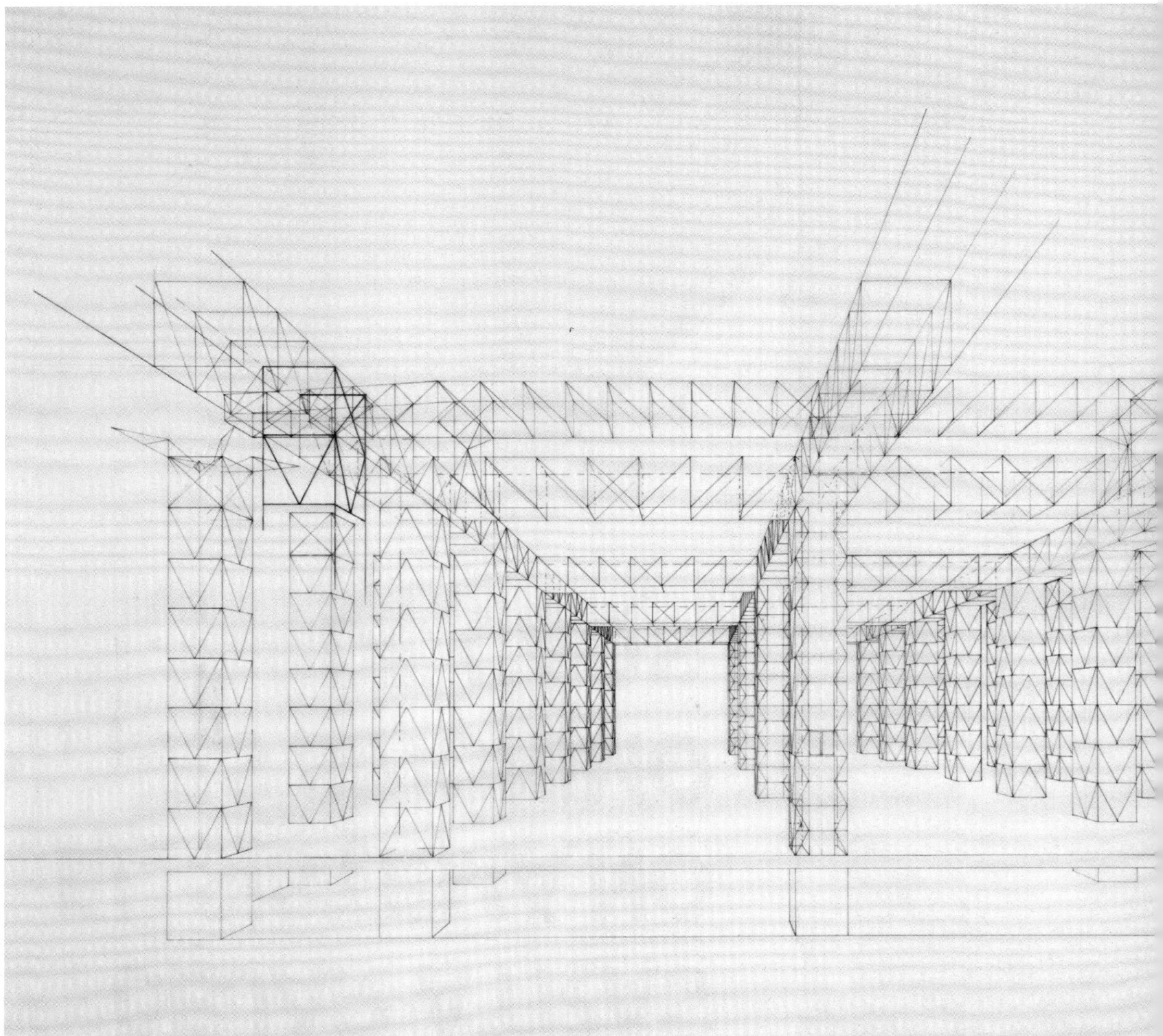

No-Fun: Fun Palace and the Cult of Flexibility

DEJAR ATRÁS
EL SISTEMA NO
ES SINÓNIMO
DE CAOS.

Keller Easterling

To Play Space

Rather than encouraging innovation, architecture's eager embrace of new media technologies may, paradoxically, reinforce default cultural scripts. Designers are usually focused on making objects and representing them with media, where that term refers to visual communications technologies. But returning to broader uses of the word media that describe surrounding elemental environments like air and water suggest that designers might explore medium design—the design of the matrix in which objects are suspended.[1]

Space itself is the information system—a temporal fluid medium and a mixing chamber for many different information systems. Designers can shape ground instead of figure, field instead of object. At any scale from intimate to planetary, the field does not resolve only as a single object or event.[2] Designing the medium means managing the potentials and relationships between objects. It is like determining the growth medium, the rules of the game, or the operating system that links and activates objects.

In a constant dialogue with humans, spatial technologies have no destined use and do not exist within a steady state. Yet even though their potentials are always changing in this human/nonhuman exchange, default cultural scripts about technologies cling to notions about right answers, destinies, and ultimates. And hackneyed media vehicles convey their messages.

Just as medium design inverts the typical focus on object instead of field, it may also invert these default cultural scripts and offer different approaches to problem solving, politics, and aesthetics. But medium design also calls for alternative approaches to media. Designers may need to invent their own documents or media mixtures to make this bigger surrounding medium palpable. And these mixtures might also lead the way to a different audience—not only private and public clients, but also a broad popular culture.

Default Scripts

One default cultural script confirms modernist arguments that the newest technology automatically delivers some essential intelligence and updates tired old thinking with the fresh information needed to survive the cresting wave of future events. The newer thing is also the smarter thing. It delivers the right answer. New technologies transcend politics with a totalizing solution to replace the previous order, and to hesitate in adopting them is to hold back an inexorable progress of successive ideas in a linear timeline.

1 Some of these theorists would include John Durham Peters, "In Media Res" and "Understanding Media," in *The Marvelous Clouds: Toward a Philosophy of Elemental Media* (Chicago: University of Chicago, 2015), 1–52; Antonio Somaini, "Walter Benjamin's Media Theory: The *Medium* and the *Apparat*," *Grey Room* 62 (Winter 2016), 6–41; and Francesco Casetti, "Genealogies of the Excessive Screen" (forthcoming).

2 Rosalind Williams, "Cultural Origins and Environmental Implications of Large Technological Systems," *Science in Context* 6, no. 2 (1993), 395.

Consider the TED Talk–style PowerPoint deck—an upbeat, "jaw-dropping" presentation of new ideas typically associated with new technologies or new paradigms. However innovative the ideas may be, they are often laced with the swagger of the new, or they move step-by-step toward the solution or the right answer. Whatever the approach, the logics of successive thinking suggest that the newest technology delivers the greatest intelligence. Any self-respecting TED Talk–style crusader would be embarrassed to suggest otherwise or, if given the choice, would never dream of favoring a lumpy analog world over one governed by new digital devices.

Or consider social media networks—an arrangement between humans and new technologies that is, in TED language, a game changer. How could it be anything else? Even when one of the primary filters on this network generates a relatively dumb binary of likes and dislikes, and even when its disposition becomes primitive and violent, the crudeness of the network is tolerated for fear of missing out on the network's supposedly advancing newness.

Similarly, responding to persuasions about the smart city, the internet of things, or autonomous vehicles (AVs), designers look to digital devices as the means to finally animate the city's stiff solids. The city, now bristling with sensors, is a subject of apps and data visualizations that even claim to make a software for urbanism—another return to determinate solutions.[3] The right algorithm will deliver the right answer, and the old technologies, deemed obsolete, will be replaced. Even when these technologies begin to centralize information in ways that violate privacy, the fear is that to not fully convert to smart-city technologies is to be left behind in a cultural backwater.

For what seems like the perfect self-parody of the optimistic scripts of the new and ultimate, consider the hilarious cocktail of kitsch utopias in urban promotional videos for free zones and other ersatz cities. As if following a mandatory template, these promotions invariably begin with a view of earth from outer space. Stirring music that you might hear in a thriller or over the thundering hooves of a Western accompany a drop from the stratosphere to locate a new center of the earth. A Star Wars–style fly-through inspects a field of digital skyscrapers sprouting from the ground before the camera swoops through industrial areas, container ports, and resorts. "What a Feeling," the theme from *Flashdance*, plays as one video advertises its city's logistical apparatus.[4] Or a Yanni-like soundtrack accompanies another's magnificent claims of global connectivity or world city urbanity enjoyed by doughy human figures rhythmically waddling along boulevards or ploughing forward stone-faced in speedboats. A population of villas flips into place as more animated figures weightlessly pad through the lush gardens instantly appearing around them. As a finale, along with swelling music from *Titanic*, confetti, glowing sunsets, and bursting hearts precede a pan back into the stratosphere past fireworks and orbiting satellites. Even North Korea has created ecstatic videos that shift frantically through a number of up-tempo musical themes—a synthesized harp or run on the piano keys transitions between organ polkas, patriotic marches, high-pitched accordion jigs, emotional lullabies, and waltzes.[5]

3 MIT City Form Lab developed such a software to crunch data about a "reach" or "closeness" metric or an "in-betweenness index," all of which can describe relationships about traffic, real estate values, and business locations. City Form Lab, "Urban Network Analysis Toolbox for ArcGIS," http://cityform.mit.edu/projects/urban-network-analysis.html/.

4 "#KAEC—King Abdullah Economic City 2015," YouTube (January 19, 2015), https://www.youtube.com/watch?v=cjyn5BP38_4/; "New City Lazika," YouTube (January 16, 2013), https://www.youtube.com/watch?v=fKa3qgnZLpw; "Aras Free Zone," YouTube (August 12, 2008), https://www.youtube.com/watch?v=P199kZcBAqo/.

5 "North Korea on its special economic zones," YouTube (May 30, 2015), https://www.youtube.com/watch?v=kocPh9l934Y/.

Swinging from utopian to dystopian, another common script regards technology not as a redemptive universal, but the cause of apocalyptic failure. Within these tragic templates, often a favorite of even the most forward-looking tales of science fiction, new technologies have a dark conspiratorial intent that will foil our hero or cause the cataclysmic end of everything. In these dystopian scripts, new technology is sometimes treated as so impactful or so dangerous that there is no longer anything to design. So tragic is the impossibility of design that designers may turn away from making design proposals and instead use the very technologies they critique to work within the realm of rhetorical commentary or reportage.

The designer is now a filmmaker, documentarian, or data modeler. Documentaries about the city, if not in the upbeat TED style, frequently adhere to this genre of sci-fi tragedy. Cue the brooding music as the footage slowly surveys a hopeless landscape or constructs an exposé in which there are clear enemies and innocents. In this case, a nonspatial instrument like a film is not intended as a design tool—something that will shift habits with spatial consequence. Instead, it is the end in itself. The work—a film, program, or data visualization—circulates among galleries and other institutions where it is absorbed as a visual or sculptural artifact. At its best, the work sharpens a critical stance and galvanizes political movements. But it also sometimes satisfies both the impulse to design and a residual need for the new in its use of the most cutting-edge technologies, while inoculating against the difficulties and inevitable embarrassments associated with making a proposal.

Medium Design

If, in medium design, space itself is treated as an information system, digital devices are not necessarily smarter than relationships within spatial arrangements. Even without electronic devices, the spatial medium is wired. It computes. The disposition of that medium can be assessed in terms of its potentials, routines, and repertoires of activities. Digital devices can be smart or dumb, and the lumpy heavy solids of the city can also be smart or dumb. Working together, spatial and digital systems can make each other smarter or dumber. Both durable and ephemeral social spaces can refilter or remix the interactions of humans in ways that are more information rich or in ways that even reduce the violent dispositions immanent in networks.

For instance, networks of autonomous vehicles are treated as the means to perfect driving, reduce emissions, and increase productivity. But there may be some essential variables from the broader spatial medium that are missing from the equation. If these cars provide the same hands-free ride as transit does, and if they are used in lieu of transit, they will create unprecedented congestion. Imagine the space of a transit seat inflated to the size of a car. Even with carpooling and platooning, the very smart vehicle would be trapped in very dumb congestion. Medium design might respond with a physical spatial volume that acts like a switch in the larger spatial information system. An intermodal switch within the network encourages upshifting and downshifting to transportation modes of different capacities while delivering riders to both transit and autonomous vehicles. Designing that switch is medium design, even though it works hand in hand with—and creates the need for—the customary design of buildings and objects.

Benefitting from an artistic curiosity about reagents and spatial mixtures, medium design also suggests different ways to register the design imagination. Beyond buildings, master plans, declarations, laws, or standards, might architects design switches, multipliers, or protocols—time released organs of interplay like bargains, chain reactions, and ratchets? Beyond the geometric dimensions of urbanism, a changing set of relationships—even a changing set of routines, uses, or programs playing out over time—adds a temporal dimension that allows organizations to respond to shifting conditions.

Rather than a master plan that arranges fixed geometries, designers might establish protocols for an interdependency between urban components—a ratio or calculus function that would remain in place as the city grows. A city might link any number of factors. The total area reserved for green space might be linked to core densities. Or a city might like to transpose foreign investment from the free economic zone back to the city and make that investment support transit serving both citizens and businesses. As the city grows, it maintains counterbalancing forces rather than a geometric outline. Something like an anti-zone protocol might propose managing foreign investment in existing cities rather than exurban enclaves. How might an urban protocol develop a ratcheting effect that allows a city to make a better bargain with its assets?

Functional or Structural Complexity

In medium design, communication media—an image, film, or post—is not the end in itself, but another active form—another multiplier of spatial consequences. It not only represents space; it enacts spatial change. The proliferation of zone videos accelerated the spread of those cities by the thousands around the world. While sometimes portrayed as a rational economic instrument, the zone also became an object of desire through its various portrayals. Medium design can position nonspatial stories and media artifacts as countercontagion with the deliberate intent of further manipulating cultural habits and routines. The aesthetic regimes of medium design then require precision in both their direct and indirect intent.

A distinction that media theorist Vilém Flusser offered regarding media imagery is helpful in this regard. Arguing that "synthetic images"—like those produced in media and through computation—potentially have a power greater than words, Flusser observed that systems of imagery can either be structurally or functionally complex, meaning either the way they are made or the way they are used can be complex. He describes how a structurally complex system like television elicits a very simple functional use, whereas a structurally simple system like chess can elicit a functionally complex use.

> It is a fact that functionally complex systems are a challenge to creative thought, whereas functionally simple systems are stultifying, idiotic. Now the complex systems which now are coming about are complex in a structural sense, whether they will be functionally complex or not, depends on us.[6]

Many urban documents are arguably functionally primitive. Prepared for and consumed by a client or a small number of municipal decision makers, a master plan often organizes the world with geometry and produces "money shots" filled with happy people cartwheeling past real estate volumes. Maybe that is why more and more hyperbolic versions of the forms are so easy to reproduce in the back offices of global development companies. For those rhetorical artifacts that remain in the gallery, however structurally complex they may be, the role of spectator or consumer often overwhelms all other possibilities for interactivity.

What are the aesthetic practices deployed in functionally complex documents of medium design that shift potentials in a spatial matrix either through instructions and specifications of a proposal or persuasions with deliberate spatial intent? Both the switch and the anti-zone protocol are organs of interplay that, unlike a master plan, are structurally simple and functionally complex as they play out over time with contributions from multiple actors. The medium to communicate the idea might also be functionally complex if it can create a persuasion that changes how urban space is used or desired, or if it can simulate mixtures of different urban conditions from simple spatial variables.

The physical manifestation of the switch rewires space, but a spatial idea with any hope of gaining traction relies not only the specifications of relationship and dimension, but also on the spin that propels it in culture. For instance, car advertisements present a strong persuasion about the sexiness and freedom of driving alone at top speed on wet curving roads. But the designer of a spatial switch would create soft-focus ads for new "mobility companies" that demonstrate the appeal of being able to manage the complicated itineraries of life without driving. The interconnected space is a smart object. The contact with other people is the sexy experience. The hands-free face-to-face contact with family and others is the aspiration. Urbanity is the luxury. Reverse engineering the persuasions that encouraged sprawl, this story is the multiplier that changes a desire that could in turn change thousands and thousands of acres of space.

6 "Vilém Flusser—1988 interview about technical revolution (intellectual level is lowering)," YouTube (January 13, 2011), https://www.youtube.com/watch?v=lyfOcAAcoH8/.

Documents, prepared for citizens as well as officials, that essentially place the user's hands on the faders and toggles of urban growth might also be a compelling popular form that plays different time-lapse futures for the city with different settings and different linkages in different sequences of interplay. Beyond data visualization, the designer might create spatial engines that crunch data about, for instance, sea-level rise, storm surge, foreclosures, and house values, to encourage retreat from flood plains related to sea-level rise. Imagine an interface in which owners could establish linkages between property sales and moves that would result in relocation to higher ground as a way of triggering lower insurance, mortgage adjustments, and lower risk for all. While market incentives usually exacerbate climate change, this kind of functionally complex device could generate a multiplier that uses market incentives to relieve the crisis. Working with a live feed of changes, properties could play the field and even band together for the best deals. Real estate engines like Zillow that collate large amounts of information for sales have already become pop culture addictions.

"Playing" any of these fragments of a spatial imagination might be like playing a music video or like playing a game compelling in ways specific to design practices. Designers are already introducing books that, like the architectural equivalent of a graphic novel, insist on telling stories about global decisions that give authority to not only white papers and economic analysis, but also measured drawings.[7] Since photography now contains extremely accurate measurements keyed into the structure of the pixels, motion pictures might facilitate design's responsibilities to measure. This high-resolution imagery might be the building block for a measured cinema different from film in that it contains temporal and geometric dimensions, and different from design's the usual disciplinary documents in that it contains time. Beyond the pop culture obsession with staring slack-jawed at before-and-after makeovers for hours each night on television, how can medium design convey another set of ongoing specifications and instructions about scales of intervention from the individual house to the planet?

Medium design might operate with different logics from conventional design, but as it opens onto new fields of endeavor, it leaves behind a number of architectural precipitants and spatial enterprises. It suggests a means to engage the powers of more immaterial media in a way that avoids either cultural defaults or the abdication of material design. It may even suggest that designers can have another popular appeal as artists and practitioners who know how "to play space."

7 See Jesse LeCavalier, *The Rule of Logistics* (Minneapolis: University of Minnesota Press, 2016); Pierre Bélanger and Alexander Arroyo, *Ecologies of Power: Countermapping the Logistical Landscapes and Military Geographies of the U.S. Department of Defense* (Cambridge, MA: MIT Press, 2016); or Clare Lyster, *Learning from Logistics: How Networks Change Our Cities* (Basel, Switzerland: Birkhäuser, 2016).

UNA VEZ DECAPITADOS, ¿QUÉ QUEDA SOBRE NUESTROS HOMBROS?

Beatriz Colomina
with Shayari de Silva,
Dante Furioso
& Samantha Jaff

Interview with Beatriz Colomina

10.14.2017
Public Hotel, NYC

Perspecta **51: Your work across the years has been important to our understanding of media within the discipline of architecture. We find your recent work on the "City of Social Media"[1] particularly interesting. Do you consider this work to be a continuation of** *Privacy and Publicity*?[2]

Beatriz Colomina: For me it is a continuation, yes, but I do see a major break in the way in which we operate as architects. We are in an unprecedented situation today that parallels the revolution in media that architects from the first decades of the twentieth century lived through, when they confronted the arrival of photography and the illustrated architecture magazine, film, radio, et cetera. It not only changed the way they disseminated their work, but radically changed their notions of what was inside and what was outside, what was public and what was private. They had to rethink what they were doing in fundamental ways. Now we are in the midst of a revolution of at least the same dimension, if not bigger. The internet and social media are redefining the spaces in which we live and our relationships to objects and to each other. Social media is a new form of urbanization, the architecture of how we live together.

P51 In understanding the contemporary, even if it's looking back to understand the contemporary, this question of medium is very chameleon-like. At one moment it's space, and the next moment it's a way of understanding space. Have you encountered that?

BC I don't make a distinction. I think space is a medium, as much as photography is a medium. I don't make those separations. For example, with *Privacy and Publicity*, **at first I thought I was working in the more traditional understanding of what media is: photography, film, publicity—**

P51 Mass media, right?

BC Mass media, of course. But the most interesting part of this book, in my view, is the turning point—the point at which I understood that architecture itself was changing, and that the medium of space was communicating a new idea of what was public and what was private, what was inside and what was outside, that corresponds to the new technologies of communication. From there, the close readings of the interiors of Adolf Loos and Le Corbusier try to demonstrate that architecture also plays a deliberate role in this transformation. You cannot separate architecture from media. Architecture is media.

P51 Would you be willing to talk a little bit about the process that led to *Privacy and Publicity* **and the personal interests you had that led you there?**

BC *Privacy and Publicity* **was actually my dissertation, which took several unexpected turns, as usually happens. At first, I thought I was working on Loos,**

and the first version of the chapter that in the book is called "City" was published as an article in a magazine called 9H with the title "On Adolf Loos and Josef Hoffmann: Architecture in the Age of Mechanical Reproduction."[3] Then somehow I became interested in Le Corbusier and the media and went to Paris to work in the Le Corbusier archive. I actually thought I was going to work on *L'Esprit Nouveau* magazine—a very traditional understanding of media: this is an architect, and this is the magazine that he edited. I was also curious about the network of avant-garde magazines of the 1920s, looking for evidence of their exchanges through the lens of *L'Esprit Nouveau*.

So I arrived at the archives of the Fondation Le Corbusier, which were only open from 2 to 6 p.m., and you had to have an appointment months ahead, and of course they want to know exactly what you are working on. As if you knew! So I said *L'Esprit Nouveau*, and they said that there were many boxes, but they could only bring one at a time. And I say okay, and half an hour later the first box arrives and I open it and it's a catalog of this, an advertisement of that, a clipping from a newspaper, and I thought to myself, "Oh, I got the junk mail box," because it doesn't make any sense to me. It is all catalogs of department stores, catalogs of Delage cars, catalogs of Hermès bags, of Innovation filing cabinets, of Farman airplanes. ... So I returned that box and asked for another one, and, of course, another half an hour passes, and here comes the other one, and you know, basically it's the same thing. And by the time I go through it, it's already time to close and I have to come back the following day and it is the same thing all over again. Long story short, after several days of going through what I thought was the junk mail, looking for the elusive letter from Walter Gropius or Theo van Doesburg—which are indeed lost in there in the middle of all of this—it comes to me that the catalogs and advertisements are the really important thing for Le Corbusier. He was actively asking for these catalogs in long elaborate letters, writing to makers of airplanes, of cars, of lamps, of trunks: "Please send me one of your beautiful catalogs with the great photographs." I also realized that some images were missing from the catalogs, and I started putting things together: he was clipping photographs that were then used as illustrations in *L'Esprit Nouveau* and later in his 1920s books: *Vers une architecture*, *L'art décoratif d'aujourd'hui*, *Almanach*, et cetera.

In the meantime, there are all these letters from the avant-garde that remain for the most part unanswered! He doesn't give a damn about the network of the avant-garde. I remember an exasperated Van Doesburg asking for the material that he had sent for publication. If *L'Esprit Nouveau* was not going to publish it they could at least return it, he argues. Of course, the magazine never published the work of any other architect. They were not interested in that. But the amazing thing is that he doesn't even bother to answer, while he doggedly pursues all these manufacturers for their catalogs. At a certain point it dawned on me that this was the topic, actually. The media is the topic.

So, I went back to the first box and to each one of them to look again more closely at how he had constructed first the magazine and then his own books out of all this everyday publicity material, newspapers, magazines, and catalogs. Le Corbusier's books are so revolutionary, in the sense that there are images of the Parthenon next to images of cars or airplanes, turbines, ventilators, filing cabinets. The first thing for me was to understand the relationship between Le Corbusier and the media of his time: modern publicity, photography, film, radio, and what effect it had on his own publications—*L'Esprit Nouveau* magazine and the books that came out of that experience. It was a huge amount of work already. I was in the archives for so long that I became friends with everybody who came around, and there were many people, because the centennial of Le Corbusier's birth in 1987 was coming up and they were preparing exhibitions everywhere. Stani von Moos was doing an exhibition on Le Corbusier in Zurich, and I published an article on Le Corbusier and photography for his catalog. Then Jean-Louis Cohen and Bruno Reichlin were preparing a big exhibition on Le Corbusier at the Centre Pompidou, and they commissioned the piece on publicity for their catalog, which was an encyclopedia. In the meantime, *Assemblage* was starting here in the United States, so I published another fragment there as well. So it was also myself experimenting with media.

But the turning point for me—I know that's what makes the book important—was a conceptual turn. Most people don't realize it. They'll say, "Oh, it's so great when you do the readings of the interiors of Adolf Loos," but it's actually the conceptual turn to start thinking of architecture as a medium that's important—that's why the subtitle is "Modern Architecture as Mass Media."

P51 So if that was the moment of mass media and this is the moment of social media, do you see this as a continuation of the trajectory, or do you see it as a second turning point?

BC It's a second turning point, because social media radically changes the way in which we live, the way in which we communicate with others, the way in which we work, even the way we love. We are living in nineteenth-century cities, with the radical separation between the place of work, the office, and the place of living, which is already obsolete. We are actually already living and working in very different kinds of spaces, coworking spaces that are products of a sharing economy, new forms of domesticity, working from bed, in a park, or actually anywhere in the world. ... We have all become digital nomads. The physical reality of our cities is changing, whether architects are aware of it or not.

P51 It's almost as if the architecture is disguising all these changes because the architecture remains constant.

BC Yes, exactly, because it's so slow to change. But I guess it took us a while to change in the nineteenth century too, with the separation of the place of work (the office or the factory) and place of living. People used to live on top of where they worked in medieval times. You would have your atelier downstairs ... and now we are returning to that, except it's all collapsing into the bed.

P51 Like the medieval bed even, which would have been actually a more public place back before the days of enfilade when rooms were connected and people walked from one room to the next.

BC Yes! The bed was a public space for a long time.

P51 So in a lot of ways we're going full circle.

BC Yes.

P51 Except it's not a social or public space with physical people now.

BC No, it is too sometimes.

P51 It is, but more so it's this network or platform as you said. But it's interesting to think about this relationship between the premodern bed, the medieval bed as the social space, and now the modern social bed.

BC The modern social bed? It is social inasmuch as you are engaging through social media with so many people in personal relationships, work relationships, et cetera. I focused precisely on the question of the bed for a long time because for me it's the epicenter of this new transformation—the fact that so many people do so many activities in what used to be a place that was only for your eight hours of sleep. Through the internet and social media, you are connected to the whole world from your bed: to India, to China, to Latin America, to Europe, at different times of the day. People are waking up in the middle of the night to answer emails, to Skype. ... This kind of 24/7 culture that we are living in has architectural consequences and urban consequences that we need to think about.

P51 It seems like one of the most salient examples you've worked on is the example of Hugh Hefner as an icon of that condition. It's particularly interesting because he recently passed away. Had you met him?

BC No, I hadn't met him personally. But I did all this research with my students and we put together an exhibition, several exhibitions actually, that were in the Netherlands Architecture Institute (NAI) Bureau Europa in Maastricht and the NAI in Rotterdam, in the Deutsches Architekturmuseum (DAM) in Frankfurt, and more recently in the Elmhurst Art Museum in Illinois and the Centre de Cultura Contemporània (CCCB) in Barcelona. The moment Hefner passed, all these magazines and even CNN wanted to talk with me about it. *[laughter]*

So yes, it's important. Hefner is a symbol in our age of this kind of work-in-bed mentality, for better or worse, in which the bed again becomes a social space. Another incredible precedent is Yoko Ono and John Lennon, who used their honeymoon bed at the Hilton International in Amsterdam as a site of protest, which is again a transformation of the bed into a public space, with journalists coming in and going out in a very precise schedule from 9 a.m. to 9 p.m. The bed replaced the street as a site of protest. And there are many other examples.

P51 You also talk about Richard Neutra.

BC Well, Neutra is interesting to me because he is an architect who felt he could work in bed and even attend to clients in bed and draw in bed—do everything in bed to use his time more effectively. And this is actually all at midcentury, at the same time that some writers and other creative people were also working from bed. As Truman Capote reportedly said in an interview, he is a "completely horizontal author" and "he can't even think unless he is lying down." He wrote everything in bed.

P51 In *Privacy and Publicity* you talk about different kinds of subjectivities that can be produced. Do you think social media is providing this kind of break in subjectivity or a turning point in that sense as well?

BC It's a producing a new subject. Yes, of course it is.

P51 And even the multiplicities of personalities that one could choose to project.

BC Exactly. Already at the beginning of the twentieth century people spoke about the need for a mask in the metropolis and about the need to protect your personal inner self in the interior, with the architecture of Loos, for example. The mask could be fashion, but it could also be the ways in which you interact with others without revealing too much about yourself. You know the way in which we all know the codes in New York for example—in the subway not to look people in the eyes, to hide yourself behind this *[gestures to an iPhone]*, behind that, behind the newspapers, et cetera. So, today we are in an acceleration of that condition inasmuch as we create a different identity to deal with different situations. You are not the same at work as on your Tinder or on your Grindr or on whatever it is that you are using, and you're not the same on your Instagram account as you are on your Snapchat or your Facebook, because your mother is on Facebook and you have to be careful about what you say and who you befriend. And then, you have to be careful about work too. So, there are these ways in which we reveal a lot, but we also try to protect some parts, particularly because this has become a major problem. Everything you say in social media could come back to haunt you—in your personal relationship, your workplace, your reputation in the world, et cetera. It exists forever.

P51 Right. The most ephemeral thing is also the most permanent.

BC It remains there on view for so many people and it's super exposed, right?

P51 Do you use social media?

BC No, I don't use social media. I am intensely concerned about privacy. But I think about it. Social media has a lot of issues. At some point, it seemed like it was incredibly liberating and progressive and was going to democratize the world. Remember the initial optimism of the Arab Spring? And now it's turned against us with the Russian hacking and the intervention in the elections in the US and in other places too, like Catalonia. In the space of a few years we went from thinking that this was the best thing that could happen to all of us, to seeing the darker side of it too.

P51 In a very short span of time.

BC Yes, exactly. And it is crucial to understand that it's an urban condition, an architectural system. That's what I'm saying—that there is a city of social media. We have to think of social media as an urban condition and we have to be aware of this architecture.

P51 And that's the struggle, right? Because architecture can't change as a discipline in five years.

BC No, it's very slow.

P51 And the condition we're trying to be a part of is changing before we can get on board.

BC Right. On the one hand there's that; on the other hand there has been social media since the year 2000, so ... about time, right?

P51 Right, and we're still learning to use computers in architecture.

BC Well, since the 1980s we have been using computers.

P51 Which is still pretty recent in the grand scheme of things.

BC It is really recent. The paperless studios at Columbia University, the digital generation, the first software ... and now it's evolving really rapidly.

P51 And you would have come to Columbia just before that, is that correct?

BC Oh no, I came much earlier, in the early 1980s. I saw the arrival of the first personal computers. I had a Kaypro around 1982. Most people didn't have a computer until much later. People would come to my apartment and ask, "What is that?"

P51 And before that you had studied in Spain.

BC I studied architecture in the school of architecture of Barcelona, which was very good at the time. Fantastic people were teaching there—people like Rafael Moneo, Oriol Bohigas, Ignasi de Solà-Morales, and so many others. It was very important to me because I didn't grow up in Barcelona. I was born in Madrid and grew up in Valencia, but went to Barcelona because it was the best school in Spain at that time. Spain was still a dictatorship. Franco died the last year of my studies, and during all that time we were all very much activists, constantly in the streets, in demonstrations. Demonstrations were part of the curriculum.

P51 So, does your interest in all of these radical magazines and the use of media as a kind of tactical tool come from that experience?

BC Yes, yes it does in a way, because I used to be involved with of one of those little magazines that we did in Barcelona with young faculty and students in the late 1970s and early 1980s.

P51 It's interesting to understand that your work has this basis in activism.

BC When I was a student and a young faculty member in Barcelona, I already had a kind of sensitivity toward the media. One of the first classes I taught at Columbia University was about the avant-garde journals of the early twentieth century. We would go to MoMA and look at all the *De Stijl* and *L'Esprit Nouveau* and all these well-known magazines, but also magazines like *Pásmo* and *Red* and *Stavba* and Polish and Czechoslovakian magazines. It was really fascinating. From there to the research on the little magazines of the 1960s and 1970s that I did with my students at Princeton University, there has been this continuous interest in architectural publications.

P51 And you did that with the work with Craig Buckley—the amazing *Clip/Stamp/Fold*.[4]

BC Actually, the team for the exhibition and the research was much bigger and included great people like Lydia Kallipoliti, Urtzi Grau, Lisa Hsieh, Daniel López-Pérez, Alicia Imperiale, Anthony Fontenot, and Irene Sunwoo, but the book was put together by Craig, Urtzi, and me. *Clip/Stamp/Fold*, the website and the collaborative platform, existed before the book. We thought it was better to have a platform, and people could add things, and so on. But wherever we went with the exhibition, and we went to more than twelve cities globally, people would ask, "When are you coming out with the book?" and we would say, "What book?" *[laughter]* But then we thought we had better come up with a book because we have all this material and there was clearly a desire for such a book. It was a huge amount of work. The same thing is happening to us now with the *Radical Pedagogies* project, which I also did with Princeton students. It was first an exhibition and a platform with all the case studies we had developed, but practically every week, and still today, we get emails from people all over the world—Latin America, Australia, New Zealand, wherever—that say, "Oh, do you know about this little school that was here?" Most of the contributions, and there are by now more than a hundred, are from people who have nothing to do with Princeton. So this is more like an open-source project, which I love. But still, wherever we go, people ask us, "When is the book coming out?" So we are going to have to do something about it soon.

P51 But in a way it's fulfilling something you had wanted to do with *Clip/Stamp/Fold*, which was to have it be more of a forum, have it be more interactive.

BC Yes, but as I say people keep asking us when the book *Radical Pedagogies* will come out. So, I think we have to do the book, because in the age of new media, the ironic thing is that we have become very attached to physical books.

P51 As editors of books, we are on board with this. *[laughter]*

BC And I'm more than on board with this, too. So, I have decided that yes, even if the electronic platform continues and you can never close a project like this, and it opens up a new interactive and collaborative community sharing their archives and ideas—which is fantastic—as a new mode of research more in tune the current world, if you do a book too then you have something that can become useful to people in another way, like an archive or resource for research. Different rhythm, different layers. I am for multimedia. Our world, our architecture, is multimedia.

P51 There's also something nice about setting the limits and having to define what the most important thing is, because otherwise it can just become infinite.

BC Right. But books can be infinite too. Books can ask questions rather than answer them. What matters is that the electronic platform is sharing knowledge in a way we didn't do before.

P51 It makes sense, because you mentioned that your early work in publications was tactical. It was for a reason, so you understood that it existed beyond just being a nice, pretty object. It had a purpose.

BC Yes. It absolutely had a political purpose. There were the politics of the journal itself and trying to change the situation in Spain, but also at the same time, trying in a school of architecture to say that

there are more ways of doing research and writing history. We offered examples of new kinds of work, saying, here's the way in which we are learning from Michel Foucault and Manfredo Tafuri and others how to do research and writing in architecture today. And now we are again in a much more complicated and vastly different situation. No longer a small set of role models, but a wider and more interdisciplinary group of very committed people changing the way in which we engage history, right?

1 **Beatriz Colomina,** *The City of Social Media*, **multimedia installation in the 2017 Seoul Biennale of Architecture and Urbanism,** *Imminent Commons*, **developed in collaboration with Evangelos Kotsioris and Weiwei Zhang. See also Colomina, "The City of Social Media," in** *Imminent Commons: Commoning Cities* **(Seoul: Seoul Biennale of Architecture and Urbanism and ACTAR, 2017).**

2 **Beatriz Colomina,** *Privacy and Publicity: Modern Architecture as Mass Media* **(Cambridge, MA: MIT Press, 1994).**

3 **Beatriz Colomina, "On Adolf Loos and Josef Hoffmann: Architecture in the Age of Mechanical Reproduction,"** *9H* **6 (1982): 52–58.**

4 **Beatriz Colomina and Craig Buckley, ed.,** *Clip/Stamp/Fold: The Radical Architecture of Little Magazines, 196x–197x* **(Barcelona: ActarBirkhäuser, 2010).**

Calabasas 91302: "It's weird and boring but I'm obsessed[1]"

Talking about the post-internet city often leads to sweeping statements and a feeling of irresolution. There is a sense that everything is being transformed, absorbed, and mined, that something profoundly novel is taking shape, but everything still looks and feels deceptively the same. If the changes to society brought by social media and the digital are evident, they haven't yet translated into architecture. Nevertheless, there are symptoms of how social media might interact with architecture—and the City of Calabasas in California is one example, perhaps even a prototype of sorts, if not a paradigm of this change.

Calabasas is the world capital of social media in the way Hollywood is the world capital of cinema. A disproportionate number of the most influential accounts on Instagram, Twitter, Snapchat, and Vevo are run by its inhabitants. Since Instagram's launch in 2010, about half of the ten most-followed accounts have been Calabasians'. By comparison, the rest of the United States has fewer followers on Instagram than Calabasas alone.

Fig. 1. Instagram accounts with most followers by location

No.	2012 (Apr)	Followers in million	2013	Followers in million	2014 (Jan)	Followers in million	2015 (Oct)	Followers in million	2016 (Dec)	Followers in million	2017 (Oct)	Followers in million
1	Instagram	1.8	Instagram	--	Instagram	--	Instagram	--	Instagram	199	Instagram	227
2	Justin Bieber	1.6	Justin Bieber	--	Justin Bieber	12	Taylor Swift	50	Selena Gomez	103	Selena Gomez	128
3	Kim Kardashian	1.5	Kim Kardashian	--	Kim Kardashian	12	Kim Kardashian	48	Taylor Swift	94	Ariana Grande	115
4	Selena Gomez	1.4	Rihanna	--	Rihanna	11	Beyoncé	47	Ariana Grande	91	Cristiano Ronaldo	113
5	Taylor Swift	1.3	Ariana Grande	--	Beyoncé	8.9	Selena Gomez	46	Beyoncé	89	Beyoncé	107
6	Kendall Jenner	1	Kendall Jenner	--	Ariana Grande	8.4	Ariana Grande	45	Kim Kardashian	88	Taylor Swift	104
7	Kylie Jenner	0.9	Taylor Swift	--	Miley Cyrus	8.2	Justin Bieber	--	Cristiano Ronaldo	83	Kim Kardashian	104
8	Rihanna	0.8	Beyoncé	--	Kendall Jenner	8.1	Kendall Jenner	--	Kylie Jenner	80	Kylie Jenner	100
9	Zooey Deschanel	0.6	Khloé Kardashian	--	Taylor Swift	7.4	Kylie Jenner	--	Dwayne Johnson	72	Dwayne Johnson	95
10	Barack Obama	0.6	Kylie Jenner	--	Khloé Kardashian	7.4	Khloe Kardashian	--	Nicki Minaj	70	Justin Bieber	92
11	Snoop Dog	0.6	--	--	Kylie Jenner	6.9	Miley Cyrus	--	Kendall Jenner	70	Kendall Jenner	84
12	MTV	0.5	--	--	Kourtney Kardashian	6.4	Nicki Minaj	--	Nike	66	Nicki Minaj	84
13	Rob Kardashian	0.5	--	--	Selena Gomez	6.1	Rihanna	--	National Geographic	63	National Geographic	83
14	Wiz Khalifa	0.5	--	--	Harry Styles	6.1	Neymar Jr.	--	Neymar	62	Neymar Jr.	83
15	Chris Brown	0.5	--	--	Kevin Hart	4.9	Kourtney Kardashian	--	Lionel Messi	59	Lionel Messi	83
16	Starbucks	0.5	--	--	Niall Horan	4.8	Katy Perry	--	Khloe Kardashian	59	Nike	75
17	Lauren Conrad	0.4	--	--	Drake	4.6	Cristiano Ronaldo	--	Katy Perry	58	Miley Cyrus	74
18	Trey Songz	0.4	--	--	Lebron James	4.5	Kevin Hart	--	Miley Cyrus	56	Khloe Kardashian	70
19	Alicia Keys	0.4	--	--	Nicole 'Snooki' Polizzi	4.2	Demi Lovato	--	Jennifer Lopez	53	Jennifer Lopez	70
20	Ryan Seacrest	0.4	--	--	Akon	4.2	Harry Styles	--	Demi Lovato	50	Katy Perry	70
% of top-ten living in Calabasas	50,00%		50,00%		40,00%		60,00%		40,00%		50,00%	

Top Instagram accounts by followers

Living in Calabasas
Living in Los Angeles
Living in the rest of the world
Non-human account

Instagram was launched in 2010. No data before 2012.

Data retrieved from various sources, including Mashable, The Roosevelts, Forbes, Statista, Socialblade, Variety, BusinessInsider, TeenVogue.

Like earlier media, social media's spatial distribution is uneven. But why is the suburban neighborhood of Calabasas so attractive to the stars of this new spectacle? Why has this city lent itself to smartphone-augmented life in ways other places have not? This question, which has been repeatedly posed by tabloids and international lifestyle magazines in recent years, also deserves to be answered architecturally.[2]

Fig. 2. Aerial photos of Calabasas

To position Calabasas in relation to Los Angeles, simply follow Mulholland Drive. The notorious road sinuously crosses the hills from east to west, from the bottom of the Hollywood Sign to the mall of Calabasas. When David Lynch stated, “You feel the history of Hollywood in that road,” on the release of his film *Mulholland Drive*,[3] perhaps he was not only talking about the many celebrity mansions located along the road and the impressive panorama of LA onto which it intermittently opens. Nor was he simply referring to the water engineer William Mulholland, who made the California dream possible by bringing the city a sufficient water supply, and inspiring Roman Polanski’s legendary movie *Chinatown* (1974).[4] Instead, perhaps Lynch prophetically sensed that the history of Los Angeles that had started in Hollywood with cinema would reach its pinnacle in Calabasas with social media—and perhaps its demise.

Released in October 2001, Lynch’s *Mulholland Drive* hinges on this periodization. It is both an homage to a lethargic Hollywood and a venture into post-cinema spectacle. Los Angeles is rendered as a city lost in its own dreams, where reality eventually gives way to fiction, and identity to performance. Rita, who has forgotten who she is after a car crash on Mulholland Drive, is desperately searching for an identity. She meets aspiring actress Betty, who helps her live her life as a performance. “It’ll be just like in the movies. We’ll pretend to be someone else,” Betty says to comfort Rita.[5] Freed to be anybody while cursed to never be real, Lynch’s protagonists could very well be remarking on the struggles of selfhood after social media, something that has become an art form in its own right, especially in the city of Calabasas.

Fig. 3. Map of Southwestern Los Angeles County
Fig. 4. Map of Calabasas

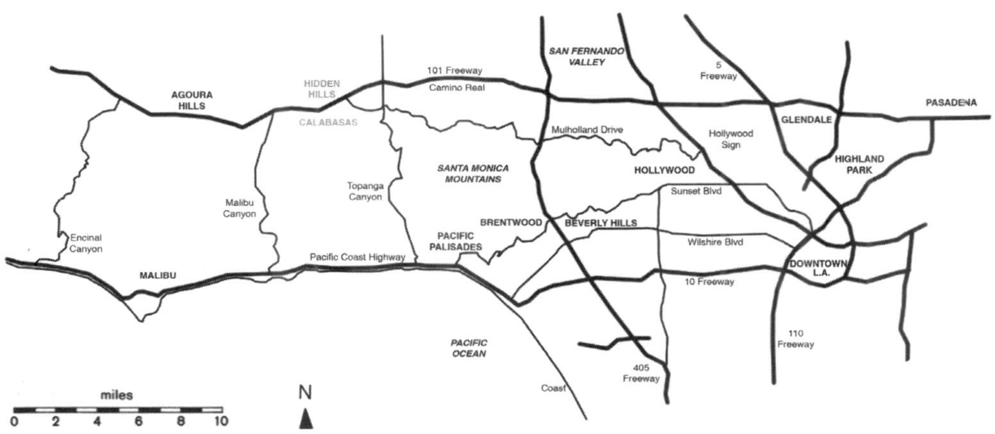

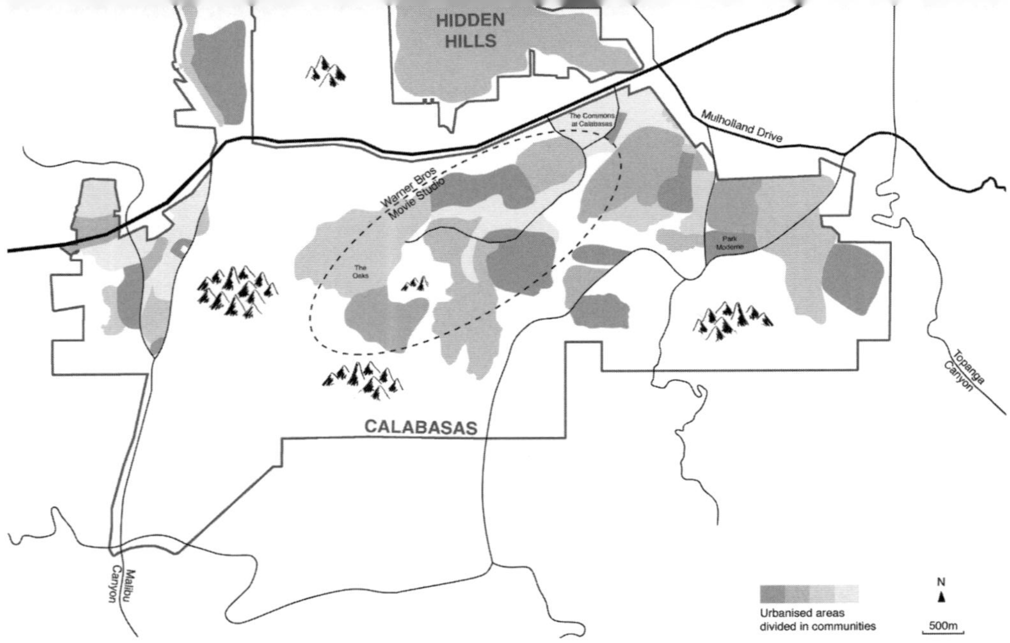

A city of walled cities

While Calabasas is known by the majority of Angelenos as an exceptional haven for celebrities, it is generally regarded as a boring, white, wealthy, conservative area with no distinctive features. It is the caricature of a suburb, a place remarkable for being familiar and deceptively normal. Its urbanism is entirely dominated by the enclave. It is a fortress city in the sense of Mike Davis's 1990 *City of Quartz* and an enclave in the sense of Reyner Banham's 1971 *Los Angeles: The Architecture of Four Ecologies*. As such, it is very much an archetype of Los Angeles urbanism.[6] Calabasas is an impenetrable network of walls and gates, a conglomerate of fortified territories made of many fortified cells, a stark contrast with the rhetoric of access and openness so dear to the internet.

The vast majority of the urbanized land of Calabasas is occupied by thirty-two residential communities.[7] These communities are on the wealthier end of the real estate development that has spread vastly in the Los Angeles area and throughout the United States since World War II. Each residential community has its own rules, its own private security and guards, its own maintenance and garbage collection, and its own community spaces within its walls, effectively dividing Calabasas into a city of many private sub-cities, each with specificities advertised in its own real estate brochure.

The majority of Calabasas's communities are gated, making the residential roads mostly inaccessible to visitors.[8] Gated communities are not unusual in the United States, but whereas in other places gates isolate a small proportion of a city, Calabasas stands out as almost completely compounded. There is hardly anything accessible to the public in Calabasas apart from the malls, the walls, and the community gates themselves.

The communities of Calabasas range from the gateless suburban development of Calabasas Village (where the price of a house starts at $200,000) to the luxury community the Oaks, where a second layer of gates encloses a fifty-property extra-exclusive community called the Estates at the Oaks, where the price of a house starts at $6 million. The most exclusive community in Calabasas, however, is Hidden Hills. Although very much inseparable from Calabasas in practice, Hidden Hills is legally autonomous. It was incorporated as its own city in 1961, thirty years before Calabasas, and is likely the aspirational model for neighboring gated communities. Hidden Hills enjoys the ultimate luxury of a border wall; the only territory outside the city walls are the city hall and the Los Angeles Pet Cemetery.[9]

Historically, the urban typology of the walled city has more to do with the age of feudal lordship than the modern capitalist state, and yet the walled city of Hidden Hills is quite popular among the heroes of new media. The Osbournes moved to Hidden Hills after their eponymous reality TV show, and most of the Kardashian family members reside there, as well as artists Jennifer Lopez, Kanye West, and Drake. Drake, who calls his house the "safe house," raps, "This is a gated community, please get the fuck off the property" in "Versace (Remix)" on Migos's album *Y.R.N. (Young Rich Niggas)* (2013). Calabasas officials, realtors, and tabloids agree on one point: celebrities love the hyper-privacy of the city because it balances their hyper-public presence. Accordingly, they are only searching for a bit of intimacy, a life without paparazzi or intruders, and the freedom to walk down the street to visit their friends, neighbors, and to enjoy life like everyone else.[10]

Fig. 5. Screenshot from Kylie Jenner's Instagram feed

Extrastate Communities

All the communities of Calabasas are common-interest developments (CID) run by homeowner associations (HOA). CIDs and HOAs offer the legal and financial framework to facilitate the initial real estate development while allowing the occupants to structure the governance of the development. They allow developers to build and advertise a project, sell the units to residents, and later transfer residents' stakes to the HOA, which includes the by-laws and fees accepted by the residents ahead of buying their properties. This legal structure is responsible for the gates and guards, the funding of community spaces, and collective services like garbage collection. In this way, the communities are a blend between exclusive members' clubs, city states, cooperatives, and corporations.

Today, CIDs and HOAs dominate contemporary urban development in the United States, just as similar liberal mechanisms do across the rest of the world.[11] In the 1970s, there were an estimated 10,000 HOAs in the US, totaling 2.1 million residents. In 2016, the estimate was 342,000 HOAs with a total of 69 million inhabitants, which amounts to more than one fifth of the US population.[12] In this sense, Calabasas is the avant-garde—a city solely composed of this new breed of real estate products, having done away entirely with more traditional forms of municipal functions. As Keller Easterling argues, these extrastate zones are powerful because they provide the infrastructure necessary to the expansion of global capitalism. Could the city of Calabasas be a glimpse of what a fully extrastate urbanity would be like, a city composed of different inhabitable lifestyle products suited for the branded lives of the contemporary spectacle?[13] Could the compounded nature of Calabasas be more contemporary than the fluid typologies of space that are usually associated with late capitalism?

The rise of CIDs and HOAs has been both an engine and a symptom of the neoliberalization of cities. They act as real estate companies that guarantee certain types of amenities and atmospheres to those who can afford it. They oppose the idea of the city as a right and instead propose the city as a service that can be bought by individuals organized as a community of neighbors. The legislative framework allows the wealthy to segregate themselves into highly serviced communities that are dependent on, but inaccessible to, the rest of the city. They do so without infringing upon anti-discrimination acts by invoking harmless concepts such as the *community* and the *neighborhood* through their very nomenclature. As political organizations founded on private property, CIDs actively divide the city between those who own property and those who do not. Property ownership becomes a condition for basic services, rights, and representation. Instead of the "one body, one vote" principle of modern democracy, CIDs follow a principle of "one plot of land, one vote." This social ethic equating rights with property is closer to feudal rights than modern rights, although this contemporary lordship isn't "by nature" or "by blood" in its constitution, but instead abides by the pseudo-egalitarian liberal rule of "whoever can afford it." Feudalism is openly evoked by Calabasas planners, who named its shopping mall The Commons at Calabasas,[14] as well as by celebrity residents like Scott Disick, who explains how to live like a king in his TV show *Lord Disick: Lifestyles of a Lord* (2013–present). After all, the decentralized court does watch the staged daily life of the lords of Calabasas quite similarly to the way the courtesans attended to the staged routine Louis XIV in Versailles. Power is exercised through spectacle.

Fig. 6. Hidden Hills gates

City Branding / Self-Branding

The *Dr. Housing Bubble* blog calls Calabasas "the quintessential SoCal bubble city,"[15] which seems fair considering that house prices have been particularly volatile over the last two decades, that the city has been subject to various media hypes, and that the social makeup of the city is precisely the middle class with access to high credit responsible for the 2008 financial crisis. (The richer creditors involved in large financial montage participated more significantly to the crisis than the poorer subprime creditors, who are usually considered responsible for the crash.)[16] Judging by local press and advertisements, real estate speculation seems to be one of the dominant cultural activities in Calabasas. Investments, house flipping, lifestyle branding, home decoration, artificial scarcity: everything is geared toward this form of production of value.

Fig. 7. Flip your own home

The legal structure of the residential developments directly participates in the culture of real estate speculation. HOAs and CIDs incentivize the residents to inflate their property value collectively because it increases both the neighborhood's worth and the value of individual properties. Conversely, misrepresenting or criticizing your own neighborhood would damage its brand, its reputation, and its value. This form of control is very much aligned with the one dominating digital platforms and social media, which are themselves modeled after the financial market. As Michel Feher argues individuals are made into "investors in their own human capital ... as managers of a portfolio of conducts pertaining to all the aspects of their lives."[17] The branding of the city logically implies the branding of the self. In this context, it comes as little surprise that social media platforms found a fertile space to develop in the communities of Calabasas. They only augment the already aspirational culture of the communities by providing more space for it to develop.

Calabasas's celebrity magnetism emerged from the combined effects of the financial crisis and the explosion of the new social media economy that followed the release of the first smartphone (Apple's iPhone) during the summer of 2007. The steep drop in housing prices due to the financial crisis made the lavish homes of Calabasas affordable for a nascent breed of pop stars. The presence and self-display of the artist-residents in the exclusive compounds infused the communities with an exposure and a relevance they never had, which grew the appeal and the value of the communities beyond any expectations and reversed to some extent the effects of the crash on housing prices. The artists moved into an existing city and rebranded it by living there. It is an unusual case of gentrification, involving new celebrities in a wealthy conservative neighborhood, but it still bears all its other traits.

Fig. 8. Bomber jacket with the map of Calabasas, The Kids Supply 2017 collection

CALABASAS REVERSIBLE SILK BOMBER

100% WASHED SILK QUILTED FILLED AND EMBROIDERED

SOLD OUT

Kanye West and Drake, who live within walking distance from each other in Hidden Hills, announced their upcoming collaboration by installing a billboard stating, “Calabasas is the new Abu Dhabi,” at the center of Hollywood. (The project never happened.) West’s clothing brand Yeezy embraced the Calabasas lifestyle as its ethos. As West says, it is “about embracing where me and my family live, where my kids are growing up, embracing the attitude and style of the Valley.”[18] Many of the clothes, shoes, and accessories made by Yeezy bear the word “Calabasas” written in the distinctive Planet Kosmos font. The children’s line that West launched with his wife, Kim Kardashian, also draws heavily on Calabasas. Many of its pieces spell out the name of the city, and a bomber jacket even features a map of Calabasas that shows the city limits, the park next to one of the schools, the shopping mall, and their gated community of Hidden Hills. The pioneers of the new media have collectively branded Calabasas as not merely a city, but a lifestyle. It is illustrative of the relationship that social media subjects have with their spatial environment.

Fig. 9. Billboard by Drake and Kanye West in Hollywood, August 2016

Calabasas has been reinvented by the smartphone. It is already much more than a neighborhood. It is a culture, an aesthetic, a subjectivity, and it is the archetypal representation of life on social media, like Hollywood has been in cinema. In fact, Hollywood and Calabasas are both real estate developments repurposed into monuments and then into to global media industries. Both mainly exist on screens. One was shaped by the car and the other by the smartphone.[19] *In Learning from Las Vegas* (1972), Denise Scott Brown and Robert Venturi argued that the city seen through the car could only be captured on film. What does it mean to experience a city through a smartphone? Glass is not only looked through but caressed all day. It is all simultaneously intimate and publicized, open and privatized, present and disembodied.

Hollywood 2.0

Calabasas’s 2003 reality television debut was on the series *Newlyweds: Nick and*

Jessica, showing the beginning of Jessica Simpson and Nick Lachey's marriage in their Calabasas house. But what most decisively established Calabasas as a home for social media celebrities was the 2007 reality TV show *Keeping Up with the Kardashians*. Now a decade old, after 195 episodes, thirteen seasons, and several spin-offs, the series has also led the seven-member family to build a half-billion dollar empire of apps, games, lifestyle products, fashion collections, and beauty lines.[20] The reasons for the global success of the Kardashians are manifold, but the journey of this not-too-standard upper-middle-class entrepreneurial matriarchy from semi-fame to global stardom was decisively fostered by the radical publication of their private lives and their proactive use of new platforms to develop narratives. Sharing everything was their main business strategy, admits Kris, the mother and manager.[21] They demonstrated a commitment to the new media and pioneered many of the practices that later became the norms for social media influencers, especially how to make them profitable. Today, one earns about $0.05 per follower, and a single post by Kim is estimated to be worth $500,000.

The smartphone and tablet game *Kim Kardashian: Hollywood* contains a particularly revealing detail about the economy of the new media. The game lets players achieve global celebrity by guiding an avatar through fashion choices, famous friends, and social media. To prevent the avatar from running out of energy, a player can either wait, watch advertisements to shorten the waiting time, or buy energy bars. The player's attention is directly equated with advertisements and money. The attention given to the avatar is not only the goal of the game, but it is also the real currency funding it.

Fig. 10. Screenshot from the game *Kim Kardashian: Hollywood*

When attention is value, aspiration is business, and personal life is devoted to an audience, the environment of the everyday is subject to different rules. It must be a relatable backdrop and a place that can be easily staged. The suburbia of Calabasas is first and foremost, in spite of its eccentricities, a hypernormal version of the suburbs that everyone, anywhere in the world, is familiar with after decades of Hollywood movies, TV shows, and celebrity news. The complete inaccessibility and fantasy of the lives depicted in Calabasas is balanced with radically familiar spaces. The aspirations of the new media rely on this relatable aesthetic. The familiarity is currency, a frame of equivalence known by the audience through which to appreciate the daily mise-en-scène in spite of the distance, and therefore sway the larger audience and profits beyond the United States.

The "show" produced in Calabasas is made possible by heightened security and coded aesthetics, which prevent unscripted drama and image leaks. Kim Kardashian's robbery in Paris on October 3, 2016, was the traumatic demonstration that the control and artifice of Calabasas does not easily travel beyond its gates. Thus, both the show and the lives of the protagonists of the new spectacle are highly susceptible to the unpredictability of noncorporate spaces.[22] In Calabasas, the celebrities can count on the city as a set. It is a mix between *The Truman Show* and *Groundhog Day*, "a time warp" according to the former mayor of Hidden Hills, a veteran TV producer.[23] Calabasas introduces a new parameter for urbanism: safeguarding the mise-en-scène.

In fact, for a good part of its history, Calabasas was home to the Warner Ranch, the Warner Brothers' studio. Active from 1935 to 1959, the ranch was on the land now developed into the fancier gated communities along Parkway Calabasas. Countless Westerns and other exoticizing tales were filmed there, including *Casablanca*, *Rebel Without a Cause*, *The Oklahoma Kid*, and *The Adventures of Robin Hood*. There was a Western town, a Mexican village, a ranch, and a Western fort. The old stables of famous Laramie Street still stand in the middle of what is now the Calabasas Country Club golf course, where every hole bears the name of a movie filmed there. Uncannily mirroring the social media celebrities who turn their homes into film sets, actor James Garner recalled that the movie ranch "was just like home to [him]," and he could not walk three feet in any direction where he hadn't filmed a scene.[24] The Kardashians could say that Calabasas is a studio, after ten years of reality TV and daily posting from there.

Calabasas used to be the place where the heroic story of American settlers was reenacted daily, before it became the place for the wealthy white elite to reenact the ideal of suburbia. The communities of Calabasas were built for just that, to conserve time. The residents are "a community of people drawn together by a shared vision and respect for the original concept," which was based on visions of cars yielding to horseback riders and neighbors stopping to buy lemonade from children's stands on street corners.[25] But will the idealized suburbia survive the assaults of the new media? The recent influx of celebrities in Calabasas could very well be another facet of the current crisis of American suburbia, whose undead convulsions have seemed particularly susceptible to reality TV and social media, as the election of President Donald Trump testified.

The Architecture of the New Spectacle

The extravagance of the celebrities in Calabasas is at odds with the traditional ethos of the gated community. They challenge the gated community's original concept, since they are not withdrawing there to consume the suburban lifestyle as advertised in the brochures. There are many reports about their deviant behaviors: Drake building himself a mansion in violation of the planning rules, Kylie Jenner's parties letting large (and "wrong") crowds through the gates, Justin Bieber's ruthless driving and loud arrogance as reported by many neighbors, and the silent disapproval of Caitlyn Jenner's gender transition.[26] As a group, Calabasas celebrities are more racially diverse than the rest of the area's residents.[27] The entrepreneurial matriarchy of the Kardashian empire also dramatically contrasts with the gender income gap in Calabasas: women in Hidden Hills earn approximately half the income of their male counterparts, well below the national average of eighty percent. In Hidden Hills this figure drops even further, to forty percent; women earned $80,000 on average, and men earned $196,000.[28]

Fig. 11. Mutant suburbias of Hidden Hills and the Estate of the Oaks, Calabasas.

The deviations of the celebrities and other hyperwealthy (mostly entertainment industry–related) residents who leached off of the peacefulness of the communities are particularly visible in the architecture of their houses. The constructions are monstrous versions of the typical American suburban home. Extremely spacious, often with six or more bedrooms and even more bathrooms,[29] their scale and wealth more closely resemble the palaces of the early industrial bourgeoisie than the nuclear family dwellings of typical suburbia. Drake lives a bachelor dream home designed primarily for parties (with its Playboy-like pool grotto among other features), while Kylie Jenner owns three houses in Hidden Hills, as well as one in the Oaks: one is her home, another is her office, the third is an old house she hasn't had time to sell, and the fourth is a new house she hasn't had time to move into.[30] The celebrity houses might respect the aesthetic codes of a typical wealthy suburb (the dominant styles in Hidden Hills and the Oaks are the Ranch House, Spanish Revival, and Hampton's Style), but they are mutant houses with extrusions and extensions popping off all sides. They are bodybuilders who spent too much time on their physique, injected with all sorts of supplements. They look grandiose when the photographs are taken from the right angles, but the plans are ugly, the volumes are out of scale, and the construction is cheap. It would be easy to say that the body culture reflects on the architecture, but no architecture has yet been invented to respond specifically to the needs of celebrities' lives—for instance, to stage the continuous theatrical performance of their selves or to integrate the large number of lower-class people involved in making their lives possible, two aspects that were central to the architecture of the late aristocracy (Versailles) and the bourgeoisie (hôtels particuliers).[31]

The golden era of Calabasas in the last decade appears to be already coming to an end. Celebrities are moving out to equally wealthy, less-conservative neighborhoods such as Bel-Air, Brentwood, Beverly Hills, and Hollywood. Whether the Calabasas bubble will be only a two decade-long anomaly or whether it will set a precedent for post-internet architecture remains to be seen. History suggests that media empires become architecture eventually. Disney became Disneyland and Epcot; *Playboy* became a mansion and a model for the postwar bachelor pad.[32] The Kardashian matriarchy could very well prove to be a continuation of *Playboy* as the forerunner of a "new relationship between production and consumption materialized within the process of communication."[33] After all, Kim Kardashian was featured on the December 2007 cover of Playboy a couple of months after *Keeping Up with the Kardashians* began (and the first iPhone was released).[34]

Why has the City of Calabasas lent itself to smartphone-augmented life in ways that other places have not? There might be something to learn from Calabasas, considering the way the actors of the new media found a fertile environment to venture into post-cinema spectacle. Now what remains to be defined is how the new breed of lifestyle media realizes themselves into architecture and whether this reality will ever transcend the sleek materiality of the screens.

This text is an edited version of the research conducted by Octave Perrault during the residency of his collective, åyr, at the MAK Center / Schindler House in Los Angeles, CA, during spring and summer 2017.

1. "The Kardashian Curse," *Keeping Up with the Kardashians*, season 12, episode 6, aired June, 12, 2016.

2. See, for example, *032c* (November 2016); *Vanity Fair* (July 2016); *Forbes* (July 2016).

3. Scott Macaulay, "The Dream Factory," *Filmmaker Magazine* (Fall 2001).

4. Coincidentally, William Mulholland's granddaughter, Catherine Mulholland, was a Calabasas resident. She wrote *William Mulholland and the Rise of Los Angeles* (Berkeley: University of California Press, 2000), a biography of her grandfather, with the intention of adding nuance to the bad reputation that he was granted after Roman Polanski's film *Chinatown* (1974). She also wrote *Calabasas Girls: An Intimate History*, 1885–1912 (Berkeley, CA: Mulholland, 1976), gathering letters from Calabasas residents at the turn of the century.

5. *Mulholland Drive*, directed by David Lynch (2001; New York: Universal Pictures, 2002), DVD.

6. Mike Davis, "Fortress L.A.," in *City of Quartz: Excavating the Future of Los Angeles* (1990; London: Verso, 2006), 221. Reyner Banham, "The Art of the Enclave," in *Los Angeles: the Architecture of Four Ecologies* (New York: Penguin, 1971), 137. In fact, both of the books indirectly referenced Calabasas to illustrate the enclave nature of Los Angeles. Davis writes about Hidden Hills, one of the gated communities of Calabasas, as a "Norman Rockwell painting behind high-security walls." Banham writes about Rolling Hills, designed by A. E. Hanson, the same landscape architect and gated-community developer responsible for Hidden Hills. In the film *Reyner Banham Loves Los Angeles* (1972), he is prevented entry at the gates of Rolling Hills before calling it "a private city."

7. The communities of Calabasas are Hidden Hills, Hidden Hills West, Calabasas Hills, Calabasas Park Estates, The Oaks, Mulholland Heights, Mulwood, Las Villas, Bellagio, The Ridge, Creekside, Clairidge, Calabasas Country Estates, Calabasas Highlands, Mountain Park, Abercrombie Ranch Estates, Cold Creek, Park Moderne, Mountain View Estates, Monte Nido, Deer Springs, Stone Creek, El Encanto, Mont Calabasas, Malibu Canyon Park, The Colony at Calabasas, Avalon Calabasas (formerly Archstone Calabasas), Mont Calabasas, Calabasas View, Saratoga Hills, Saratoga Ranch, Deer Springs, and Steeplechase.

8. Parkway Calabasas is a two-mile-long road leading nowhere to the public: all of its off-streets are gated entrances to exclusive communities. Google Street View isn't available beyond the gates.

9. The Los Angeles Pet Cemetery appears to be legally part of Calabasas, although it is located just next to one of the gates of Hidden Hills, between the city's limits and the 101 freeway.

10 "So why have so many famous names settled into this affluent area known for its rustic canyons and manicured cul-de-sacs? It's the privacy, the safety (even if an inordinate number of houses boast panic rooms anyway) and the value of property vis-a-vis the Westside." (Gary Baum, "Why Celebrities like Justin Bieber Are Flocking to L.A.'s Suburbia," *Hollywood Reporter*, May 31, 2012.) "Indeed, real-estate moguls say that celebs have fallen for Hidden Hills because this is finally a place where they can do normal things such as put their baby in a pram and take it for a walk down the road, something which would cause a paparazzi pile-up anywhere else. As there are no paps inside Hidden Hills, and everybody else is famous too, nobody cares. Indeed, Kim K tweeted just the other day about going for a 'casual stroll thru Hidden Hills,'

while J-Lo is said to enjoy taking her kids for fresh air in its country lanes—which all have bucolic names such as Round Meadow and Long Valley." (Sophie Heawood, "Hidden Hills: The LA Celebrity Enclave with All the Allure of Totnes," *Guardian*, May 7, 2015.) "Even though its gates promise exclusivity and privacy from cameras, Hidden Hills has hosted lots of reality-TV stars who don't exactly shun the glare of media attention." (Molly Lambert, "Welcome to Calabasas," *Grantland*, July 16, 2014.) "Jaden moved out of his parents Calabasas compound and into a $4 million home in the gated community [of Hidden Hills]. One draw to Hidden Hills may have been his friend Kylie Jenner, 19, who lives less than a mile away in a $12 million mansion." (Jill Ishkanian, "The Fresh Prince of Hidden Hills," *Daily Mail Online*, February 16, 2017.)

11. Evan McKenzie, *Privatopia: Homeowner Associations and the Rise of Residential Private Government* (New Haven, CT: Yale University Press, 1996); Keller Easterling, *Enduring Innocence: Global Architecture and Its Political Masquerades* (Cambridge, MA: MIT Press, 2007).

12. Data from the Community Associations Institute, *The Community Associations Factbook 2016*, accessed August 2017, https://www.caionline.org/AboutCommunityAssociations/Statistical%20Information/2016StatsReviewFBWeb.pdf/.

13. Keller Easterling, *Extrastatecraft: The Power of Infrastructure Space* (London: Verso, 2016), 12. "[T]he more rationalized these spatial products become the better suited they are to irrational fictions of branding, complete with costumes and a patois of managementese. This familiar confetti of brightly colored boxes nestling in black asphalt and bright green grass—the same in Texas or Taiwan—weaves elaborate, emotional stories about Starbucks coffee, Beard Papa cream puffs, and Arnold Palmer golf communities."

14. The Commons at Calabasas (opened 1998) was developed and is owned by Rick J. Caruso. It stands as a prototype for the new generation of successful malls that emerged in Los Angeles in the last decades. The Grove in Los Angeles (opened 2002) and The Americana in Glendale (opened 2008) were both developed by Caruso after the model tested in Calabasas.

16. Manuel Adelino, Antoinette Schoar, and Felipe Severino, "Loan Originations and Defaults in the Mortgage Crisis: The Role of the Middle Class", *Review of Financial Studies* 29, no. 7 (July 1, 2016): 1635–70.

17. Michel Feher, "Self-Appreciation; or, The Aspirations of Human Capital," *Public Culture* 21, no. 1 (2009): 30.

18. Kanye West, quoted by Dirk Standen, "Exclusive! Kanye West Talks Yeezy Season 4, the Casting Call Controversy, and His Calabasas Connection", *Vogue*, September 17, 2017, accessed January 2018, https://www.vogue.com/article/kanye-west-spring-2017-interview/.

19. The Hollywood Sign is originally an advertisement for a real estate development inviting the new wealthy class car owners to settle in a part of town free from poorer, darker, non–car owners. Kevin Starr, *Material Dreams: Southern California Through the 1920s* (Oxford: Oxford University Press, 1991), 94. See also Paul Bahn, *The Archaeology of Hollywood: Traces of the Golden Age* (Lanham, MD: Rowman & Littlefield, 2014); and Leo Braudy, *The Hollywood Sign: Fantasy and Reality of an American Icon* (New Haven, CT: Yale University Press, 2012).

20. Leslie Bruce, "The Kardashian Decade: How a Sex Tape Led to a Billion-Dollar Brand," *Hollywood Reporter*, August 16, 2017.

21. Ibid.

22. "Paris" and "The Aftermath," *Keeping Up with the Kardashians*," season 13, episodes 2 and 3, aired March 2017.

23. Gary Baum, "Celebrity Suburbia," *Hollywood Reporter*, May 29, 2012.

24. David Walstad, "For Years, This Was How the West Was Done," *Los Angeles Times*, August 13, 2003.

25. "Living in Hidden Hills," Homeowner Association of Hidden Hills, accessed

August 2017, http://www.hiddenhills.org/living.php.

26. Jeff Weiss, "Unlocking the Mysteries of Calabasas and Hidden Hills," *Complex.com*, January 2016.

27. The data here is mainly for Hidden Hills, for which there is much more extensive public data. Although all the information leads us to believe that the tendency applies to Calabasas at large too.

28. US Census Bureau, 2012–2016 American Community Survey 5-Year Estimates.

29. Zillow.com, location filter: Hidden Hills, accessed January 2018, https://www.zillow.com/hidden-hills-ca/.

30. Karen Hua, "This $4.5 Million Mansion Will Become Kylie Jenner's Cosmetics Headquarters," *Forbes.com*, August 19, 2016. Emily Silverman and Sara Tardiff, "Kylie Jenner Loses Big Money on the Sale of Her Calabasas Home," *Elle Decor Online*, July 26, 2017. Mark David, "Mogul Kylie Jenner Rumored to Ink Deal to Sell Calabasas Starter House," *Variety.com*, July 7, 2017.

31. The flows of cars going in and out of the gated communities of Calabasas reveals the divide. White people in expensive cars leave in the morning and come back in the evening (residents). Darker people in cheap cars or maintenance trucks entering in the morning and leave in the evening (cleaners, janitors, and gardeners).

32. Richard R. Beard, *Walt Disney's Epcot Center: Creating the New World of Tomorrow* (New York: Harry N. Abrams, 1982). Paul B. Preciado, *Pornotopia. An Essay on Playboy's Architecture and Biopolitics* (Brooklyn, NY: Zone Books, 2014).

33. Preciado, *Pornotopia*, 54.

34. *Playboy*'s contemporary description of the ideal playmate is uncannily fitting for the Kardashians: "Playmates are multi-dimensional. The Playmate is the perfect combination of personality, beauty and lifestyle. We [*Playboy*] are and always have been a lifestyle brand after all." *Playboy.com*, accessed August 2017. It continues, "Personality: A Playmate leads with her personality; she is entrepreneurial, confident, passionate and a team player. ... Beauty: A Playmate is stunning both inside and out. ... She is of all shapes, sizes, backgrounds and ethnicities. ... Lifestyle: A Playmate's lifestyle is aspirational, she pursues her passions and keeps up with her hobbies, however eclectic. Examples from the past range include piloting helicopters, to pursuing artistic talents, to building a company, to crafting a multi-million follower brand. A Playmate is not solely social media driven, she uses it to amplify her voice, brand and passions outside of the social realm."

G
GRADUADO

P
PUPPET

Let us consider two species of media architecture: one new and one old. And for the sake of orientation and comparison, let us focus on a single city—say, Venice, Italy. Our first stop, as it would be if we were visiting in the flesh, is Venice Marco Polo Airport (VCE), the fifth busiest airport in the country.[1] Originally opened in 1960, the airport introduced in 2002 a new passenger terminal, designed by locals Giampaolo and Giovanna Mar, which nods subtly to Aldo Rossi in its geometric form and masonry construction. Its canopies resemble those of the Gaggiandre in the old shipyards in Venice's Arsenale. Inside, we encounter exposed wooden trusses, plenty of glass and natural light—and the typical tempest of traveler tips and tutelage: wayfinding signage and flight status monitors, touch-screens and security instructions. Mixed in with the logistical communications are TV screens, bookshops, cell-phone charging stations, and WiFi to serve our entertainment and business needs.

1. Venice has another airport, Treviso, which focuses on low-cost carriers, leaving VCE to handle flights to major European cities and some international destinations in North America, Africa, and the Middle East.

Fig. 1
Aerial view of Venice Marco Polo Airport, situated on the mainland outside Venice.

Fig. 2
Venice Marco Polo Airport, designed by Studio Architetto Mar (2002).

Fig. 3
Interior view of the Venice Marco Polo Airport terminal.

Named after a thirteenth-century merchant-traveler who emblematizes a distant age of geopolitics, Marco Polo Airport, like all airports, encompasses a variety of spatial ontologies: security zones, international zones, spaces of legal exception and suspended national sovereignty, logistical spaces, restricted spaces, wormhole-like portals for staff that traverse a variety of terrains, and so forth. The boundaries between those zones are typically demarcated by architectural barriers—different floors, locked doors, bollards, cones, fences or, more commonly in public areas, transparent walls—as well as mediated markers and data-imbued thresholds. As geographers Rob Kitchin and Martin Dodge explain, air travel requires the transversal of a constellation of "code/spaces," and "the decision as to whether people and luggage can progress from one code/space to the next is more than ever before taken by systems that operate in an automated, autonomous, and automatic way."[2] Boarding passes, barcodes, bag tags, and passports grant us, and our stuff, the right of passage. Illustrated signage tells us how to pack our liquids and gels, and how to disassemble ourselves at the security check, so that our bodies and carry-ons, too, can pass scrutiny. All this screening and scanning of codes and anatomies makes for an integral *rite* of passage in what Rachel Hall, in *The Transparent Traveler*, calls the "cultural performance of risk management."[3] We've learned the script: passports open to the photo page, shoes off, laptops out.

2. Rob Kitchin and Martin Dodge, *Code/Space: Software and Everyday Life* (Cambridge, MA: MIT Press, 2011): 137.

3. Rachel Hall, *The Transparent Traveler: The Performance and Culture of Airport Security* (Durham, NC: Duke University Press, 2015): 2.

Opened shortly after September 11 shook the global travel industry and raised the stakes for airline security, VCE was "equipped with the most up-to-date technological systems for data-management and communication, an avant-garde security system, and suitable commercial areas" to serve 6.5 million passengers.[4] In 2015, as the airport began work on another expansion, it also linked to other European airports through the EUROCONTROL "airport collaborative decision-making" process. This involves sharing flight data throughout the European system, thus consolidating all phases of a flight—"from the flight plan to airport operations, from take-off to en-route to landing, with the corresponding turn-around"—into a "single process" that ties geographically disparate runways and terminals together into a holistic aerospace.[5] So, while the airport-as-architecture is growing on the ground, the airport-as-aerial-jurisdiction, as code-space, is expanding in the air and through networked databases.

4. Studio Architetti Mar, "Marco Polo Terminal Venezia."

5. "Venice Becomes 3rd A-CDM Italian Airport," EUROCONTROL, January 26, 2015.

Contemporary airport architecture materializes this logic of continuity and connection, suggesting a correspondence between its administrative and material spaces. Transparency, as manifested in VCE's glass walls and glowing screens, has become the obligatory trope of international travel. Evoking Colin Rowe and Robert Slutzky's distinction between "literal" and "phenomenal" transparency (that is, the difference between actually transparent materials, like glass, and the *perception* of multiple, simultaneous spatial conditions), Hall suggests that transparency is the "aesthetic of choice" for risk management, particularly in airports, because it simultaneously exteriorizes and incorporates. It "reveals what it enfolds."[6] Glass walls and open floor plans, emblems of the modernist paradigm, here evoke unfettered freedom, openness, adventure—ideals befitting a tourist airport like VCE—while also accommodating surveillance. Our bodies freely traverse endless corridors and expansive food courts, while our coded subjectivities are constantly scanned and registered.

6. Rachel Hall, *The Transparent Traveler: The Performance and Culture of Airport Security* (Durham, NC: Duke University Press, 2015): 32. Colin Rowe and Robert Slutzky, "Transparency: Literal and Phenomenal," *Perspecta* 8 (1963): 45–54.

There are of course grave consequences for mistaking the perceived transparency, the seeming unfetterdness, of the airport for actual borderless abandon. An alarm will readily alert us if we've accidentally passed into restricted territory. A team of armed security guards might magically appear if we speak too freely (there are certain words we should not say in a security queue!) or pack too liberally. Given the stakes of underestimating the limitations of the airport's transparency, we often look for mediated markers, like the green light on the body scanner, and other spatial cues, including architectural fixtures and furnishings, to direct our actions.

The airport's signature furnishings—baggage carousels, ticket counters, customs stations, turnstiles, body scanners, even lounge chairs at the gate—inhabit liminal zones between different kinds of space. And the frictions and frustrations we inevitably face in our encounters with each of these furnishings (they're never *comfortable* experiences) remind us that, as we pass through various borders defined by geopolitics and logistics and biometric data, we simultaneously traverse different spatial orders. Those furnishings, however un-ergonomic and uncomfortable they might be, function as both logistical and epistemic gateways that help to mediate the transitions between these zones. And, in some cases, they provide our only clues that those transition zones even exist.

The baggage carousel signals our proximity to freedom and fresh air. We retrieve our luggage, pass through the automated sliding doors, exit into the sunshine, and head toward the water taxis on the lagoon. We soon find ourselves standing before the Biblioteca Nazionale Marciana, a Renaissance marvel on the iconic Piazza San Marco—both named in honor of Saint Mark, the city's patron saint. Noted architect and sculptor Jacopo Sansovino designed the library and oversaw its construction between 1537 and 1553.[7] Yet the idea for the library, and the gathering of its collection, began much earlier. In 1362 Francesco Petrarca—Petrarch of the eponymous sonnet—bequeathed his personal library to the city, provided it kept the collection intact and secure and made it available for use by nobles and scholar-citizens in what would have been among the first public, or common, libraries (as opposed to private scholarly or family libraries) in western Europe. Yet Petrarch's books and manuscripts never arrived. A century later, in 1468, humanist scholar and collector Cardinal Bessarion gifted 750 Greek and Latin codices, 250 manuscripts, and several *incunabula* (early printed books) to the city, but even this bequest didn't find a permanent home for decades—not until Doge Andrea Gritti commissioned Sansovino.[8]

7. When Sansovino passed away in 1570, Vincenzo Scamozzi oversaw the addition of five additional bays, which extended the library down to the embankment.

8. For more on the library collection's evolution, as well as its organization and how it was catalogued and made available for public access, see Dorit Raines, "Book Museum or Scholarly Library? The 'Libreria di San Marco' in a Republican Context," *Ateneo Veneto: Atti e Memorie Dell'ataneo Veneto*, vol. 2 (2010): 31–50.

Fig. 4
Nineteenth-century engraving of the Biblioteca Marciana (1560) by Dionisio Moretti, printed in a book published by Antonio Moretti in 1831.

Fig. 5
The monumental facade of the sixteenth-century Biblioteca Marciana, designed by architects Jacopo Sansovino and Vincenzo Scarmozzi. It is one of the oldest public manuscript archives in the world.

Arriving at the airport for a departing flight, we either crawl in through its subterranean transit station, lumber in from its parking garage, or stumble from a cab onto a chaotic curb. The spacious Piazza San Marco, by contrast, offers ample room to behold Sansovino's masterpiece: a classical two-story, twenty-one-bay columned structure with copious ornamentation: angels, garlands, lion heads, and rooftop statues and obelisks. His design fulfilled the Senate's 1515 decree that the library should "emulate the ancients" in its classicism, yet it represented a distinctively Venetian take on Vitruvian principles.[9] As architectural historian Deborah Howard explains, "florid skylines," like those at the library, were "a distinctive feature of the Venetian townscape," as were elaborate stone facades and liberal use of glass.[10]

9. Quoted in Deborah Howard, *Jacopo Sansovino: Architecture and Patronage in Renaissance Venice* (New Haven, CT: Yale University Press, 1975): 26.

10. Howard, 27. For more on the library's architecture, see Howard, 17–28; Eugene J. Johnson, "A Window in the Venetian Mint and the Libreria di San Marco," *Journal of the Society of Architectural Historians* 69, no. 2 (June 2010): 190–205; and the work of Manfredo Tafuri, referenced in Johnson.

Fig. 6
The Biblioteca Marciana occupies a prominent place framing the iconic Piazza San Marco.

Fig. 7
The monumental room in the Biblioteca Marciana.

Inside, its walls and ceilings feature paintings by the likes of Titian, Veronese, and Tintoretto and statuary representing philosophy, classical mythology, and other allegorical figures of wisdom and virtue.[11] Originally, the library's books were chained to walnut lecterns, as was the case in many early modern libraries seeking to protect their precious collections. But sixteenth-century Venice, home to more than 450 printers, publishers, and booksellers, was a center of European print production; among its creations, according to art historian Bronwen Wilson, were myriad maps, atlases, travel chronicles, and guidebooks, reflecting Venice's position as a mercantile center and a departure point for travelers.[12] Many of those publications made their way into the library's collection thanks to a 1603 law that established the Biblioteca Marciana as a local "library of deposit," obligating all those Venetian printers to file copies of each of their publications.[13] Donations and legacy bequests, acquisitions from monasteries, and purchases further added to the collection, which, by the end of the seventeenth century, had been unchained and moved to cabinets lining the walls. By the early twentieth century, the library had to expand next door into Sansovino's Pallazzo della Zecca, the former state mint.

11. Biblioteca Nazionale Marciana Venezia, "Pareti e Soffitto," accessed August 18, 2016.

12. Bronwen Wilson, *The World in Venice: Print, the City, and Early Modern Identity* (University of Toronto Press, 2005).

13. Biblioteca Nazionale Marciana Venezia, "Storia." Today, the Biblioteca Nazionale Centrale serves as Italy's library of deposit (just as the Library of Congress does in the US, and the British Library in the UK). And government agencies are often required to submit their data assets to a central repository, where many data sets are made publicly accessible.

Today, the library holds approximately one million printed books.[14] The full collection offers a particularly rich representation of Venetian print history, but its scope is famously cosmopolitan, and that worldliness is reflected particularly well in its extensive assortment of cartographic objects.[15] At the center of the Sansovino salon we find two massive, seventeenth-century Vincenzo Coronelli globes, one terrestrial and the other celestial. Marco Polo's will and testament is here, too. Yet Fra Mauro's ca. 1450 map of the world, exhibited at the top of Sansvovino's staircase, is among the library's most notable holdings. Curator Nat Williams describes the cartographer-monk's large-scale (2.2 square meter), densely inscribed work as a unique integration of "three predominant medieval map forms—the portolan chart, the *mappamundi* and the Ptolemaic atlas—with knowledge drawn from the latest maritime exploration to create what was, in effect, a compendium of current knowledge about the world."[16]

14. "Patrimonio Librario," Biblioteca Nazionale Marciana Venezie, accessed August 18, 2016. Other notable items in the collection include 24,000 *cinquecentine*, or works published in the sixteenth century, and historical musical works by Venetian composers.

15. Other holdings include the woodblocks used to print the Haji Ahmed's 1559 *A Complete and Perfect Map Describing the Whole World* (which, notably, depicts a land-bridge between Siberia and Alaska); and Jacopo de Barbari's 1500 *View of Venice*, an extraordinarily detailed woodcut of the city that fancifully depicts Mercury in the sky and Neptune in the harbor.

16. National Library of Australia, *Mapping Our World: Terra Incognita to Australia* (Canberra: National Library of Australia, 2013): 43.

Fig. 8
The Fra Mauro Map.

While the library's collection might promote fluid inquiry across disciplines and languages and forms of expression and documentation, while it might provide the conditions for "emulating the ancients" in the pursuit of classical humanist values, while its global literatures and travel collections and cartographic materials might inspire wonder at the world's breadth and humanity's dreams of exploration, this heterotopic realm of possibility and phenomenal transparency is far from literally transparent. Yes, Sansovino generously fenestrated his library, and the new reading room in the old mint courtyard is topped with a grid of skylights. But the institution's interior spaces are rigidly demarcated, their boundaries made seemingly impenetrable by opaque materials, opulent ornamentation, and furnishings of containment: columns, balustrades, statues, cabinets, vitrines, long wooden tables, heavy drapery, thick frames. Such were the epistemological architectures of the Renaissance, before the age of steel frames, glass walls, and open plans.

While Marco Polo's final papers live alongside Fra Mauro's famous medieval map, the Mappamondo, a reincarnation of the explorer's enterprising, adventuresome spirit lives on eight miles away at his namesake airport. Despite their widely disparate architectural languages, these two sites—both stuffed with media in their historically appropriate forms—can be read, like the mappamundi, as compendia of their own ages' "current knowledge about the world." Both are institutions mediating between security and access, between private and public. Both reflect the epistemologies and politics of knowledge characteristic of their eras, and their architectures reinforce and reflect these values. The library's media are regarded as invaluable artifacts of cultural heritage worth preserving for posterity, and the library building that houses them is emblematic of that heritage. Meanwhile, the airport's media—its flight data and magazines, passenger biometrics and security-camera footage—are valued primarily for their timeliness: their immediate use for logistical and security purposes or their ephemeral entertainment value. If the airport's data flows and fleeting media content are captured and preserved, it's likely for the purposes of tracking airline or vendor performance or for conducting forensic investigations in the case of malfunction or disaster. Unlike those books on the library's shelves, or those manuscripts that we can cautiously peruse only after donning white gloves, the airport's preservation-worthy information is typically "black-boxed," both literally (as with an airplane's flight data recorder) and phenomenally.[17] The data worth saving are seen only by those with the highest levels of security clearance. For the rest of us, we see only a transient architecture that reflects the transience of its occupants—human, machinic, mediated.

17. See Greg Siegel, *Forensic Media: Reconstructing Accidents in Accelerated Modernity* (Durham, NC: Duke University Press, 2014).

This movement also manifests, on a larger institutional scale, as an array of phenomenal and political approaches to exploration and globalism. Marco Polo and Saint Mark, fellow travelers, both lend their names to Venetian institutions that manifest the legacies of colonialism and mercantilism, as well as the timeless struggle between knowledge and faith (faith in a messiah, faith in a ship captain or a map, faith in airline security or air traffic control). Their fifteenth- and twenty-first-century infrastructures reflect how these perennial concerns are materialized in different political-economic, technological, and cultural ages.

In 2015, another traveling merchant, New Zealand–born artist Simon Denny, secured the patronage of prime ministers and private collectors and ventured to Venice to throw those epochal regimes into juxtaposition. In the thirteen years that had passed since VCE opened, social media, digital cartography, new rising global superpowers, and a host of other emerging forces had transformed the world's geopolitical and techno-cultural landscapes. Pundits who had only a decade earlier proclaimed the ascendance of a flat, post-national global order, were now, in the age of ISIS and nationalist cyberbattles, reconsidering the relevance of the nation-state. Denny had been chosen to represent New Zealand at the 2015 Venice Biennale, a global art gathering that, since 1907, has used the nation, and national exhibition territories, as its primary organizational structure—a model that has elicited much criticism in recent years for its anachronism and Occidentalism.[18] While roughly sixty nations maintain their own permanent pavilions, others rent temporary spaces. New Zealand is among the itinerant, so Denny chose to stage his work, *Secret Power*, across two sites: the Biblioteca Marciana and Venice Marco Polo Airport, each representing different ages and forms of nationalism, globalism, and intelligence.[19] By productively *mis*placing the two sites' media and media-furnishings he hoped to highlight the institutions'—and their respective eras'—material and visual codes of intelligence and to examine how those codes flow through, or fracture between, different spatial ontologies.[20]

18. See, for instance, George Baker, "The Globalization of the False: A Response to Okwui Enwezor," in Elena Filipovic, et al., *The Biennial Reader* (Bergen, Norway: Bergen Kunsthall, 2010), 446–53.

19. Denny's installation is named after Nicky Hager's book *Secret Power: New Zealand's Role in the International Spy Network* (Nelson, New Zealand: Potton & Burton, 1996).

20. Much of my description of Denny's installation is drawn from *New Zealand at Venice*, "Secret Power."

Figs. 9, 10
Simon Denny, *Secret Power* (2015), Venice Marco Polo Airport floor. Photo: Nick Ash.

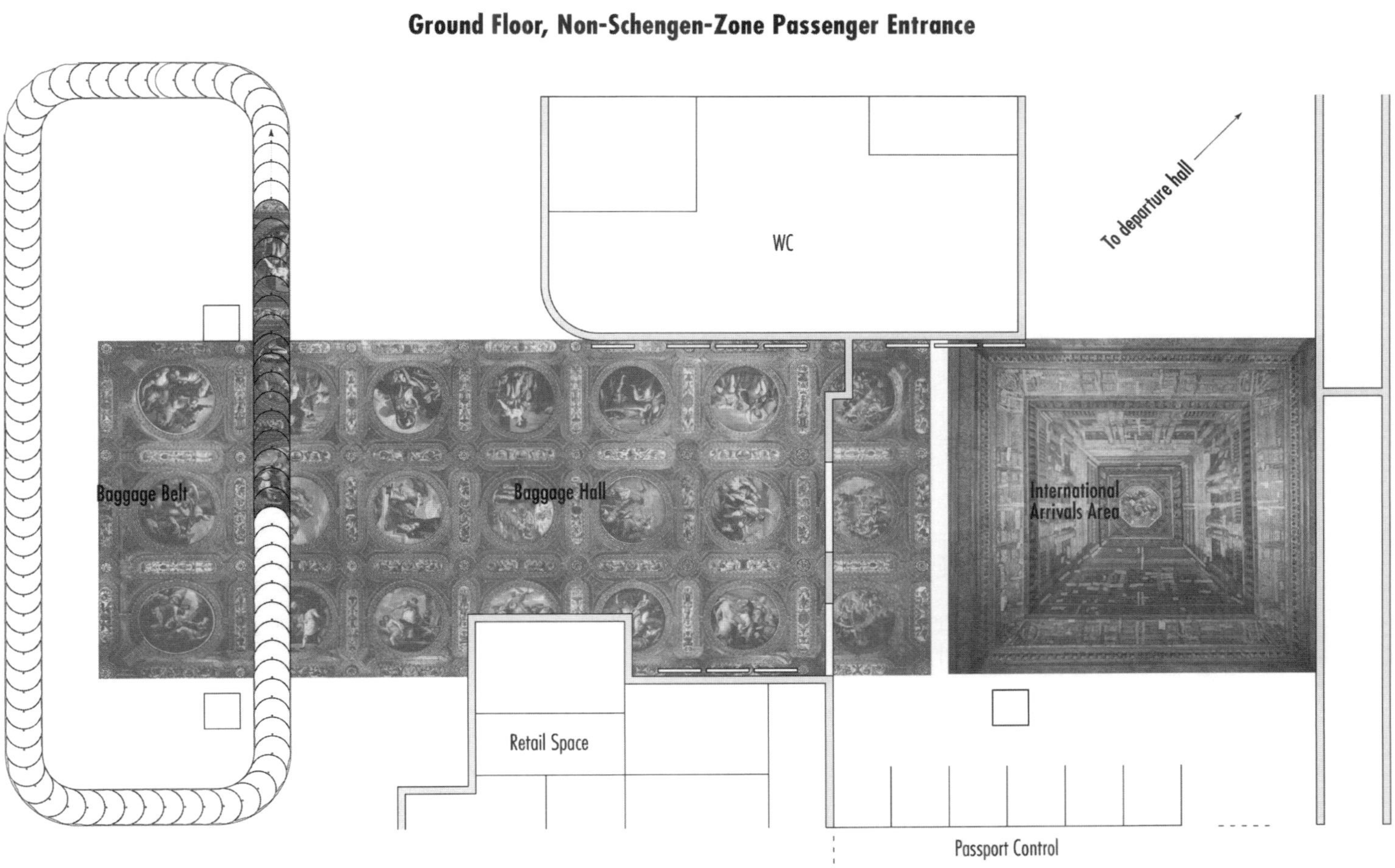

Fig. 11
Simon Denny, *Secret Power* (2015), airport plan.

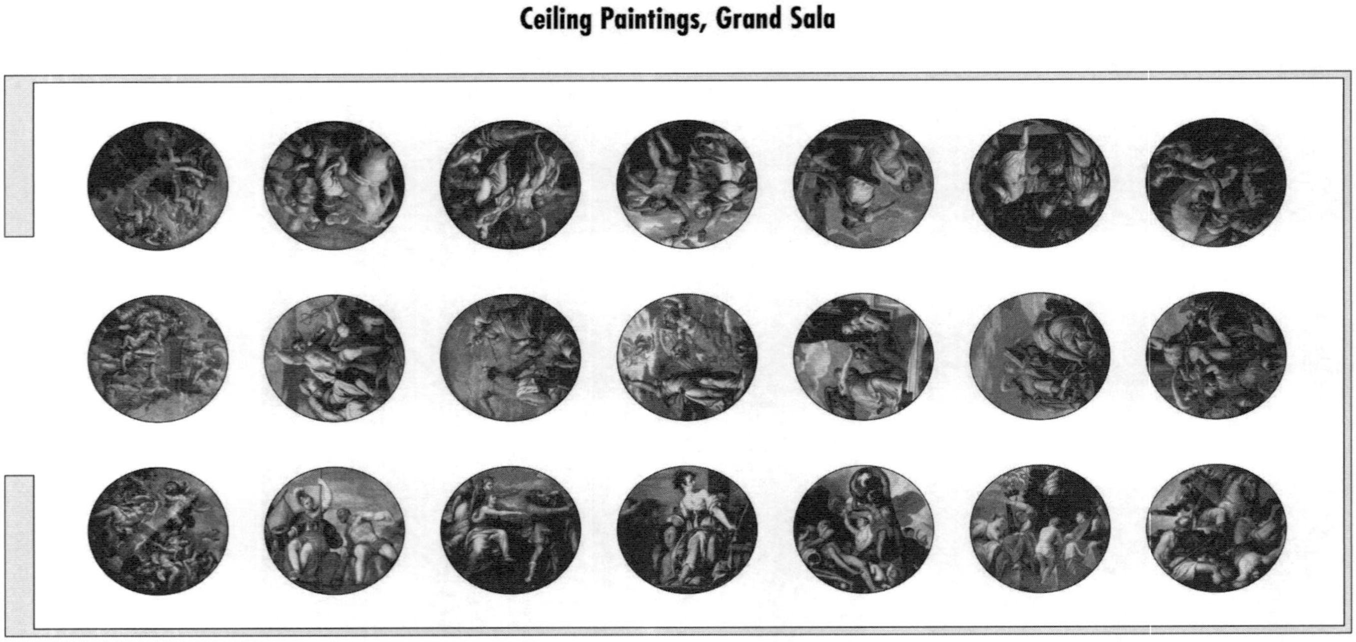

Fig. 12
Simon Denny, *Secret Power* (2015), library ceiling plan.

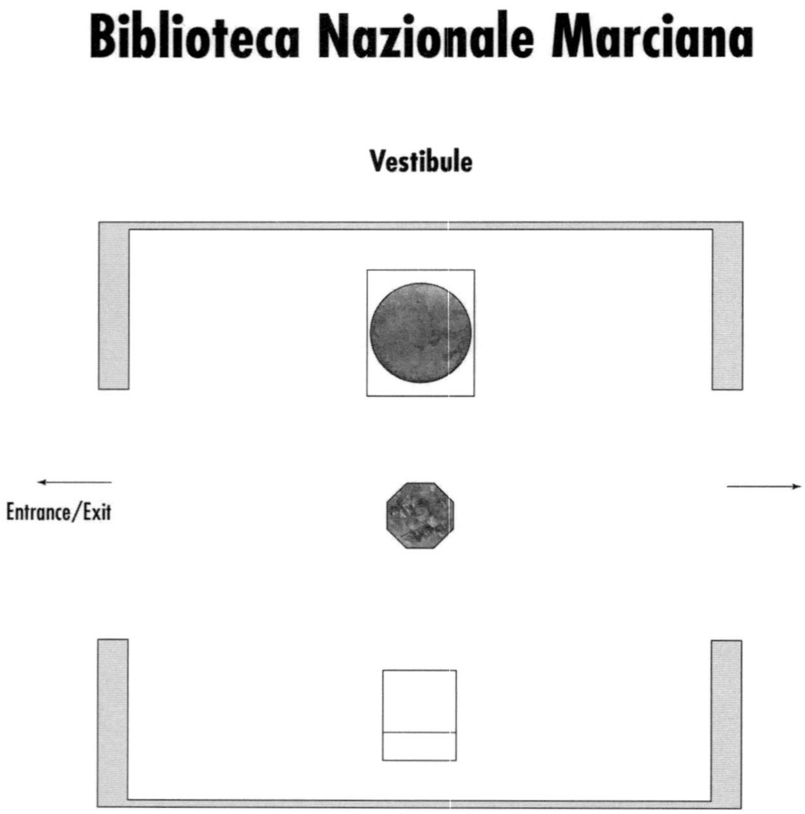

Fig. 13
Simon Denny, *Secret Power* (2015), library plan.

Into the library's monumental rooms, with their massive globes and masterful paintings, Denny inserted another room of a very different character: a server room with a modified Herman Miller office workstation at one end (perhaps a metaphor for the chained lecterns that formerly occupied the library?). His modified ("modded") glass-fronted, LED–lit server racks—which contained servers and cables—doubled as vitrines for an installation exploring the visual culture and graphic identity of the US National Security Administration (NSA) and Five Eyes–era geopolitics. Curator Robert Leonard called it a "server-room-cum-wunderkammer," evoking yet another historical architecture for pedagogical presentation.[21] The didactic materials on display took stylistic inspiration from two unlikely sources: the PowerPoint slide decks released by Edward Snowden, an NSA contractor who leaked classified information in 2013; and the work of David Darchicourt, former NSA creative director and exhibition designer for the National Cryptologic Museum, Maryland, whom Simon commissioned to create new illustrations for Venice (without informing Darchicourt how those illustrations would be used—another secret!).[22] Denny found that the graphic and textual language in these documents, while comically garish (art critic Chris Kraus describes it as "heavy-metal infused gamer-cartooning"), revealed a subtle political sensibility, with slight visual variations cueing different degrees of confidentiality.[23] In these modded monumental rooms, PowerPoint slides were the new manuscripts; network diagrams, the new portolan charts; hackers, the new merchant-explorers. "The effect," reported *ArtAsiaPacific*, "was a humorous yet chilling rendition of mass surveillance's bureaucratization, and offered today's achievements as a sad culmination of the Enlightenment's quest for knowledge."[24]

21. Quoted in Denise Tsui, "Robert Leonard: Meticulous Enabler," *ArtAsiaPacific* 93 (May/June 2015): 67.

22. See Linda Herrick, "Venice Biennale: Creepy Take on Power," *New Zealand Herald*, May 7, 2015. Denny said: "Darchicourt is a very playful image-maker. … He makes cartoon-based imagery to summarize things that are very complicated or boring and make them more attractive to people working within that institution."

23. Chris Kraus, "Here Begins the Dark Sea," in *Simon Denny: Secret Power* (Milan: Mousse Publishing, 2015), 23.

24. "New Zealand Pavilion: Simon Denny 'Secret Power,'" *ArtAsiaPacific*, almanac supplement (2016): 219.

Fig. 14
Simon Denny, *Secret Power* (2015). Photo: Nick Ash.

Fig. 15
Simon Denny, *Secret Power* (2015). Photo: Nick Ash.

In his room-within-a-room, a site of phenomenal transparency, Denny juxtaposed disparate architectures; disparate furnishings and fixtures for storage and display (ornate, built-in wooden cabinetry and austere metal shelves, gilded frames and hacked vitrines, wall labels and metadata); and disparate means of manifesting and aestheticizing knowledge (corny corporate iconography and data visualizations of bureaucratic communication, and artifactual and gilded art-historical language of maps and allegorical paintings). Despite their stylistic differences, all the work in this room—whether classical painting or comic-book illustration, whether born during the age of exploration or the age of ubiquitous surveillance—grappled with geopolitical power.[25] And through their juxtaposition, those artifacts, and those nested spaces, posed ontological and political questions about the nature of our media, our institutions, and our forms of intelligence. By inciting friction between the old and the new, Denny explains, *Secret Power* asked us to consider "how the world is mapped and imagined today, at a time when wide-ranging surveillance of global information exchange is normal."[26]

25. "Although separated by centuries," the library's Renaissance iconography and Denny's graphic insertions "rhyme," according to curator Robert Leonard. "Both levels feature representations of bearded wise men, soldiers, weapons, and battles. Ideas about strategy, territory, and conquest, power and knowledge, and social hierarchy and civic duty ricochet between them." Robert Leonard, "Too Much Information," in *Simon Denny: Secret Power*, 15.

26. Quoted in Jacob Proctor, "Simon Denny Talks about *Secret Power*," *Artforum International* 53, no. 9 (2015): 338–41

The airport is just such a space of surveillance and global information exchange, and Denny's exhibition strategy there was similarly confrontational. Within this contemporary terrain of globalization, where intelligence is equated with logistics and risk management, Denny again created a heterotopia. He placed (or, as several art critics quipped, "dragged-and-dropped") full-scale reproductions of the library's ceiling murals onto the floors and baggage carousels in the airport's arrival halls for both Schengen and non-Schengen Area travelers, and he posted reproductions of the library's historic maps on the airport's walls, where they resembled advertisements for the Sansovino exhibition.[27] The maps reminded Venice's leisure and business travelers of other ages—the days of Polo, Vespucci, Columbus—when travel not only *felt* different, but implied a different spatial epistemology: different ways of knowing about the world we lived in. The floor murals—portraying wisdom and virtue and other classical values—both physically and symbolically traversed the airport's security borders and geopolitical zones. As Denny explained:

> half [of the floor mural] is in international space (before you clear customs) and the other half is in Italy (where you pick up your baggage); each half is visible from the other. The calculated staging of opacity and transparency is crucial to the way airport architecture operates everywhere, and for me, this resonates with how online communication works.[28]

27. The Schengen Area comprises twenty-six European countries with a common visa policy; there is no border control for passengers traveling between these countries.

28. Quoted in Proctor, "Simon Denny Talks about *Secret Power*."

Even the *inconvenience* of Denny's exhibition was part of its pedagogical value: "I like that it's hard to see," he said; if you're a non-Schengen visitor, "you have to show your passport even to get to the installation."[29]

29. Kevin McGarry, "New Zealand's Contribution to the Venice Biennale: A Library and an Airport, Transposed," *T: New York Times Style Magazine* blog, May 1, 2015.

The mediated "secrets" Denny revealed include classified security data, initially "unsecreted" by Snowden, and national cultural treasures secured, but hardly obscured, in one of Italy's historic libraries. But the secret *powers* he revealed are the infrastructures that contain those media: the furnishings and architectures, organizational logics and conventions of presentation that our dataspaces and knowledge institutions employ to generate, collect, store, preserve, classify, and make intelligence publicly available—or not. In Denny's world of rooms within rooms and cabinets within cabinets, where ceilings become floors and maps become territories, we feel the friction of different epistemological, ontological, and political regimes clashing. That clash generates what Michel Foucault would call an epistemic rupture: a revelation that all those ordering structures *exist*, and that their orders—intellectual property, colonialism, surveillance, information capitalism—"are perhaps not the only possible ones or the best ones."[30]

30. Michel Foucault, *The Order of Things: An Archaeology of the Human Sciences* (New York: Vintage, 1994), xx.

Yet we often have similarly revelatory experiences in more mundane settings. Consider the librarian who unchains his collection of early codices, the airline security officer or passenger who acclimates to a new body scanner, the pilot who familiarizes herself with new cockpit interfaces, the cataloguer who adopts a new data-management system, the cubicle worker who moves to a newly configured workstation. All experience the friction of transition, which shines light on the habits of mind and senses of space that were so natural, so transparent in the old arrangement. When we rearrange our epistemic fixtures and furnishings, we see how those systems, those once-secret powers, give shape to thought, how they inform our own thinking, how they embody a logic of their own place and time. We recognize our architectures as mediated: not only skinned and stuffed with mediating objects, but also coded with data and modeled after the epistemic systems of their ages. And we appreciate the seeming banality of bureaucracy and logistics—book stacks and turnstiles and circulation patterns—as political infrastructures that define our access to space and information, program our subjectivity, and delimit our power to know and shape our world.

Shawn Maximo

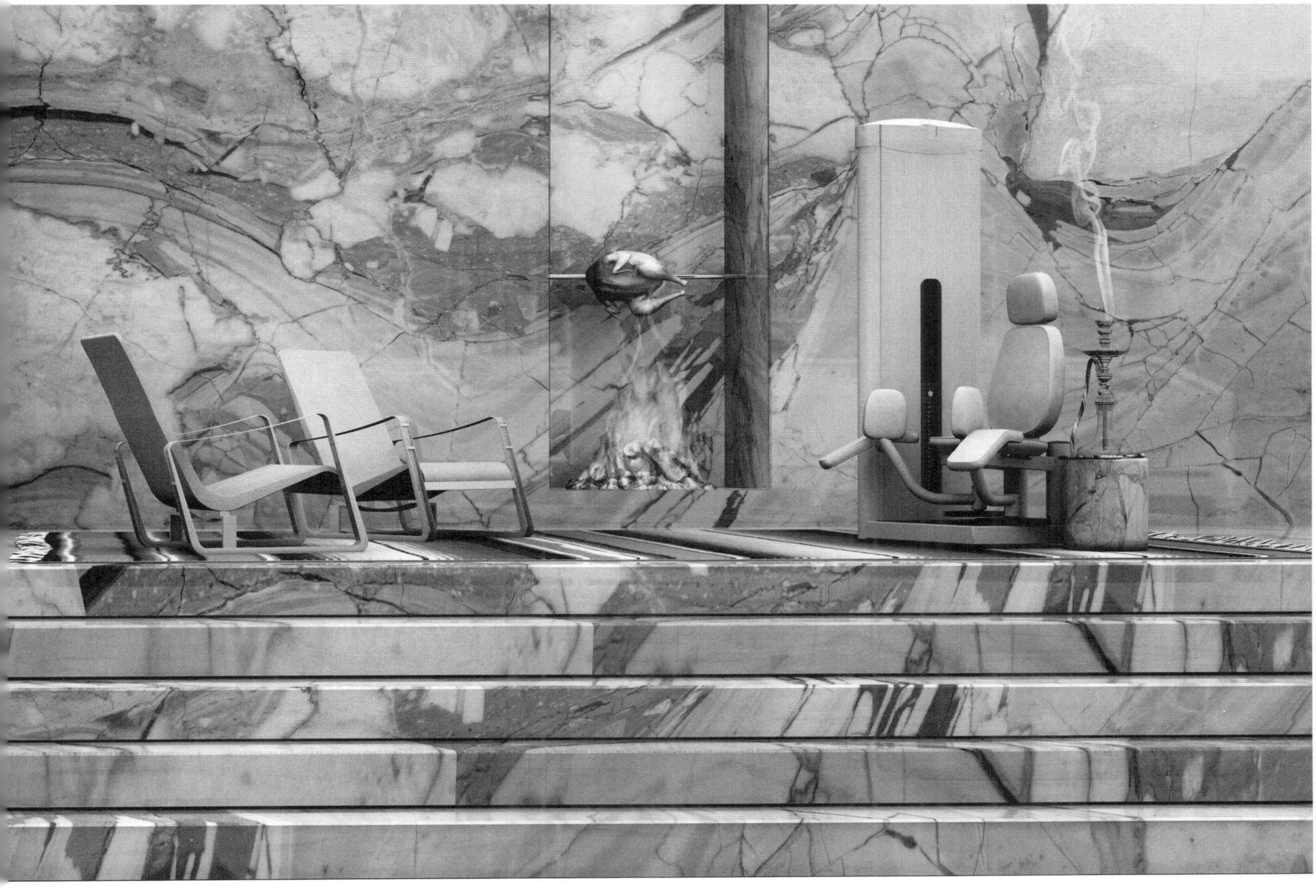

ATM
Welcome

SyncMaster 206bw
SAMSUNG

Shamsher Ali
is a writer and photographer. He was part of the Cybermohalla Ensemble (2001–13), and coauthored innumerable books, broadsheets, and art works with the Ensemble. Notable among them are *Trickster City: Writings from the Belly of the Metropolis* (Penguin India, 2010, first published in Hindi as *Bahurupiya Shehr* by Rajkamal Prakashan in 2007), and *Cybermohalla Hub* (Sternberg, 2012). During the *Sarai Reader 09* exhibition process (Gurugram, 2012–13), he initiated a program that evolved over nine months inside the 1:1 prototype of the Cybermohalla Hub building designed by Hirsch and Müller. Shamsher cofounded the art collective Kosh in 2013. He works at the Raqs Studio in Delhi as fabrication convener and 3D graphics designer.

Nick Axel
is an architect, writer, critic, and editor based in Rotterdam. He is currently Deputy Editor of e-flux Architecture, where his work focuses on generating new audiences and experimenting with the temporal logics of the architectural project. Previously, he was Managing Editor of *Volume Magazine* (#44–49), Researcher at Forensic Architecture, and resident at DAAR (Decolonizing Architecture Art Residency). Nick has taught architecture, design, and theory at Strelka, Design Academy Eindhoven, KABK, Bauhaus-Universität Weimar, and The Bartlett.

åyr
(formerly AIRBNB Pavilion) is an art collective whose work focuses on contemporary forms of domesticity. It was founded in 2014 by architects Fabrizio Ballabio, Alessandro Bava, Luis Ortega Govela, and Octave Perrault. They have recently exhibited work at the Stedelijk Museum, the Ludwig Museum, the Berlin Biennale, and Venice Architecture Biennale.

Aleksandr Bierig
is a doctoral candidate studying architectural and urban history at Harvard University. His current research focuses on the intersection of the built environment, the natural environment, and political economy, particularly in eighteenth- and nineteenth-century Britain. Before beginning his PhD, Bierig worked for architectural firms in the United States and Europe. He has written for *Log, Clog, Architectural Record, The Architectural Review*, and *Pidgin*, among other publications.

Francesco Casetti
is a film and media theorist who has written extensively on the semiotics of film and television, as well as genres, intertextuality, and enunciation. His most recent book, *The Lumière Galaxy: Seven Key Words for the Cinema to Come* (Columbia University Press, 2015), reflects his current research on early film theory, the relocation of cinema in new spaces and on new devices, and the screen as an optical apparatus and component of our "mediascapes." Casetti is the Thomas E. Donnelley Professor of Humanities and Film and Media Studies at Yale University.

Beatriz Colomina
is Professor of History and Theory in the School of Architecture and founding director of the program in Media and Modernity at Princeton University. She has written extensively on questions of architecture, art, sexuality, and media. Her books include *Are We Human? Notes on an Archaeology of Design* (Lars Müller, 2016), *The Century of the Bed* (Verlag für Moderne Kunst, 2015), *Manifesto Architecture: The Ghost of Mies* (Sternberg, 2014), *Clip/Stamp/Fold: The Radical Architecture of Little Magazines 196X–197X* (Actar, 2010), *Domesticity at War* (MIT Press, 2007), *Privacy and Publicity: Modern Architecture as Mass Media* (MIT Press, 1994), and *Sexuality and Space* (Princeton Architectural Press, 1992). She has curated a number of exhibitions including *Clip/Stamp/Fold* (2006), *Playboy Architecture* (2012) and *Radical Pedagogies* (2014). She was curator with Mark Wigley of the third Istanbul Design Biennial (2016).

DIS
is a New York–based collective composed of Lauren Boyle, Solomon Chase, Marco Roso, and David Toro. Its cultural interventions are manifest across a range of media and platforms, from site-specific museum and gallery exhibitions to ongoing online projects. Across its various endeavors, DIS explores the tension between popular culture and institutional critique, while facilitating projects for the most public and democratic of all forums—the internet.

Keller Easterling
is an architect, writer, and professor at Yale University. Her most recent book, *Extrastatecraft: The Power of Infrastructure Space* (Verso, 2014), examines global infrastructure as a medium of polity. A forthcoming e-book essay is titled *Medium Design* (Strelka Press, 2017). Another recent book, *Subtraction* (Sternberg, 2014), considers building removal or how to put the development machine into reverse. Other books include: *Enduring Innocence: Global Architecture and its Political Masquerades* (MIT Press, 2005) and *Organization Space: Landscapes, Highways and Houses in America* (MIT Press, 1999). She has published web installations including: *Extrastatecraft, Wildcards: A Game of Orgman*, and *Highline: Plotting NYC*. Her research and writing has been included in the 2014 and 2018 Venice Biennales. She lectures and exhibits internationally. She is a past contributor to *Perspecta*.

Georgios Eftaxiopoulos
is an architect living and working in London, He has taught at the Berlage and at the University of Navarra on the topic of the city. In 2016, he was awarded the AA-CCA Research Grant.

Moritz Gleich
is a scientific assistant for architectural theory at the Institute for the History and Theory of Architecture (GTA) at the Swiss Federal Institute of Technology Zurich (ETH). His research interests draw from the intersections of cultural sciences, media studies, and the history of architecture. He is currently preparing a dissertation on the genealogy of machinic concepts in architecture. Among his recent publications are "Stirling's Arrows" with Laurent Stalder in *AA Files* 72, and "Liquid Crowds: Regulatory Discourse and the Architecture of People Flows in the Nineteenth Century," in *Grey Room* 66.

Evangelos Kotsioris
is an architectural historian currently completing his doctoral degree at Princeton University. His research interests center on the intersections of architecture with science, technology and media. Kotsioris was the assistant curator of the 3rd Istanbul Design Biennial "Are We Human?" and the 2016–17 Emerging Curator at the Canadian Centre for Architecture (CCA) in Montreal. He has presented his research in conferences and symposia of the Society of Architectural Historians, Harvard University, Columbia University, Princeton University, Boston University, and Georgetown University, among others. Kotsioris has authored and coauthored chapters and articles for edited volumes, catalogs and journals, such as *The Architectural Review, New Geographies, Volume, Conditions, On Site, Pidgin, Uncube,* and others.

Nashin Mahtani
is Research Director of anexact office in Jakarta, Indonesia, where she is currently conducting research for the exhibition-led inquiry *The Architecture of the Brain*. She is also Project Co-Manager and Lead Designer of PetaBencana.id, an Indonesian disaster-mapping foundation, where she creates data-visualization strategies and new representational forms to explain information and communication technologies and systems. With a background in architecture, Nashin's research and design work investigates the relational complexities of urban infrastructure, computation, and neuroscience.

Reinhold Martin
is Professor of Architecture at Columbia University, where he directs the Temple Hoyne Buell Center for the Study of American Architecture. At Columbia, Martin also chairs the Society of Fellows in the Humanities and is a member of the Committee on Global Thought. A founding coeditor of the journal *Grey Room*, Martin's books include *The Organizational Complex: Architecture, Media, and Corporate Space* (MIT Press, 2003), *Utopia's Ghost: Architecture and Postmodernism, Again* (University of Minnesota Press, 2010), and *The Urban Apparatus: Mediapolitics and the City* (University of Minnesota Press, 2016). He is currently working on a history of the American university as a media complex.

Shannon Mattern
is Associate Professor in the School of Media Studies at The New School in New York, where she was Graduate Program Director from 2006 to 2009. Her writing and teaching focus on archives, libraries, and other media spaces; media infrastructures; spatial epistemologies; and mediated sensation and exhibition. She is the author of *The New Downtown Library: Designing with Communities*; *Deep Mapping the Media City*; and *Code and Clay, Dirt and Data: 5000 Years of Urban Media*, all published by University of Minnesota Press. In addition to her dozens of published journal articles, she contributes a regular long-form column about urban data and mediated infrastructures to the online publication *Places*.

Shawn Maximo
is an artist and architect working in sculpture, digital media, and design. His work has been featured in the *New York Times*, *Zeit Magazin*, *frieze* and *Artforum* magazines, and has been exhibited at the Vitra Design Museum, Kunsthalle Wien, ZKM Center for Art and Media Karlsruhe, Musée d'Art Moderne de la Ville de Paris, Perez Art Museum Miami, MoMA PS1, and at the 9th Berlin Biennale.

Marshall McLuhan (1911–1980)
was a Canadian professor, philosopher, and public intellectual. His work is viewed as one of the cornerstones of the study of media theory, with practical applications in the advertising and television industries. He was educated at the University of Manitoba and the University of Cambridge; he began his teaching career as an English Professor at several universities in the US and Canada before moving to the University of Toronto, where he remained for the rest of his life. He contributed to *Perspecta* 11 (1967).

Scott McQuire
is Professor of Media and Communications in the School of Culture and Communication at the University of Melbourne, Australia, where he is a founding member of the Research Unit for Public Cultures. He undertakes interdisciplinary research linking the fields of digital media, contemporary art, urbanism, and social theory. He is the author and coeditor of seven books and over 100 essays in journals, scholarly books and exhibition catalogues. His book *The Media City: Media, Architecture and Urban Space* (2008) won the Urban Communication Foundation's 2009 Jane Jacobs Publication Award. Scott is Deputy Director of the Melbourne Networked Society Institute, and a member of the advisory board of the Microsoft Centre for SocialNUI established in 2013. He currently leads funded research projects on participatory public space, and digital storytelling. His most recent book, *Geomedia: Networked Cities and the Future of Public Space*, was published by Polity in 2016.

Markus Miessen
is an architect, spatial designer, consultant and writer. He is Full Professor in Design at the Academy of Design (HDK), University of Gothenburg, Sweden. The initiator of the Participation tetralogy, Miessen's work revolves around questions of critical spatial practice, institution building, and spatial politics. He is the author of *Crossbenching* (Sternberg & Merve, 2016) and *The Nightmare of Participation – Crossbench Praxis as a Mode of Criticality* (Sternberg, 2010). Together with Nikolaus Hirsch, Miessen is the editor of the Critical Spatial Practice book series at Sternberg Press.

Ginger Nolan
is a postdoctoral fellow in Urban Studies at Basel University. She works on histories and theories of architecture, media, and race. Her work has been published in various journals, including *Grey Room*, *The Journal of Architecture*, *Log*, and *Architecture Theory Review*. She currently has two books forthcoming from the University of Minnesota Press.

Shveta Sarda
is an editor and translator based in Delhi, who likes collectives and multitudes. She coedited Cybermohalla Ensemble's *Cybermohalla Hub* (2012), and edited Raqs Media Collective's *With an Untimely Calendar* (2014). Between 2001 and 2013, during her time at Delhi's creative adventure called Sarai, she worked with writers and practitioners in working-class neighborhoods across the city. She is the translator of *Trickster City* (2010). Sarda's works with individual authors include the translations *Mansion* and *Basanti* by the late Bhisham Sahni (2016). She was editor of *Blueprint* and *Mise-en-scène* of the 11th Shanghai Biennale (2016–17).

Jeffrey Schnapp
is a cultural theorist, media historian, designer, and experimentalist. He teaches at Harvard University and is the founder and faculty director of metaLAB (at) Harvard University, faculty co-director of the Berkman Klein Center for Internet and Society, and CEO of Piaggio Fast Forward. Among his recent books are *The Electric Information Age Book* (2012), *Modernitalia* (2012), *The Library Beyond the Book* (2014), *Blueprint for Counter Education—Expanded Reprint* (2016; a reprint edition of Maurice Stein and Larry Miller's 1970 work of radical pedagogy); and the bolted book *FuturPiaggio: Six Italian Lessons on Mobility and Modern Life* (2017).

Dubravka Sekulić
is an assistant professor at the IZK—Institute for Contemporary Art, Faculty of Architecture, TU Graz and a PhD fellow at the Institute for History and Theory of Architecture, Department of Architecture, ETH Zürich. She wrote *Glotzt Nicht so Romantisch! On Extralegal Space in Belgrade* (jan van eyck, 2012), *Constructing Non-alignment: The Case of Energoprojekt* (msub, 2016), and coedited, together with Žiga Testen and Gal Kirn, *Surfing the Black* (jan van eyck, 2012). She was a fellow at the Akedemie Schloss Solitude, Stuttgart, and Jan Van Eyck Akademie, Maastricht. She was a founding member of the Parity Group at the Department of Architecture, ETH Zürich. She is an amateur-librarian at Public Library/Memory of the World, where she maintains feminist and space/race collections.

Prasad Shetty
is the cofounder of the School of Environment and Architecture (Mumbai), where he also teaches. His works with Rupali Gupte have been shown in many exhibitions, including *Manifesta 7* (Bolzano), *Sarai Reader 09* (Gurugram) and the 56th Venice Biennale. He and Gupte were chief architects of the 11th Shanghai Biennale, and they curated *When is Space?*, an exhibition on contemporary architecture at Jawahar Kala Kendra (Jaipur, 2018). Prasad is an urbanist and one of the founding members of the urban research collective, CRIT. His work involves research and teaching on contemporary urbanism, including architectural practices, studies of postindustrial landscapes, housing, archiving post liberalization developments, entrepreneurial practices, and urban property. Alongside teaching, he also works with the Mumbai Metropolitan Region—Environment Improvement and Heritage Conservation Society, Mumbai.

Molly Wright Steenson
is an associate professor in the Carnegie Mellon School of Design. She researches the history of design, architecture, computation, and artificial intelligence from the 1950s to the present and is completing a book titled *Architectures of Interactivity* that explores these linkages with a focus on the practices of Nicholas Negroponte, Cedric Price, Christopher Alexander, and Richard Saul Wurman.

Neyran Turan
is an assistant professor at the University of California-Berkeley, and a partner at NEMESTUDIO, an architectural office that has been recognized with several awards, including the 2016 Architectural League New York Prize for Young Architects, multiple citations at the 2016 and 2017 Architects' Newspaper Best of Design Awards and a Built Environment Notable Award at the Core 77 Design Awards 2017. Turan's work focuses on alternative forms of environmental imagination within architecture and their capacity for new aesthetic and political trajectories within architecture and urbanism. Her forthcoming book, titled *Architecture as Measure*, positions climate change as a cultural and political idea that requires a renewed architectural imagination.

Etienne Turpin
is a philosopher and the Founding Director of anexact office, a design research practice based in Jakarta and Berlin. From 2013–17, he codirected PetaBencana.id. Following this work, Etienne cofounded User Group, a London-based cooperative developing and supporting open source software projects for environmental monitoring and disaster response. He is a co-editor of *Fantasies of the Library* (MIT Press, 2016), *Art in the Anthropocene* (Open Humanities Press, 2015), and *Jakarta: Architecture + Adaptation* (Universitas Indonesia Press, 2013), and editor of *Architecture in the Anthropocene* (Open Humanities Press, 2013).

Christina Varvia
is an architect, researcher, and Deputy Director of Forensic Architecture (FA). Her previous research includes studies on digital media and memory, as well as the perception of the physical environment through scanning and imaging technologies deployed through time-based media. Christina has worked in architectural practice and was part of the Unknown Fields Division before she joined the FA (FA) team in 2014. At FA, she has coordinated the *Rafah: Black Friday* report, *Saydnaya: Inside a Syrian torture prison* project, *77sqm_9:26min: A counter Investigation*, as well as many other projects and exhibitions.

Richard Vijgen
is a designer whose Arnhem-based Studio for Contemporary Information Culture investigates new strategies to find big stories in big data through research and design. Vijgen creates interactive data visualizations and installations ranging from microscopic to architectural in scale and uses space, code, and pixels to visualize the invisible. In addition, he writes about digital culture and teaches Information Design and Information Spaces at the Arnhem School of Art and Design (NL). He has lectured at a wide range of design schools and universities in the Netherlands and abroad.

The editors greatly acknowledge the permissions granted to reproduce the copyrighted material in this publication. Every effort has been made to trace the ownership of all copyrighted material and to secure proper credits and permissions from the appropriate copyright holders. In the event of any omission or oversight, necessary corrections will be made in future printings. Unless otherwise noted, all images are public domain and/or courtesy of the author.

Jeffrey Schnapp

Fig. 1 Public domain courtesy of the US National Archives.
Fig. 3 Public domain courtesy of the Library of Congress.
Fig. 4 Public domain photograph published in Matthew Luckiesh, *Artificial Light: Its Influence upon Civilization* (New York: The Century Co, 1920).
Figs. 5–6 Courtesy Otto K. Olesen Illuminating Company.
Fig. 8 Public domain courtesy of the United States National Coast Guard.

Francesco Casetti

Figs. 1–10 Illustrations courtesy Dimitri Brand and Gregory Cartelli.

Christina Varvia

Fig. 2 Courtesy of Forensic Architecture.
Fig. 3 Courtesy of Richard Mosse.
Fig. 4 © The National Gallery, London.

Ginger Nolan

Figs. 1–7, 9 © J. Paul Getty Trust. Getty Research Institute, Los Angeles (2008.M.51).
Fig. 8 Getty Research Institute, Los Angeles (2008.M.51).

Nashin Mahtani & Etienne Turpin

All images courtesy of PetaBencana.id.

Richard Vijgen

Fig. 2 By Michael Gauthier, Wireless Networking in the Developing World [CC BY-SA 3.0 (https://creativecommons.org/licenses/by-sa/3.0)], via Wikimedia Commons.

Molly Wright Steenson

Figs. 1–3 © Asymptote. Asymptote Architecture New York Stock Exchange project records, Canadian Centre for Architecture. Gift of Asymptote Architecture.

Marshall McLuhan

Illustrations by Seokhoon Choi and Carr Chadwick, based on illustrations by Keith Goddard for *Perspecta* 11.

Nick Axel

Figs. 1–4 Photographs by Enric Duch, courtesy of Studio Miessen and Omer Fast.
Figs. 5, 6 Photographs by Markus Miessen, courtesy of Studio Miessen.
Fig. 8 Photograph by Chiara Figione, courtesy of Studio Miessen.
Fig. 9 Photograph by the Center for Contemporary Art, Tel Aviv, Israel, and courtesy of Studio Miessen.
Fig. 10 Photograph by Artists Space, NY, and courtesy of Studio Miessen.
Fig. 11 Photograph by Bob Goedewaagen, courtesy of Studio Miessen.

Aleksandr Bierig

Figs. 1, 2, 6 Courtesy of Albert Kahn Associates.
Fig. 4 Courtesy of Time Life.
Fig. 5 Public domain from Bentley Historical Library, University of Michigan.

Evangelos Kotsioris

Fig. 1 Courtesy of the Canadian Centre for Architecture, Montreal.
Figs. 2, 6, 7, 14 Public domain from US Patent and Trademark Office.
Figs. 3, 4 Courtesy of *Popular Mechanics*.
Fig. 10 Courtesy of *Architectural Record*.

Neyran Turan

All images courtesy of NEMESTUDIO.

Georgios Eftaxiopolous

Figs. 1–4 Courtesy of Canadian Centre for Architecture, Montreal.

åyr

Figs. 1, 3, 4 Courtesy of Octave Perrault and Tatjana Patzschke.
Fig. 2 © Alamy Stock Photo and courtesy of Octave Perrault.
Figs. 5, 8–10 Courtesy of åyr.
Figs. 6, 7 Courtesy of Octave Perrault.
Fig. 11 Courtesy of Mapdata © Google 2018, Imagery US Geological Survey.

Shannon Mattern

Fig. 2 Photograph courtesy of Paolo Monello.
Figs. 9, 10, 14, 16 Photographs by Nick Ash, courtesy of the studio of Simon Denny.
Figs. 11–13 Courtesy of the studio of Simon Denny.

DIS

All images courtesy of DIS. Graphic design by Chris James.

Perspecta 51 is indebted to a great many individuals who provided us with support and guidance over its long gestation. We would like to thank all of our professors at Yale University, especially Francesco Casetti, Peggy Deamer, Sheila de Bretteville, and Alan Plattus for their insight and counsel. Keller Easterling deserves our profound gratitude for providing us with encouragement and inspiration, particularly in the nascent stages of this project. We would also like to thank Dean Deborah Berke for inviting us to her office and offering feedback as we entered the final stages of the project. Thank you to Richard DeFlumeri and A. J. Artemel for answering all our questions and keeping us on track. Mahdi Sabbagh and Russell LeStourgeon deserve our sincerest thanks for tirelessly providing insight into the editorial process, as do all the past editors of *Perspecta* who helped us find our way. We are especially thankful for the exacting copy editing of Stephen Hoban, who helped unify the work of three editors and more than twenty writers. Thank you to Will Morningstar for thoroughly proofreading the final version of this journal. Keith Goddard, designer of *Perspecta* 11, generously shared his experience with our designers. To our contributors: thank you for your time, patience, and generosity throughout this project. The exceptional talents and remarkable conceptualization by our designers, Seokhoon Choi and Carr Chadwick, helped us clarify and strengthen the production of our own medium—thank you! Most of all, we would like to thank our families and friends for putting up with countless phone calls, Skype meetings, and Sunday editorial meetings over the three years spent creating this journal.

Perspecta 51: Medium

Editors
Shayari de Silva
Dante Furioso
Samantha Jaff

Designers
Carr Chadwick
Seokhoon Choi

Copy Editor
Stephen Hoban

Printed by
NPN Drukkers, the Netherlands

Paper
Magno Gloss 100gsm
Olin Rough High White 90 gsm
Olin Smooth High White 90 gsm

Perspecta 51 would like to thank the following donors for their ongoing generosity in supporting this journal:
Marc. F. Appleton, '72 M.Arch
Hans Baldouf, '81 BA; '88 M.Arch
Austin Church III, '60 BA FamilyFund
Fred Koetter and Susie Kim
Cesar Pelli, '08 DFHA
Robert A.M. Stern, '65 M.Arch
Jeremy Scott Wood, '64 BA;'70 M.Arch
F. Anthony Zunino, '70 M.Arch

Perspecta, The Yale Architectural Journal is published in the United States of America by the Yale School of Architecture and distributed by the MIT Press.

Distributed by the MIT Press
Massachusetts Institute of Technology
Cambridge, Massachusetts 02142
http://mitpress.mit.edu

Library of Congress Control Number:
2018941584